FOUR DECADES
OF
MASSACHUSETTS POLITICS

FOUR DECADES
OF
MASSACHUSETTS
POLITICS

1890-1935

By

Michael E. Hennessy

BOOKS FOR LIBRARIES PRESS
FREEPORT, NEW YORK

First Published 1935
Reprinted 1971

INTERNATIONAL STANDARD BOOK NUMBER:
0-8369-5700-8

LIBRARY OF CONGRESS CATALOG CARD NUMBER:
76-150187

PRINTED IN THE UNITED STATES OF AMERICA

Dedicated to my friends who made possible the publication of this book

FOREWORD

THIS volume, covering four decades of Massachusetts politics will, it is hoped, give the reader a comprehensive idea of the leading events in an important epoch in the history of this State, in which it was the good fortune of the author to play the part of an observer in his capacity as reporter for the *Boston Daily* and *Sunday Globe.*

A gradual and distinct change has taken place in the social, political and economic life of its 4,000,000 population, nearly half of whom are foreign born. Her Puritanism has been softened by the great influx of immigrants and their children. While Massachusetts is no longer a Puritan Commonwealth, happily many of the ideals of its founders have been preserved, thanks to that efficient melting pot—the public school.

The Bay State has not lagged behind in the forward march of progress. She has generally been in the vanguard. Other States with greater reputations as progressive Commonwealths have copied her advanced laws and followed in her wake in the enactment of legislation on behalf of education, labor, social welfare, protection of life and property, the encouragement of thrift and industry and bringing government nearer to the people.

Her material growth is told in the almost fabulous figures of her savings banks, representing the thrift of her people, the number of her home owners, the diversity and success of her industries.

Her government activities in behalf of the welfare of its people are continually increasing. Her people give to charity until it hurts. She has always led in education. She fosters with lavish hand art and science.

Evidence is abundant to prove that the old rebel colony of Massachusetts, which led in the fight for American freedom, is still the friend of human rights within and without its borders.

That has twice been proven in the period covered by this volume—in the Spanish War, when her troops were first in the field to aid Cuban independence, and the World War, when her volunteer soldiers were the first National Guard to step on French soil. In both conflicts Massachusetts men added new laurels to the martial glory of the Commonwealth.

Her political and economic progress is shown by the adoption of the secret or Australian ballot; abolition of the poll tax as a prerequisite to voting; free text books in the public schools; laws reducing the hours of labor for men, women and children; workmen's compensation; factory inspection for the protection of employees; the initiative and referendum; direct primaries; minimum wage; the probation system; pure food laws; a pension system for public employees; old age pensions; and savings banks life insurance at lower rates than those offered by private companies.

Massachusetts was a pioneer in good roads. Millions were put into a great Boston pier to attract ocean com-

FOREWORD   ix

merce. The State parks and reservations are unsurpassed anywhere. Her laws regulating public utilities were among the first in the United States and have been adopted as models by sister Commonwealths, as were her care of the insane and her social welfare policy.

To secure these laws required years of agitation, but Massachusetts is fortunate in that she is rich in public spirited men and women, willing to devote their time, money, energy and talents in behalf of every good cause.

Advanced as she is in these matters, it is not a wild dream to predict that in the next four decades, the people of the State will enjoy things provided by the Commonwealth unthought of to-day.

For years Massachusetts was steadfastly Republican nationally. Since the formation of the Republican party in the late 50's, she gave her electoral vote every four years to that party until 1912, when the Bull Moose split it in twain and Woodrow Wilson was the first Democrat to receive its electoral support. Sixteen years later Massachusetts voted for Alfred E. Smith, Democrat, for President on a straight out and out two party contest. Four years later she repeated her 1928 record, casting her electoral vote for Franklin D. Roosevelt.

Occasionally she elected Democratic Governors, usually on issues which divided the ranks of the Republicans. The election of Joseph B. Ely, Governor and Marcus A. Coolidge, United States Senator, Democrats in 1930, is important to remember, for the Republicans that year also lost two important State offices—Treasurer and Auditor and the Democrats increased their representation in the

Legislature. This was repeated two years later and in 1934, James M. Curley, Democrat, was chosen Governor. The Democrats came within an ace of winning the Legislature and the Executive Council. The only Republican candidate on the State ticket elected that year was the Secretary of State.

These events point unerringly to a change in the politics of the State. Whether this change is to be permanent remains to be seen. Unless the Republicans succeed in retrieving their losses soon, Massachusetts may be a total loss to them. But they can take comfort in the saying that their best asset is the Democratic party and they may yet return to power through the mistakes and bickerings of that party.

The old Republican order has passed. If the Republican party is to control the State government again, there must be a more liberal leadership and a way found to win back to its fold the thousands of Republicans who deserted them in the last election. The Republican party has a chance to prove that it can thrive without patronage. It has a glorious past, but a political party cannot live on the past.

M. E. H.

Boston, March 1, 1935.

ILLUSTRATIONS

	FACING PAGE
MICHAEL E. HENNESSY	*Frontispiece*
GOVERNOR EUGENE N. FOSS	12
SINCLAIR WEEKS, LOUIS K. LIGGETT, COUNCILOR FRASER, ARTHUR LYMAN, FRANK A. GOODWIN, DANIEL J. LYNE	28
CHARLES SUMNER BIRD	42
B. LORING YOUNG, THOMAS J. BOYNTON, CHARLES S. O'CONNOR, CHARLES E. HATFIELD, CONGRESSMAN WIGGLESWORTH, BERNARD J. ROTHWELL	56
WILLIAM M. BUTLER	72
DANIEL J. GALLAGHER, HENRY H. PIERCE, PROFESSOR SIMPSON, CONGRESSMAN MARTIN, HENRY PARKMAN, JR., U. S. MARSHAL MURPHY	90
SENATOR DAVID I. WALSH	116
COLONEL JOSEPH F. TIMILTY, ELIOT WADSWORTH, COLONEL GASTON, WILLIAM H. COOLIDGE, CONGRESSMAN RUSSELL, ERNEST L. GOULSTON	138
JOSEPH P. MANNING	150
JOSEPH P. LOMASNEY, ANDREW J. PETERS, ERLAND P. FISH, EDITH NOURSE ROGERS, JOHN RICHARDSON, CONGRESSMAN MCCORMACK	168
SENATOR MARCUS A. COOLIDGE	186
HENRY I. HARRIMAN, JAMES H. BRENNAN, CHARLES H. INNES, EDWARD L. DOLAN, MORGAN T. RYAN, THOMAS C. O'BRIEN	206
EBEN S. DRAPER	226

EX-CONGRESSMAN CARTER, SLATER WASHBURN, LEOPOLD M. GOULSTON, HENRY L. SHATTUCK, CONGRESSMAN TINKHAM, JAMES ROOSEVELT 246

GOVERNOR FRANK G. ALLEN 260

JOHN W. WEEKS, COL. CHARLES R. GOW, BAYARD TUCKERMAN, SAMUEL L. POWERS, GENERAL EDWARD L. LOGAN, J. OTIS WARDWELL 284

JOSEPH P. CARNEY 304

SHERMAN WHIPPLE, J. J. STORROW, CHARLES F. COTTER, SHERIFF KELIHER, CONGRESSMAN TREADWAY, ARTHUR D. HILL 326

JOSEPH A. MAYNARD 350

GOVERNOR ALVAN T. FULLER 364

ALFRED E. SMITH 384

MAYOR MANSFIELD 408

GOVERNOR JOSEPH B. ELY 420

LIEUTENANT GOVERNOR GASPAR G. BACON 438

STATE TREASURER CHARLES F. HURLEY 458

POSTMASTER GENERAL JAMES A. FARLEY 478

LIEUTENANT GOVERNOR JOSEPH L. HURLEY 492

SPEAKER LEVERETT SALTONSTALL 510

GOVERNOR JAMES M. CURLEY 520

GENERAL CHARLES H. COLES 530

PRESIDENT FRANKLIN D. ROOSEVELT 540

FOUR DECADES
OF
MASSACHUSETTS POLITICS

WILLIAM EUSTIS RUSSELL
Governor 1891-1894

THE election of William Eustis Russell of Cambridge, Democrat, Governor in 1890, over Governor John Quincy Adams Brackett, Republican, running for reëlection by a plurality of 9000 votes, broke the Republican succession for the first time since Benjamin F. Butler, running on the Democratic ticket against Robert R. Bishop, Republican candidate eight years before.

It was Russell's third try for the Governorship. As the young and accomplished mayor of his native city, he had attracted State wide attention by the high character of his administration of its municipal affairs. He pitched his gubernatorial campaigns on a high level. He had an attractive and winning personality and he was an orator of marked ability. His speeches and public utterances showed an intelligent grasp of public questions. The campaign of 1890, was one of the most spirited since the Butler-Bishop contest, but unlike that campaign, it was free from personalities and mud slinging. It was fought on National and State issues, chiefly the tariff, progressive labor laws and home rule for cities and towns.

The Prohibitionists, chafing under the procrastination of the Republicans on temperance legislation, made every effort to muster their strength and cast 15,000 votes for their gubernatorial candidate the year before. In 1890 they nominated William Blackmer of Springfield for Governor. Their hope was to weaken the Republican candidate by pulling the temperance Republicans away from Brackett to their own candidate for Governor and they conducted a lively campaign for their ticket. The Republicans renominated Governor Brackett for a second term and in their platform reaffirmed their "fidelity to the principles of temperance," pledged their support of legislation to "suppress the dram shop and the saloon" and condemned "the evils of the blighting curse of drink."

The passage of the McKinley tariff by Congress, increasing the cost of living, went into effect thirty days before election and was a great help to the Democrats. Their brilliant campaigners made the most of the tariff increases and they were aided by the Young Men's Democratic Club, whose membership worked in harmony with the Democratic State committee, directed by such able executives as Nathan Mathews, Jr. and Josiah Quincy, both in their early thirties.

The liquor question played an important part in deciding the election. For some time the Drys had been demanding a prohibitory amendment to the State constitution. The Republicans put through the Legislature the dry amendment demanded by the Prohibitionists. A special election was ordered for April 22, 1889, and the day made a legal holiday. The amendment was rejected by a two to one vote. The Drys believed that they had been double crossed by the Republicans. With an idea of mollifying the temperance people, Governor Brackett discussed the liquor question in his inaugural of 1890, pointing out that eighty-two per cent of the cities and towns of the State were dry and that the existing law specifically stated that where liquor was sold the public bar was prohibited. If further restrictions were deemed necessary to curtail the sale of liquor, he expressed the hope that the Legislature would pass them.

Under Governor Brackett's interpretation of the law, the Police Commissioners of Boston, a State board, appointed by the Governor, two of whose members were Republicans and the third a lukewarm Democrat, out of step with his party, proceeded to enforce the law as interpreted by the Governor. Every bar in Boston was ordered screened by the police board. Patrons of saloons were obliged to sit at tables and order food with their drinks. The saloons resorted to the free lunch plan. People went into saloons to drink, not to eat, and, as a rule, spurned the free lunch, usually an uninviting looking sandwich, often made to do duty over and over again by the thrifty saloon keeper. The ridiculous ruling aroused intense indignation and resentment. Boston became the laughing stock of other cities, the butt of the vaudeville stage and the newspaper humorist. At their first opportunity at the following election the voters voiced their protest by voting for Russell.

As a protest against the new tariff law, many Republicans voted the Democratic Congressional ticket and that party elected seven of the twelve Representatives to Congress. The Democrats also increased their representation in the lower House of the Legislature to 98 members, elected twenty of the forty members of the State Senate and for the first time since the Republican party came into power in the State, elected its candidate for State Auditor, William D. T. Trefry of Marblehead.

Trefry's election was due to a quarrel among the Republicans. Major J. Henry Gould, a prominent Grand Army man, defeated the State organization candidate, State Auditor Charles R. Ladd, for the nomination, but Major Gould's victory was short lived. His opponents charged that he had been a carpet bagger in one of the Southern States, following the Civil War and that he had been involved in some questionable financial transactions. There was a hurried conference of the party leaders on the heels of his nomination. Major Gould was forced off of the State ticket and Ladd, the man he had defeated for the nomination was substituted for him. Gould's friends felt that he had been harshly dealt with and enough of them bolted Ladd to bring about the election of the Democratic candidate.

The Democratic candidates for Congress were successful in the Third, Fourth, Fifth, Eighth, Ninth, Eleventh and Twelfth districts. Up to this time the only safe Democratic district in the State was the Fourth, or Boston district, represented by Joseph H. O'Niel, who was re-elected. Among the Democrats elected to Congress in this landslide were young Sherman Hoar, son of Judge E. Rockwood Hoar of Concord and nephew of Senator George Frisbie Hoar; John F. Andrew, son of the Civil War Governor, John A. Andrew and George Fred Williams. All three had bolted the nomination of James G. Blaine for President in 1884 and went into the Mugwump movement, which played such an important part in the defeat of the "Plumed Knight" and the election of Grover Cleveland, his Democratic opponent.

Moses T. Stevens, an old line Democrat and a rich woolen manufacturer of Andover, defeated Frederick T. Greenhalge, up for reëlection in the Lowell district. Frederick S. Coolidge of Ashburnham, another old line Democrat was successful in the Eleventh district and young John C. Crosby in the Twelfth or Berkshire district.

The Democrats in the Lynn district were anxious to beat Henry Cabot Lodge for reëlection as Representative in Congress, but nobody in the district was willing to make the fight and the nomination was given to Professor William Everett of Quincy, an outsider. Dr. Everett was a militant Mugwump, son of the famous orator and statesman, Edward Everett. Dr. Everett was headmaster of an academy in Quincy, a pedagog by day, a politician by night. He had been a Harvard professor and was an accomplished public speaker. He made a colorful and vigorous campaign, attracting wide attention. While he did not succeed in depositing Mr. Lodge in a cavity, to use one of his own campaign phrases, he whittled down his plurality to a bare 1000 votes.

The Legislature was safely Republican as was the Executive Council, the confirming power of the Governor's appointments. The rest of the Republican State ticket the Auditor excepted, was saved by comfortable margins and assured that party of control of the State government. Congressman Joseph H. Walker of Worcester, who joined the Mugwump movement in 1884, but returned to the G.O.P. fold, characterized the Democratic victory as "a combination of Harvard College and the slums." Governor Brackett took his defeat manfully and promptly congratulated the victor.

Russell's election attracted Nation wide attention and he was hailed by his party leaders as a promising candidate for President. He was the idol of his own party and thousands of Republicans gave him their support at the polls. He was inaugurated Governor, January 8, Jackson Day, in the Democratic calendar. With the exception of George S. Boutwell, he was the youngest man ever inaugurated in that office. There was a slight delay in the organization of the Senate, due to the demand of the twenty Democrats of that body, who wanted to elect a member of their own party President, but wiser counsel prevailed and an agreement was reached to divide the committee chairmanships evenly between Democrats and Republicans and Henry B. Sprague, Republican, was re-elected as presiding officer.

In the presence of a distinguished gathering of members of the Legislature, past and present, public functionaries who by law and custom are required to be there, the youthful Chief Executive delivered his inaugural address, a document of progressive ideas in government, most of which he had eloquently advanced in his three gubernatorial campaigns. He asked for the repeal of the law which required the payment of a poll tax as a prerequisite to voting, pointing out the hardships to voters and candidates alike by its continuance. It was a drain on the candidates of all political parties, especially in the cities and large towns, where thousands of voters neglected to pay the tax, depending on their party leaders and the candidates for office to do so for them. It often happened that a rich man had the advantage over a poor man, who had not the means to meet this necessary election expense. There had been cases in Congressional districts where candidates had to pay from $10,000 to $15,000 for poll taxes of their party followers.

To curb the corrupting influence of the State House lobby, he suggested the passage of a law regulating the activities of the "Third House" during sessions of the Legislature. He advocated the abolition of free railroad passes to members of the Legislature and State officials and suggested that the railroads be required to issue passes to the members of the Great and General Court to be used by them during the session. The railroads, he observed, could hardly object to such a law.

He called attention to the variety of opinion as to the meaning of the statute forbidding the keeping of a public bar and said that the administration of the law in Boston did not tend to promote temperance and urged its repeal. He asked for a corrupt practices act which would call for the publication of campaign expenses. "Expenses which cannot bear the light of day ought not to be made," he said.

After his election, it was discovered that the State constitution required that the Governor of Massachusetts must be possessed of a freehold of at least $5000. Mr. Russell's friends were obliged to use their wits to comply with this archaic law. In his inaugural, he called attention to this section of the constitution and asked that it be abolished, which request was promptly granted.

Governor Russell's military staff was a notable aggregation of leading Democrats, but he retained the Adjutant General, Dalton, a Republican. While the lawmakers declined to adopt all of his suggestions, Governor Russell was able to wring from an unwilling Legislature a number of important acts in his first term. It repealed the objectionable law forbidding the sale of liquor over a bar and divided the State into 13 new Congressional districts as required by the apportionment law enacted by Congress on a basis fair to both political parties.

A new drunk law, permitting arresting officers to discharge without court proceedings first offenders was passed. A weavers fine bill was enacted, but was subsequently declared unconstitutional by the State Supreme Judicial Court. Another act permitted cities and towns to engage in the manufacture and sale of gas and electricity. A collateral inheritance law was enacted putting a tax of five per cent on inheritances on estates valued at more than $10,000.

The first sweat shop bill was passed this year, prohibiting the sale of clothing and garments made outside the State in tenements and unsanitary shops. A rapid transit bill was passed for Boston, authorizing the investigation of the subject, the commission to report its findings to the next Legislature.

Restrictive legislation was proposed affecting fraternal and beneficiary organizations which had sprung up like mushrooms all over the land. The public had gone mad over this form of insurance. Many sharpers reaped a harvest in the formation and manipulation of these organizations at the expense of a credulous public. There was a general demand that the State impose strict regulation on these organizations through its insurance department, but those who had made money out of the business employed able counsel and successfully fought off action by this Legislature, which referred the subject to the next General Court.

An initiatory appropriation of $75,000 was made for the Massachusetts exhibit at the World's Columbian Exposition to be held in Chicago, the following year, commemorating the 400th anniversary of the discovery of America by Columbus.

General John W. Corcoran, the Governor's loyal and devoted friend and running mate on the Democratic ticket and Judge Advocate General on his military staff, was made chairman of the commission. The Massachusetts building at the Fair was a reproduction of John Hancock's house—a compliment to the first Governor of the Commonwealth under the Constitution.

REËLECTED 1891

Throughout the Legislative session this year the Republicans were planning and building to redeem the

Governorship. Several aspirants for gubernatorial honors appeared to thwart the leaders' plans for a united front against the popular Democratic Governor. Two major booms were under way by early summer, one for Ex-Congressman William W. Crapo of New Bedford and the other for Ex-Congressman Charles H. Allen of Lowell. Allen, the younger of the two, made the most aggressive campaign for the nomination and was preferred by the younger element. He was nominated on the first ballot in the State Convention held in Boston. Lieutenant Governor William H. Haile of Springfield, a colorless figure in public life, but wealthy and a liberal campaign contributor was again nominated for second place.

Henry Cabot Lodge presided over the convention and aroused great enthusiasm by a forceful and eloquent speech in which he did not spare the Democrats or their party. The platform was written by former Congressman Greenhalge of Lowell, a victim of the political cyclone of the year before.

It denied the Democratic charges of extravagance by Congress in enacting new pension laws, favored the further restrictions of emigration, declared for the purity of elections, came out strongly for sound money, roundly condemned the Democrats for their leanings toward free silver, affirmed its fidelity to the protective tariff, favored the further restriction of and the suppression of the evils arising from the sale of intoxicating liquors and contained a labor and educational clause calculated to please those interested in such subjects.

The Democrats held their convention in Worcester and

renominated their old ticket, Russell and Corcoran. Their platform condemned the Republican attitude toward State boards and commissions, claiming that they were beyond the control of the Governor and responsible to nobody. It declared for free text books for public schools and reaffirmed its former position favoring an efficient system of manual training and the increase of the school age. It demanded the repeal of the McKinlay tariff bill, denounced the recent silver legislation by the Republican Congress and opposed the free coinage of silver in the absence of any international agreement.

The Prohibitionists nominated Charles E. Kimball of Lynn, who received 8908 votes at the polls. The Socialist Labor party appeared in Massachusetts for the first time this year, nominating Harry W. Robinson of Lynn, as their standard bearer, but his vote was small.

The Peoples Party fired the first gun in the campaign, nominating Henry Winn of Malden, for Governor. Major Winn was well known to the members of the Legislature. For years he had appeared before them in behalf of many political reforms, notably on taxation. He was a disciple of Henry George and an ardent advocate of the latter's single tax ideas. The platform of this party contained many of the tenets of the Farmers Alliance whose growing strength among farmers in the Nation's corn and wheat belts disturbed Republican leaders. Major Winn polled only a handful of votes.

The Republicans felt confident that in their candidate, Allen, they had a man who could match Russell. Allen opened his campaign with a big meeting in Boston, at which he made the mistake of telling a dialect story regarding a mythical Mr. Casey, who sucked his torch. In introducing him that same evening, ex-Governor Long, the presiding officer, who had served in Congress with Allen, remarked that the Republicans were not in the habit of putting all their big apples on the top of the barrel. The Democrats seized this playful remark, fastened the title of "Little Apples" on the Republican candidate and made the most of the torch story which offended a large element of the population.

Allen was unable to stand the strain of a hard campaign. His throat gave out and he was obliged to cancel several important speaking engagements.

There was a joint debate in Boston at the height of the campaign between Henry Cabot Lodge and John E. Russell. Two better speakers would be hard to find. Mr. Lodge was the idol of the younger and militant element of his party and John E. Russell, "the Gentle Shepherd of Leicester," as he was affectionately known by his friends—a title by the way, conferred on him by William McKinley of Ohio, a member of Congress, when Russell represented the Worcester district at Washington and was debating the wool schedule in a tariff bill. Mr. Russell was elected to Congress in 1886 in the Worcester district on a free trade platform. He was a man of means and lived the life of a gentleman farmer. As an orator, he had few equals in the State and ably presented the case of his namesake. Mr. Lodge did the same for Mr. Allen. Probably very few votes were changed by the oratorial battle of the two scholars in politics, but it added

GOV. EUGENE N. FOSS

zest and gaiety to the contest and gave both candidates a chance to present their side to the voters through two able debaters.

The vote for Governor was: Russell, 157,982; Allen, 151,515. The political complexion of the Legislature elected was: Senate, 24 Republicans, 16 Democrats; House, 149 Republicans, 90 Democrats, 1 Prohibitionist. Russell was the first Democrat to be reëlected Governor since the advent of the Republican party to power in the State. His two predecessors since the Civil War, Gaston and Butler were yearlings.

One year in office had convinced him more than ever that the time had come when the Legislature should make a thorough examination of the methods of executive administration work "and the adoption of such changes as will bring into complete responsibility to the people, and will simplify machinery at present complex, without system or uniformity" he said in his second inaugural address.

He briefly sketched the gradual but large growth of executive work and executive offices in the more than 100 years that had elapsed since the institution of constitutional government in the State. "There are over 25 State commissions and more than 100 trustees of public institutions. Whether this number can be reduced by abolition or consolidation of offices has been considered by a special committee of the last Legislature, who will submit to you the result of its investigation," he said. Only eight officers, Russell pointed out, could be removed by the Governor alone upon his own responsibility. This, he explained, was the extent of his responsible executive control.

The Executive Council composed of eight Republicans and one Democrat, was not disposed to give him a free reign in removals and appointments. The Governor, in his first term, had removed from office Police Commissioner Osborne of Boston for political activities. Mr. Osborne was a Republican, had been president of the Common Council of Boston and a factor in local politics. He was a cousin of Congressman William McKinley of Ohio, who afterwards became President of the United States. Osborne was made a political issue in the campaign just closed. The Democrats charged that he used his influence as a police commissioner to get votes among liquor dealers for the Republican candidate for Governor. Many Democrats advocated the abolition of the Council, but the Governor did not go as far as that in his second inaugural. The Constitution, he said, created the Council "for advising the Governor, not for tieing his hands, not for dictating his appointments, not for exercising coördinate and equal power with him." He believed that there should be a confirming power in appointments to office by the Executive Council, but nothing came of his suggestions.

He reviewed the creation of the State Board of Police for the city of Boston in 1887, always a favorite topic with Democratic politicians who have never ceased to condemn the act as destructive of the principle of local self-government. Since then the city government of Boston has had no power over the police department. He recommended that the control of the police be restored to the city but his recommendation fell on deaf ears.

The Senate and House of 1892 contained several able men, some of whom later acquired national fame in public affairs. In the House, the foremost figure on the Republican side was Samuel W. McCall, who was elected that Fall a member of Congress and was destined to occupy a prominent place in the party councils at the National capital for the next 20 years, when he retired from Congress. Returning to political life after a brief absence of one year, he was elected Governor in 1915, the first Republican in six years to be chosen.

George von L. Meyer who became a member of President Theodore Roosevelt's cabinet after serving as Ambassador to Italy and Russia, represented Ward 9, Boston. The veteran Democrat "Jim" Parker sat for Methuen, Wellington E. Parkhurst of Clinton, brother of Dr. Parkhurst of New York, famous for his fight against Tammany, was one of the militant Republicans of the House of 1892. Bentley W. Warren, afterwards legislative counsel for street railway corporations, represented the Brighton district of Boston. Others who sat in the same house were: Frank P. Bennett of Everett, Henry W. Ashley of Westfield, General Francis H. Appleton of Peabody, Benjamin Butler Barney and George Fox Tucker of New Bedford, Colonel Richard H. Barrett of Concord and Daniel H. Coakley of Cambridge.

Among the important laws passed that year were: An act prohibiting railroads issuing passes to the Governor, Lieutenant Governor, Councilors, Judges and members of the Legislature. Mileage was fixed for the legislative session at $2 per mile in lieu of passes.

Championed by Samuel W. McCall, an act was passed forbidding corrupt practices at elections, defined the purposes for which candidates might expend money to secure an election and set forth the manner returns should be made. It forbade committees to solicit campaign contributions, but of course contributions could still be made voluntarily. It was made a crime punishable by a fine of $100 to compel an employe to agree not to join a labor organization. Another law in behalf of organized labor fixed the hours of employment of women and minors in manufacturing establishments at 58 hours a week. The Weavers fine bill was repealed and a substitute was enacted in its place.

Lotteries were prohibited and the appointment of persons not residents of the State as special police was prohibited, the latter, at the behest of the labor representatives.

Medford and Everett was incorporated as cities and a general law was passed under which towns of 12,000 might become incorporated as cities. West Tisbury was set off as a separate town from Tisbury.

The salary of the Governor was raised from $5000 to $8000 and $10,000 was set aside for the State Firemen's Fund for the relief of firemen's widows and families. A law was passed regulating the organization and conduct of fraternal beneficiary societies.

The Naval Brigade was established and a law was passed punishing the fraudulent marking of ballots.

THIRD ELECTION

GOVERNOR RUSSELL's popularity was undiminished and he decided to run again. The Republicans figured that in a Presidential year they stood a good show to elect their candidate for Governor. By common consent the nomination went to Lieutenant Governor Haile. Roger Wolcott of Boston was nominated for Lieutenant Governor. Governor Russell was nominated by acclamation by the Democrats. James B. Carroll of Springfield was nominated for Lieutenant Governor.

The Prohibitionists were the first to hold their State Convention, nominating Wolcott Hamlin of Springfield for Governor, adopted their usual platform on the liquor question and put in a strong plank on the public schools, intended to catch some A.P.A. votes. The A.P.A., the so-called American Protective Association, had begun to make itself felt and all the political parties, except the Democrats, began to cater to them by incorporating in their platforms high sounding phrases about church and State, the public school and Americanism, designed to please those who professed to believe that the country and its institutions were in danger of foreign control. Like the predecessor of a generation before, the Knownothings, it found men high in party councils willing to deal with them.

The Republicans stressed national issues and their electoral ticket swept the State by a vote of 202,874 against 176,813 for the Democratic electors, but the unbeatable

Russell squeezed by again with 3000 plurality. He received 10,000 more votes than the Democratic electors. Mr. Haile had 19,000 less than the Harrison electors.

Roger Wolcott was an easy winner over James B. Carroll, the vote was 180,358 to 170,121. The Republicans elected 10 Congressmen, the Democrats three, although one of the latter, Michael J. McEttrick, was classed as an Independent, a gain of five seats for the Republicans.

The State Senate chosen was made up of 30 Republicans and 10 Democrats. The House, 165 Republicans, 74 Democrats and one tie. On the question of striking out of the Constitution the property qualification of the Governor the vote was Yes 141,321, No 68,045.

PRESIDENTIAL CAMPAIGN OF 1892

THE name of Governor Russell was frequently discussed as a possible candidate for President in Democratic circles. Massachusetts stood ready to present his name at the nominating convention if the opportunity presented itself; but he and most of his friends believed that the wisest course would be to renominate Grover Cleveland.

There was an attempt in the State Convention which elected the delegates-at-large, to start a demonstration for Governor David Bennett Hill of New York, but General Patrick A. Collins promptly objected to being hitched to the tail of Hill's kite, informed the convention that he wore no man's collar and would go to the convention free to do what he believed to be the best thing for the party.

The Delegates-at-Large were: Patrick A. Collins, John E. Russell, John H. Sullivan and Albert C. Houghton. General John W. Corcoran was elected a delegate-at-large, but having been appointed by Governor Russell, judge of the Superior Court, he named John H. Sullivan one of the alternates to act for him. General Collins made one of the seconding speeches for Mr. Cleveland.

The Democrats held their convention in Chicago and again nominated Cleveland for President. The feeling between the followers of Cleveland and Governor Hill of New York was intense. Thirty of the Massachusetts delegates voted for Cleveland, five for Hill and one for Russell. Governor Russell was a guest of Mr. Cleveland at Gray Gables, during the convention proceedings. The 72 votes of New York were cast for Governor Hill.

William W. Crapo of New Bedford was the chairman of the Massachusetts delegation to the Republican convention. His associate delegates-at-large were: ex-Governor Brackett, Congressman Cogswell and W. Murray Crane, the latter a new name in the councils of the party and destined to play an important part in the politics of the State and Nation a few years hence. General Cogswell was chairman of the Committee on Credentials and ex-Governor Brackett was placed on the Committee on Resolutions. President Harrison was not a popular public figure. Some of his party associates said mean things about him. Thomas B. Reed referred to him as "the ice man." There was quite a sentiment running among Republicans in behalf of William McKinley, Jr. of Ohio, author of the McKinley tariff bill, repudiated at the polls in 1900. The Republican leaders decided to renew the battle on tariff lines in 1892 and defiantly put Major McKinley into the presiding officer's chair of the convention.

Massachusetts voted, Harrison, 18; McKinley, 11; Blaine 1. Mr. Blaine received 182 votes in the convention, showing that some Republicans still clung to the "Plumed Knight." Blaine had resigned in a huff as Secretary of State in Harrison's cabinet a few weeks before the convention and his friends voted for him for the nomination to show their disapproval of Harrison's treatment of him. He was still the idol of many Republicans.

Whatever the cause of Mr. Blaine's resignation from the Cabinet, intimate friends knew at the time that he was far from being a well man. He died the following January. Major McKinley's vote was the same as Mr. Blaine's, showing that a substantial element in the convention had not been reconciled to General Harrison. An attempt was made to nominate Thomas B. Reed of Maine for Vice-President. In view of Mr. Reed's personal opinion of General Harrison as President, such a move would have been an open insult to the President. Mr. Littlefield of Maine appealed to the delegates not to nominate Reed, as nobody had any authority to present his name as a candidate. Whitelaw Reid of New York, editor of the Tribune, was nominated for second place by acclamation.

There was no heart in the Republican campaign and

Cleveland landed back in the White House, with a Democratic Congress. Massachusetts remained fast to her Republican moorings, but the Harrison electors had only a measly 26,000 plurality. The Congressional delegation was unchanged.

Mr. Cleveland was generous to his Massachusetts friends in his distribution of Federal plums. Richard Olney, a successful corporation lawyer was made Attorney General. Later, Mr. Olney became Secretary of State. Few of the Democratic rank and file knew Mr. Olney, but the older men of the party, particularly the lawyers, enthusiastically endorsed him. He was a sound lawyer, an able advocate and an incorrigible Democrat. He was the kind of a man who would appeal to Mr. Cleveland—conservative, secretive, and inclined to be imperious. He came to know Mr. Cleveland as a fellow Summer Cape Codder. As Secretary of State he twisted the British lion's tail when it attempted to place its paw on Venezuelan territory. The Anglomaniacs of the country were astonished when they read the virile letters that were exchanged between the American Secretary of State and the British foreign office. Olney insisted that John Bull must let go of what she thought she had and arbitrate the disputed questions. After a lot of blustering, England consented and the Monroe Doctrine was again made a living American political principle.

Patrick A. Collins was named Counsel General to London. Among some of his friends there was a feeling that Mr. Cleveland had made a great mistake in his first administration in not tendering a place in his cabinet to the

Bostonian. No Democrat in New England had the following of General Collins.

The New England member of Mr. Cleveland's first cabinet was William Endicott of Massachusetts, who was Secretary of War. Evidently Mr. Cleveland did not intend to make the same mistake twice. A day or two after the election of 1892, General Collins, accompanied by General Corcoran, went to New York. He was a dinner guest of William C. Whitney who had managed Mr. Cleveland's campaign. The question of patronage was freely discussed. The feeling was that General Collins might be invited into the second Cleveland cabinet, but this he did not care for. He could not afford it he said. A foreign ambassadorship was suggested to him at another conference, but he was not interested in that. He intimated that if Mr. Cleveland was disposed to honor him he would consider the Consul Generalship at London, the juiciest Federal plum the administration had to bestow. When Collins' selection for this post was announced, the question was raised: would the appointment of an ex-Fenian, a Land Leaguer and Irish Nationalist like General Collins be offensive to England? But assurances were received from the Gladstone ministry that there was no disposition to object to the appointment. On the eve of his departure for London, General Collins was given a complimentary banquet by 100 leading Bostonians representing various races and religious views.

Josiah Quincy was made Assistant Secretary of State but he did not remain long. He was regarded as the headsman of the department. He had served on the Democratic

National Committee in the campaign and knew the deserving men of the party. Charles S. Hamlin of Massachusetts, a young tariff reformer was named Assistant Secretary of the Treasury.

RUSSELL'S THIRD TERM

DEEPLY grateful to the people of Massachusetts for their thrice expressed confidence in him, Governor Russell was inaugurated for the third time January 4, 1893. The novelty of inaugurating a Democratic Governor in rock ribbed Republican Massachusetts had by no means worn off, judging from the number of people present. The inaugural address took the form of a valedictory, the Governor observing that he construed the duty of the Legislature and the Executive "to deal with broader matters than the specific recommendation of departments— and to suggest principles of legislation and necessary reforms, rather than to perfunctorily indorse or transmit details of administration."

He felt that as he had made his last two campaigns largely on the issue of more power over administrative boards and commissions by the chief executive, he was justified in again urging the passage of laws widening the sphere of gubernatorial authority over such boards and commissions and in demanding that the council be shorn of its power to prevent the removal of State executive officials in whom the Governor had lost confidence.

He again renewed the suggestions and recommendations for the abolition of unnecessary state offices and commissions, that steps be taken to simplify and systematize the machinery for administrative work and that full responsibility to the people be vested in the Governor, who should have the power to remove for cause any executive officer appointed by him. He asked that the Legislature give the people an opportunity thrice recommended by one of his Republican predecessors, John D. Long, to express their opinion on the need of an elected executive council by submission to them of a constitutional amendment providing for the abolition, but the Legislative branch ignored his request.

He deprecated the growing tendency of the Legislature to exercise its paternal power over the cities and towns of the Commonwealth as a violation of the principle of home rule and local self-government. "A law," said he, "founded on a mistrust of the people, removing government beyond their reach and officials beyond their control, is certain to lead to grave abuses. Such has been our experience with state control of the police of Boston. The Board of Police by its acts has deservedly lost the confidence of the citizens of Boston and the people of the Commonwealth. I again earnestly recommend the separation of the powers of this board; that the control of her police, which is a purely administrative function, be restored to the city of Boston; that the control of licenses, which is judicial in its nature, be placed in a board of such character, appointment and tenure as to be judicial in its action."

It was not until some years later in the administration of Curtis Guild, Jr., that the Legislature consented to do in part what Governor Russell asked it to do in his time. In Governor Guild's term, the power of granting the licenses was transferred to another commission, a Licensing Board, being created for this purpose, but the Legislature still refused to give back to Boston the control of its police force.

The incorporation of safe deposit and trust companies, like savings and coöperative banks, under the scrutiny and authority of the Savings Bank Commissioner, instead of being, as then, a matter of special legislation was recommended and a general law passed. He asked the Legislature to consider the expediency of providing a general law for the sale of new railroad stock by auction, or other disposition of it at its market value where such value is in excess of par, instead of its distribution to its stockholders at par as then permitted.

The important questions affecting Metropolitan Boston, relating to sewerage, rapid transit, parks, and water supply were called to the attention of the Legislature and showed that he favored good roads and advocated closer trade relations with Canada, Uncle Sam's best customer, but the Legislature did nothing to encourage either suggestion.

This year witnessed the authorization of the Boston Transit Commission. The charter of the Cape Cod Canal Company lapsed because of the failure of the company to undertake the building and a new company was chartered called the Old Colony and Interior Canal Company.

The affairs of the Bay State Gas Company were investigated at this session and the Legislature decided that it had violated the law by issuing obligations of $4,500,000. An act was passed annulling the charter unless the company cancelled them and the company complied with the law.

A law was enacted, providing that all new issues of railroad corporation stock must first be offered to the stockholders at the market price thereof and all stock not so taken must be sold at public auction. A law was passed to wind up the affairs of Endowment Orders, so-called, doing business under the Act of 1888 and further operations by them prohibited. The Metropolitan Park Commission was created. Nine hours a day was established for manual labor on State work.

Two constitutional amendments were acted on, viz., relative to the mileage of the members of the General Court proposed by the session of 1892 was approved and provisions made for its submission to the people at the November election. Another amendment proposed was the abolishing of the requirement that commissioners of insolvency be elected by the people.

Governor Russell participated in the inaugural ceremonies of President Grover Cleveland and was easily one of the favorites in the imposing parade, astride a richly caparisoned mount escorted by members of his military staff. He was a fine horseman and his escort, in their showy uniforms, fittingly represented the old Bay State.

LODGE ELECTED UNITED STATES SENATOR

THE most important political happening in the Legislature of 1893, was the election of Henry Cabot Lodge a member of Congress from the Lynn district, United States Senator to succeed Henry L. Dawes. Mr. Dawes was in his 77th year and had indicated his desire to retire and spend his declining years in his native Berkshire hills. He had served in the Senate since 1875 and was a member of the House from 1857 until his election as Senator.

Prior to his service at Washington he had served in both branches of the General Court. He was an experienced legislator at the time of the Constitutional convention of 1853 and was regarded as one of the ablest lawyers of that body. From the office of district attorney, he went to Congress. In all, he had spent 45 years in public life. He was as poor at the end of his senatorial career as when he entered public life. He had seen associates in Washington grow rich in the public service, but to him a good name was to be preferred to great riches. A position was provided for him at Washington as chairman of the Commission to the Five Civilized Tribes of the Indian Territory, which he held until his death in 1903. Friends tendered him a banquet in Boston on his retirement and presented him a purse of gold,—ample for his simple life. He spent the next ten years with his books at his Pittsfield home, occasionally journeying to Washington in the discharge of his official duties.

When Mr. Dawes decided to retire, Mr. Lodge and his friends lost no time in getting into the senatorial canvass. There was some talk of William W. Crapo of New Bedford, but when the Republican caucus was held Mr. Crapo received but 30 votes. The rest were cast for Lodge. When the Legislature balloted, Mr. Lodge had every Republican vote cast. Patrick A. Collins received the Democratic vote. Mr. Lodge was admirably equipped for his new duties. Possessed of ample means, with a liberal education, broadened by foreign travel and intimate acquaintance with many of the leading public men at home and abroad, a student and writer of American history, a polished speaker and a strong party man, Mr. Lodge took his seat in the Senate, March 4, 1893, under a Democratic President, Grover Cleveland, his certificate of election signed by a Democratic Governor.

From a party standpoint he had earned the right to aspire to fill the seat. In his early manhood the temptation to bolt his party more than once beset him. The Tilden campaign for the Presidency lured many Republicans from their party. The nomination of Blaine in 1884 was distasteful to a large number of young Republicans and Mr. Lodge preferred another candidate, but he remained loyal to the Republican nominee. To him more than any one man in the State was due the victory of the party in 1883, when, as the tireless, energetic resourceful Chairman of the State Committee, he directed the Robinson campaign and defeated Governor Butler for reëlection.

He had served in the Legislature and had been elected

MAYOR SINCLAIR WEEKS

LOUIS K. LIGGETT

COUNCILLOR FRASER

ARTHUR LYMAN

FRANK A. GOODWIN

DANIEL J. LYNE

to the 50th, 51st and 52nd Congresses. His voice had been heard in every nook and corner of the State for years in behalf of his party and its candidates. A hard hitter, with a sharp tongue capable of lashing a political opponent into fury, the Democrats and not a few of his own party, regarded his a favorite political target. Called "the Scholar in Politics," yet he was always practical. The election of Lodge as Senator made it necessary to hold a special election in the seventh congressional district to fill the vacancy. William E. Barrett, Speaker of the House, was the Republican candidate and Dr. William Everett of Quincy, the Democratic nominee. This time Dr. Everett successfully deposited his opponent in a cavity, and was elected by a small plurality, the vote being, Everett, 9763; Barrett, 9699, making the Congressional delegation nine Republicans and four Democrats.

DEATH OF GENERAL BUTLER

GENERAL BENJAMIN F. BUTLER died January 11, 1893, at the age of seventy-five. For half a century he had been a prominent figure in the political, military and legal life of the State and Nation. Like most men of strong character he had many enemies. He had changed his politics often. He was regarded by his friends as a great statesman. His opponents looked upon him as a tricky politician. Those who care to revive the controversy whether he was a great man or a person of average ability as a lawyer, soldier, congressman and Governor, will find plenty of literature pro and con on that question. A disinterested observer, however, would not be likely to accept for example, Senator Hoar's low estimate of General Butler's character, nor would one care to take General Butler's own high estimate of himself as set forth in "Butler's Book."

The State paid its mark of respect by sending to his funeral a delegation from the Legislature and Governor Russell attended with his staff. For many years friends of General Butler tried to secure the passage of a resolve through the Legislature authorizing the erection of a statue of him on the State House grounds, but just as regularly Butler's opponents defeated it. The same people who prevented a statue to Butler made no objections to the erection of effigies on the State House grounds of General Nathaniel P. Banks and General William Devens, two Civil War soldiers and Republican politicians of mediocre ability and parochial reputations, whose military records contain no dazzling successes. General Butler had offended many of the leading Republicans and not a few Democrats, who carried their grudges to his grave.

A NEW RUSSELL IN THE FIELD

It became known early in Governor Russell's third term that he would not seek another reëlection. His determination to retire from the Governorship caused a flurry in the ranks of the Democracy and every Democrat turned confidently and hopefully to his namesake, John E. Russell of Leicester. When the convention met, the scholarly Leicester Democrat was the unanimous choice of the Democracy. James B. Carroll was again named for Lieutenant Governor.

The platform favored the direct election of United States Senators by the people, declared that the Executive Council should be abolished and endorsed the demands made by Governor Russell in his last inaugural for authority to remove State officials without advice or consent of the Council. It denounced the "subserviency" of the Republican Senate to corporate influence, in preventing the passage of the anti-stock watering law. It also demanded that important matters of legislation be referred to the people for their approval and it went on record for substantial taxes on legacies and successions direct and collateral.

On the Republican side there was considerable rivalry for the gubernatorial nomination. Ex-Mayor Thomas N. Hart and Attorney General Albert E. Pillsbury were candidates, but ex-Congressman Greenhalge of Lowell had the call and was an easy winner in the convention. The Republicans entered the contest with more confidence of success than they had since their first defeat by William E. Russell.

The A.P.A. (American Protective Association) was becoming quite a power in state politics and the Republican platform contained a plank designed to please this unAmerican organization. It eulogized the free public school as "the bulwark of freedom" and declared: "We shall stand by it no matter who shall assail it." It also declared that "The Republican party will have no common interest with the saloon or the groggery," this to catch the temperance vote. It favored a law that would reach all bequests and inheritances, direct and collateral. It met the Democratic demand for preventing stock manipulation by corporations by declaring in favor of drastic laws against such practices. It favored the referendum on local matters "under reasonable restrictions."

Governor Russell made several speeches for the ticket. Some of John E. Russell's old congressional friends came into the State and spoke for him. The election was a Republican sweep. The Democratic vote dropped to its normal size and the Republicans swelled their totals, swamping the Democrats by a plurality of 36,000. The Legislature was more Republican than the year before, the Senate standing 33 Republicans and seven Democrats; the House, 183 Republicans and 56 Democrats.

FREDERIC T. GREENHALGE

Governor 1891–1894

THE country had passed through a financial and business depression when Frederick T. Greenhalge was inaugurated Governor, January 4, 1894—the first Republican to be elected in three years. Though an Englishman by birth, Governor Greenhalge was American to the core.

He came with his parents to this country at an early age. His education was received in the public schools of his adopted city, Lowell, and at Harvard College. His young heart beat warmly for the Union cause and he was a volunteer in the Federal Army, but at the end of five months campaigning in the South, he was honorably discharged owing to illness contracted in the service. He studied law, engaged in politics and became a member of the city government and was elected Mayor of Lowell. He was a delegate to the Republican national convention of 1884 and the next year was a member of the General Court. He was a member of the 51st Congress, but was defeated for reëlection in 1890 by Moses T. Stevens of North Andover, his Democratic opponent.

In every public office he held, Mr. Greenhalge displayed signal ability, high courage and intelligence. He had an engaging personality and was an attractive public speaker. His tribute to the Commonwealth of Massachusetts in the peroration of his first inaugural address, is worthy of a place in any book of modern orations.

How familiar this inaugural inhibition sounds even 40 years afterwards, uttered by Governor Greenhalge in 1894; "The circumstances in which we find ourselves must convince us of the necessity of retrenchment and economy. In our present condition, it would be inconsistent and unwarrantable to permit even the semblance of extravagance, luxury, or unnecessary expenditure of any sort in the management of the public business entrusted to us at a time of crisis and trial."

On the question of public education Governor Greenhalge said that there was no room for narrowness, for intolerance, for prejudice. He was a firm believer in the public schools and gave as his opinion that no other agency welded the decisive elements of the population together as good as the public schools.

He favored local option for the regulation and sale of liquor. He recommended that "Suitable legislation be enacted to prevent the watering of the stock of quasi-public corporations, either through the instrumentality of construction companies or otherwise, and also to prevent the issue of bonds as a bonus to parties who subscribe for stock; to confine the expenditures of these corporations as strictly as possible to the purposes for which they are organized, and to insure honesty in dealing both with the stockholders and with the public."

He heartily concurred in the recommendation made by his immediate predecessor for the abolition of the Fast Day, and as a substitute therefor the observance by solemn and patriotic ceremonies of the 19th of April. "It is vain to attempt," said he, "to maintain a custom which has become 'more honored in the breach than in the observance.'" One of the earliest men in public life in Massachusetts to favor votes for women he recommended in his inaugural address limited municipal suffrage for them. The House passed such a bill but the Senate rejected it.

The Senate organized with William M. Butler of New Bedford, President, and the House chose George von L. Meyer of Boston, Speaker.

A law was enacted which prohibited saloons within

400 feet of a school house. Among the other important acts was the incorporation of the city of Beverly, another providing for the decennial taking of the census, authorizing cooking in the public schools, the investigation by the State board of statistics of the liquor traffic in relation to crime, pauperism and insanity, regulating fraternal beneficiary societies, prohibiting the marriage of any male under 18 and any female under 16, establishing the office of fire marshal, and regulating the use of bicycles in public streets.

The Legislature was prorogued July 2, the longest session since 1883, except that of 1900, which lasted four hours longer. It was the last session of the House held in the old part of the State House.

CAMPAIGN OF 1894

THE Republican platform on which Governor Greenhalge ran for reëlection in 1894 was written by Senator George F. Hoar. It consisted of 28 short, pithy paragraphs, several of which contained but two words. It was the last platform which the venerable senator was destined to write for his party, and he tells the story of how he came to prepare this unique political document in his interesting autobiography. He had put off the preparation of the platform until the last minute owing to a press of public business. He jotted down on a few sheets of paper a list of the topics about which he thought there should be a declaration in the platform. It occurred to him that it would be a relief and a commendable change in the style of platform making if he submitted his headings for the platform instead of the old-fashioned style of "viewing with alarm" Democratic policies and "pointing with pride" to the achievements of the Republicans.

The phrase "No barbarous queen beheading men in Hawaii" in the platform was regretted afterwards by Senator Hoar, who discovered that the source of information on which the declaration was based was faulty, that Queen Liliuokalani to whom it referred was a good Christian woman and that there had been no beheading in the Sandwich Islands where the United States had intervened and restored the government. He took occasion more than once to express in the Senate his respect for her and his regret for the injustice he had done her.

The Democrats nominated John E. Russell for Governor and Charles E. Stratton of Boston for Lieutenant Governor. Their platform reaffirmed the demand for tariff reform, endorsed the Wilson bill, and reiterated its position in favor of free raw materials, approved the principle of the income tax, favored the extension of the national civil service law and roundly denounced the A.P.A. movement by declaring against distinction of birth or religion in the rights of American citizenship. It also favored proportional representation.

It was a walkover for the Republicans, their plurality exceeding 66,000. The A.P.A. made a special mark of Lieutenant Governor Wolcott and the result was that his vote was considerably below that of the head of the ticket. Democrats elected but one member of congress that year, John F. Fitzgerald in the Boston district. The State Senate elected stood, 36 Republicans, 4 **Democrats.** The House of Representatives: Republicans 191, Democrats 48, Socialist 1. The Democratic party was at its lowest ebb in years.

GREENHALGE'S SECOND TERM

GOVERNOR GREENHALGE delivered his second inaugural address January 3, 1895, in the new chamber of the House of Representatives. The country was gradually recovering from the business depression. The Republicans had elected a majority of the National House and they once more controlled the Senate of the United States. They had made practically a clean sweep of Massachusetts and the vote for the Democratic candidate for Governor had dwindled to 123,000. The Republican majorities in both branches of the Legislature were very large.

In his address, the Governor asked the Legislature to look into the irregularities and defects in the State taxation system. Not a teetotaler himself, he remarked, referring to the demand of the temperance people for new and more stringent laws governing the sale of liquor: "Energetic action under existing laws may produce quite as satisfactory gains as feverish efforts to secure new legislation."

The subject of State commissions and boards was dismissed with the renewal of the recommendation that the office of Commissioner of Foreign Mortgage Corporations should be abolished, and the work of that office placed under the control of the Commissioner of Corporations. "United in the principle of administration, simplicity of system, are to be preferred to the loose, slovenly method of creating an executive board or office which seems to be an unconnected and unrelated part of the body politic," said the Governor. He reviewed the work under prosecution by the important State commissions and commended the work of the police boards of Boston and Fall River, two Democratic cities, the members of which are appointed by the Governor instead of the mayors of those cities.

The term of Senator Hoar expired March 3 and he was reëlected without opposition from his own party in the Legislature. The Democrats voted for John E. Russell, their unsuccessful gubernatorial candidate.

One of the most important Legislative acts of the year was the creation of the Metropolitan Water Board for providing an ample water supply for Greater Boston. The State was authorized to issue bonds to the amount of $27,000,000. Important changes were made in the charter of the city of Boston. The term of the mayor was made two years instead of one year. Instead of three-headed commissions for the fire, water and institutions departments, they were made single headed commissions with a view of securing better administration of city affairs. The old registrars of voters board was changed to the Ballot Law Commission, consisting of four commissioners, two

MASSACHUSETTS POLITICS

Democrats and two Republicans. The office of city surveyor and city architect were abolished and the work transferred to other city departments.

The establishment of textile schools was authorized and provided for. North Adams was incorporated as a city. The sale of intoxicating liquors on February 22 and July 4 was prohibited. Further regulation of the Sabbath was also passed this year, prohibiting entertainments except those for charitable purposes on the Lord's Day. Another act gave preference to veterans for employment in the public service.

STATE CAMPAIGN OF 1895

CONGRESSMAN ELIJAH ADAMS MORSE of Canton, "Rising Sun" Morse, as he was called, because he manufactured Rising Sun stove polish, opposed Governor Greenhalge for the nomination for Governor at the State Convention of 1895. It was generally understood that the A.P.A. element in the party supported him, but the Governor was overwhelmingly renominated. Elijah Morse was a unique figure in Massachusetts politics. He was always immaculately attired and sported a huge diamond in his white expansive shirt bosom. A preacher of temperance, he never questioned the size of the liquor bills of his campaign managers. He encouraged the tradition that he was one of the famous Adams family that clutter the pages of American history, but the Adams' denied his claim.

Lieutenant Governor Wolcott had no opposition for renomination.

The platform condemned the Democratic tariff. It was for the gold standard of money and opposed the free coinage of silver at any ratio not established by international agreement. The national administration was criticised for its bond issue through private bankers. It declared for the enforcement of the Monroe doctrine, civil service reform, restricted immigration and contained the usual catch phrase on the liquor question.

The Democrats nominated George Fred Williams of Dedham for Governor and James S. Grinnell of Greenfield for Lieutenant Governor. The latter was an old line Democrat and a brother-in-law of John E. Russell. The platform commending President Cleveland's administration, congratulated the manufacturers of the State on the successful operation of the Wilson tariff bill, and denounced the Republicans for trying to reopen the tariff question. It was strong for the gold standard and declared that the government should not engage in the banking business. It again declared for home rule for cities and condemned the Republicans for their efforts to centralize the police power of the cities in the Governor of the state.

There were tickets in the field also of the Populist, Prohibition and Socialist-Labor parties. The vote for Governor was: Greenhalge, 186,280; Williams, 121,599; Kendall, Prohibitionist, 9170; Brown, Populist, 776; Ratherm, Socialist-Labor, 3249. Municipal suffrage for women was defeated on a referendum by a big vote.

ROGER WOLCOTT
Governor 1897–1900

On New Year's Day, 1896, Governor Greenhalge took the oath of office for the third time. Always eloquent and polished in his public utterances and possessing to a remarkable degree the faculty of clothing his thoughts in language that delighted the ear and touched the heart, it was remarked by his close friends that they had never seen the Governor in better form than he was on that occasion.

He wasted no words in the opening of his inaugural address and hurriedly sketched the great enterprises then in progress under the supervision of the State authorities, including the metropolitan water supply system, metropolitan sewerage, metropolitan park system, the subway, the public docks project, the improvement of the harbor in Boston and the construction of State highways, in which Massachusetts was one of the pioneers.

Towards the end of his address he reminded the Legislature of the dangers of corruption creeping in and of the baneful influence of the lobby, which had once more become active if not defiant of the law enacted to curb its activities at the State House.

The influence of the A.P.A. in the ranks of the Republican Legislature was strong enough this year to defeat Edward A. McLaughlin, a Democrat, for election as Clerk of the House of Representatives. Mr. McLaughlin had served every legislature since 1883, when he succeeded

George A. Marden of Lowell, a Republican, whose assistant he had been. His removal was regretted by many of the leading Republicans of the State, but the A.P.A.'s grip on the legislators was tight and they compelled the delivery of enough votes to turn out an official, whose qualifications were of highest character. His absolute nonpartisanship in his office was acknowledged by thousands of men who had served in the House in the 22 years he had held the office. His successor was George T. Sleeper, whose chief qualification for the position was membership in this secret political organization. He lasted but one term. The House was fortunate in having at its command the services of James W. Kimball, who had been Mr. McLaughlin's chief assistant for many years. Most of the labor of the office of clerk fell to him after the change and the next House eagerly embraced the opportunity of dropping Sleeper and electing Kimball.

On February 22, ex-Governor George D. Robinson, General Butler's successful opponent for governor in 1883 died. The Legislature took appropriate action, naming a committee to attend his funeral and setting aside a day for his eulogy.

Within a fortnight the State was shocked to hear of the death of Governor Greenhalge. He was the only Governor of Massachusetts of foreign birth since Thomas Gage, 120 years before. Governor Gage, the British governor of the rebellious colony in the revolutionary time left town rather hurriedly. Lieutenant Governor Roger Wolcott was sworn in and carried out the public policies of his departed chief.

CHARLES SUMNER BIRD

Several important laws were enacted at this legislative session. Perhaps the most important was the act authorizing the building of the South Station, Atlantic Avenue and Summer Street, whereby the Boston & Providence, Boston & Albany, Old Colony and New York & New England Railroads were brought together under the roof of one terminal. Prior to the building of the South Station each road maintained separate terminals in different sections of the city.

The plan for a Greater Boston was referred to the next General Court and while the subject was for years afterwards discussed and is still discussed, nothing came of the suggestion, the suburban cities and towns fearing that they would lose their identity and be swallowed up by Democratic Boston. Their leading politicians also felt that in such a plan they would also lose their influence and they have never given the scheme any real support.

Congressional regulations of the hours of labor and making them uniform was favored in a resolve. Provision was made for the erection of a suitable tablet on the battle field of Antietam, commemorating the services of Massachusetts troops engaged in that important Civil War battle. The collection and circulation of information regarding the abandoned farms of the State was provided for and the splendid equestrian statue of General Joseph Hooker in front of the East Wing of the State House was authorized. $100,000 more was appropriated for the extirpation of the gypsy moth.

The demands of the textile operators for less hours and more pay and the claims of the manufacturers that Massachusetts industries would be unable to compete with those of the South where wages were lower, living costs less, led to an order being passed, permitting the committee on Mercantile Affairs to visit the Southern mill centers, where they had a chance to see for themselves the conditions.

A commission charged with the investigation of the unemployed reported its findings to the Legislature. The hard times had thrown many out of work and the commission made an exhaustive investigation of conditions among the unfortunate people. Their report said that they found that most of the trouble resulted from the influx of a large number of unemployed from other sections of the country and recommended that so far as possible only residents of the state be employed on public works.

NATIONAL CAMPAIGN OF 1896

IN the campaign of 1896 the Democrats were badly split on the money question. The Bryan, or Silver Wing of the party in this State, was led by George Fred Williams. The Gold wing, or Palmer and Buckner faction, nominated Frederick O. Prince for Governor. Mr. Prince had been secretary of the Democratic National Committee for 25 years, was one of the best known Democrats in the State, and had a wide acquaintance with the leading Democrats of the country. He had been a popular Mayor of Boston. A "sound money" man, he refused to accept the Bryan 16 to 1 free silver theory, regarding the doctrine un-Democratic, if not dishonest, and declined to support the nominee of the Chicago convention. Almost every Democrat with a check book left the party that year and either openly espoused McKinley, the Republican presidential nominee or voted the Gold Bug ticket. Practically every prominent and influential Democrat in this State was against free silver.

Mr. Williams' conversion to free silver was quite sudden. In the Spring of that year he had been elected one of four delegates-at-large to the Democratic national convention. His associates were General John W. Corcoran, John E. Russell and James "Smiling Jim" Donovan of Boston. The convention which elected these delegates-at-large declared unreservedly for the gold standard and endorsed ex-Governor Russell as Massachusetts' choice for President. A few weeks later and on the eve of the National Convention which met in Chicago in July it was whispered that Mr. Williams, who, in the 52nd Congress had ably championed the gold standard and condemned the effort to rehabilitate silver, was coquetting with the white metal men. His conversion meant that he must repudiate the platform on which he was chosen, cast his lot with new friends and fight those with whom he had waged many a hard political contest in this State.

When Williams came out for free silver, the gold Democrats aroused and incensed at his action, prevailed upon ex-Governor William E. Russell to go to Chicago and join a group of the prominent Democrats headed by

William C. Whitney and David B. Hill of New York, to prevent the adoption of a 16 to 1 silver plank in the platform. President Cleveland and his cabinet were practically a unit against free silver. The contest at Chicago between the two wings of the Democracy was waged with bitterness.

Governor Russell with the proxy of a Cambridge Democrat sat in the convention and made one of the closing speeches against the 16 to 1 plank. His right to participate in the proceedings of the convention was questioned by Williams, but the Dedham man's objections were not sustained. The free silverites were in the saddle and all opposition to their program was ruthlessly swept aside as they pushed through their platform and nominated William Jennings Bryan, "The Boy Orator of the Platte," for President. A few minutes before, Mr. Bryan who had gone to the convention in his capacity as a reporter for an Omaha paper, had made his famous "Crown of Thorns and Cross of Gold," speech in advocating the 16 to 1 plank in the platform, taking the delegates off their feet by his fervid oratory and carried off the nomination for the Presidency.

The Gold Democrats left Chicago disheartened. Among them was ex-Governor William E. Russell. Worn out by his long hours and heat of the convention city, retired for a brief rest at his summer home and then went to the New Brunswick camp of a friend, Benjamin F. Dutton, a prominent Boston merchant, where he hoped to mend his shattered nerves. He had hardly bade his friends in Boston good-bye when the news of his death was received casting a gloom over the entire state. Governor Russell died July 16, 1896, cut off in the flower of his young manhood at 39.

Williams had but few supporters in his flop to silver in the Massachusetts delegation and the Bay State delegation that year presented the spectacle of a divided house before the convention. It was said that if he had been able to muster any considerable following from New England at the convention he would have been the Vice-Presidential nominee instead of Arthur Sewell an old time Democrat and ship builder of Bath, Maine. As it was, Mr. Williams received 76 votes for that office on the first ballot which dwindled to nine on the fifth when Mr. Sewell was nominated.

The Delegates-at-Large to the Republican National Convention this year were Senator Lodge, Lieutenant Governor Crane, Eben S. Draper and Curtis Guild, Jr. Massachusetts went to St. Louis for Thomas B. Reed of Maine, but the cards were stacked by Mark Hanna for the Ohioan and William McKinley was nominated on the first ballot. Twenty-nine of the thirty Massachusetts delegates voted for Reed. When the roll of the convention was called on the nomination of candidates and the State of Maine was reached Senator Lodge of Massachusetts nominated Speaker Reed in a short and eloquent speech. But it was all over except the shouting. A new political manager, Mark Hanna a business man using business methods had it fixed for Major McKinley. Senator Lodge withdrew the name of Mr. Reed and moved to make the nomination of McKinley unanimous.

DEMOCRATS NAME TWO STATE TICKETS

On his arrival from Chicago, Williams' friends welcomed him with a band and a public meeting at which he defended his course as a delegate. The "Gold Bugs" were not idle. They too were organizing and preparing for the battle election day.

The Republicans had little to do but enjoy the Democratic fight. Few Republicans were attracted to the Bryan-Sewell-Williams banner in Massachusetts. When the time arrived to nominate State tickets the Silver Democrats saw in the movement of the Gold Wing of the party a plan to control the State convention, repudiate the Chicago convention and nominate a candidate for Governor opposed to Bryan.

On the evening of September 25th, there was a public meeting in Music Hall in behalf of the Democratic National ticket and for the purpose of arousing interest among the voters in the State ticket which was to be nominated the next day. Just as the meeting was about to adjourn Mr. Williams declared that there was a plot on the part of the Gold men in the party to shut out the Bryan-Williams men at the convention. He asked all his followers to remain in the hall that night and hold it against their opponents.

Plenty of volunteers were found and when the officers of the State Committee appeared at the hall at eleven o'clock next morning they found the old edifice in control of the radical wing of the party. All efforts to compromise matters failed. The Williams men held their convention in Music Hall while the State Committee and their friends gathered at Faneuil Hall. Both conventions nominated the same State ticket headed by George Fred Williams for Governor and Christopher T. Callahan, afterward judge of the Superior Court, for Lieutenant Governor. Williams declined the Faneuil Hall nomination, knowing that few of those who participated in that Convention intended to support him.

Mr. Bryan came to New England to visit his associate on the ticket, Arthur Sewell of Maine. Boston gave him a noisy welcome. 100,000 tried to hear him on the Common, where he spoke in the evening, but when the votes were counted in November, McKinley carried Democratic Boston by 18,000 plurality. Nevertheless, against all the odds which Mr. Bryan had to contend he rolled up a popular vote of 6,502,925 against 7,184,179 for McKinley. The electoral vote was: McKinley, 271; Bryan, 176.

In this State the Democrats were badly beaten, Governor Wolcott's plurality rising above 150,000. Only one Democrat was elected to Congress, John F. Fitzgerald. On a joint ballot the Legislature stood: Republicans 232; Democrats 44; Independent Republicans 3; Citizen Democrat 1.

When McKinley came to select his cabinet, he named as secretary of the Navy, ex-Governor John D. Long of Massachusetts. Mr. Long had served in Congress with him and there was a bond of friendship between them. Some of the local political leaders objected, but Mr. McKinley was determined to appoint his old congressional colleague. Governor Long's appointment was regarded by many as an incongruous selection because for many years he had been prominent in a Peace Society which abhorred war, but for four years directed the affairs of the Navy Department with signal ability, bringing the department up to a high standard of efficiency.

He had for his assistant Theodore Roosevelt of New York, then on the threshold of his great public career. It was Secretary Long who selected George Dewey for command of the fleet in Asiatic waters, destined to shed new lustre on the fame of the American navy in the Spanish American war by his brilliant victory in Manila Bay, destroying the Spanish fleet and silencing the forts which led to the capturing of the Philippine Islands.

WOLCOTT EASY WINNER

GOVERNOR ROGER WOLCOTT had served in the Common Council of Boston and in the State Legislature. He was never too proud to fight in the ranks of his party in municipal or State campaigns. He stood for clean politics and never hesitated to condemn wrong doing, even though he hurt the feelings of his own party associates. He held some independent views on public questions. He was not an office seeker, but he did not decline party honors when they came to him. When he was Lieutenant Governor during Governor Russell's last term, he treated the Democratic Chief Executive with the greatest respect.

In his first inaugural address to the Legislature Governor Wolcott cautioned the members about growing state expenses and the increasing public debt. He discussed and urged the necessity of improving Boston harbor. The pressing needs of the Metropolitan Boston were pointed out. He praised the State Nautical Training School and commended the appointment of the Commission for the study of tax laws, which was ordered by the Legislature to report to that body October 1, 1897. He warned against making the bank laws too easy to set up trust companies and urged the Legislature to shorten its session and to keep down the number of new laws, most of which were of a special character.

President Lawrence of the Senate was again chosen to preside over the upper branch of the Legislature and a new face appeared on the Speaker's rostrum in the House —John L. Bates of East Boston, who was just beginning a brilliant political career, which was cut short, however, after two years in the office of Governor and had an unhappy ending.

Because of the split in the Democratic party at the November election, many Democratic votes were diverted from the regular channel and for the first time in many years a Republican appeared to be elected in the Fourth Councillor district, the State's only Democratic district. The Republican nominee was Isaac B. Allen, a prominent colored politician of the ward heeler type, who preyed upon rich and ambitious Republicans. His Democratic opponent, John H. Sullivan a leading member of that party, declined to follow the Bryan-Sewell-Williams flag and the Silverites got a lot of satisfaction in his defeat by a colored man.

The most important act of the Legislature of 1897 was the granting of a charter to the Boston Elevated Street Railway Company, which later leased the West End Street Railway Company and took over the transportation system of Boston. The Governor was authorized to appoint a commission to investigate the relations of the street railway companies and the municipalities, naming as the commissioners Charles Francis Adams, William W. Crapo and Elihu B. Hayes.

Through the efforts of Senator Hoar the manuscript of Governor William Bradford's "History of the Plymouth Plantation" was returned to the people of the State. It was supposed to have been taken by the British soldiers on their evacuation from Boston during the Revolutionary war.

STATE CAMPAIGN 1897

AGAIN there were five State tickets in the field at the election in 1897. The Republicans renominated their ticket of the year before, Wolcott and Crane. The Gold wing of the Democracy kept up the fight against the Bryan-Williams Democrats and nominated Dr. William Everett for Governor. The Regular or Silver Democrats named their old ticket of last year, Williams and Callahan. Thomas C. Brophy was nominated for Governor by the Socialist-Labor party. The Prohibitionists named John Bascom and the People's party again fused with the Bryan-Williams Democrats. Because of the division in the ranks of their opponents, the Republicans didn't have to do much campaigning. Their platform confined mostly to local issues declared for the free, unsectarian school and for the enforcement of the liquor laws, waved the flag and marched on to another victory.

The Democratic platform declared for municipal ownership of public utilities, a reform in the tax laws of the State, abolition of irresponsible commissions, popular election of United States senators, eight-hour day for labor, better inspection of factories and an amendment to the employees liability law.

Williams' vote was the record low vote for a Democratic gubernatorial candidate in years. Many Democrats disliking Williams and his leadership and refusing to subscribe to the radical policies of William J. Bryan, either withheld their votes or voted for Governor Wolcott.

SPANISH-AMERICAN WAR

GOVERNOR WOLCOTT entered upon his full term of office, January 6, 1898—a year which was to be the most memorable in his career as a public official. In his inaugural address he again called attention to the fast mounting public debt, but the Legislature heeded not his warning. There was the usual review of the State institutions and their work, and here and there a suggestion to remedy some slight fault. He again referred to the question of a franchise tax on street railways, which the last Legislature had referred to a special committee of the members to report to the present body. The general taxation question was still open, the commissioners named to investigate the subject being unable to agree. The Governor recommended more stringent laws regarding assessment insurance and touched upon education, harbor improvements and the building of the new State dock in South Boston. He suggested that the Cape Cod Canal be built by prison labor. Nothing came of the suggestion. A few years later, August Belmont, a New York financier, took hold of the project and built the canal, opening it to shipping in the summer of 1914. Later the United States Government was induced by a well paid lobby to take over the ditch at a handsome profit for the owners and spent millions to improve it and make a real canal of it.

In reviewing the work of the Metropolitan commissions, Governor Wolcott suggested the continuance of the Transit Commission of Boston, whose official life would end in July, unless new legislation were passed extending it, which was done. He urged State control and care of the insane. He was of the opinion, he said, that all offenders against the laws of the Commonwealth should be subject to final State control. He favored the referendum on all special laws affecting municipalities. The subject of tuberculosis in cattle was discussed quite fully as its importance demanded and he expressed the hope that the Legislature would determine a general policy in dealing with this source of danger to public health.

He was not impressed with the soundness of assessment insurance and regarded it a real danger. He favored higher salaries for the justices of the Supreme and Superior courts. The Legislature passed a law limiting the height of buildings in the vicinity of the State House so that the capitol would not be overshadowed and shut in by the modern skyscraper.

The year 1898 marked the centenary of the old State capitol. The State authorities took possession of the State House on January 11, 1798 and the 100th anniversary of this event was celebrated in a fitting manner by State officials and both branches of the Legislature. The report of the special commission to investigate the relations of street railways and municipalities and towns was received and a law was passed embodying its most important recommendations. The street railways were put under the jurisdiction of the railroad commissioners.

After years of agitation a law was passed regulating fraternal beneficiary insurance associations. Hanging for capital crimes was abolished and a law provided that thereafter the death penalty shall be inflicted by electricity. Greylock Mountain in the Berkshires was made a State reservation and an appropriation of $25,000 was made for the enterprise. Woman suffrage was unable to muster enough votes in the House to secure a roll call on the question.

George E. Smith succeeded George P. Lawrence as President of the Senate. Speaker Bates was reëlected and both branches settled down for a long session, lasting until June 23, destined to be one of the most historic in recent years because of the outbreak of hostilities between Spain and the United States.

As in the Revolution and in the Civil War, so in the Spanish-American War, Massachusetts was first in the field in defense of freedom. On April 15, Governor Wolcott asked the Legislature for $500,000 to be extended in defraying military and naval expenses. Within 25 minutes the law was passed, engrossed, and received the signature of the Chief Executive. This is said to be the record time on legislation. All rules were suspended and the unanimity displayed showed that Massachusetts was of but one mind and that to once more demonstrate that the patriotism of the State and its loyalty to the Government at Washington was unsurpassed by any of her sister commonwealths. Massachusetts troops were in the field the day after war was declared. The State treated its soldiers and sailors with its customary liberality.

The quota of the State under the two calls of the President was 7388, but it is estimated that between 10,000 and 12,000 men volunteered in the army and navy during the war. The regiments that left the State fully equipped for service were the 2nd, 5th, 6th, 8th and 9th. The 2nd and 9th were a part of the force engaged in the reduction of Santiago and the 2nd was engaged with the enemy.

The appearance of the 6th regiment in the streets of Baltimore on its way to Camp Alger, Virginia, was an event of national interest and importance. Thirty-seven

B. LORING YOUNG

THOMAS J. BOYNTON

CHARLES S. O'CONNOR

CHARLES E. HATFIELD

RICHARD W. WIGGLES-
WORTH

BERNARD J. ROTHNELL

years before, a command with the same regimental number on its way to defend the National capital at the outbreak of the Rebellion, was mobbed and the blood of Massachusetts' troops flowed in the streets of the Oriole City, a hot bed of secession. The second appearance of Massachusetts troops was happily quite different. They were received with open arms and shown many courtesies, proof that the old sectional animosities of the great conflict between North and South had disappeared.

MORE REPUBLICAN VICTORIES

WHEN the political season opened in the Fall of 1898, the Democrats gathered in convention at Worcester. The Free Silver element had control of the convention machinery and under the leadership of George Fred Williams removed from the office of National Committeeman, General John W. Corcoran, who was not in sympathy with that wing of the party. The platform adopted endorsed every principle of the last Democratic national convention, free silver and all. It took strong ground against Imperialism, as the acquisition of the Philippines was called. The planks on public ownership of public utilities of the previous year were reiterated and the party stood squarely for the initiative and referendum. None but Free Silver Bryan men were nominated on the State ticket. The candidate for Governor was Alexander B. Bruce of Lawrence.

The Republicans renominated Governor Wolcott. Their platform followed largely the national platform of their party, commended the Dingley tariff law, praised President McKinley for his conduct in peace and war, glorified the deeds of the American army in the war just closed and declared for a larger army and navy.

As the Democrats were still divided, although the Gold wing of the party made no nomination for State officers this year, the Dutch captured Holland again. The vote for the head of the ticket was: Wolcott, Republican, 191,146; Bruce, Democrat, 107,960; Peare, Socialist-Labor, 10,063; Shapleigh, Prohibitionist, 4734; Porter, Socialist-Democrat, 3749.

The Senate elected was: Republicans 33, Democrats 7; House, Republicans 165; Democrats 65; Independents 10. The Republicans elected 10 out of the 13 congressmen.

WOLCOTT'S THIRD TERM

In his third and last inaugural address to the Legislature, January 5, 1899, Governor Wolcott called attention to the fact that the United States for a half century had waged no war against a foreign foe and said, in reviewing the event of the year passed: "There is no doubt in my mind that this war was entered upon by the great majority of the people of the United States, without distinction of party or locality, with high and unselfish purpose; nor do I doubt that its results will be promotive of civilization and enlightenment." With pardonable pride he referred to the splendid patriotic spirit Massachusetts manifested in responding to the call of the National government for the assistance even anticipating that war coming four days before war was declared.

Under the head of Municipal Legislation, Governor Wolcott protested against the mass of legislation passed every year affecting the city of Boston and declared that there was danger in carrying this too far.

One of the first and important political happenings of the year was the reëlection of United States Senator Lodge. Alexander B. Bruce, who had been the Democratic candidate for Governor in November, received the Democratic votes.

Governor Wolcott vetoed the bill giving Spanish war veterans a preference in the civil service. There were further amendments to the election laws. Important laws affecting education were passed, among them the establishment of 40 scholarships at the Worcester Polytechnic School, the authorization of vacation schools and the establishment of additional textile schools. A retirement law was passed for justices of the Supreme and Superior courts on three-quarters pay. Woman suffrage was turned down again, as was the effort to allow them to vote on liquor licenses.

In the Fall, the Democrats nominated Robert Treat Paine Jr., for Governor. Mr. Paine was one of the few men of wealth and high social standing in the State who supported Bryan and Free Silver in 1896. The platform was largely a reiteration of the previous one. The war in the Philippines was characterized as 'criminal aggression." It demanded that the life tenure of judges be repealed.

Governor Wolcott having served the customary length of time announced his decision to retire from politics at the close of his term and Lieutenant Governor Crane was moved up. Speaker Bates was made Crane's running mate on the State ticket. The Republican gubernatorial ticket won by a plurality of 68,000 and the Legislature retained its big Republican majority.

WINTHROP MURRAY CRANE
Governor 1900–1903

WHEN Lieutenant Governor Crane took the oath of office as Governor on January 4, 1900, and read his inaugural message, he was but 37 years old. It was the first time he had addressed a public assembly. Mr. Crane was a unique figure in Massachusetts politics. He lacked much of what people generally regard as necessary in a successful man in politics. He had not a commanding presence nor was he given to the glad hand habit, so common among public men, but he possessed many attractive personal qualities which endeared him to his neighbors and friends.

He might have gone to college and brought home a degree, but he preferred to engage in business with his father in the manufacture of paper. For generations the Cranes of Dalton had made the paper for the United States Treasury and still continue to make it. From earliest times the Cranes of Dalton were men of influence and standing in Western Massachusetts. They took pride and an interest in the affairs of their town, county and State, proving it by serving in various public capacities.

Winthrop Murray Crane early displayed an interest in politics. In 1892 and 1896, he was one of the Delegates-at-Large to the Republican National Conventions. In the latter year he defeated Colonel Samuel E. Winslow of Worcester for the nomination of Lieutenant Governor. From thence on until his sudden death in October 1920, he played an important but unobtrusive part in State and National politics. On the death of Senator Hoar, Governor Bates named him to fill the unexpired term. He soon became a trusted counsellor and a leader of his party in Congress. President Theodore Roosevelt offered him a place in his cabinet, but Mr. Crane preferred to continue in the Senate.

His three inaugural addresses were more of the nature of business documents than political harangues or reviews. The affairs of the Commonwealth were discussed frankly and the law making power was admonished to go slow about piling up more public debt. As a practical and successful business man, the financial condition of the State alarmed him. He spread the figures of the State debt, some $45,000,000, before the members of the Great and General Court and the public, and declared for rigid economy. He advocated a revision of State Commissions in the interest of economy and efficiency. He asked the Legislature to memorialize Congress to widen and deepen the channel of Boston Harbor, recommended that the cost of maintaining the State highways be assessed on the counties, cities and towns, declared that there must be no letting down the restrictive bars on liquor selling and condemned the tendency of the Legislature to interfere too much in the local affairs of cities and towns.

The Legislature was heavily Republican. James J. Meyers was chosen Speaker of the House in a lively contest, defeating Frank P. Bennett of Saugus and Charles R. Sanders of Boston. George E. Smith once more presided over the Senate. An effort was made to repeal the old law by which Roger Williams was banished from Massachusetts because of his religious views, but the Legislature refused to do it on the ground that even if they did repeal the statute, Mr. Williams would not return.

The repeal of the poll tax law was also refused. Saloons were ordered closed election day. Cities and towns were authorized to grant pensions to teachers and firemen. The House went on record for the election of United States Senators by the people. A resolution was adopted in favor of the Boers of South Africa and hoping for freedom of the Transvaal in its fight for independence against British aggression. The leases of the Fitchburg Railroad to the Boston & Maine and the Boston & Albany to the New York Central were authorized.

NATIONAL AND STATE CAMPAIGNS OF 1900

LED by George Fred Williams, Massachusetts Democrats journeyed to Kansas City in 1900 to help renominate William J. Bryan for President. Many leading Democrats of the State still held aloof from their party. They refused to contest with Mr. Williams for the control of the delegation and made up their minds to vote for McKinley if the Democrats insisted on Bryan and free silver again.

Ex-Governor David Bennett Hill of New York worked hard to prevent a 16 to 1 Silver plank, but he was outvoted. He bowed to the will of the majority and supported the ticket. Four years before as one of the leaders for sound money he retired to his home after his defeat and remained silent in the campaign. He was one of the members of the committee on resolutions at the Kansas City Convention and aroused a lot of enthusiasm by announcing his intention to support the ticket, although he did not believe in the money plank in the platform. A majority of the Massachusetts delegates followed Mr. Williams on all questions.

Senator Lodge headed the Massachusetts delegation to the Republican convention in Philadelphia. His associates were Samuel W. McCall, a member of Congress, William B. Plunkett of Adams, a personal friend of President McKinley and Walter Clifford of New Bedford. Senator Lodge was made permanent chairman of the convention. Colonel Roosevelt was nominated for Vice-President. After much urging and persuasion he consented to accept the nomination. He was Governor of New York and head of the New York delegation to the convention. He felt that some of the New York political bosses were trying shelve him politically when they suggested him for Vice-President. He was interfering too much with their carefully laid political plans and was too independent for them.

The Massachusetts delegates were glad to vote for Roosevelt for Vice-President. He was Senator Lodge's old and intimate friend. Six months after President McKinley took office for a second time he was shot by a demented man while holding a public reception at the Buffalo Exposition and was succeeded by the Vice-President whom political bosses thought they had shelved by nominating him as McKinley's running mate.

The Republicans carried the State for McKinley and Roosevelt by more than 80,000, elected 10 of the 13 Congressmen and a Legislature heavily Republican. The vote for Bryan, 156,997, showed that the Democracy of Massachusetts was getting back its normal strength, but the vote for their candidate for Governor, Robert Treat Paine, was a disappointment to the Bryan men. His vote was 26,000 less than that cast for Mr. Bryan. Crane carried the State by almost 100,000.

The Democratic nominee for Lieutenant Governor was John B. O'Donnell of Northampton, a prominent lawyer in the Western part of the State and an enthusiastic Bryan man. His Republican opponent, John L. Bates, carried the State by 104,000 plurality. Boston returned to the Democratic column begrudgingly giving Mr. Bryan a scant 10,000 plurality. Democratic Congressmen were elected in the 3rd, 9th and 10th districts.

GOVERNOR CRANE'S SECOND TERM

In his second inaugural address Governor Crane paid a feeling tribute to his predecessor, Roger Wolcott, who had passed away. He renewed his recommendation of the year before against further and unnecessary expenditures in the metropolitan districts. The work in progress by all of the State commissions was reviewed and concisely set before the Legislature, together with helpful suggestions for improvements in the administration of various departments. He advocated the consolidation of the Metropolitan Water and Metropolitan Sewerage boards on the grounds of efficiency and economy. He entered an emphatic objection to further appropriations for the topographical survey and map of the Commonwealth, started in 1884 on an appropriation not to exceed $40,000, but which had exceeded $250,000. He urged the appointment of commissioners to revise the public statutes. The last revision he pointed out was in 1880.

As a big successful, liberal business man, Governor Crane took pride in the growth and healthy condition of the State's industries which at the time had reached the billion dollar mark annually, giving employment to

500,000 wage earners. He did his part and practised what he preached in keeping down expenses of the State government, but the same cannot be said of the Legislature. The session of 1901 lasted until June 10. Rufus R. Soule of New Bedford was President of the Senate and James J. Meyers, Speaker of the House.

Senator Hoar, whose term as United States Senator was expiring March 3rd following, was reëlected for his fifth term. He was out of step with the Philippine policy of the administration at Washington, but that did not make any difference in the attitude of the Legislators of his party towards him. Richard Olney, who had been Attorney General and Secretary of State in the second Cleveland administration received the Democratic vote.

During the Legislative session Vice-President Theodore Roosevelt visited the State House, made a brief address and held a public reception.

All the Greater Boston schemes were sent over to the next General Court. A new grade crossing law was passed on the lines suggested by the Governor. The Governor vetoed the Washington Street Subway bill and insisted on the city building it and leasing it to the street railway company, a policy which had been pursued by the municipality since it undertook to improve the transit facilities of Boston. The veto was a popular one and made many friends for him.

The Metropolitan Water and Sewerage board was created consisting of three members. The office of Prison Commissioner was abolished and a board of Commissioners was appointed. The liquor laws were stiffened.

It was made a misdemeanor to sell or give away cigarettes to those under 16. A Bucket Shop bill was passed, putting that class of "stockbrokers" in the class with the gamblers and practically wiped them out of existence.

Street railways were authorized to carry United States mail and newspapers. A new law was passed making kidnapping punishable by 25 years imprisonment. The pure food law was strengthened to protect the public against antiseptic and preservative substances.

When the Legislature was prorogued it was to meet again November 13 for the purpose of considering such revision of the statutes as a special committee should recommend. At this special session the report of the committee on the revision was accepted and 7500 copies were ordered printed. Resolutions on the death of President McKinley were adopted at the adjourned session, the President having died at Buffalo, September 14th.

At the November election the Republicans carried the State without much effort, reëlecting their ticket of the year before. The Democrats nominated Josiah Quincy for Governor who consented to lead the forlorn hope. The truth was that the people were satisfied with Crane's administration conducted in a businesslike way with a minimum of politics and it was hard to arouse enthusiasm. The vote for Governor was: Crane, 185,809; Quincy, 114,362; Lewis, Prohibitionist, 4780; Wrenn, Democratic-Socialist, 10,671; Berry, Socialist-Labor, 8898. The Legislature was heavily Republican.

CRANE'S THIRD TERM

IN his third and last inaugural address, Governor Crane called attention to the mounting debt of the State and cautioned the Legislature against extravagance. He recommended an appropriation of $5,000,000 to be spent at the rate of $500,000 a year for the abolition of grade crossings. He contended that the street railways having lines upon crossings to be abolished should bear some of the expense of abolition. He urged the passage of a law which would prevent the control of savings banks by National banks and prohibit officers of a National bank serving as President or Treasurer of a savings institution. At the time there were in Massachusetts 186 savings banks with aggregate deposits of $560,000,000. The number of depositors in the savings banks, November 1, 1901, was 1,593,640. The Governor believed in safeguarding the people of the State. To this appeal the Legislature was responsible and a law embodying the Governor's idea was passed. He recommended that certain commissions be abolished and their powers and duties be transferred to other existing boards.

This year Prince Henry of Prussia, brother of the Kaiser, visited Boston and the two Socialist members of the House protested the invitation of the Legislature to the distinguished visitor to meet the members of the Great and General Court in joint convention. The Prince came and his visit was a most enjoyable one. Receptions, luncheons and dinners were crowded into the few hours that he was in Boston.

During the hearings before the Committee on Constitutional amendments organized labor numbering 700 marched into the State House and asked that the committee report a bill which would allow on petition of 50,000 legal voters constitutional amendments be submitted to the people.

Carrying out the suggestion of the Governor, the Legislature merged the offices of State Aid Agent and Pension Agent and created the office of State Aid Commissioner. The duties of the Fire Marshal were transferred to the State police. Vaccination was made compulsory, the speed of automobiles was regulated and the first Sunday in July in each year was designated as Old Home Week. The Sunday laws were further liberalized by permitting the sale of candy and soda on the Lord's Day. The Governor approved the bill for a 10 hour day and a 58 hour week for women and children employed in manufacturing and mercantile establishments.

President Roosevelt appointed Chief Justice Oliver Wendell Holmes of the Supreme Judicial Court of Massachusetts an Associate Justice of the Supreme Court of the United States, a position he filled with distinction for years. In place of Chief Justice Holmes, Governor Crane named Justice Marcus P. Knowlton of Springfield. The Legislature authorized the appointment of three additional judges of the Superior Court and the Governor named Charles A. DeCourcey, Robert O. Harris, Lemuel L. Holmes.

Quite a stir was caused when Governor Crane refused for some time to surrender a negro criminal on the requisition of the Governor of North Carolina. Although the Governor of North Carolina had promised him protection against violence the fact that two lynchings had taken place under his administration was used by opponents of his return to prove that he could not get a fair deal if he were returned, but Governor Crane finally honored the requisition.

In September, 1902, when President Roosevelt was completing his tour of New England, he visited Governor Crane at the latter's residence in Dalton. While returning from a visit to the venerable United States Senator Dawes, at Pittsfield, and on the way to Stockbridge where he was to board his special train, the carriage containing the President, Governor Crane and Secretary Cortelyou, was struck by an electric car, resulting in the death of the President's personal body guard, seriously injuring the driver of the carriage and throwing its occupants into the street. The President and Governor Crane received a severe shaking up. The motorman of the car, Luke J. Madden, was arrested and at his trial Governor Crane appeared as one of the witnesses for the prosecution. Madden was sentenced to a short term in the County jail.

Probably the most noteworthy act of Governor Crane's administration was the settlement of the great teamsters' strike of March, 1902. For days he devoted himself to the task of relieving the situation. All his personal and official influence was brought to bear upon the leaders of both sides. Both sides were for a time inexorable but Governor's diplomacy won in the end. The striking teamsters and railroad men returned to work.

JOHN L. BATES

Governor 1903-1905

THERE was a new deal in Republican State politics in the Fall of 1899, forced by the anti-machine men. When Lieutenant Governor Crane was moved up to the head of the State ticket, the organization leaders planned to nominate Curtis Guild, Jr. for second place, but a new political factor had sprung up, a young representative from East Boston, John L. Bates. He had made a good impression in the popular branch of the Legislature. When Speaker Meyer left the chair to become Ambassador to Italy, this young East Boston man was elected to succeed him as presiding officer of the House. As Speaker he ruled the lower branch of the Legislature with dignity and firmness.

The son of a Methodist minister, Speaker Bates was strong with the "church vote." A good campaigner who uttered commonplace facts with great unction, possessed with the art of pulpit and platform oratory, he was a valuable man for Mr. Crane who couldn't make a speech.

Mr. Crane took no part openly in the contest for second place on the ticket, but Bates' victory was not objectionable to him.

Curtis Guild, Jr., Bates' opponent, represented the "better element" of the party. He was a well known and popular figure in the parties of the State. He loved the classics and quoted liberally from Greek and Latin scholars in his public speeches and writings. Bates was an easy victor and Mr. Guild had to wait until Mr. Bates succeeded Governor Crane before he was permitted to get aboard the party esculator.

In his inaugural address Governor Bates asked the Legislature to appropriate money for the State's representation at the St. Louis Exposition. The needs of additional legislation affecting public education, textile schools, the militia, the control of the foot and mouth disease among cattle, the need of additional accommodation for the insane, the more humane treatment of prisoners and their employment on waste lands, harbor improvements in Boston and the abolition of the fee system were discussed. He advocated party enrollment to better protect party nominations. He favored preference of employment of Massachusetts citizens in State construction work, a limited referendum law, a tax for public franchises from corporations or individuals to which such privileges were granted and he took a stand against public officials seeking favors from public service corporations. He advocated two additional judges of the Superior Court because of increasing litigation. He urged more stringent laws for the protection of those who had invested

WILLIAM M. BUTLER

their savings in life insurance and favored liberalizing the corporation laws.

The Legislature remained in session until June 26, having spent 171 days in adding more than 500 new laws. Resolutions on the death of Ex-Senator Henry L. Dawes who died during the session were adopted as were resolutions favoring legislation by Congress to protect the forests of the White Mountains by including them in a national park. Permanent control and ownership of anthracite coal mines prompted by the country wide suffering caused by the great coal mines strike was favored in resolutions adopted by the Legislature. One constitutional amendment was proposed, where by a petition of 50,000 voters they may submit amendments to the State constitution.

Dr. William Everett, one of the original Mugwumps and a unique character in the politics of Massachusetts, died February 16, 1903. Eccentric, independent and courageous, he added spice to every campaign in which he participated.

By the death of John E. Russell who died October 22, the Democracy of Massachusetts lost one of its ablest champions and the State one of its gifted sons. He was a Democrat of the old school. He might have graced the cabinet of Grover Cleveland or represented his country abroad, Mr. Cleveland having tendered him his choice of a portfolio in his cabinet or an important diplomatic post, but he preferred his own fireside among the hills of Worcester County to the Capitals of Europe or the passing glory of a place in a President's cabinet.

STATE CAMPAIGN OF 1903

IN the gubernatorial contest of 1903, the Republicans renominated the ticket of Bates and Guild. The platform was read by Ex-Governor Crane. Congressman Samuel L. Powers was chairman of the State convention and Senator Hoar made the nominating speech for Governor Bates. It was the last State convention in which the venerable statesman participated.

The Democrats renominated Colonel Gaston and John C. Crosby for Governor and Lieutenant Governor, respectively. Gaston proved that he was a good vote getter. His strength compelled the Republicans to call out their reserves the year before. Republican leaders, aware of Bates' weakness with certain Republicans and Gaston's strength among business men, made the campaigns of 1902 and 1903 largely personal contests against Colonel Gaston, calling attention to his banking, street railway and gas company connections. But the Republicans were not alone in that phase of the campaign. The Williams Democrats, smarting under defeat in the convention of 1902 when they lined up against Gaston for Hamlin, charged that the Democratic State leaders sold out the party to the corporations and that certain public corporations with which Colonel Gaston was connected supplied the campaign funds. The work of Gaston and his friends in organizing the Democrats of the State was effective and his vote of the year before showed that there was a steadily growing opposition to the Republicans and that once more the Democracy, which had been buried time and time again, was showing signs of life.

Governor Bates' first year in office was not a happy one. Several of those who had been among his most active supporters for the nomination were in open rebellion against him. The first serious split came when these men submitted to him their choice for chairman of the Boston Police Board, in place of Albert F. Clark whose term expired. The Governor rejected their candidate and named a personal friend and neighbor, Judge Emmons, of the East Boston District Court. Emmons' appointment proved to be unpopular. The Governor instructed the State police to see that pool selling at horse races was stopped. That aroused further opposition to him.

In the midst of the campaign, a prominent lawyer and ex-member of the Legislature took the stump and charged that Governor Bates had borrowed money from an insurance lobbyist, Walter J. Holden, who had been one of the Governor's most enthusiastic backers in his contest for Lieutenant Governor and Governor. Photographic copies of the checks drawn by Holden to the order of Bates were exhibited and created a mild sensation. The Governor acknowledged his borrowings from Holden, but said that he had repaid the loan with 6% interest.

The Democrats felt that the check exposure, Judge Emmons' unpopular administration of the Boston police department and the enforcement of the anti-pool selling law would cost Bates a lot of votes. The Republicans seeing that they had a hard fight on hand redoubled their efforts and pulled the head of the ticket through with a plurality of 35,000. The dwindling Republican plurality for Governor was evidence that the Republicans were heading for the political toboggan.

For the second time Governor Bates took the oath of office on January 7, 1904. His inaugural was a lengthy review of State affairs with little new or startling in his recommendations.

The General Court passed 460 acts and 110 resolves. Among the most important acts passed were those establishing the school for Crippled and Deformed children, transferring the powers and duties of the Fire Marshal's office to the State police, making the number of Aldermen in the City of Boston 13 instead of 12 and dividing the city into 13 aldermanic districts, taxing coupons and stamps used in the sale of merchandise, a new charter for the City of Pittsfield, an act relative to the expense of candidates for public office, another relative to the instruction of prisoners, a law relating to children bound out in families, another relative to the powers and duties of the bar examiners and the admission of attorneys at law to practice, incorporation of the Y.M.C.A. evening Law School and amendments to the caucus laws.

Reverend Dr. Edmund Dowse, for 25 years chaplain of the Senate resigned and was succeeded by Dr. Edward A. Horton.

Governor Bates named Lloyd E. White and Lorance E. Hitchcock new judges of the Superior Court.

In the Fall of this year Judge Phelps of the Lee Police Court, imposed a fine of $25 on Hugh Gurney, third secretary of the British Embassy at Washington for overspeeding an automobile in Lee. Gurney refused to plead, whereupon Judge Phelps ordered a plea of "not guilty" to be entered and fined the British attaché $25 for contempt of court. Gurney appealed to the British Ambassador and the case was laid before the State Department, creating a tempest in the diplomatic tea pot and was the subject of extended despatches between Washington and London. Judge Phelps was only a Trial Justice—not even a lawyer. He was not aware that members of the diplomatic corps are immune from arrest. The Secretary of State demanded an explanation from Governor Bates. The Governor apologized for the Judge's mistake and the Judge, through Governor Bates and the State Department made amends to Mr. Gurney.

The dedication of the imposing equestrian statue of General Joseph Hooker, one of the noted Union commanders during the Civil War, a native of Massachusetts, took place during the year as did the annual encampment of the Grand Army of the Republic, affording Governor Bates opportunities to strengthen his hold on the veterans of the Civil War.

NATIONAL AND STATE CAMPAIGNS
1904

DEMOCRATS and Republicans named their delegates to their National Conventions in April. The former chose as their delegates-at-large, Patrick A. Collins, Colonel William A. Gaston, William L. Douglas and Congressman John R. Thayer. The Bryan men with George Fred Williams as leader made a determined fight for delegates favorable to the widely known newspaper publisher, but the Conservatives were in the saddle, and the most the Bryan-Hearst men could muster in the State convention was 270 votes cast for Williams.

Into the trained hands of Charles S. Hamlin, Guy W. Currier, Josiah Quincy and James B. Carroll, the Gaston or Conservative forces placed their fortunes for the day. John J. Flaherty of Gloucester was made permanent chairman of the convention. Richard Olney, who had been Grover Cleveland's Attorney General and Secretary of State was endorsed as Massachusetts' choice for the Democratic Presidential nomination. George Fred Williams opposed the resolution instructing the delegates for Olney. In the course of his speech Mr. Williams prophesied that if the resolution was passed, there would be a contest on the question before the National convention. He argued that the State convention had no right to instruct the district delegates, several of whom, he declared, favored another candidate.

On his arrival in St. Louis, Mr. Williams found that the delegates and most of the Democratic leaders were bent on ignoring Bryan. Leader after leader denied their old master. Staunch political lieutenants of former battles deserted him but Mr. Bryan kept his temper and saved his strength for the contest in the committee on resolutions, where his political principles were in danger of being rejected. He was willing to abandon a specific 16 to 1 declaration for the sake of harmony. His popularity and influence had suffered in four years. It was apparent that the convention would nominate Judge Parker of New York and that it would refuse to be guided in any matter of importance by the twice nominated candidate for President, Mr. Bryan.

On the first ballot the 32 votes of Massachusetts were cast for Richard Olney under the unit rule. It should be said in justice to Mr. Olney that he never encouraged his followers to believe that he could be nominated and he was reluctant to allow the use of his name. The Olney boom got little encouragement from outside this State. General Collins carried a letter written by Mr. Olney withdrawing from the contest to be used at his discretion, but the delegation insisted on Olney's nomination and also on voting for him. Parker was nominated on the first ballot. Mr. Olney had 38 out of 1000 votes in the convention. Parker had 669 and Hearst 194. The six votes Mr. Olney received outside of this State came from Maine 4, Nebraska 1, Oklahoma 1.

The Massachusetts member of the committee on resolutions was Charles S. Hamlin. He declined to support Bryan and Free Silver in 1896 and stumped the State for the Gold Democratic National and State tickets. The St. Louis platform as reported and adopted by the convention was silent on the money question. After Judge Parker had been nominated and learning that the platform had not taken a stand on the money question, the nominee sent a telegram to William C. Sheehan of New

York, his personal representative in St. Louis, in which he said that he regarded the gold standard irrevocably established and as the platform was silent on the subject his views should be made known to the convention and if unsatisfactory to a majority, he requested Sheehan to decline the nomination for him. The telegram created a sensation when it was read in the convention. There was a heated discussion over the attitude of the nominee and as to what course the convention should pursue. It was finally voted to send the following telegram to Judge Parker:

"The platform adopted by this convention is silent on the question of the monetary system, because it is not regarded by us as a possible issue in this campaign and only campaign issues were mentioned in the platform. Therefore there is nothing in the views expressed by you in the telegram just received which should preclude a man entertaining them from accepting a nomination on said platform."

The convention voted to allow the platform to stand as adopted. The Massachusetts delegates got into line with the rest and nominated Henry Gassaway Davis of West Virginia for Vice-President and returned home feeling that they had at least succeeded in shaking off Bryan and his radical political ideas.

The four delegates-at-large, to the Republican National convention at Chicago, were Senator Lodge Chairman, ex-Governor Long, ex-Governor Crane and Colonel Everett C. Benton. President Roosevelt was nominated by acclamation, but there was a lively contest for Vice-

President. It was the first convention of the Republican party since its formation that Ohio did not have a candidate to offer for the Presidency. Elihu Root was temporary chairman. In the time intervening between the issuing of the call to the meeting of the convention, Mr. Hanna, chairman of the National Committee, died.

Senator Lodge was the personal choice of President Roosevelt as Chairman of the committee on resolutions and on the second day of the proceedings, when he stepped upon the stage with his White House inspired typewritten platform, he read it in an impressive manner, evoking frequent and hearty applause. Twenty years before, Mr. Lodge and Mr. Roosevelt as delegates sat in the convention in the same city. What a change had come over the political fortunes of both in two decades! In 1884, both were young and inexperienced in public affairs. The nomination suited neither of them. Many of their personal friends bolted the nomination and joined the Mugwump movement in that memorable campaign. Lodge and Roosevelt were not enthusiastic over Blaine, but they remained regular.

Ex-Governor Long was one of the committee named to escort Speaker Cannon from the Illinois delegation to the platform where "Uncle Joe" received the gavel from Mr. Root and piloted the convention proceedings from that out as its permanent Chairman.

Mr. Roosevelt was the first Republican Vice-President to be nominated for President and the first Vice-President to be nominated for President by a leading party since Martin van Buren, nearly 70 years before, for Millard

Fillmore was only the choice of the "Knownothings" and John C. Breckenridge of a faction of the Democrats. Martin van Buren owed his nomination to his alliance with the all powerful Jackson. One more precedent was violated by this convention. It was the first time that the Republican party went to the State of New York for a presidential candidate. William H. Seward in 1860, Roscoe Conkling in 1876 and Chester A. Arthur in 1884 were rejected. The Republican party never but once before, when it nominated Blaine, had crossed the Alleghenies for a standard bearer and then it went to defeat. This precedent was to be broken by Mr. Roosevelt at the polls in November.

DOUGLAS DEFEATS GOVERNOR BATES

COLONEL GASTON disappointed his followers by refusing to run again. A man of wealth who spent his money liberally, he had done a lot of organizing work and the Democrats were more united than they had been since the days of Cleveland and Russell. The diehard Bryan men disliked Gaston's corporation connections and were ready to oppose his nomination. He felt that the party had had all the quarreling the voters would stand and announced that he was out of the running. He and his friends supported William L. Douglas the wealthy Brockton shoe manufacturer, a life-long Democrat who had always shown a friendly interest in party affairs.

The State convention accordingly nominated Douglas for Governor and John C. Crosby of Pittsfield for Lieutenant Governor. Douglas was not objectionable to the radical wing of the party and he was on good terms with labor organizations. Mr. Douglas had been for years a large advertiser in the newspapers. His picture always accompanied his advertisements and his features were as well known to the people of the Commonwealth as those of Lydia Pinkham and Father John, adorning their patent medicine ads. A big advertiser in the newspapers has a great advantage over a non-advertiser. Newspapers are commercial enterprises and the counting room cannot be expected to offend good customers.

Governor Bates' veto of the Overtime bill offended the labor men and they flocked to the Democratic standard. Under the proposed overtime law, no woman or minor under 18 years could work in any factory more than 10 hours a day, except to make up for time lost through the breaking of machinery on a previous day of the same week, or to make up time so that a Saturday half holiday might be had. Labor leaders organized "Flying Wedges" and went after the Governor's political scalp with vengeance.

Governor Bates' appointment of Judge Emmons as chairman of the Boston Police Board was a very unpopular move. The Judge was a good man personally, but he attempted to run a cosmopolitan city like a country village and the public rebelled. Many practical politicians who had helped Bates beat the Republican machine candidate for Lieutenant Governor and worked hard for him for Governor, took delight in knifing him because he had refused to do their bidding. The tide was running against him.

Everything seemed to be going the Democrats' way. Douglas' successful business record helped him with the business men. Several years previous, he had served in the House and Senate. He was popular in his own section. Republicans opposed to Governor Bates turned to him. The few speeches that he made dealt with the tariff. Mr. Douglas was in favor of free raw material, especially free hides and leather of which he was a large consumer. The Republicans charged him with being a free trader but the issue was not free trade, it was Douglas *vs.* Bates. Boston was strongly Democratic that year. Patrick A. Collins, its Mayor, and the party organizations worked like beavers for the ticket. The first returns indicated Democratic victory. As early as six P.M. it was known that Douglas was elected. The final tabulation of the votes gave him a plurality of 35,000 over Bates.

The pluralities for the National and State tickets, with the exception of that of Governor, assured the continued ascendency of the Republican party in the Legislature and the large percentage it retained in the congressional delegation, electing 10 of the 13 representatives, proved that the election was a personal drive against Bates. He accepted the verdict good-naturedly. This unfortunate man became involved in financial difficulties a few years later. Complaint was made against him by clients to the Bar Association who claimed that he had not accounted for monies entrusted to him as their legal representative and he was disbarred, the only Governor of Massachusetts to suffer such punishment.

DEATH OF SENATOR HOAR

THE venerable and venerated Senator Hoar died at his home in Worcester, September 30, 1904. He was 78 years old and had been engaged in public life almost a half century. In his long and notable public career at the Nation's capital, he saw men in politics grow rich, some honorably and others not over scrupulous how they acquired their wealth, but the breath of avarice never polluted his nature. His partizanship, at times was intense, but he never hesitated to say that his party or his associates in public life were wrong, if that was his belief. He inherited his independence from his Puritan ancestors. Puritan of Puritans, Senator Hoar was cosmopolitan and broad-minded. A Unitarian in religion, he respected the religious views of his fellow citizens who worshipped at different altars from him. To the immigrant he extended the hand of fellowship. His great heart went out to the poor, and to the suffering, struggling peoples of the world. His eloquent voice was ever raised for freedom.

His friendship, once formed, was as true and as constant as the needle, which guides the mariner across the pathless sea. The beauty and purity of his home life and his devotion to his family and friends were among his strong traits of character. Few among his contemporaries could sway an audience as he could. He was a courageous fighter in any cause he undertook to champion. He gave and received heavy blows in politics. His conception of his duty to his conscience was demonstrated when he stood in his place in the Senate of the United States and parted political company with friends of a lifetime, because he could not bring himself to believe that President McKinley's "benevolent assimilation" of the Philippines, conformed with American ideals of popular self-government.

In the great contest which he made against the Imperialistic policy of his party, he invited political and social ostracism, but he suffered the loss of neither. When his term as Senator was about to expire, the Legislature of Massachusetts approved of his independence and unanimously reëlected him for another term. That one act of his native State meant more to him than the plaudits of the entire country. He spoke of it in his autobiography and printed the resolution endorsing him. It was a chivalrous act and proof that the spirit of independence and generosity was not dead among Massachusetts politicians.

He lived to see his old enemies of the South growing out of the secession, regard him as their best friend and invite him to their shattered firesides after that dreadful conflict between North and South over slavery. He often arose above the slough of partizanship to pay tribute to the worth and character of a political opponent. He lived in modest quarters in Washington which many a department clerk would rebel at. He kept neither coach nor footman. He couldn't afford such luxuries, even if he cared for them. The street car was his favorite conveyance in Washington and at home. His modest dwelling in Worcester was a store house of cultivated intellect and meant more to him than the castle of a king. He was carried back to his boyhood home, Concord, where his remains were laid beside her who shared his joys and sorrows for more than a half century.

The people of Senator Hoar's home city reared a monument to his memory. The sculptor was Daniel C. French, one of America's leading artists, who did full justice to his subject. The statue was erected with subscriptions ranging from one cent to $100 from 30,000 individuals, residents of Worcester. There were 2648 subscriptions of one cent, mostly from school children, 22,820 from one cent to 25 cents, 3139 from 25 cents to $1 and 15 above $100. The list included subscriptions from 128 societies. All classes, races and creeds, mindful of the public services of the man, gathered at the dedication ceremony to show their appreciation of his worth and character. His old and intimate friend, Rev. Dr. Edward Everett Hale the Unitarian divine offered the prayer.

Governor Bates was called upon to name a successor to Senator Hoar pending the meeting of the Legislature, which would select a Senator to fill the unexpired term. Several candidates were mentioned, but he named ex-Governor Crane, whose selection was confirmed by the Legislature when that body met in January and met with general satisfaction of all classes of citizens all over the State.

WILLIAM L. DOUGLAS
Governor 1905-1906

WILLIAM L. DOUGLAS was the fourth Democrat chosen Governor since the Republican party came into power in the State. Twelve years had come and gone since the Democrats had elected a Governor. They were naturally elated over their victory and they flocked to the State House to speed the parting Republican incumbent and welcome the incoming Governor of their own political faith. The booming of cannon on the Common, saluting the new Chief Executive, was followed by the applause of enthusiastic followers who overran the Capitol as their gubernatorial choice stood on the Speaker's rostrum in the Chamber of the House to read his inaugural address. With gratitude to the people and a full realization of the responsibilities placed upon him Governor Douglas said, he entered upon his duties with the determination to be the Chief Executive of all people of the State and to do all in his power to promote the welfare of the Commonwealth and its inhabitants.

That part of his inaugural in which he recommended the enactment of a law returning to Boston and Fall River the control of their own police force naturally pleased the Democrats. He charged that the high cost of living was due to the Republican tariff and observed in his discussion of that subject that "high wages and low labor costs go hand in hand." He agreed on the necessity of other States enacting child labor laws and the employment of women, similar to those of Massachusetts. Being one of the largest shoemakers in the United States, it was only natural that Governor Douglas should favor free hides. He coupled free coal with the same demand. "Coal," said he, "the great source of power for our factories and heat and light for our homes, is one of the essentials to our industrial life. It should be as cheap as possible." Congress finally granted free hides, but the shoe manufacturers soon had a new excuse for raising the price of their goods and the consumer was not benefited by such action. He favored direct legislation. He asked for generous appropriations for industrial and trade schools.

He recommended legislation giving to cities and towns wider powers in the conduct of business which derived its profits from the necessities of the community. "The powers already granted have proved the economy and wisdom of the conduct of such business by the community itself," said he. That was a longer step in this direction than any of his predecessors had taken on this subject for many years. Coming from a successful business man the suggestion caused quite a flurry among opponents of municipal ownership. The lobby and the high priced legislative counsel, to be sure, had to do a little more button-holing of members than usual and the Governor's public ownership ideas were rejected by the Legislature.

A very important announcement was made regarding the State militia. He said that he had asked the War Department to detail Lieutenant General Nelson A.

Miles, U. S. A., retired, to report to him under the provisions of the "Dick Militia Act" and that he had been notified by the Secretary of War that the request would be granted. Forty-four years before, Nelson A. Miles, a native of this State had raised and equipped at his own expense, a company of volunteers when President Lincoln asked for defenders of the Union. His rise was rapid, winning promotion after promotion by conspicuous bravery. He was in every engagement of the Army of the Potomac, with one exception, until the surrender of Lee to Grant at Appomattox. At 25 he commanded an army corps, numbering 25,000 men. Three times wounded, he was mustered out at the close of the war as a Major General of volunteers. Entering the Regular Army at the close of the Civil War he served on the frontier, fighting Indians. He was the terror of "Sitting Bull" and other famous old Indian warriors. No man who wore the uniform of the United States in his day had more public honors heaped on him than General Miles, but he got out of favor at the White House during President Roosevelt's term, was snubbed and retired.

General Miles was one of the foremost soldiers of the State and country and yet he had never seen the inside of a military school until after he had won his commission as Major General. General Miles had been away from his native State so long that he felt like a stranger on his return. He came without much show or trappings, took the desk assigned him in the Adjutant General's department and gave the State the benefit of his wide experience and military knowledge. With the pass-

DANIEL J. GALLAGHER

H. H. PIERCE

PROF. FRANK L. SIMPSON

CONGRESSMAN MARTIN

HENRY PARKMAN, JR.

U. S. MARSHAL MURPHY

ing of the Douglas administration General Miles departed as quietly as he came.

Governor Douglas gave his support to the movement to establish juvenile courts for handling the cases of minors under 16.

With a Republican Legislature and a Republican Executive Council, with the other elected State officials on the State ticket Republicans, Governor Douglas began his administration by appointing William R. Buchanan of Brockton, a newspaper proprietor and business associate, a Republican, his private secretary. Mr. Buchanan came to be regarded as a Deputy Governor. He knew practically none of the Democratic politicians and made no attempt to cultivate their acquaintance or friendship. Pretty soon the complaint was heard that Democrats couldn't get at Governor Douglas. Rightly or wrongly Buchanan was blamed. Many leading Democrats stopped going to the Executive department to see the Governor.

John J. Flaherty of Gloucester, chairman of the Executive Committee of the Democratic State Committee and John C. Crosby, who had been a party draught horse for years and Douglas' running mate on the State ticket, were made judges of the Superior Court, Charles H. Cole, succeeded Judge Emmons, police commissioner of Boston. That was about all the big jobs that were handed to the faithful. The small fry got only a few patronage crumbs from the Douglas table.

Governor Douglas vetoed four Legislative acts, only one of which was passed over his veto. Very few of the changes in the organic laws proposed by Governor Douglas were adopted. His was a colorless administration.

Mayor Patrick A. Collins of Boston, died suddenly at Hot Springs, Virginia, September 13, 1905, where he had gone for a brief rest. The news of his death came as a shock to his friends and Boston was plunged into genuine grief and mourning. He was easily the foremost man of his race and yet he was genuinely American in every fibre of his body. For a quarter of a century he had been regarded as one of the big Democrats of the Nation. His counsel and advice was sought by the party leaders in National, State and city affairs. Honest, sincere, upright in character, he hated shams and meanness and stood head and shoulders above most of his party associates in politics.

A grateful public erected a noble monument to him in the Fenway, hard by the effigy of the friend of his youth, John Boyle O'Reilly, whose memory is also perpetuated in bronze by his admirers.

DEMOCRATS NOMINATE BARTLETT

ONE term was enough for Governor Douglas. When the announcement was made that he would not be a candidate for reëlection, the Democratic leaders began to troop up Beacon Hill and ask him to reconsider his disinclination. Men who had openly criticized him joined in the procession and begged him to run again, realizing that a business man like Douglas, was an asset to the party, but he wanted to return to his lasts and awls. Colonel Gaston was asked to run. He, too, refused. Finally, General Charles W. Bartlett, a well known lawyer and member of Governor Douglas' military staff was agreed upon and nominated. General Bartlett had never been prominent in party affairs, although he had shown some interest in ward politics when he lived in Dorchester. New Hampshire born and bred, he inherited his politics from a long line of Granite State Democrats. His nomination was a popular one and he had the support of all factions of the party.

Before he was nominated, however, there were a lot of things requiring the attention of the party doctors. For second place, it was agreed beforehand, that Henry M. Whitney of Brookline, a prominent Boston business man and promoter of big enterprises would be nominated. Mr. Whitney had long been an advocate of Canadian reciprocity. He came of an old Democratic family. His father, General James S. Whitney, was a Jacksonian Democrat. He was Collector of the Port of Boston before the Civil War. His son, Henry M., inherited his father's aptitude for big business. Another son, William C. was Secretary of the Navy in President Cleveland's first cabinet.

Besides being engaged in the steamship business, Henry M. Whitney had brought about the consolidation of all the street railways of Boston. He was a director in the Boston & Maine Railroad. He had dabbled in the gas combine in Boston and the suburbs and was still looking for other business worlds to conquer. The Republicans charged that he was working for selfish purposes, pointing out that under reciprocity—merely another name for free trade they claimed—the products of Whitney's Nova Scotia coal and iron mines would be admitted free into the American markets. The paramount issue of the campaign with the Democrats was relief from unnecessary and burdensome tariff restrictions. Aside from a little eruption over the manner in which the State committeemen-at-large were to be selected, the convention was as harmonious as could be desired.

Lieutenant Governor Guild was nominated by acclamation by the Republicans, on motion of Ex-Governor Bates who made the nominating speech for him in the convention. There was a three-cornered contest for the second place on the ticket and also for the position of Attorney-General. Eben S. Draper was an easy winner over August H. Goetting and Frank S. Hall for second place and Dana Malone had a walkover for Attorney General. The Reciprocitarians were represented in the Republican convention by Henry B. Blackwell, husband of Lucy Stone, and Eugene N. Foss, but they were disarmed at the start by the phraseology of the tariff plank in the platform. General William F. Draper, brother of the nominee for Lieutenant Governor, disapproved of the effort of the Republican leaders to pacify the reciprocity element and denounced the tariff plank of the platform as weak.

Beaten in the convention, the Reciprocity advocates resented their treatment and denounced the tariff plank as meaningless. Guild's position was satisfactory to them and they decided to make their fight on Draper, an opponent of their ideas. A delegate who had the audacity to offer a resolution favoring the election of United States Senators by popular vote was rebuked by the chair which ruled his motion out of order, amid shouts of approval by the delegates.

The campaign on both sides started off with a rush. The Republicans realized that they were up against two good campaigners in Bartlett and Whitney. A few of the extreme radicals in the Democratic ranks declined to support Whitney. Foremost among them was George Fred Williams, who wrote an open letter to Mr. Whitney charging him with using corrupt methods in securing legislation for his street railway consolidation measure many years before. Mr. Williams reviewed the famous West End legislative investigation of 1890 in which Mr. Whitney figured. Mr. Williams at the time was a representative from Dedham and took a prominent part in the investigation.

At the election, Guild's plurality was 22,558 but Draper's was less than 2000. Interest in the contest between Draper and Whitney was intense. Election night, the Democrats, through Arthur Lyman, Chairman of the State committee, sent a telegraphic despatch to the chairman of the Democratic town and city committees asking them to prepare petitions for a recount of the vote for Lieutenant Governor. The recount did not change the result and the official vote gave the election to Mr. Draper by the narrow margin of 1941 votes. The Legislature and Executive Council remained heavily Republican.

DEATH OF EX-GOVERNOR BOUTWELL

Ex-Governor George S. Boutwell passed away, February 27th. He had lived and labored beyond the biblical age of three score and 10, serving his State and country with distinguished ability every office he filled. Originally a Democrat, he became a Free Soiler and was one of the founders and leaders of the Republican party. He was the friend and confidant of Lincoln, Andrew, Sumner and Wilson, advisor of President Grant and his Secretary of the Treasury. Under Lincoln he organized the Federal Internal Revenue Department. He was a Representative and Senator in Congress and one of the Committee of the House in the impeachment proceedings against President Andrew Johnson. In the evening of life, he became estranged from the party he had helped organize over its Philippine policy and was a leading anti-Imperialist. In the campaign of 1890, when feeling ran high on the subject, Congressman Moody remarked, in a speech before the Essex Club, that "He (Boutwell)" at least might spare epithets to the party that had showered upon him every honor within its gift except the Presidency."

Mr. Boutwell replied, saying that if he had applied any disparaging epithets to the Republican party he was not aware of it, recounted his party services and what the party had done for him and concluded by saying: "If a mercantile account current could be written it might appear that my obligations to the Republican party are not in excess of the obligations of the Republican party to me." He died poor in purse, but rich in the legacy of noble life dedicated to his country and his fellow citizens.

CURTIS GUILD, JR.
Governor 1906–1909

IN nominating Curtis Guild, Jr., for Governor, the Republicans carried out their policy of promoting the second man to first place on the State ticket. The escalator system still worked smoothly. He was heir apparent to the gubernatorial chair by inheritance. As Lieutenant Governor under Governor Douglas he had treated the Democratic Governor in all of his official dealings and personal relations with great courtesy. While a strong partizan, he had occasionally refused to enthuse over some of his party's local candidates for public office.

He came of good Yankee pioneer stock. He moved in the best society, but he was democratic in his ways, mixed with the common people, sympathized with and worked for many political reforms. For years he had been one of the most popular stump speakers of the State. When the Spanish War broke out, he resigned his commission as Lieutenant Colonel in the State militia and went out as Adjutant and Lieutenant of the old, historic 6th Massachusetts regiment. Later, influential friends at Washington, procured for him an appointment on the staff of General FitzHugh Lee, in command of the 7th Army Corps, as Inspector General with the rank of Lieutenant Colonel. The 7th Army Corps saw no fighting.

Years before he was chosen Lieutenant Governor, Eben S. Draper served as chairman of the Republican State Committee and took an active interest in the success of the party. The Drapers of Hopedale were among the most cheerful givers to their party campaign funds. As manufacturers of cotton machinery they were interested in a high tariff on cotton goods and their own products. The success of the Republican party in the State and Nation meant much to them in a business way. The new administration of Guild and Draper was sworn in January 4, 1906. Governor Guild took occasion to answer in his inaugural the Democratic charge that Massachusetts was decadent, attributable they charged, to the high tariff.

He suggested the extension of the corrupt practices act to limit the amount to be spent by candidates and the prohibition of campaign contributors by corporations, warning the Legislature not to "make it impossible for some future Samuel Adams to be a candidate for Governor." He did not believe in rich men buying office and sought to prevent them from doing so. A lifelong advocate of civil service reform, he recommended that an adequate salary be paid, at least to the chairman of the Board, from whom he said the needs of the work demanded daily attention. Touching on State finances, he urged more economy by the Legislature.

Adverting to the Insurance laws and the scandalous

showing made by the investigation of the big companies in New York, he said that "Not one hint of graft, or even of political interference, is directed, in this general storm of criticism, against the Insurance Departments of this Commonwealth. At such a crisis, with a patent wrong crying for redress, a Commonwealth with such a record cannot relinquish leadership."

He favored putting telegraph and telephone companies within the jurisdiction of the Highway Commission with regulatory powers. Calling attention to Virginia's celebration at Jamestown, the first English settlement on American soil, he said that Massachusetts should be adequately represented at the exposition. He took issue with the Democrats on the police system of Boston and justified the State's interference. He recommended the establishment of an Excise Board which should be given the power to grant and regulate liquor licenses, then possessed by the Board of Police and advocated a single Police Commissioner for Boston. Both of his recommendations respecting the Police Board of Boston were adopted by the Legislature and he named Stephen O'Meara former editor of the Boston Journal, as the new Police Commissioner. Mr. O'Meara's appointment, made while he was on a European tour, took the Boston police out of politics, though he was an uncompromising Republican. His administration was free of politics and the Boston police regained their standing and respect of its citizens. Mr. O'Meara was reappointed by Governor Foss.

The Legislature adopted resolutions memorializing Congress praying that the Federal Government establish uniform hours of labor in all the States. It also passed an amendment of the Constitution authorizing the Governor and Council to remove justices of the peace and notaries. The Governor and Council were authorized to spend the sum of $5000 for a portrait bust of Senator Hoar for the State House and $2100 for a portrait of Abraham Lincoln, to be hung in Memorial Hall. The Governor was empowered to name five commissioners to have charge of the Massachusetts exhibit at the Jamestown Exhibition and the board was authorized to spend $50,000 for the State exhibit.

It was the period of street railway consolidations and the New York, New Haven & Hartford Railroad Co. was authorized to acquire several lines in Western Massachusetts, which proved to be a poor investment and later, under the Wilson administration at Washington, it was forced to unscramble its street railway and steamboat lines, by orders of the Justice Department which made a drive against transportation monopolies.

DEFEATS JOHN B. MORAN

IN 1906 the radical wing of the Democratic party found in John B. Moran, District Attorney of Suffolk County, a new and vigorous leader. Moran had been elected District Attorney the year before over Michael J. Sughrue, who had the nominations of the Democrats and the Republicans. Moran had a sharp tongue and used it on his opponent with telling effect, criticizing the conduct of the District Attorney's office. Always independent in politics, he didn't like the party machine leaders and they disliked him. He had supported Republicans for Mayor and Governor and he had long been given up by leading Democrats as irreconcilable.

His opponents charged him with using the great power of his office to make political capital for himself. Men of high standing in the community were haled before him and questioned as an old time police magistrate would examine a culprit. He brought before him legislators and aldermen on graft charges. He hunted grafters big and little and for a time his presence at Pemberton Square had a wholesome effect. When the Democratic convention was held, Moran's friends had control of the State committee and ran things their own way. Moran's friends dropped the Gastons, the Thayers, the Burnetts and the Quincys and substituted George Fred Williams and his friends.

William R. Hearst was nursing the fond hope of being the Democratic candidate for President in 1908 and had organized the Independence League, manned it by employees of his newspapers and was making a lot of political noise in his Boston organ. To satisfy the Hearst men and the labor element, the Moran campaign managers nominated Eldridge Gerry Brown of Brockton for second place on the State ticket. Moran's control of the State Committee marked the passing of the control of the State organization from the "safe and sane" wing of the party, led by Gaston, Currier, Quincy and John A. Sullivan, to the radicals, headed by Moran, Williams, Feeney, Timothy W. and Daniel H. Coakley.

It was a Moran convention, unanimous from beginning to end, except for the endorsement of William Jennings Bryan as the Democratic nominee for the Presidency in 1908. Mr. Moran's campaign manager, Granville S. MacFarland, an editorial writer on Hearst's paper, took the platform and emotionally opposed the proposition of his political sponsor and tutor, George Fred Williams, to indorse Bryan for the Presidency, but when the motion was put only three of the delegates voted no.

The platform was an elaboration of the Moran declaration of principles, issued some time before the convention when Mr. Moran announced his candidacy. In addition to the Democratic nomination Mr. Moran had the nomination of the Prohibitionists and Mr. Hearst's Independence League.

The Republican State Convention was a love feast. Ex-Governor Bates was the presiding officer and Guild and Draper were nominated. The platform, read by William H. Moody, Attorney General in President Roosevelt's cabinet, was a glorification of the State and National administrations. The convention was devoid of incident save the oratory of Bates, Guild, Lodge and Moody.

The campaign proved to be the most exciting and sensational witnessed in years. Moran drew big crowds and he made many charges against Governor Guild, among them that he had named Senator Dana to the bench of the Superior Court, because the latter had as President of the Senate, prevented the Overtime bill going to him—

the same measure, by the way, that helped to defeat Governor Bates. Governor Guild denied the charge and said that he would have signed the bill had it come to him. Moran accused Governor Guild of accepting money for a eulogy on William McKinley and also of protecting a grafting State commissioner.

The Republicans struck back at Moran and claimed that about all he had done as District Attorney was to use the office to further his own political fortunes. Several times during his stumping tour of the State, Moran collapsed on the platform. It was charged by his opponents that this was done to gain the sympathy of his audience, but his intimate friends knew that he was then suffering from the disease which ere long was to kill him. The Moran campaign chest was practically empty. The expenses of the campaign were defrayed from the lean pockets of the candidate and his friends. He declined financial assistance from corporations and the few rich men who supported him. The cost of his rallies was usually borne by the local committees. Moran's campaign ended in Boston with a great indoor meeting and an overflow on the Common of several thousand people.

Governor Guild was reëlected by 30,000 and Draper by 9,000. The Republicans elected 11 of the 14 Congressmen and the Legislature chosen had its customary Republican majority in both branches. Many Democrats voted for Guild rather than risk the reins of the government in the hands of Moran. They did not relish the idea of Moranizing the State Capitol and being compelled to submit to the same "reign of terror" on Beacon

Hill which obtained for a time in Pemberton Square, while he was District Attorney.

GUILD'S SECOND TERM

It was "with high appreciation" of the trust imposed in him by the people that Governor Guild for the second time took the oath of office. He had met and defeated one of the best vote getters in the State. Few men in his party could have stemmed the tide which was running against the Republicans. Many Democrats found it easy to vote for him, because of his fine sportsmanship and broadness on public questions.

In the opening of his second inaugural address, Governor Guild discussed the relations between capital and labor. He urged uniformity of legislation between States concerning such matters as cannot be constitutionally controlled by the National government. State finances were discussed at considerable length. He was happy to say that during his first year as Governor, the State debt had been reduced $12\frac{1}{2}\%$. He set up the claim that the whole corporation tax belonged to the State instead of to the cities and towns. In his opinion the State should receive one-half the liquor license fees in order to help defray the expenses entailed by the liquor traffic.

Calling attention to the overcrowded condition of the State House, he said business sense and sound economy alike required the immediate construction of an office building for State Departments. He favored a graduated tax on direct inheritances. Automobile regulation and a stricter examination of drivers of cars on the highways and a tax on motor cars was recommended. He urged amendments to the eight hour bill and a real enforcement of the factory laws.

Referring to the dissatisfaction with railroad passenger and freight service, which was then agitating the public, Governor Guild said that "railroads themselves have it in their power materially to relieve congestion and in cases where they have shown no disposition to exert such power, they should be compelled to do so" and added a warning against transportation monopoly in New England. He was for safeguarding of the savings of the poor and adequate protection of money deposited with foreign banking corporations. Governor Guild was a consistent and persistent opponent of the "bucket shop" and asked the Legislature to prohibit it from doing business in the State, a request which the Legislature heeded with several other of his recommendations.

Speaker Cole of the House was reëlected and William D. Chappel was chosen President of the Senate. To meet the needs of the Superior Court owing to the increase of business the Legislature authorized the appointment of two additional judges. The Legislature of 1907 put 587 new laws and 133 resolves into the Blue Book. Six acts were vetoed by Gov. Guild. The legislative session lasted 178 days and the Legislature was prorogued Friday, June 28, at 11.14 P.M. Among the memorials to Congress were resolutions favoring a further prosecution of the work of exterminating the gypsy moth in conjunction with the State authorities, another favoring a Federal law for the extermination of dogfish, regarded as a menace to the fisheries of the State. Both branches went on record favoring international peace. Resolutions were passed condemning the New York Central Railroad for its inadequate freight facilities and approved the demand of the public for better freight accommodations. One of the important acts passed by this Legislature was to prohibit bucketing and bucket shopping and to abolish the bucket shop so-called.

A board for the establishment of three sanatoriums for tubercular patients was authorized. The election laws were once more overhauled and former statutes were repealed inconsistent with the new laws affecting primaries and elections. Additional subway facilities for Boston were provided by another act. The Insurance laws were strengthened in behalf of the policy holder as suggested by the Governor in his inaugural.

"PINK TICKET" CONVENTION

MORAN's big vote of the year before—the largest a Democratic candidate had ever received for Governor—encouraged the Democrats to believe that they were within hailing distance of the governorship, but early in the year, Moran announced that his health would not permit him to make another campaign. His retirement opened wide the field but no Radical of prominence stepped into the breach. The "safe and sane" Democrats, taking courage, began to plan for their return and the control of the State organization and trotted out as their candidate for Governor, Henry M. Whitney.

A poll of the Democratic members of the House and the Senate showed that Whitney was the choice of a large majority of them. Whitney sentiment cropped out all over the State. Mr. Whitney was convinced that there was a real demand for him and he began an active, dignified campaign for the nomination. General Bartlett envinced a desire to be considered again and placed himself "in the hands of his friends." Mr. Whitney opened his campaign with a big mass meeting at Combination Park, Medford. While Mr. Whitney was speaking, a man named O'Keefe, a member of the State Committee, interrupted the prospective gubernatorial candidate with the question: "How about the mer-ger?" using the hard *g* in the last syllable in merger. Mr. Whitney, a bit hard of hearing, asked the man to repeat the question, and answered that he would state his position on that question later in the campaign.

It proved to be the rock, or one of the rocks on which the Democrats split in the campaign. The question of a merger of the Boston & Maine Railroad and the New York, New Haven & Hartford Railroad was then so far advanced that people began to wonder if Mr. Whitney's candidacy was in any way connected with it. As a Boston & Maine director, as a former head of the Boston Chamber of Commerce and identified with large business enterprises, many believed that his candidacy was in some way related to the scheme to monopolize the railroads of the State.

The Bartlett men made the merger the leading issues of their campaign against Whitney. General Bartlett opposed it. The Independence League's candidate for Governor, Thomas L. Hisgen of West Springfield, an oil dealer, was opposed to it. The anti-Whitney men, controlling the State Committee, chose Springfield for the holding of the State convention.

The afternoon before the convention, a special train from Boston carried the delegates from the eastern sections of the State to Springfield, where the State Committee was to meet that evening, select the permanent chairman of the convention and agree on other details. The Whitney men didn't lack funds and no Whitney delegate was obliged to absent himself from the convention because he couldn't afford the expense. Somebody financed the anti-Whitney wing—some said it was Thomas W. Lawson, the broker. Lawson had quarrelled with Whitney and to many there seemed to be a motive on Lawson's part for making trouble for his whilom State Street friend. In the entourage of General Bartlett at Springfield, were many faces unfamiliar to Democratic convention goers. The train had not left the South Station before the report was started that the anti-Whitney men had secured the services of a lot of strong arm, disreputable characters, picked up from the under-world to "rough house" the convention. As proof of their deftness, one of this class relieved Mr. Whitney of his pocket book containing a considerable money and some railroad passes. "If those men are allowed in the convention tomorrow it will be the gravest mistake that can be made by the men who seek the defeat of Mr. Whitney," said Congressman Keliher, a Whitney manager. "It is an element which must be controlled and suppressed the first minute of the convention, or else the Democratic party's interest will suffer."

It was nearly midnight when the first test of the relative strength of the two candidates in the Democratic State Committee disclosed the control of that body resting in the adherents of General Bartlett, and also made the Bartlett men a majority in the State Committee and forced the selection of Daniel J. Kiley for temporary chairman over Joseph A. Conry by a vote of 23 to 21. When the matter of selecting a chairman on resolutions was reached, the Bartlett supporters again had their way and named George Fred Williams. Congressman Joseph F. O'Connell was made chairman of the Committee on Credentials.

Chairman John P. Feeney of the State Committee personally assured the Whitney managers that he would give everybody a square deal in the convention. The Bartlett men having control of the convention, gave out pink tickets to their followers, admitting them to the convention. From these tickets the convention got its name. By nine o'clock the next morning, the holders of the pink tickets began to move over from their hotel to the Court Square Theatre. They had no difficulty getting in, but the Whitney men with their credentials, many of them among the best known Democrats of the State, were kept waiting in line for hours before they were admitted. When they were admitted to the hall they found the theatre filled with Bartlett "delegates." Although but one convention was called, there were two conventions held, both in the Court Square Theatre. The Bartlett convention held the stage. Joseph A. Conry acted as chairman of the Whitney convention in the rear of the hall.

Bartlett was nominated by acclamation by his followers with John Alden Thayer of Worcester for Lieutenant Governor. General Bartlett accepted the nomination then and there, but Mr. Thayer sent word that he would not permit his name to stand on the ticket. Later he appeared before the Whitney delegates and repudiated the nomination of the Bartlett convention and announced that he would support Whitney. The Whitney forces went through the motions of nominating Whitney for Governor and Ex-Senator George A. Schofield of Ipswich for Lieutenant Governor.

The legality of the Bartlett nomination was brought before the State Ballot Law Commission. That body found that General Bartlett was not legally nominated and that Mr. Whitney was the Democratic nominee. George Fred Williams declared the decision to be the worst political scandal in the history of the State.

General Bartlett ran as an anti-merger candidate. The campaign on the Democratic end was lively, but, of course, the party was doomed to defeat. The Republicans prosecuted their campaign with vigor. They had the significant Moran figures of the year before in mind and took no chances. The vote for the three leading candidates for Governor was: Guild, 188,068; Whitney, 84,379; Hisgen (Independence League), 75,499; Bartlett, 11,194. The combined vote of three minor party candidates totalled 13,430. Draper for Lieutenant Governor received 173,619. The combined vote of Schofield and Browne, 166,819. The State was slipping away from the Republicans. All that was needed to complete the overturn was a united opposition.

GOVERNOR GUILD'S ILLNESS

GOVERNOR GUILD took the oath of office for the third time, January 2, 1908. He told the Legislature that the State must control public service corporations, but he counseled against "sensational onslaughts on property shattering public confidence," and "checking investments, reducing alike earnings of capital and the employment of labor."

Again he prodded the Legislature to pass an additional law to further safeguard the savings of the people. Railroad and other transportation corporations were discussed and he submitted for the consideration of the Legislature and he asked that they consider as a matter of general policy, the following questions:

"1. Shall a steam railroad be allowed to control trolley lines? The intent of the law of Massachusetts clearly prohibits such control. The competition in passenger service, and, since the law of 1907, in express service, between them and street railroads, is, I believe, healthy and should be maintained.

"2. Should an express company be permitted to control a railroad and through a railroad freight rates? I believe that the influence of express companies in the control of railroads hampers their development and tends to damage the general interest of the public. I believe that the ownership of railroad stocks by express companies should be discouraged.

"3. Should railroad companies be permitted to own or to control or to establish steamship lines?"

He took a firm stand against outside control of Massachusetts railroads.

The previous Legislature had passed an act forbidding corporations under the supervision of the Commonwealth to contribute to political candidates or campaigns. He asked them to broaden the act to shut off all corporation contributions. He called for a law prohibiting churches, benevolent and charitable associations soliciting money from candidates for public office. He favored an act correcting the distribution of the corporation tax, instancing glaring examples of the unfairness of the law as it stood. He proposed further regulation of child labor, calling for a medical certificate before any minor was set to work at any occupation. A lover of the flag of this State and country, one who always uncovered in the presence of Old Glory, he asked that the State flag be protected and preserved by law.

MASSACHUSETTS POLITICS 113

The presiding officers of both branches of the Legislature of the year before was reëlected for the session of 1908.

A few weeks after inauguration, Governor Guild was stricken with a severe illness and for weeks his life was despaired of. He was unable to attend to his duties as Governor for a period of four months, during which time Lieutenant Governor Eben S. Draper discharged the duties of the office. The illness of Governor Guild cast a gloom for some time over the whole Commonwealth and his popularity among the people was demonstrated in many ways. Race, creed and politics were forgotten for the time being and everybody joined in the prayer that he be spared and restored to his duties. Again in August, Governor Guild was stricken with appendicitis. For the second time Draper was acting Governor.

The presiding officers of both branches of the Legislature of the year before were reëlected for the session of 1908. The Legislature lasted 165 days and adjourned June 13, at 6.14 P.M. Six hundred and fifty acts and 146 resolves were passed. Seven acts and one resolve were allowed to become laws without the signature of the Governor and nine acts and two resolves were vetoed relating to special legislation for individuals.

VAHEY *vs.* DRAPER

GOVERNOR GUILD followed the long established Republican party custom of stepping aside for the Lieutenant

Governor, at the close of his third term and Lieutenant Governor Draper was unanimously nominated for Governor at the State Convention. Congressman Augustus Peabody Gardner, Senator Lodge's gifted and popular son-in-law, was the chairman of the convention. For second place there was a three cornered fight, the candidates being John N. Cole, Robert Luce and Louis A. Frothingham. All three had been prominent figures in the Legislature. Frothingham and Cole had been Speakers. Luce was the author of election and caucus laws.

Albert E. Winship of Somerville, who was to have presented the name of Mr. Luce to the convention, was taken ill at the last moment and Mr. Luce decided to present his case to the delegates in person. This he did, modestly and eloquently. Frothingham had a big lead over his competitors, who united in making his nomination unanimous.

Congressman Gardner made a spirited defense of Lieutenant Governor Draper, who, he said, had been the victim of more malevolent misrepresentation and vituperation than any other man within his recollection. He had been maligned as an employer of labor. But the people of Hopedale knew whether he was an oppressor or not. They had a chance to register their opinion of their employer at the polls and only 17 were against him. This, Mr. Gardner argued, was an emphatic denial of the charges against him as an employer.

The Massachusetts platform was in entire agreement with the National platform adopted at Chicago in June.

Satisfied that John B. Moran's health would not permit him to enter the gubernatorial race, Senator James H. Vahey of Watertown announced his willingness to become the Democratic standard bearer. It seemed like a hopeless and thankless task for any Democrat to try to get together the warring factions of the party, but by tact and diplomacy, Mr. Vahey succeeded remarkably well. With the aid of a few loyal friends, he stumped the State and made a good impression on the Democratic voters. The Democratic State convention was held in Boston. Congressman Andrew J. Peters was the permanent chairman. David I. Walsh of Fitchburg was temporary chairman. Both made speeches scoring the Republicans for their failure to entrust the people with their own government.

Under the heading "Hypocrisy of Republican Senators," the platform adopted declared: "We believe in an eight-hour day. We believe that women and children should not be compelled to work more than 54 hours a week. We denounce the action of the Republican Legislature which defeated the bills regulating the hours of labor for women and children, and for peaceful persuasion in industrial disputes. We point to the hypocrisy of Republican senators who reported favorably upon the latter measure, and then voted against their own report."

Vahey had no opposition for the nomination for Governor. Charles J. Barton of Melrose, an old time Democrat, was named Vahey's running mate. A new set of State Committeemen-at-Large were chosen and a slate for Presidential electors was nominated.

Hearst's Independence League nominated William N.

Osgood of Lowell for Governor. Some years before, Mr. Osgood was prominent in the Democratic party. The Prohibitionists put up Willard O. Wylie of Beverly, as their candidate. James F. Carey of Haverhill again ran on the Socialist ticket and Walter J. Hoar of Worcester was the choice of the Socialist-Laborites.

The campaign was tame. The Republicans figured that the Democrats couldn't possibly win and counted on their "reserve vote" to come out in the Presidential year and did not think it necessary to conduct a very vigorous campaign. Draper's plurality was 60,000. Bryan carried Boston by a scant 200, Vahey's plurality in Boston was over 11,000.

Frothingham led Draper by 12,038. His plurality over Barton, his Democratic opponent, was 96,307. Both the Independence League and Socialist party secured more than the necessary 3 per cent to retain their entity as political parties.

In the case of Congressman O'Connell, whose plurality dwindled to a scant four votes, his Republican opponent, J. Mitchel Galvin, contested his seat unsuccessfully. Congressman Peters, Democrat, a popular Democrat, had a close shave, getting by with a plurality of 494. The Legislature remained Republican.

PRESIDENTIAL CONTEST 1908

LONG before the Spring campaign for delegates to the Republican National Convention in 1908 began, Presi-

DAVID I. WALSH

dent Roosevelt had decided on William Howard Taft of Ohio, his Secretary of War and former Governor of the Philippines, as his successor in the White House. Mr. Taft was United States Circuit Court judge at the time of his appointment as Governor of the Philippines by President McKinley. He came from fine old New England stock. His mother was from Millbury, Massachusetts, his father from Vermont. When a lad, Taft spent his summer vacations with his Aunt Delia Torrey in Millbury. He had a splendid record as Governor of the Philippines. He was by nature peculiarly fitted for this task.

A big, broad, humane American, he made the yoke of Government as light as possible for the little brown brother and held out to the Filipinos the hope of self-government, "as soon as they were deemed capable of managing their own public affairs." Having accomplished the difficult task given him in the Orient, President Roosevelt called him home and made him Secretary of War. A lot of Republicans disliked the idea of Roosevelt picking his own successor. It smacked too much of a perpetuation of a Roosevelt dynasty in the White House, they said. Mr. Roosevelt had incurred the enmity of a large and important faction of his own party. "You'll take Taft or me," President Roosevelt was often quoted as saying during the campaign for delegates.

The opposition to the White House candidate was known as the "Allies." Its candidate was Vice-President Fairbanks. To Ex-Congressman Samuel L. Powers of Newton, a close personal friend of Secretary Taft, was assigned the duty of lining up the Republicans of Massachusetts for Taft. Senator Crane was one of those in the inner circle of "The Allies." He wanted uninstructed delegates to the National convention. Mr. Taft, in his "swing round the circle," came into New England territory and his supporters made the most of his visit. Defeated in a majority of the district conventions, the anti-Taft men kept up the fight against instructions until long into the morning of the day of the State convention, when a compromise was reached and the promised fight on the floor of the convention was abandoned.

The Taft managers consented to a declaration in which it was stated that for party reasons it was not considered wise to indicate any preference for President in the party platform, but recognized that a majority of the delegates desired the nomination of Mr. Taft. The lions of the Taft league led by Senator Lodge and the lambs of the "Allies" led by Senator Crane lay down together. Politicians who sat up the night before the convention hurling defiance at the senatorial combination, Lodge and Crane, who dominated the situation, came into the convention hall the next day to the tune of the "Merry Widow" waltz, and were ready to eat out of the hands that had smote them a few hours before.

TAFT NOMINATED

WHEN the convention was held in Chicago, the Roosevelt-Taft forces beat the Allies to a "frazzle," to use

President Roosevelt's own term. Senator Lodge was permanent chairman of the convention by request of Mr. Roosevelt. The Massachusetts delegation went to the convention with a Guild boom for Vice-President, but they found another Massachusetts man on the ground with headquarters going full blast and an announcement sent broadcast that he was a candidate for second place on the ticket. John Hays Hammond, the eminent engineer and capitalist, who figured so prominently in the Jameson Raid in South Africa and whom President Kruger of the Boer Republic came near hanging, had recently purchased a summer home in Gloucester and declared his intention of becoming a resident of Massachusetts, was the man. He was Taft's friend. Aside from that, nobody seemed to know why he should be thought of as a candidate. Mr. Hammond's boom collapsed just before the assembling and he announced his withdrawal from the contest. Hammond was suspected of entering the fight to help the candidacy of Taft's choice for second place, James S. Sherman of New York.

On the fourth day of the convention, Senator Lodge arose and presented the name of Governor Guild. Chase S. Osborne of Michigan seconded it. On the ballot, which nominated Sherman by a large majority, Guild received 75 votes. When the result of the ballot was announced, Senator Crane moved on behalf of the Massachusetts delegation that the nomination of Sherman be made unanimous. There was really no heart in the Guild movement. Both Massachusetts Senators knew he hadn't a chance to be nominated. Later they and the administration furnished ample salve for the Governor's wounded feelings in the shape of a special embassy to Mexico on the occasion of the celebration of the Centennial of Mexican independence and later on as ambassador to Russia.

Senator Crane was reëlected on the National Committee. The new chairman of the Republican National Committee who ran the Taft campaign, Postmaster Frank H. Hitchcock, was credited to Massachusetts. It was true that he claimed a voting residence in Newton, but he had lived in Washington for several years after his graduation from Harvard and was unknown to most Massachusetts people.

DEMOCRATS ENDORSE OLNEY

THE Democratic State Convention met in Faneuil Hall, Boston, in May for the election of four delegates-at-large and four alternates to the National Convention. The chairman was Frederick J. Stimson of Dedham, afterward American ambassador to the Argentine, under Woodrow Wilson, a scholar, a recognized authority on international law and a novelist, whose pen name is "J. S. of Dale." It was a Williams-Bryan convention from beginning to end.

The riotous scenes of the Springfield convention the Fall before were repeated in the old Cradle of Liberty. In a session lasting nearly four hours, during which pandemonium reigned for a considerable part of the time, making deliberation impossible, the Bryan men, who insisted on instructions for the delegates-at-large, won over the anti-instructionists who leaned to Governor Johnson of Minnesota for the Presidential nomination.

The anti-Williams or anti-Instructionists ticket was headed by Robert M. Burnett of Southboro. The other candidates were the same as on the Williams ticket—Moran, Coughlin and Doherty. In putting through the Bryan program, Mr. Williams had the powerful influence of Martin M. Lomasney. Not that Mr. Lomasney loved Williams more, but he loved those who were fighting the Dedham man less. When the battle of words and epithets raged the fiercest, it was Lomasney who jumped into the thick of the fight and routed the "Corporation Democrats" who, he charged, were trying to create discord in the party. While Williams enjoyed the emoluments of the convention, it was Lomasney and the latter's lieutenants who did the work. Chairman Stimson lost control of the convention early in the proceedings and didn't recover it until he called the police to his aid.

The first break occurred when the platform was read. Professor Alexander F. Chamberlain of Clark University, Worcester, who sat with Charles Haggerty of Webster and Eben S. Stevens of Dudley, the latter a brother-in-law of Richard Olney, arose and shouted his disapproval of the Bryan instructions. The chair ruled him out of order. Mr. Chamberlain made for the platform and landed at the foot-lights on the historic stage quicker than it takes to tell it. He moved that all reference to

Bryan in the platform be stricken out. Chamberlain's voice was drowned for a few moments in the catcalls, hisses, jeers and cries of "Put him out" from the supporters of the Nebraskan. But the Worcester man possessed excellent lung power and demonstrated that he had good staying qualities.

Professor Chamberlain characterized Bryan as a dead one and predicted that if the delegation was tied to the Nebraskan it would be as dead politically as the candidate, but the platform was adopted "unanimously" so the chair ruled. After further wrangling and shouting and the police cleared the stage, the ballot for delegates resulted in the choice of George Fred Williams, Dedham, John B. Moran, Boston, Daniel F. Doherty, Westfield, John W. Coughlin, Fall River.

On the way to the convention city, Denver, the delegates called at Mr. Bryan's home, "Fairview" a suburb of Lincoln, Nebraska. Dr. John W. Coughlin of Fall River was elected National Committeeman. There were things to do at Denver and the Bryan men determined to do them and to put none but Bryan men on guard. Christopher T. Callahan of Holyoke, was made chairman of the Committee on Credentials. Williams was made a member of the Committee on Resolutions.

Neither presidential candidate came to Massachusetts that year, the Republicans deeming the State solid for Taft and the Democrats regarding it as a waste of time. Mr. Taft's plurality was 108,000. The congressional delegation remained the same as the last Congress and the Legislature was heavily Republican.

EBEN S. DRAPER
Governor 1909–1911

THE State was to enjoy the benefit of another business man at the helm in Eben S. Draper for a short time. Men in public life with convictions like his usually displease many. There was nothing mealy mouthed about Eben S. Draper. He had the courage of his convictions, published them and fought for them. He had no use for frauds or shams and he did not hesitate to denounce them. Organized labor was his unrelenting opponent. The labor union leaders had opposed him ever since he entered public life. For many years he had taken a prominent and active part in politics. He denounced the Canadian reciprocity movement as a delusion and a snare and declined to cater to those who headed the agitation. His three terms as Lieutenant Governor, several months of which were spent as Acting Governor, during the severe illness of Governor Guild, familiarized him with the duties of that office.

His first inaugural address was a business document. Naturally, his first concern was the finances of the State and these he treated with a refreshing frankness. Like his predecessor, he urged economy on the Legislature and a consideration of the fact that the burden of taxes falls on the people. It is an old trick of legislators to provide snug berths for some of their number in the shape of recess appointments. In the opinion of Governor Draper, recess committees were unnecessary and expensive and he sat down hard on this policy. To him is due the credit for suggesting and insisting on the passage of laws for the better regulation of operating automobiles. He recommended that the boards of Registration in Dentistry, Registration in Pharmacy, Registration in Veterinary Medicine and Registration in Medicine be consolidated on the ground that four separate organizations for this work seemed unnecessary. He asked the Legislature to keep down the number of new laws.

Joseph Walker of Brookline was chosen Speaker of the House and Allen T. Treadway of Stockbridge President of the Senate.

The most important act of the Legislature was the Boston Charter bill. It was opposed by substantially a unanimous vote of the Democratic party. It was designed to clip the wings of the then Democratic Mayor of Boston, John F. Fitzgerald. Among some of the important measures of a non-partisan character passed were the bills consolidating the Board of Education and the Industrial Commission into a new Board of Education. The bill regulating the use of automobiles and laying a graded tax on the same so that the Commonwealth would collect something like $200,000 a year more from the owners of these machines than before, which money was used for the repair of State roads, was passed. It was the beginning of the unfair drive on automobile owners, singled out by legislators as a profitable source of income.

FOSS JOINS DEMOCRATS

Vahey's candidacy of 1908 demonstrated that when a real Democrat ran he could get the party vote. He succeeded in welding the warring factions together and at the outset made it plain that his only motive was to offer every Democrat an opportunity to return to the fold. His vote of 168,000, one year after the "Pink Ticket" convention, was a remarkably good showing and caused thoughtful Republicans to regard him as more than a mouthing politician. It also proved that the Democracy had more lives than the proverbial cat and must be reckoned with even though its recent behavior had been far from ideal. Most Democrats take the ground that a thing worth having is worth fighting for. Being usually the minority party in the State, they have a freer rein in public discussion of party affairs and public policies and there is less of the cut and dried program in their political conventions. Republicans generally do their fighting behind closed doors and their feasting in public. Democrats reverse this.

A new figure on the Democratic political horizon loomed up quite unexpectedly in the summer of 1909. The Democratic managers felt that if they could draft or drag a man with money into the campaign, they could fight the people's battles with more heart and courage. For some time the chairman of the State Committee, Frederick J. McLeod, and the candidate for Governor, Mr. Vahey, had been flirting with such a man. A few days before the State convention, it was announced that Eugene N. Foss, foremost in the Reciprocity movement and a lifelong Republican, had consented to accept the Democratic nomination for Lieutenant Governor.

Leading Republicans heaved a sigh of relief and most of those prominent in Republican party affairs joined in exclaiming: "Good riddance to bad rubbish!" Mr. Foss, with his Canadian reciprocity and tariff ideas had been a thorn in the side of the Republicans for years. The Democratic managers had some difficulty convincing some of their friends that the nomination of Foss was the right thing to do. The Foss boomers pictured thousands of reciprocity and tariff revision Republicans following him into the Democratic party election day. Better still, he would finance the campaign. Mr. Foss had the reputation of being a liberal spender in political campaigns. He had not, however, proved that he was much of a vote getter. He had been the Republican Congressional candidate in the 11th district, but was defeated by John A. Sullivan. The Democratic leaders succeeded in nominating Mr. Foss for second place without much opposition.

Representative Thomas P. Riley of Malden was the temporary chairman of the State convention and Charles S. Hamlin the permanent chairman. Mr. Riley was the Democratic floor leader in the Legislature this year and in his convention speech he reviewed the work of that body, condemning the Republicans for their "subserviency to the railroads and the corporations" and the Governor's veto of the Eight Hour Bill. The tariff and the income tax were the burden of Mr. Hamlin's speech.

The platform was a rehash of former resolutions. Ex-Mayor John T. Coughlin unexpectedly bobbed up as a candidate for the gubernatorial nomination but Vahey easily defeated him.

Foss's nomination slipped by on greased ways. There was no nominating speech for him. His promoters figured that the fewer speeches, the easier it would be to nominate him.

The Republican State Convention met at Symphony Hall, Boston, October 2, 1908, and renominated the old ticket of Draper and Frothingham. Few saw the handwriting on the wall and it was destined to be the last Republican State Convention for six years to nominate a winning gubernatorial ticket. Ex-Mayor Edwin U. Curtis of Boston was the permanent chairman. Ex-Governor Bates, always useful and ornamental about a Republican State convention, read the platform which praised everything Republican and condemned everything Democratic. Both Draper and Frothingham appeared and accepted their nomination in brief speeches.

The campaign was waged with old time vigor on both sides and almost every Republican spellbinder took a whack at the Democratic candidate for Lieutenant Governor. Mr. Foss's candidacy attracted more Republican attention than Vahey's. Organized labor was very active against Draper. Its slogan was "Remember the Eight Hour bill!" In a speech at Worcester, his opening gun of the campaign, Governor Draper created no little consternation by asserting that one of those who urged him to veto the Eight Hour bill was the Democratic candidate for Lieutenant Governor. When the Democrats denied it, the Governor produced the original petition signed by Eugene N. Foss, but labor refused to drop Foss and kept on fighting Draper.

Election night the early returns didn't look very good for the Republican party. At one time during the evening Vahey and his friends believed that Draper was defeated but the idea was dispelled an hour or so later when it was found that Draper had a reduced but safe margin over Vahey of about 8000 and Frothingham over Foss about the same. Again the Republicans maintained control of the Legislature.

DRAPER'S SECOND TERM

THE "renewed expression of confidence" for which Governor Draper thanked the people in opening his second and last inaugural address to the Legislature caused the cynics to smile. A gubernatorial candidate who drops in one year from a plurality of 60,000 to 8,000 must needs be an optimist to see "renewed confidence" in such a dwindling vote. Frothingham's 96,000 plurality of 1908 also shrunk to an insignificant 8000 in 1909. The Republican vote was growing smaller and the Democratic strength was increasing. It needed no prophet to see what was going on in the minds of the voters. In addition to their own burdens the Republicans were carrying the load of the National Administration. Taft's administration at Washington became unpopular the moment he signed the Payne-Aldrich tariff bill. Republicans had reason to view with alarm the show of strength by the Democrats. The Republicans were on the eve of a political upheaval in State and Nation, which was to dethrone them from power.

State finances were carefully treated by the Governor in his inaugural. He asked the Legislature to practice economy and advised that no large, new undertakings be started which were not absolutely necessary. During the past year the treasurer of the town of Framingham had made away with the public funds by pledging the town's credit to banking houses. Governor Draper advocated a reform in the method of issuing municipal loans in order to prevent what had happened in Framingham. Little real important legislation was recommended by the Governor and the Legislature once more settled down for a six months' stay on Beacon Hill.

The Republican State Committee undertook to advise with the majority party at this session and began cultivating the friendship of the Republican legislators by giving them a banquet early in the session. Chairman Hatfield of the State Committee appealed to the Republican members of the Legislature to coöperate with the party organization to maintain the party in power. Speaker Walker threw the fat into the fire by declaring against dictation. He asked if the leaders of the party were getting out of touch with the rank and file of the party and if the party was losing the confidence of the plain people.

He entered his objections to a few party leaders selecting the party candidates for the State ticket and declared that the State convention should be a free for all arena. He didn't relish the close relationship existing between certain Republican leaders and certain monopolies. On the tariff, he wanted more light. He was not satisfied with the last Republican tariff.

President Treadway of the Senate did not agree with the pessimistic view of Speaker Walker. He praised the management of State affairs and pointed out that in passing the resolve to create a commission to investigate the high cost of living, the Republicans had not stolen Democratic thunder as had been charged, but that the legislative action was passed on the order of a Republican Senator, Ross, of New Bedford. If he had any criticism to make, he said that he would say that too frequently the party welfare had been lost sight of in legislating. Too often, he said, he had seen Republican legislators voting with the minority party and furnishing campaign ammunition for the Democrats.

There was a lively contest over what was known as the "Bar and Bottle Bill"—a measure proposed by the temperance people to separate the liquor business into a strictly bar business and a bottle business. It was argued by the proponents of the measure that it would have a tendency to reduce drinking and drunkenness. The liquor interests fought the measure, but the temperance people had the votes to pass it.

Columbus Day, October 12, was made a legal holiday. The Governor's suggestion that the bonds of the Railroad Holding Company be made a legal instrument for savings banks stirred up a lot of opposition. Bank men objected and the idea had to be abandoned, so pronounced was the opposition, but they beat the devil around the bush in another way, giving the company permission to issue preferred non-taxable stock.

The Eight Hour bill for public employees which Governor Draper vetoed the year before was passed again and again vetoed by him. A bill was passed permitting direct nominations in representative and senatorial districts where the voters desired them. Democrats made a hard fight for a resolve declaring in favor of the direct election of United States Senators, got it through the House, but the Senate rejected it. A saner Fourth of July bill was passed and signed by the Governor. One piece of legislation important to labor men was the law compelling advertisers for help in case of a strike to state in their "ads" that a strike was on.

Prorogation took place on the evening of June 16, the last act being the passage of the State tax bill amounting to $5,500,000, the biggest State tax bill up to that time.

DEATH OF GENERAL DRAPER

JANUARY 28, 1910, General William F. Draper of Hopedale, the Governor's eldest brother, who had been the American Ambassador to Italy under President McKinley, died at his Washington home at the age of 68. General Draper had a fine Civil War record. He had represented his district in Congress and was at the head of the Draper Company of Hopedale. He was a staunch and uncompromising Republican, warm hearted, frank and democratic in manner, positive in character and a man of strong likes and dislikes.

FOSS' ELECTION TO CONGRESS

CONGRESSMAN William C. Lovering of Taunton, representing the 14th district, died in Washington, February 4th, 1910. Governor Draper issued a rescript for a special election in the district to fill the vacancy. The Democrats tried to induce Charles S. Hamlin to accept their nomination. Mr. Hamlin procrastinated and finally declined to make the run. The nomination was offered to Eugene N. Foss who had, only a few weeks before, changed his political coat and he accepted.

On the Republican side, three men wanted the nomination—Judge Robert O. Harris of Bridgewater, Dr. Frank G. Wheatley of Abington and William R. Buchanan of Brockton, former Secretary to Governor Douglas. In the caucuses Buchanan got the largest number of delegates and when the convention was held he was nominated. The Republicans didn't take any more kindly to him than the Democrats when he was secretary to Governor Douglas. A lot of Republicans were suspicious of his party loyalty. "How could a loyal Republican serve a Democratic Governor?" they asked. Buchanan's nomination was not popular.

Mr. Foss didn't live in the district. He was a resident and voter in the 11th district, where he had run twice as the Republican nominee and was defeated at the polls by John A. Sullivan, the Democratic candidate. Foss declared against Cannonism and Aldrichism, said that he stood with President Taft for an income tax and that he agreed with Theodore Roosevelt on the latter's conservation policy. The high cost of living was the chief issue put forward by Foss. He promised that he would go to Washington without a party collar and represent all the people of the district regardless of party. Leading Democrats bestirred themselves for Foss.

Senator Lodge came on from Washington to speak for Buchanan. At a rally at Middleboro, Foss said that if elected he would join the Progressive Republican "Insurgents" of the House. In all his speeches he stressed the importance of Canadian reciprocity to Massachusetts and called Buchanan a "Standpat" Republican. The Republicans did everything they could to stir up interest in behalf of Buchanan but without success. Governor Draper stumped for Buchanan and took a fling at Foss, his old reciprocity opponent, predicting that Foss would try to disrupt the Democratic party as he had endeavored to do with the Republicans.

Election day, March 22, Foss swept the district. Buchanan's defeat was overwhelming. Foss' plurality was 5647. Two years before, Lovering, the Republican candidate, carried the district by 14,356. Foss carried Brockton, Buchanan's home city. He had a plurality in 33 of the 44 towns of the district. Democrats all over the country were jubilant. Some of them maintained that it was a rebuke to Lodge. Champ Clark said it was the best political news since the close of the polls in 1892. When Mr. Foss appeared in Washington to take oath of office, arm in arm with his brother, Congressman Foss of Chicago, one of the Republican leaders of the House, he was made much of by the Democrats. Republicans were curious to see the man who had turned a Republican plurality of 14,000 into a Democratic victory of 5,000. Representative Foss took very little part in Congressional proceedings, however, spending little time at the capital. He delivered one speech on the tariff while in Congress.

EYE ON GOVERNORSHIP

MR. Foss had arrived politically. He had been a candidate in the Republican party for Lieutenant Governor and was laughed out of court. He had been a candidate for delegate to the Republican National convention and was defeated. He won the Republican nomination for Congress in the 11th district twice after spirited contests, but was defeated at the polls. He had the reputation of being a free spender when he was personally interested in a cause. Vahey, one of his Democratic sponsors, congratulated him on election, adding: "We must now set about to give Massachusetts proper representation in the Senate of the United States," but Mr. Foss did not jump at the senatorial bait. His mind was set on the Governorship. His submarines were busy with their under sea warfare on Vahey. One of his chief supporters was Chairman Mcleod of the Democratic State Committee.

The Foss gubernatorial movement gained momentum and by the middle of April, Mr. Vahey felt it necessary to announce that he was a candidate for a renomination.

Things drifted until the picnic and outing season arrived—July and August—when the Foss talk got a new impetus, but Mr. Foss declared he would not lift a finger for the gubernatorial nomination. Charles S. Hamlin, believing that there was to be a contest for the nomination, threw his hat into the ring and published his platform. One by one, Vahey found his supporters slipping away from him and going over to the Foss or Hamlin camp.

Nobody had won enough delegates in the caucuses to nominate in the convention. The campaign for the nomination was renewed after the caucuses and every delegate was canvassed. The State Convention was held at Faneuil Hall, October 6th. District Attorney Pelletier of Suffolk County was temporary chairman and Ex-Congressman John R. Thayer of Worcester permanent presiding officer. It was a good old fashioned Democratic convention, lasting from forenoon until long after midnight.

Foss led on the first two ballots. On the first ballot Foss lacked 113 of the necessary number to nominate, while on the second ballot he came within six votes of the nomination. Vahey and Hamlin were nearly even on the first ballot, the former leading by only seven votes. On the second ballot, several Hamlin delegates went to Vahey. The result was that while Foss still led on the second ballot he was only 13 votes ahead of Vahey.

The candidates were under the impression that the nominations must be filed the next day, October 7th, at 5 P.M., with the Secretary of State. There was no hope of the convention being able to nominate and after the second ballot a conference of both sides was suggested. The chair named a committee and the conference agreed on recommending to the convention that Frederick W. Mansfield, a supporter of Vahey, should be nominated in order to file the certificate, that a nominating committee of four be named by the presiding officer of the convention, they to select a fifth member and when the nominating committee agreed on a candidate Mr. Mansfield should withdraw. Mr. Mansfield agreed to the arrangement and the convention ratified the agreement unanimously.

Mr. Vahey explained to the delegates that it would be futile to attempt to nominate either himself or Mr. Foss, the leading candidate, because of what happened in the convention. It was evident, he declared, that neither would be satisfactory after what had transpired It didn't look as if the nomination would be worth the paper it was written on.

At times the convention was in great disorder. Delegates engaged in blows. In some respects the scenes of disorder exceeded anything witnessed in the Democratic convention at Springfield three years before.

The convention did not attempt to select a candidate for Lieutenant Governor from the field of five, but also left that to a committee. Clifton R. Loring, executive clerk at Democratic headquarters, was named temporarily. Like Mansfield, he was a "Stop-Gap" candidate. The committee to select a candidate for both places consisted of Chairman Frederick J. Macleod of the State Committee, William P. Hayes of Springfield, Joseph A. Maynard of Boston, and Robert J. Crowley of Lowell. The four were unable to agree on a fifth member. It was discovered after the adjournment of the convention that the time for filing nomination certificates did not expire at 5 P.M. October 7, but on Monday following. The committee had until 5 P.M. October 24 to substitute for their selections, ample time in which to arrive at an agreement.

The day following the convention, Mr. Foss declared that he was out of the contest. Vahey was more emphatic and positive. He said that he was only not a candidate but that his name would not appear on the ballot election day. For several days the nominating committee met and conferred but were unable to agree on a candidate. Macleod and Maynard were for Foss, Hayes and Crowley were for Hamlin. Foss suggested a new convention. Hayes and Crowley stoutly opposed this scheme. Macleod and Maynard supported it. The committee finally agreed on the following plan and it was adopted in the form of a resolution:

"Resolved that a special delivery letter be mailed to every regularly elected delegate to the recent State convention, with a special delivery return envelope enclosed, addressed to William P. Hayes, Secretary, Committee of Four, having power to select a candidate for Governor, requesting their reply immediately, stating their preference for the most available candidate for Governor at this time for the information and guidance of the special committee by the convention named."

The State Committee summoned the special committee before them. Major Crowley refused to go, saying that he was not a member of the State Committee, and that he didn't consider the State Committee had anything to do with the nomination of the candidate for Governor. Hayes took the same position, but the State Committee went on with its plan of nominating a gubernatorial candidate by mail and the Hamlin men reluctantly agreed to abide by the result of the poll.

When the Hamlin men learned that the special delivery letters to the delegates bore a number on the flap of the envelope they charged that the State Committee had "keyed" the delegates, that is, each delegate was numbered and the number on the flap of the envelope corresponded with the number beside his name on the list of delegates in the possession of Chairman Macleod and a member of the nominating committee.

It would have been an easy matter for State Committee officials to keep track of those who had not replied by checking off the number on the list at headquarters as

LT. COL. TIMILTY

ELIOT WADSWORTH

COL. WILLIAM GASTON

WILLIAM H. COOLIDGE

CONGRESSMAN RUSSELL

ERNEST L. GOULSTON

the return envelopes arrived, addressed to William P. Hayes, Secretary of the Convention Committee on nomination. To prevent this Mr. Hayes had the mail held for him at the post office until a certain date, when he called for it and it was publicly opened at State headquarters.

At the appointed time the Nominating Committee met to open the mail ballot and count the votes. When they were tabulated, the result was as follows:

Whole number of votes cast	989
Necessary for a choice	495
Foss	495
Hamlin	484
All others	10

As soon as Mr. Hamlin was informed of the vote he despatched a brief note to the committee withdrawing his name. Ex-Senator Thomas F. Cassidy of Adams was nominated for Lieutenant Governor. Mansfield withdrew and the last act was over in this exciting political melodrama. Foss was the platform.

REPUBLICANS DEFEATED

In the Republican camp there was peace and harmony. Governor Draper, Lieutenant Governor Frothingham and the other candidates for places on the State ticket were nominated in a convention devoid of popular interest.

The convention attracted few spectators in comparison with the attendance of other years. More than 400 accredited delegates remained away and sent no substitutes. There was not a sound in disapproval of a single proposition in the platform. Even Colonel Butler Ames, who was a candidate for senatorial honors, permitted the indorsement of Senator Lodge without dissent. The delegates cheered for President Taft and Colonel Roosevelt and gave Senator Lodge a rousing reception.

The presiding officer, Congressman Robert Luce, in discussing the tariff said: "We are reaching a point where we cannot support ourselves without help from abroad." He advised a revision of the tariff, one schedule at a time, by a commission of experts. He deplored the scheme of letting Congress do it. "Business men want the tariff taken out of politics," said Mr. Luce. He was enthusiastic in his commendation of the Bar and Bottle bill, and said the Republican party would go still further to suppress the evils of the saloon.

The platform adopted was largely commendatory of what the party had done and this was the note most often sounded by the permanent chairman, Robert Luce. Praise of the National administration, a demand for tariff revision by a commission of experts and an indorsement of direct nominations were features of the platform. After their nomination, Governor Draper and Lieutenant Governor Frothingham appeared before the convention and made brief speeches of appreciation.

By all the rules of fair play the Democratic nomination for Governor belonged to Vahey who had led two forlorn hopes. During the pre-convention fight the Vahey adherents attacked Foss' labor record and quoted Samuel Gompers, head of the American Federation of Labor, against him. Mr. Gompers didn't like Mr. Foss' labor record in Congress, but in E. Gerry Brown, one of his new political lieutenants, prominent in labor circles, Mr. Foss found a ready champion who claimed that Mr. Foss' labor record was satisfactory to organized labor. Foss gathered about him a staff of ready letter writers and immediately after the nomination began to bombard his opponents with typewritten statements.

The campaign on the Republican side was well under way before the Democrats had settled their party differences and Mr. Foss felt the necessity of speeding up his campaign. Governor Draper and his associates fully realized that they had a hard fight on their hands. They knew that with Foss in the field the Democrats would not want for sinews of war, and they had seen Democrats fight among themselves before and then unite against their opponents. Republicans could not close their eyes to the fact that the tide of public sentiment was setting against them. They had witnessed the Democrats increase their strength to 182,000 votes at the last State election. To add to their troubles the Payne-Aldrich bill was unpopular. Besides, they had to contend against the high cost of living.

Like Champ Clark, the Republicans observed that the most sensitive nerve in the human body was that which leads to the pocket book. People rebelled at high prices and were ready to make a change in their government.

They were willing to give the Democrats a chance to carry out their promise to reduce the living costs. Republican spellbinders countered by declaring that the trouble was really the cost of high living, but their contention fell upon deaf ears.

Foss knew that his wealth afforded the Republicans an opportunity to critize him. He "beat them to it," however, issuing a broadside against Senator Lodge and Congressman Gardner, the former's son-in-law, saying that they were among the worst offenders in the spending of money in elections. In a speech before the New England Postmasters' Association Senator Lodge had decried the use of money in elections, saying that it would be a sorry day for the country when the result of an election would be determined by votes bought and sold. That gave Foss his opportunity and he took advantage of it. Mr. Foss wrote in an open letter to the Senator in which he said that Mr. Lodge and Mr. Gardner had done more to debauch and corrupt the electorate by the lavish expenditure of money than any other two men in the State. Mr. Lodge made taut reply, saying that the question was whether Mr. Foss could buy the Governorship and added that he did not believe the State was for sale.

Senator Lodge was Mr. Foss' favorite target in the campaign. The Senator's term was expiring in March, 1911, and the Legislature to be elected would choose a Senator in January. Congressman Butler Ames was a candidate against Lodge. Ex-President Roosevelt spoke for the Republican State ticket on the evening of October 21st and made a special appeal for the reëlection of Senator

Lodge. He spoke to a great crowd at the Arena, from a raised platform roped off like a prize fight ring. It was heralded abroad that the Colonel would "knock 'em over the ropes." In his speech he made a savage attack on Foss saying that, "It would be scandalous for the Commonwealth to elect as Governor, a man, who, having tried to dominate one party and failed, having made money in stocks, seeks to rise in public life not by his record, but by force of effrontery and power that comes from money." The attack on Foss stirred the Democrats who declared that the statement was far from the truth and unworthy of a man who had occupied the highest office in the land. They followed up the Roosevelt meeting with one of their own at Tremont Temple, at which all the big guns of the party in Boston were present, including Hamlin and Vahey.

In the last week of the campaign the labor men, who supported Foss, got a letter from Samuel Gompers in which the latter said that if Foss would be true to labor he ought to be supported and Draper ought to be defeated. To prove that Mr. Foss did urge Governor Draper to veto the Eight Hour bill, the Republicans produced Foss' letter signed, "B. F. Sturtevant Company, E. N. Foss, Treasurer." But labor didn't care. They were out to get the scalp of Draper. Foss was elected Governor by 33,779 plurality and Lieutenant Governor Frothingham squeezed by with 5583.

The Republicans fared better in the Congressional districts, electing 10 out of the 14 Congressmen, but most of them by greatly reduced pluralities. Representative William H. O'Brien of Boston volunteered to become the Democratic sacrifice in the 6th or Essex district. He made a lively campaign, but Congressman Gardner won by 5500. The Democrats who were elected to Congress were John R. Thayer in Worcester district, defeating Congressman Charles G. Washburn, William F. Murray in the 9th, defeating Congressman John A. Keliher, Independent, James M. Curley in the 10th and Andrew J. Peters in the 11th.

The Democrats gained six seats in the State Senate, 44 in the House, and, on a joint vote, they lacked but 15 votes to beat Lodge for Senator. Mr. Foss announced that his victory voiced the protest of Massachusetts against the Payne-Aldrich tariff bill, the high cost of living and the broken promises of the Republican party. It was another Democratic tidal wave year. Congress was to be Democratic. The year 1910 introduced Woodrow Wilson to the public eye. He was elected Governor of New Jersey that Fall. Connecticut, Ohio, Nebraska, New York and Wyoming, all chose Democratic Governors. Oyster Bay, Cincinnati and Nahant went Democratic.

FOSS FAILS TO DEFEAT LODGE

HAVING defeated Draper for Governor, Mr. Foss turned his attention to Senator Lodge. Here was his chance to even political scores with Lodge for the humiliation the latter had publicly heaped upon him in more than one

Republican state convention. Mr. Foss tried to induce Colonel Gaston to become a candidate against Lodge but he refused, as did John R. Thayer, Richard Olney and Henry M. Whitney.

Senator Lodge's friends were angry at what they termed Foss' "brazen effrontery" and they rallied to his support. It was the first real serious opposition Mr. Lodge had had in all of his long senatorial career. They declared that they "loved him for the enemies he had made." The opposition to Lodge united most of the Republicans. A poll of the legislators shortly after election showed that Mr. Lodge must busy himself. Speaker Walker, though no enthusiastic admirer of Mr. Lodge, was among the first to come to the Senator's aid. Senator Crane was early on the battle line in behalf of his colleague. Of Senator Crane's activities, Governor Foss remarked "Uncle Murray better remove his gumshoes and take to the tall timber. Gumshoeing won't accomplish what he is after this time."

Foss asked Senator Lodge to join him in a plan to defer the election of a Senator one year and allow the people at the State election in 1911, to indicate their senatorial preference. He offered to submit the suggestion to the Legislature. The offer was ignored by Senator Lodge. Then Mr. Foss announced that he would campaign against Mr. Lodge until he was inaugurated Governor and invited the opposition candidates to join him in his tour of the State. Robert Luce, a Lodge supporter, challenged Foss to a joint debate, but Mr. Foss not being a debater declined to meet a speaker of Mr. Luce's forensic abilities.

After a while the much heralded anti-Lodge tour of the State got under way, beginning on the Cape. In Mr. Foss' entourage were a number of small fry politicians. The anti-Lodge meetings fell short of Mr. Foss' expectations.

The Senator came home from Washington in January to face the music. Henry M. Whitney, Mr. Foss' oldtime coworker in more than one tariff fight, announced his support of Lodge. The Senator's friends arranged a meeting for him at Symphony Hall, where he gave an account of his 18 years' stewardship in the upper branch of Congress. His dramatic account of what he had done as Senator was applauded by an appreciative audience that packed the hall.

"Every tradition of our great State is dear to me, every page of her history is to me a household word," he said in closing his speech. "To her service I have given the best years of my life and the best that was in me to give. I believe that I have not been an altogether unprofitable servant. I have given my all; no man can do more. Others may well serve her with greater ability than I. I fervently hope that there will be many such others in the days to come, when her light will shine before men as it now shines with steady radiance in the pages of history. Others may easily serve her better than I in those days yet to be, but of this I am sure: no one can ever serve her with a greater love or deeper loyalty."

The first legislative skirmish in the Senatorial contest resulted in the unanimous renomination of Senator Lodge by the Republican caucus. All of the avowed Ames men remained away, as well as a few other anti-Lodge men, twenty-eight in all. Just before the caucus Ex-Governor Guild who had been urged to enter the contest declined to do so saying that he favored the reëlection of Mr. Lodge.

When the Democrats held their Senatorial caucus, Sherman L. Whipple of Brookline, classmate of President Taft, received their nomination. Mr. Whipple was the personal choice of Governor Foss. He was comparatively a new man in State politics but his Democracy was inbred. He was one of the ablest lawyers in the State. John R. Thayer led all competitiors up to the fourth ballot. On the fifth and deciding ballot his vote dwindled to almost one half of Whipple's and the latter had eight more than enough to nominate.

When the House of Representatives balloted Mr. Lodge received the largest number of votes, but lacked three of a majority. Immediately after the voting, Speaker Walker sent a letter to the four men who had voted for him, saying that while he appreciated the honor he must protest and ask them not to vote for him at the joint convention. At the joint convention of both Houses of the Legislature, Mr. Lodge was reëlected for his fourth term with five votes to spare.

In balloting in the joint convention, two Democratic Senators, Michael J. Murray and Martin P. F. Curley of Boston, shifted their votes from Whipple to Lodge. Representative Arkwell of Worcester who voted for Speaker Walker the day before changed his vote to Lodge.

One of Ames' men voted for Lodge. The other Walker men changed to President Lowell of Harvard who received two votes for Senator. Representative Cogswell of Lynn cast his vote for Curtis Guild, Jr. The only absentee was James H. McInerney, Democrat, of Boston,

WALKER BARELY DEFEATS LOMASNEY FOR SPEAKER

USUALLY the contest for Speaker of the Massachusetts House of Representatives is a factional fight within the Republican ranks. For years the public service corporations have made their influence felt and it is seldom that a man reaches that office who is not regarded by them as "safe and sane." Indeed, there are cases where the corporations and some of the big banking houses of Boston, actually picked the Speaker of the House and the President of the Senate and lined up the votes for them. The corporations feel that they must protect their vested interests and guard against unjust and inimical laws to them. Having paved the way for the Speaker, the next thing is to see that the legislative committees which report on proposed legislation are not unfriendly. The activities of the corporations begin at the start—the primaries—and their "grapevines" lead to every branch of the State government.

For a generation or more, the Republicans never had to worry about the Speakership of the House. Republican after Republican succeeded Republicans in that office, often a stepping stone to the Governorship. The election in 1910 gave the Republicans only a slim majority of the lower branch of the Legislature. In the organization of the House of 1911, the Democrats needed but nine more votes to control it and elect its officers. The lone Socialist would, in all probability, vote with them, they reasoned. All that was necessary then was to ensnare eight Republicans. There were plenty of Republicans who didn't approve of Speaker Walker. He wobbled too much politically to suit them.

Representative Martin M. Lomasney of Boston, a seasoned legislator and a power in politics, announced his candidacy for Speaker. Lomasney, a rough-and-tumble political fighter, had many enemies in his own party and they began to busy themselves against him. In his long political career, Lomasney had made many enemies in his own party and many friends among the Republicans. Walker and his friends were uneasy. Open war on Lomasney was decided upon.

In the House there were 127 Republicans, 112 Democrats and one Socialist. If all members were present it would require 121 votes to elect a speaker. If the Democrats and the Socialist voted for a Democratic candidate it would be necessary for that candidate to get but eight Republican votes to make him Speaker of the House. There was one Democratic stumbling block in Mr. Lomasney's way. Representative Charles F. McCarthy of Marlboro had speakership ambitions. By a vote of 78 to 4 in the party caucus Lomasney was named as the

Democratic candidate for Speaker and McCarthy made it unanimous.

To guard against deserters, the Republicans decided on a voice vote for Speaker. The fight to make Lomasney Speaker began before Governor Draper had left the rostrum after swearing in the members. On motion of Robert M. Washburn of Worcester, the roll was called and each member announced his choice. Mr. Lomasney objected, but was overruled by the chair. He appealed and lost by a vote of 125 to 109. It was the first time in 132 years that a Speaker was chosen in this manner. The custom had been to use a secret ballot. The tally of the voice vote showed that every Republican voted for Walker and were joined by five Democrats. Four other Democrats cast their ballots for Charles F. McCarthy and Walker was elected Speaker for the third time.

In the Senate President Treadway was reëlected. The 14 Democratic members of that body voted for Senator John F. Malley of Springfield.

EUGENE N. FOSS

Governor 1911–1914

EUGENE NOBLE FOSS, the 45th Governor of Massachusetts, began the first of his three memorable terms January 5, 1911. Five years had passed since the Democrats had witnessed the inauguration of a Governor of their

JOSEPH P. MANNING
Boston's Useful Citizen

party. Two thousand invitations to be present at the inaugural ceremonies were issued. The Governor's wife and two daughters, his father and mother, George E. Foss of Chicago, the Governor-elect's brother, Republican Congressman, and other relatives of the family occupied seats in the Speaker's gallery.

Thenceforth, for three years, Mr. Foss kept politicians, office holders and the public guessing what his next move would be. In his inaugural he gave the members much to think about. He began by demanding the abolition of the boss, the caucus, the nominating convention and all political machinery governing nominations. He declared for the initiative, referendum and recall. Labor's rights must be recognized and the workmen exempted from unfair injunction proceedings. He espoused a workingmen's compensation act, demanded immediate installation of vocational and trade schools, asked for legislation with a view to bring trunk lines of railroads of this country and Canada to the port of Boston, demanded its development by coöperation of the State and city in ownership of docks and terminals, and a system of waterways and canals, to supplement railroads. He denounced Holding companies.

He asked for more Superior Court Judges to speed up justice and recommended more salary for members of the higher courts; urged a State Finance Commission and declared against more State Commissions; favored creation of a Greater Boston. Demanded direct election of United States Senators and would have the States aid the Federal Government in levying income taxes. He would compel citizens to vote, and demanded a fair redistributing of the State into Congressional districts.

Governor Foss had been in office hardly two weeks when Judge Harris of the Superior Court resigned to take effect March 1st, when he was to assume his duties as Congressman from the 14th district succeeding Foss. Judge Bond of the same court had just died and Mr. Foss began his great record as a judge maker which had never been equalled by any of his predecessors in 25 years. In accordance with his announced policy of "persistent pitiless publicity," Governor Foss broke all precedents and gave out a list of names submitted to him for the two new justices of the Superior Court. No other Governor had done such a thing and it created a mild sensation in legal and political circles. Mr. Foss said the people were entitled to know who were back of their judges. He named Joseph F. Quinn of Salem and John D. McLaughlin of Boston to the two vacancies. He never published any more lists of candidates for any office. Like most of those who shout the loudest for publicity in public affairs, Mr. Foss soon became as uncommunicative as an old fashioned politician, who takes keen delight surprising the public in his selection of public officials.

The Legislature was called upon during the session to fill two important State offices. William M. Olin, Secretary of State, and Henry E. Turner, State Auditor, died. The contest over the Secretaryship which was the first to be filled was bitter and partizan. The Legislature filled the Olin vacancy by electing Representative Albert P.

Langtry of Springfield. The Democrats voted for Frank J. Donahue, prominent in politics and now a Justice of the Superior Court, named by Governor Ely. For State Auditor popular Senator John E. White of the Cape district was chosen. He had no serious Democratic opposition.

The session of 1911 was the longest in the history of the State up to that time, exceeding the Butler year of 1883, when the Legislature was in session 203 calendar days. The session of 1911 occupied 206 calendar days. 719 acts and 153 resolves were passed.

Several times the legislators manifested a desire to be prorogued. Republicans and a few Democrats treated with scorn many of the Governor's suggestions for legislation. His official message writer kept the Sergeant-at-Arms busy, trotting back and forth to the Executive Department, doing escort duty for the Governor's veto and message bearer. On several occasions, when messages were announced "from His Excellency," the announcement was received with derisive laughter and at times Democrats vied with Republicans in putting the measures over the Governor's veto.

Acts of discourtesy and open insult did not bother Governor Foss. Toward the end of the session he openly defied the members of the Legislature. In the middle of July, while the House was discussing his veto of the increase of their salaries from $750 a year to $1000, the 78th message from the Governor arrived and for the first time in the memory of the oldest attaché of the House, a message from the Governor of the State was received with groans, catcalls, hisses and unprintable remarks by the Representatives.

The newspaper men had come to refer to the Governor as the "Old Boy." The nickname stuck to him through his three terms. It was a favorite term of his own. The Constitution gives the Governor the right with the advice and consent of the Council to prorogue the Legislature and unless he consents to adjournment it must remain in session. Under the law the Legislature cannot adjourn itself over more than two legislative days. The Governor had the whip hand in this case. Local history does not record an instance of a Massachusetts Legislature turning on the Chief Executive of the Commonwealth as it did on Governor Foss when the Senate, without the semblance of debate, passed over his veto, two bills in succession by a vote of 28 to 0.

The position of the House was just as emphatic and pronounced as that of the Senate. The leaders of the Governor's own party, with few exceptions, appeared to be more vindictive than the Republicans. Leader Lomasney vehemently rebuked Leader Underhill of the Republicans for his language in reference to one of the Governor's message under discussion, but the same Democratic leader cast his vote with those who disagreed with His Excellency and voted to pass the measures over the Governor's veto.

The following day the House outdid the Senate by passing over the Governor's veto the bill for pensions of members of the State police, putting them on the same basis as that of the Boston police. Having done this, it proceeded to pass over his veto the bill to increase the salary of the members of the Legislature from $750 to $1000. It also passed over his veto, the bill to establish minimum salaries of judges and registrars of probate. During the entire session of the Legislature, the State departments and the Legislature were kept in a turmoil. There was politics on both sides. Very little of Governor Foss' ambitious Legislative program was enacted into law in the form he demanded it.

He got through his Port Directors bill and an appropriation of $9,000,000 for harbor development of Boston. At the head of this commission he named Hugh Bancroft. From this appropriation was built the great Commonwealth Dock headhouse and the locality improved. One of the commendable pieces of legislation passed, was the Loan Shark bill, regulating through a State Commissioner, the small loan business, which had preyed upon poor people and charged them excessive interest on loans. The legislation didn't accomplish all that it was hoped it would, but it brought the loan sharks under State control.

Labor didn't get all it expected. The Governor signed the 54 Hour Bill under pressure, but he vetoed the Peaceful Picketing bill. The Senate killed the Public Opinion bill. A new Corrupt Practises bill became a law, limiting the amount of money a candidate may spend in the primaries for a nomination and at the polls election day. The Governor gave his approval to the legislative invitation to the Grand Trunk Railway of Canada to build a line to Boston and at the same time he demanded the

repeal of the Railroad Holding measure, whereby the
New Haven held control of the Boston and Maine Railroad. The latter demand was not granted. The Institute
of Technology was given a $1,000,000 grant. In signing
the bill, Governor Foss said that the understanding was,
that it should be the last State aid the institution would
ask of the Commonwealth. The House killed a Sunday
baseball bill. The Senate also killed what was known as
the Lifting Jack bill, which would compel railways to
carry lifting jacks on every car.

A bill forbidding Chinese keeping restaurants, a bit of
strike legislation, designed to shake down the thrifty
celestials, was declared unconstitutional by the Supreme
Court and the attempt to pass such a law was abandoned.
The annexation of Hyde Park to Boston was authorized
and a referendum attached, submitting the proposition
to both Hyde Park and Boston voters. Woman Suffrage
was beaten by a vote of 161 to 69 in the House and in
the Senate by 31 to 6. The House went on record by a
vote of 170 to 37 favoring the direct election of United
States Senators by the people, but the Senate, on a close
vote, killed the measure.

Governor Foss' first veto was negatived in the House
by a vote of 155 to 51. The bill provided that applicants
under the Civil Service law should not be compelled to
set out in their application blanks offenses committed
before they were 16 years of age. The liquor people made
a determined fight for the repeal of the Bar and Bottle
bill but they were unsuccessful. The House ratified the
amendment to the United States Constitution on the in-

come tax. The Senate rejected it, but the following year both branches accepted it and thus closed a question which had agitated the Legislature for several years.

The Governor's veto of the Boston elementary school teachers' increase of salary brought down a storm of abuse on his head and the advocates of the measure were unable to put it over his veto. Mr. Foss took the ground that it was a question for the Boston School Board to determine, rather than the Legislature, the same position that he took on the bill lowering the height of members of the Boston Fire Department, saying that the city authorities should regulate that question.

As the session was nearing its end, Governor Foss sent a communication to the Legislature demanding an investigation of the business methods of the United Shoe Machinery Company but the Legislature sent word back that there was law enough already if an investigation were needed. The term of office of Police Commissioner O'Meara of Boston expired. As usual, the Governor kept everybody guessing. Democratic politicians were opposed to his reappointment, but the Governor sent O'Meara's name to the Executive Council for another term of five years, and he was promptly confirmed.

REËLECTED

ENOUGH votes had been cast for Foss as a Progressive in the election to constitute a political party and the Governor was in a position to hold that over the heads of the Democrats, in case they should consider turning him down as their candidate. There had been threats of that nature, but they vanished after his endorsement by the Democratic legislators. The Governor had been so busy with legislation and investigations that he had neglected to fill more than a score of good paying positions, which the Democrats naturally coveted. He kept dangling these plums before his party associates. As the primaries approached, he shook the tree gently. A running mate must be chosen. Several names were suggested, but as usual, Foss put it off until the last moment, when David I. Walsh of Fitchburg was agreed upon, Thomas F. Cassidy, last year's candidate, declining to run again.

Chief Justice Knowlton of the Supreme Court asked to be retired. In his place Judge Rugg of the same Court was appointed. Four Superior Court judges were named in midsummer, all on one day—Patrick M. Keating, John B. Ratigan, Democrats; Walter Perley Hall and Hugo A. Dubuque, Republicans. Hall had been a member of the old Railroad Commission. His place was given to Frederick J. MacLeod, chairman of the Democratic State Committee, who desired a judgeship, but the "Old Boy" decided MacLeod's experience at the bar had not been extensive enough. The vacancy on the Supreme Judicial Court was filled by the promotion of Judge Charles A. De Courcey of the Superior Court.

The Republicans had a three cornered fight for Governor—Lieutenant Governor Frothingham, Speaker Walker and Norman H. White were the candidates.

They all took a whack occasionally at the "Old Boy." Frothingham won and his nearest opponent in the race, Joseph Walker, immediately proffered him his support and subscribed handsomely to his election fund. The third man in the contest, Norman H. White, was not so demonstrative. Robert Luce of Somerville was the choice for Lieutenant Governor.

The Suffragists decided to put all candidates on record regarding equal suffrage. A big touring car, filled with well known Suffragettes trailed candidate Frothingham through Berkshire County. At Stockbridge, Miss Margaret Foley asked him if he was in favor of woman suffrage. Frothingham replied that it was a constitutional question with which the Governor had nothing to do. Miss Foley harangued the crowd saying that Frothingham's record was 100% bad. She and her associates kept up their heckling of the candidate at the various stops and made speeches to the street crowds.

The Democratic State ticket was agreed upon in advance of the primary. George Fred Williams, who had not yet broken with Foss, was selected to write the platform. The convention was a Democratic love feast. Sherman L. Whipple presided and delivered a good natured speech, containing many sharp thrusts at the Republicans. He described the Republican candidate as a young man of pleasing personality, but who was, nevertheless, "the representative of the special interests." When he got to his word picture of Senators Lodge and Crane, Mr. Whipple fairly shook with laughter. "Senator Lodge, he of the silver tongue, and Senator Crane, he of the golden tongue—Senator Lodge whose speech is silver and Senator Crane whose silence is golden," struck the delegates as being good, and they sat back in their chairs and chuckled.

Representative John F. Meany of Blackstone, the temporary presiding officer, was the Governor's personal representative on the floor of the House during the legislative session. He related what the Democrats had succeeded in doing in the session, the Eight Hour bill, twice wrung from unwilling Legislatures, only to be vetoed by a Republican Governor, was enacted into a law. The 54 Hour bill, for women and minors, sought for by the workers for a long period of years. The Union Fines and the Hoar Jury Trial Acts, giving an added measure to legitimate protection to the worker; and the Workmen's Compensation law, forced to enactment this year by Democratic insistence. The great industry of agriculture, once the mainstay of the Commonwealth, was protected against unfair and ruin-bearing legislation in Governor Foss' veto of the Ellis Milk bill, he said.

Governor Foss appeared and read a speech in which he said he welcomed the injection of the tariff in the fight.

In the midst of the campaign, the Governor named Professor Garrett Droppers of Williams College to succeed Clinton White as Railroad Commissioner and Charles G. Wood of New Bedford a member of the State Board of Conciliation and Arbitration. Droppers was rejected after the State election, but Wood was confirmed.

The Governor also nominated for the second time for clerk of the Boston Juvenile Court, William L. Reed, the colored messenger at the Governor's office, to succeed Clerk Williams, another colored man. Reed was rejected. Some time before the Governor named David Stoneman, a young Jewish lawyer, as Associate Justice of the Dorchester Municipal Court, but the Council rejected him. Governor Foss told the public of his troubles with the Council, declared it a relic of the past and asked the people to rebuke the members who had opposed his nominations.

The eve of election he demanded a Grand Jury investigation of alleged violations of laws governing political campaign solicitations and alleged illegal political advertisements of his opponents. He sent to District Attorney Pelletier a letter calling for prosecution of the Republican State Committee, Ex-President Theodore Roosevelt and other officers of *The Outlook* magazine, the two United States Senators from Massachusetts, the Republican candidate for Governor and officers of the United Shoe Machinery Company, of the American Woolen Company and the Arkwright Club, charging them with illegal campaign contributions, but the District Attorney found nothing to prosecute—after election.

Foss was reëlected by nearly 9000 plurality, falling over 40,000 below his preëlection claim. Luce, Republican candidate for second place, was successful over David I. Walsh, Democrat, by a little over 4000 votes. Mr. Luce was not in good favor with the liquor interests because of his temperance views and they worked hard to defeat him.

The House elected stood: Republican, 142; Democrats, 97; Socialist, 1. The Senate: Republican, 36, Democrats, 14.

There is little doubt that Governor's Foss' judicial appointments contributed more to his reëlection than any one factor in the campaign. For the first time in the history of the State the Democrats had been given anywhere near a fair representation on the judiciary of the higher courts. After election the Governor made three more appointments to the Superior Court: Nathan D. Pratt to succeed the late Judge Richardson, Frederick H. Chase to succeed Judge De Courcey, promoted to the Supreme Court and Richard W. Irwin to succeed Judge Sherman, retired. The two former were Democrats and the latter a Republican.

Foss was hailed by some enthusiasts as a Presidential possibility and it was not long before there was evidence that the Presidential bee was buzzing in his bonnet. Later he became an avowed candidate for the Democratic nomination.

The Progressive Republican movement had begun to manifest itself in the State. Following the State election they held a meeting in Tremont Temple, which was addressed by Governor Bass of New Hampshire and Ex-Congressman Record of New Jersey. The gathering was a forerunner of what was to be a movement of the Roosevelt men in the party to defeat Taft and the Old Guard in the next Presidential election in which Massachusetts was to play an important part.

FOSS' SECOND TERM

MR. Foss was the first Democratic gubernatorial candidate to be reëlected since William E. Russell.

Grafton D. Cushing succeeded Joseph Walker as Speaker of the House and Levi H. Greenwood, President of the Senate in place of Allen Treadway, and they settled down to listen to the second inaugural of Governor Foss rampant in advanced ideas of legislation. He again urged the adoption of all measures in his first message which the Legislature had rejected and added a plethora of new panaceas, including provision for submitting the question of woman suffrage, new and drastic conservative laws for timber and shell fish, a labor bureau, a new State prison, more liberal compensation for prisoners, a State Fair, more free scholarships for ambitious youths, but most of his suggestions got scant support from the law makers.

Sheriff Seavey of Suffolk County died in January and the Governor appointed John Quinn, Jr., the Democratic member of the Executive Council, to succeed him. The Legislature elected Edward D. Collins of South Boston to succeed Councillor Quinn. Of the numerous appointments made by Governor Foss this year, the most important were the five new Industrial Accident Board members to administer the Workingmen's Compensation Act passed the year before. The men appointed and their terms were: Chairman, James B. Carroll of Springfield, five years; Dudley M. Holman of Taunton, the Governor's Secretary, four years; Ex-Mayor David T. Dickinson of Cambridge, three years; Edward F. McSweeney of Boston, two years; Representative Joseph A. Parks of Fall River, one year.

In May, the legislators planned to adjourn, but the Governor served notice on them that he would not prorogue them until they passed certain measures, particularly the reorganization of the Railroad Commission and his bill merging the Boston & Maine with the New Haven. June 10th, after repeated unsuccessful attempts by individuals to get the Governor to prorogue the Legislature, Senator George Holden Tinkham, Republican, declared that if Governor Foss continued to sign and veto legislation, not done on its merits, the Governor should be impeached by the House, in accordance with the terms of the Constitution, which provides for such action in cases of mal-administration and misconduct by the Executive. The Governor only laughed at the suggestion but from then on the Executive and Legislative branches worked more in harmony. On the evening of June 14, he prorogued the Legislature.

He signed the Grand Trunk Bill which enlarged and extended the corporate powers of the Southern New England Railroad Company, a part of the Canadian Grand Trunk system. Although the road spent millions for construction of the new line, the world war curtailed its financial source and the death of President Hays who went down on the ill-fated *Titanic* of the White Star line on its maiden voyage, stopped its completion and the scheme fell through. There was a systematic, organized opposition to the Grand Trunk Bill by the New Haven interests. The Berkshire trolley merger, so much desired by the New Haven management, was vetoed by Governor Foss but the bill was passed over his veto.

The New Haven interests at the State House were cared for by William H. Coolidge, one of the leading corporation lawyers of the State, who had been for many years the Boston & Maine Railroad representative on legal matters, on Beacon Hill, a man of means and active in business and financial affairs. Mr. Coolidge possessed a sense of humor, which often cropped out at legislative committee hearings and investigations. One day, when a bill was before the railroad committee, providing for further public regulation of railroads, Mr. Coolidge referred in his argument against the measure to George Ade's story of how Canada and the United States treated its railroad builders.

"Two young hustling Americans," said he, quoting the Hoosier philosopher, "began railroading in the West. One went to Canada and built up a great Trans-Continental line, the other remained in this country and developed one of the big trunk lines of the West. For doing precisely the same thing the former was knighted by the King and the latter was indicted by the Federal Grand Jury."

The Legislature off his hands Governor Foss plunged into the National campaign which was well under way before the Legislature adjourned, entering the list of candidates for the Presidential nomination.

ROOSEVELT AND TAFT SPLIT

MASSACHUSETTS was one of the early battle grounds of both parties in the National campaign of 1912. Champ Clark's candidacy for the Democratic Presidential nomination appealed to a majority of the Six o'Clock Democrats of the State and a ticket with delegates favorable to him easily won in the primaries. Friends of Woodrow Wilson tried to break into the delegation, but by the time they had arrived on the scene, the Clark men had pre-empted the field. The Wilson managers opened headquarters here under the supervision of Dudley Field Malone operating through William S. McNary, prominent for many years in Democratic State politics. Governor Wilson came to Massachusetts and made speeches in Boston, Worcester, Fall River, Springfield and Holyoke, but he was unable to make much of a dent in the solid line of Clark men in the primaries.

Colonel Roosevelt paid a brief visit to Boston, late in February. He was a dinner guest of his old friend, Judge Robert Grant. That evening he issued through *The Outlook* office in New York, his favorable reply to the seven "Little Governors" who had asked him to become a candidate for the Presidential nomination. The Colonel was in fine fettle and sleepily announced that his hat was in the ring. The next day he addressed the members of the Legislature. Prior to coming to Boston he had made a speech in Ohio in which he advocated a referendum on judicial decisions involving police powers, which legislators of late years had generously appropriated. This speech cost the Colonel the support of many Republicans who were hesitating between him and Taft. They felt it was encroaching on the sphere of the Court and was dangerous legislation. From all over Northern and Eastern New England prominent Roosevelt supporters journeyed to Boston to confer with him.

President Taft came to Boston as the guest of the City Club and the South Boston Citizens' Association, March 18. He was the leading attraction at the Evacuation Day exercises. In the evening he was the chief guest at the Charitable Irish Society banquet. While in New England Mr. Taft did some campaigning in New Hampshire. On the afternoon of March 18th, the President addressed the Massachusetts Legislature taking issue with Colonel Roosevelt on what he termed an attack on the judiciary. While here President Taft conferred with his friends of the Taft League which had been organized to elect delegates favorable to his renomination.

Before the Champ Clark Democrats put their ticket into the field, they talked with Governor Foss and told him that Clark had made it a rule not to contest a State where a local candidate was in the field. If he was a candidate, the Clark men said they would not file for delegates. George Fred Williams, taking the Governor at his word, became active for Clark.

At this junction of State politics a new figure loomed on the horizon, Charles Sumner Bird of Walpole, wealthy manufacturer and the son of Frank Bird, known to the older politicians as the "Sage of Walpole." Mr. Bird was intensely Rooseveltian. He gave liberally to the Progressive campaign fund and a vigorous State wide campaign was made in behalf of that ticket for delegates to the National Republican convention.

Mr. Taft's advisers were not pleased at the way his campaign was going in Massachusetts. Congressman Gardner came on from Washington and applied the necessary stimulant. He announced that he was here to "kick that hat [Roosevelt's] out of the ring." Taft and Roosevelt returned in the primary campaign and made speeches. The President said he disliked to involve himself in a personal controversy with a man to whom he was greatly indebted, "But when you are backed up against a wall, and a man is hitting you in each eye, and punishing you in every other way, both above and below the belt, if you have any manhood in you, you have got to fight," said he in his opening speech.

Colonel Roosevelt said harsh things in his Massachusetts speeches against President Taft, accusing him of untruths and misrepresentations. In the primaries, Taft carried the State on a preference vote for the nomination over Roosevelt by almost 5000, but lost the Delegates-at-Large, due largely to the candidacy of Frank Seiberlich, who ran as an Independent, pledged to Taft. Many Republicans voted for everything on the ballot labeled Taft and the result was that thousands of Taft ballots were spoiled. Holding that a preferential vote was binding, Colonel Roosevelt renounced any claim he had on the Massachusetts Delegates-at-Large and asked them to vote for Taft, but the Roosevelt delegates refused to comply

JOSEPH P. LOMASNEY

EDITH NOURSE ROGERS

ERLAND P. FISH

ANDREW J. PETERS

JOHN RICHARDSON

CONGRESSMAN McCOR-
MACK

with the wish of the Colonel. The State delegation to the Republican National Convention was 18 for Taft, 18 for Roosevelt. The Roosevelt men were very bitter against Senator Crane because of his activities for Taft and they also refused to vote for his reëlection as National Committeeman.

Governor Foss secured seven of the delegates to the Democratic Convention. Eight delegates were pledged to Clark. The rest were unpledged but most of them favored the nomination of the Speaker of the National House of Representatives. After much wrangling, the Democrats reëlected Dr. John W. Coughlin of Fall River as Democratic National Committeeman.

NATIONAL REPUBLICAN CONVENTIONS

THE spirit of radicalism, sailing under the flag of Progressivism, was sweeping over the Republican ranks. The Old Guard raised the third term cry against Roosevelt. From all quarters came the same report—Taft was losing State after State in the primaries. Roosevelt was backed by several millionaires in his fight. The personal fortunes of some of them, it was claimed, had been affected by Taft's prosecution of trusts with which they were connected. At any rate there was no lack of campaign funds among the Progressives. The administration lined up the Southern delegates, most of them Federal office holders. Roosevelt's friends contested the right of some of these delegates to sit in the convention, and a sickening scandal ensued.

On the afternoon that Colonel Roosevelt arrived in Chicago, a great crowd welcomed him and followed him to his hotel. The Colonel stood up in his automobile, bowing and smiling at the cheering crowd. At his hotel he spoke to 10,000 people saying that Chicago was a bad place for men to try to steal. His followers claimed that the Taft managers were stealing delegates through the credential committee. "This has come down to mean a fight for honesty against dishonesty, for honesty against theft," shouted the Colonel. "The people have spoken and the politicians who oppose them will be made to understand that they are the servants and not the masters of the rank and file of the plain people of the Republic."

The tone of the Colonel's demagogic speech and the remarks of his lieutenants indicated plainly that they meant to reconstitute the old party or create a new one. On the night of the 17th of June, Roosevelt's friends held a meeting which packed the Auditorium. He announced that he would not be bound by the votes of fraudulently chosen delegates, and flayed Taft and the G.O.P. bosses. Senator Borah of Idaho presided at the meeting and discussed the steam roller tactics of the National Committee.

The following day the Old Guard had the votes to elect Elihu Root for permanent Chairman of the Convention. Root and Roosevelt had been boon companions. Root had been Colonel Roosevelt's Secretary of State. He had been an admirer of Root and in their salad days said he would crawl on his hands and knees from the

White House to the Capitol, if by so doing, he could make Root President.

The vote for Chairmanship, the key position in the convention, was 558 for Root and 502 for Governor McGovern of Wisconsin, the Roosevelt candidate. The convention settled down to nominating a Presidential ticket. Colonel Roosevelt asked his supporters to register a silent protest over the selection of Root and decline to take part in the proceedings. Three hundred and forty-four delegates followed his orders. Taft won the nomination easily and James S. Sherman of New York was named for Vice President.

DEMOCRATS

WHEN the Massachusetts Democratic delegates reached Baltimore, the Democratic convention city, they found a big row incubating between William J. Bryan and some of his old friends, over the selection of Ex-Judge Alton B. Parker for temporary presiding officer of that gathering. Mr. Bryan wouldn't listen to Parker's selection. He put on his war paint and feathers, snatched his tomahawk and started on the warpath after the Democratic reactionaires as he called them. An hour after he had hit the trail he had the palefaces of the "interests" on their knees offering him the pipe of peace, but he spurned it and said he'd not be satisfied with anything less than the scalps of the political trailers of his own tribe. When the Committee on Resolutions met, the chairmanship of that important committee was laid aside for Mr. Bryan as a peace offering. He declined the honor but retained his place as a member of the committee and dominated it.

David I. Walsh of Massachusetts was one of his willing assistants. On this occasion the Democrats named their candidate first and adopted their platform afterwards, thus reversing the order of things. The idea was Mr. Bryan's, who claimed that he wanted the platform to fit the candidate. He didn't want any more candidates amending the platform by telegraph as Judge Parker had eight years before. Some of his opponents hoped that he would bolt and nagged him. He had a special aversion against Thomas Fortune Ryan, the Wall Street financier, a member of the Virginia delegation. Mr. Ryan was too close to the "interests" to suit Mr. Bryan. He must be bottled up. When the convention met Speaker Champ Clark was the leading candidate for the Presidential nomination. His nearest competitor was Governor Woodrow Wilson of New Jersey. Senator Ollie James of Kentucky was chosen permanent presiding officer. He was a Clark man but fair to all factions.

Governor Foss went to Baltimore, the custodian of his own boom. With him went a half dozen office holders from the State House. He circulated among the delegates, talked with some of the candidates and distributed copies of a campaign circular by messenger boys, entitled: "Foss the Only Democrat Who Can Win." When Foss was suggested to Mr. Bryan as a good man to nominate, the

Nebraskan smiled and remarked: "He's still wet about the neck." The "Old Boy" asked Congressman William Sulzer of New York for his support. Sulzer replied that only once had the Democrats nominated a Republican —Horace Greeley—and, he added, "You know what happened." Foss was unable to muster the complete vote of his own State. On the 26th ballot, when Clark's vote began to break up, Governor Foss received 45 votes.

On the 14th ballot when Nebraska was called, Mr. Bryan arose amid the wildest tumult. Mounting the rostrum he announced it as his purpose to explain his vote. Stilling the clamor that his presence before the convention aroused, he declared that while he was instructed for Clark, he could not take any part in nominating a candidate where success depended upon the vote of New York and that to prevent such a result he felt free to vote for the second choice of Nebraska, Woodrow Wilson.

McCorkle of West Virginia demanded to know if he was ready to pledge himself to support the nominee of the Convention. Mr. Bryan parried by remarking that his Democracy had the indorsement of 6,500,000 Democrats and declared that he had no idea that the Convention would nominate a man for whom he could not vote. Leaning over the rail of the rostrum like a captain standing on the bridge of a ship in a storm, he challenged his foes to ask him questions, saying that if any one had a question to ask him he would be glad to help him get it off his mind. After this blow from Bryan, the Clark vote sank and continued to sink throughout the balloting.

The fight then became Wilson against the field. Clark was sent for and hurried on from Washington, but the convention adjourned before his arrival. On the 46th ballot, July 2nd, Woodrow Wilson was nominated.

Thomas M. Marshall of Indiana was nominated for Vice-President. Great sympathy was expressed for Speaker Clark. Ballot after ballot he had led and had a majority of the delegates, but not the requisite two-thirds to nominate required by the Democratic Convention from the earliest days. He was popular with the public and well liked by his associates. He was mortified over his defeat by a political novice, a school master—Woodrow Wilson. Time softened his feelings towards most of those who went back on him and he served the Wilson administration loyally, but he never forgave Bryan's betrayal of him.

BULL MOOSE

ANOTHER party was to be launched in the campaign—Colonel Roosevelt's Bull Moose party, as it came to be known. It forms an interesting chapter in the political history of the country and Massachusetts had an important part in its launching.

MASSACHUSETTS was well represented when the Bull Moose or Progressive party was organized, in August, 1912, at Chicago. Colonel Roosevelt had many influential friends in Massachusetts. It grieved his old friend Senator Lodge to see the Colonel bent on destroying the solidarity of the party of their early love, the party which had bestowed its choicest gifts on both of them. Roosevelt, cast in a different mould from Lodge, did not hesitate to ruthlessly strike down his party. Lodge remained loyal to the G.O.P.

Foremost among the Roosevelt leaders in this state were Charles Sumner Bird, Professor Albert Bushnell Hart, Matthew Hale, Richard Watson Child and Arthur D. Hill. The latter had been named District Attorney of Suffolk County by Governor Draper, on the death of John B. Moran, to serve until the voters could choose the latter's successor. The Democrats of Boston made short work of Hill and elected Joseph C. Pelletier. Hale had been, some years before, a tutor in the Roosevelt family, came to Boston, was introduced by Roosevelt's friends into politics and was elected a member of the Board of Aldermen. Bird had never been active in politics. There were others, to be sure, men like Charles H. Davis of the Cape whose liberal campaign contributions were made early and often, Ex-Congressman Lewis D. Apsley of Hudson, Rev. Dr. Perrin, James F. Magenis and Russell A. Wood. Just before the gathering of the Moose at Chicago, the Massachusetts Roosevelt followers elected 36 delegates to the convention. Eighteen Presidential electors were also nominated. Roosevelt and Johnson were endorsed as the National ticket and the delegates were instructed to vote for them "until the cows come home," on motion of Timothy W. Coakley formerly prominent in the Democratic party and brother of Daniel H. Coakley, a prominent Boston lawyer.

Like all third party movements, the Bull Moose party had its quota of cranks. It required all the tact of the presiding officer to handle them without causing a rumpus and at the same time prevent their cure-all schemes from being grafted on to its declaration of principles.

Chicago was Roosevelt mad. When the Colonel's train steamed into the La Salle Street station, there was a crowd as big, if not bigger, than the one that greeted him when he arrived in June to take personal command of his delegates in the hope of wresting the Republican nomination from President Taft.

Senator Dixon of Montana, National Chairman of the Progressive party, called the gathering to order. Ex-Senator Beveridge of Indiana sounded the keynote in an eloquent speech. It was a singing convention. They sang at the least provocation, until it seemed as if the convention had resolved itself into a religious revival.

When the chair announced that the next business of the convention was the "experience" meeting, James R. Garfield of Ohio, son of the martyred President Garfield, moved the adoption of a resolution inviting Colonel Roosevelt to address the delegates the next day. The motion was carried and the convention then adjourned until noon the next day. Colonel Roosevelt appeared and made his "Confession of Faith," as he called his speech on the occasion.

He told them that there was never a fight better worth making than the one in which they were engaged; that win or lose, there would be no faltering and that the fight would go on whatever fate overtook them. He cared nothing for the sneers of his opponents who charged him with socialism and anarchy. The new party, he said, stood as a corrective for Socialism and an antidote for anarchy, by favoring the rule of the people. With head erect, fists clenched, defiant and militant as a crusader of old, he concluded his address dramatically exclaiming:

"We stand at Armageddon and we battle for the Lord!"

On August 7th the Bull Moose Presidential ticket was nominated, Colonel Roosevelt and Governor Johnson of California accepted their nominations in brief speeches. Colonel Roosevelt was nominated by William A. Prendergast of New York, who was to have performed the same duty at the Republican convention in June, delivering practically the same speech at the Progressive convention he would have delivered at the Republican convention, had he been permitted to place the Colonel's name before that convention.

STATE CAMPAIGN 1912

THE State campaign in 1912 was a three cornered contest for Governor. District Attorney Pelletier of Suffolk county made it lively for the "Old Boy" in the Democratic primaries for the gubernatorial nomination. Pelletier went into the fight when Foss announced that he would not seek a third term. Later Mr. Foss changed his mind. Leading Democrats all over the State came to the rescue of Governor Foss and saw to it that he was renominated. John R. Murphy, a member of the Foss campaign committee, published a list of the Governor's appointments in answer to the charge that Foss had not given the Democrats enough jobs.

Mr. Murphy added in his statement that in his opinion, the criticisms made of Governor Foss by Mr. Pelletier and the latter's supporters were without foundation. Speaking as a Democrat, Mr. Murphy said he believed that the Governor had given a just, liberal, progressive and Democratic administration. He objected to interjecting un-American issues into the campaign by the opposition to Governor Foss, especially religious issues and appeals to fraternal societies, meaning the Knights of Columbus in which Pelletier was a high officer. The Murphy list was a pretty good showing from a party standpoint and helped Foss materially to win a renomination. The Governor figured prominently in settling the Elevated Railroad strike in July, which was another feather in his cap.

Joseph Walker and Everett C. Benton were the candidates for the Republican nomination. Mr. Bird, the Bull Moose hand picked candidate, had no opposition. Governor Hiram Johnson of California came into the State and spoke for the Progressives. Governor Wilson of New Jersey paid a flying visit to Massachusetts, speaking at the Barre fair, Springfield, Boston and Fall River. In the September primaries, Governor Foss had a majority of

27,000 over Pelletier and Walker won over Benton in the Republican primaries by about 10,000. All the defeated candidates accepted the decision of the voters and aided in the campaign of their party nominees. David I. Walsh was renominated for Lieutenant Governor on the ticket with Foss. Lieutenant Governor Luce was again named by the Republicans and Daniel Cosgrove, a former Democrat, was Bird's running mate.

President Taft, who summered at Beverly, remained later than usual this year and on September 28th, addressed the Essex County Republican Club, denouncing the third party for its "willingness to destroy every limitation of constitutional representative government, in order that by short cuts these various reforms, inconsistent as they may be, and many of them are, with each other, may be accomplished by the decree of a benevolent despotism to be supported by the acclaim of a hero-worshipping, emotional, undiscriminating, superficially minded and nonthinking people."

The Democratic and Republican State conventions were held in Boston, October 6th. Senator Lodge was the presiding officer of the Republican convention. He condemned the initiative and referendum and the general attack on the Constitution and the courts and declared that there were worse things than defeat. The platform adopted began with the statement that a change of party administration in the Nation would threaten prosperity, reaffirmed devotion to the protective tariff "which shall maintain American wages, and provide an adequate standard of living and provides annual employment for

600,000 persons in Massachusetts at wages higher than in other countries."

A readjustment of tariff schedules and reduction of excessive rates was favored based on "exact information." A demand was made for an international investigation of the causes of the high cost of living, and support was promised to every proper endeavor to reduce the cost. Popular recall of judges or of judicial decisions, as well as demonstrations to influence the actions of courts, were denounced as dangerous and un-American. The initiative and referendum was opposed.

DEMOCRATS

THERE was no clipping of the wings of the dove of peace at Faneuil Hall when "the unterrified and embattled Democracy of Massachusetts" as described by the blind senator from Oklahoma, Thomas P. Gore, met in State convention to nominate 18 electors and choose 16 members-at-large of the State Committee. Encouraged by the compliments and encomiums of Senator Gore, who observed that "no Walker could walk fast enough or Bird fly swift enough to pass Governor Foss on his third marathon race for the gubernatorial chair." John F. Fitzgerald who had announced his candidacy for United States Senator was the presiding officer.

On October 14 came the shocking news that an assassin had endeavored to take the life of Colonel Roosevelt, while he was campaigning in Wisconsin. Partizanship was laid aside and the efforts of the campaigners slackened, until it was discovered that the wounds were not fatal. The shooting kept the Colonel off the stump until the night of October 30, when he addressed a monster gathering at Madison Square Garden, New York.

Fitzgerald's senatorial candidacy was a favorite target for the Republicans and the Moose in the campaign Colonel Roosevelt was unable to come to Massachusetts during the campaign, but on his return to Oyster Bay, after his discharge from the Chicago hospital, where he had been under treatment for his pistol wounds, he wrote a letter asking for the support of the Massachusetts Progressive State ticket. The campaign continued without a letup until election day. Massachusetts broke its age old political precedent by giving her eighteen electoral votes to Woodrow Wilson.

Foss was elected for a third term by a plurality of about 45,000, and a Democratic Lieutenant Governor, David I. Walsh, was elected by 40,000 plurality. President Taft was second in the Presidential race. Joseph Walker, Republican candidate for Governor, led Charles S. Bird, Progressive. The Republican vote was split almost in half between the Progressives and the Republicans. In the avalanche of Bull Moose votes, the Democrats elected their candidate for Secretary of State, Frank J. Donahue. They increased their representation in the Legislature and a number of Bull Moose candidates succeeded in nosing in. Although the Republicans elected nine Congressmen and the Democrats elected seven, the total

Republican vote in the 16 districts fell 8027 behind the total Democratic vote.

The Democratic total was 195,790 and the Republican total 187,763. In 15 districts Progressives polled a total of 93,665. The biggest Republican vote was polled by Congressman Roberts in the 9th district. The biggest Democratic vote was polled in the 11th district where Andrew J. Peters was reëlected. The biggest Bull Moose vote was in the 14th where Kincaide was the Congressional candidate with 11,341.

The complexion of the Legislature was still Republican. That, of course, ended Mayor Fitzgerald's plan to succeed Senator Crane. The Republicans had 54 majority in the joint convention and a half dozen Republican candidates began to get busy to capture the Senatorial prize.

DEMOCRATIC LOAVES AND FISHES

In the contest for the Presidential nomination in 1912, the Democratic State organization was for Speaker Clark in the primaries. The White House remembered the scant courtesy Governor Wilson's field lieutenants received at the hands of the State organization. When the patronage came to be distributed, it was found that very few of the Champ Clark men got any of the plums from Washington. Edmund Billings, secretary of the Good Government Association, was made Collector of the Port, John F.

Malley of Springfield, a Wilson man, was named Collector of Internal Revenue, Charles S. Hamlin was appointed Assistant Secretary of the Treasury, all without consultation with the so-called State leaders. Billings' appointment was the hardest blow the Boston Democrats had to bear, but as a salve to their wounded feelings the Treasury Department consented to the appointment of President Joseph A. Maynard of the Democratic City Committee as Surveyor.

The neat way in which several Democratic members of Congress managed to slip into good Federal berths amused the public but angered their political associates. When Congressman Andrew J. Peters found that he would have to make a hard fight for a renomination, Francis J. Horgan having announced his candidacy, he quietly slipped into the office of Assistant Secretary of the Treasury, as the successor to Charles S. Hamlin, who was made Governor of the New Federal Reserve Board. Congressman William F. Murray was appointed Postmaster of Boston. Congressman John J. Mitchell was named United States Marshal. Congressman Gilmore, believing that a bird in the hand is worth two in the bush, decided that the postmastership of Brockton, his home city, was a great deal better than trying for a reëlection in his Republican Congressional district. The last of the big Federal plums were thus disposed of by the naming of Charles B. Strecker Assistant United States Treasurer in charge of the sub-treasury in Boston.

A few days before his second inaugural, the Governor removed from office Fred H. Walker, State Cattle Commissioner and E. Gerry Brown, Supervisor of Small Loans. Both were charged with irregularities in the conduct of their offices. Walker was a Republican, Brown, a Foss appointee. Both put up a determined fight against removal but the Executive Council backed up the Governor in his stand.

WEEKS ELECTED SENATOR

THE saving of the Legislature was the only consolation which the Massachusetts Republicans derived from the election returns of 1912. To accomplish this they bent all their energies and used all their personal and political influences. The repeal of the Bar and Bottle bill, the annexation of the cities and towns in Metropolitan Boston and the repeal of the Boston City Charter Amendments, were pictured in a circular sent out to those sections of the State where the Republican managers believed such an appeal would be the most effective. They also pictured the election of Mayor Fitzgerald as Senator Crane's successor. To the latter possibility, they attributed their success in retaining control of the Legislature more than any other issue.

The control of the Legislature not only insured the Republicans of the election of the United States Senator, but the Speakership of the House, the President of the Senate and the patronage which went with those offices. With the assurance that the next Legislature was safely

Republican, the Republican candidates for the United States Senate, Congressman John W. Weeks, Ex-Governor Eben S. Draper, Congressman Samuel W. McCall, Curtis Guild, Jr., and William B. Plunkett of Adams, did not permit any grass to sprout under their feet and immediately started their campaigns, to secure the Republican nomination to succeed Senator Crane.

Mr. Weeks mailed a letter to the Republican members elect of the Massachusetts Legislature the night after the election informing them of his candidacy for the Senate. Ex-Governor Guild, then the American Ambassador at St. Petersburg, happened to be home on department business when Senator Crane announced his decision to retire and was urged by friends to become a candidate. His position was that he would gladly accept the honor, but he returned to his diplomatic post and did nothing further about it. William B. Plunkett announced that he was against the "Old Guard" methods and machinations and that he favored "progressive legislation." The most formidable candidate to take the field against Mr. Weeks was Samuel W. McCall, who had declined to stand for reëlection to Congress after twenty years' service.

Joseph Walker who had been the Republican candidate for Governor came out in an open statement against Weeks, declaring that he was not sufficiently progressive. Weeks published a letter from Walker written right after election in which he congratulated him on his reëlection to Congress and thanked him for his support in the gubernatorial campaign.

Mr. McCall published with pardonable pride a letter

Charles W. Eliot, President Emeritus of Harvard, wrote Senator Stearns of Cambridge, urging him to vote for McCall.

No candidate was able to muster the 94 votes required under the conference two-thirds rule at the first session of the caucus. After six futile ballots the caucus adjourned to the next day. McCall led on every ballot. His nearest competitor was John W. Weeks. McCall received 63 votes on the first ballot and Weeks 56. On the second ballot McCall jumped to 71 and Weeks increased his vote to 61. Weeks now gained steadily. On the fourth ballot he had 68 votes, McCall 72. On the fifth ballot McCall had 73, Weeks lost one. The only change on the sixth ballot was the loss of one vote by McCall and the reëntrance of Plunkett in the race. Speaker Cushing gave the Guild, Weeks and Draper men a shock when he voted for McCall. His colleague, Courtney Crocker, also voted for McCall.

By January 10, 22 ballots had been taken with the same result. McCall led Weeks. The voting on the 22nd ballot was as follows:—

Total number of ballots cast	157
Necessary for choice	94
McCall	73
Weeks	71
Guild	9
Draper	2
Lawrence	2

SENATOR MARCUS A. COOLIDGE

Following the announcement of this vote, the caucus adjourned to meet again on Monday. The Republican State Committee took a hand and endeavored to break the deadlock, issuing an appeal to the Republican legislators to unite on a candidate without further delay. On Monday the caucus balloted again and on the 31st ballot Weeks got 97 votes and was declared the Republican nominee. The fight was over.

The Democrats were "watching and waiting" from the day of the first session of the Republican caucus. Representative John F. Meany of Blackstone had a long talk with Governor Foss. When he left the Governor, Meany announced that he would introduce, in the House, a bill providing for the Oregon plan for the nomination of a United States Senator and ask for a suspension of all rules, that the bill might become a law at the earliest possible moment. Under this bill the joint primary would be held February 5. Whoever received the highest vote would be the nominee and members of the Legislature would be morally bound to vote for him, whether he was a Republican, Democrat or Progressive. The Republicans ignored his request and waited until after they had agreed on their Senator before acting, when they reported "leave to withdraw" and the report was accepted.

After a stormy meeting the Democrats nominated Sherman L. Whipple of Brookline. Mayor Fitzgerald and his senatorial aspirations were early made an incidental issue which at times provoked heated outbursts. A discussion of the ex-mayor brought on a warm debate as to the relative merits of the city and the country Democrats.

Both branches of the Legislature met in their respective chambers January 14th for the purpose of electing a Senator and chose John W. Weeks. Weeks resigned his seat in Congress. A special election was held April 15 to fill the vacancy. The Democrats nominated John J. Mitchell, who had made the fight against Weeks in November. The Republicans nominated Alfred L. Cutting of Weston. Norman H. White of Brookline was the Bull Moose candidate. Mitchell won, the vote being: Mitchell, 13,134; Cutting, 8,742; White, 5,503.

FOSS' THIRD TERM

MR. Foss was sworn in for the third time as Governor, January 3, 1913. Also for the first time since the existence of the Republican party, a Democrat was sworn in as Lieutenant Governor, David I. Walsh of Fitchburg, was the new figure on Beacon Hill this year. Cheers greeted the Chief Executive and his colleague, as they filed into the House chamber to take their oaths of office. The Governor's inaugural message dealt almost exclusively with the transportation problems. He renewed his suggestions of the year before in those matters which the Legislature had not gone the distance he desired, including an appropriation of $30,000,000 for the development of the port of Boston. "Develop the Connecticut,

Taunton and Merrimac rivers and memorialize Congress to open the Panama Canal free of tolls to the ships of all Nations," he told them.

His first special message to the Legislature dealt with the number of pardons granted in 1912. He had been criticized for exercising the pardoning power too freely. Of the number released 31 were from the State Prison, 22 from the Massachusetts Reformatory, 28 from the Houses of Correction, 14 from the Womens' Reformatory, 1 from jail, 1 from the State Farm and 1 from the Prison Camp, a total of 98. Ten of those pardoned were murderers. The longest sentence served was nearly 32 years of a life sentence by David Mooney. The shortest sentences were those of Chin Toy and Won Chung, two Chinamen, each eight years of a life sentence for murder.

On January 14, the members of the Electoral College met and cast the State's 18 votes for Woodrow Wilson for President and Thomas R. Marshall for Vice-President. The following day a Democratic Secretary of State, Frank J. Donahue, was sworn in.

Governor Foss sent a chill down the spines of the Democrats when he named William P. Fowler a member of the Boston Licensing Board. Mr. Fowler was almost unique as a public servant in filling a salaried office for 11 years without accepting pay, saving the city $33,000. He was Registrar of the Institutions department for that period. In explaining the refusal of the salary Mr. Fowler said: "I do not think that I earn the salary. Most of the work is done by clerks. There is hardly a day, however, that I do not devote some time to my duties as Registrar;

some days it requires considerable time, while on others there is very little to do. I do not need the money and the work is on matters in which I am interested so that I have always been glad to give the city the benefit of my services without pay." But in the case of the Licensing Board he did not hesitate to take the money.

The House, February 10, adopted a resolution felicitating Great Britain and Ireland on the passage of the Home Rule bill. The Legislature observed Lincoln Day listening to an address by William H. Lewis, Assistant United States District Attorney, a former member of the House from Cambridge and a member of the race that Lincoln emancipated 50 years before.

As the time approached for the inauguration of Woodrow Wilson as President, Governor Foss let it be known that it would please him to see a big turnout of Massachusetts troops and preparations were made on a large scale for the inaugural parade. The State made a creditable showing in Washington, but Governor Foss did not bring back a Cabinet portfolio on his return home. Soon afterward he began to show a dislike for Democratic measures and a coolness toward Democratic leaders.

Meanwhile, the Legislature was busy with its task. John J. McDevitt of Quincy, a member of the Senate, said at a public meeting that he had been offered a bribe of $300 to vote for a certain bill. He was summoned before the joint committee on Rules and questioned. He declined to give the name of the man who offered him the bribe. At one of the hearings he mentioned the name of the Democratic members of the House in connection with the charge, but when pressed for details declared that he didn't remember. The House dropped the matter but the Senate found the charge unproven and sentenced him to a reprimand and suspension for 30 days. Senator James H. Brennan of Charlestown tried to have the vote reconsidered, whereby McDevitt was suspended, his pay stopped, a reprimand by the President of the Senate in open session ordered and an apology in writing demanded, as a condition precedent to his restoration to his rights as a member of the Senate, but reconsideration failed by a strict party vote of 9 Democrats to 28 Republicans. The full penalty was inflicted but not until the Quincy Senator had entered a vigorous protest and spread upon the records a request for a trial by the Senate. McDevitt never returned to his seat. He sought a vindication at the hands of his constituents in the primaries but was denied it.

Champ Clark, Speaker of the National House, visited Massachusetts, March 17, as the chief guest of South Boston's Evacuation Day committee. He made a brief address to the Massachusetts House in which he said he hoped that the Commonwealth of Massachusetts and this mighty Republic will go on

> "Forever and forever,
> As long as the river flows,
> As long as the heart has passions,
> As long as life has woes."

Woman Suffrage was beaten at this session, the vote in the House being 144 to 88.

While the Suffolk Law School bill was before him,

Governor Foss had a controversy with Dean Archer of the school. The bill gave the school the right to issue degrees. It was fought by other colleges and law schools and Dean Archer called on Governor Foss to present his arguments, why the Governor should sign the bill. After Governor Foss had communicated his veto to the House, Dean Archer sent to the Legislature a letter declaring that the Governor had perpetrated a cruel hoax and then "gloated over the trick" he had played on him. Archer said that at the time that he was arguing for the measure the Governor had already vetoed it, but did not inform him of his action. This the Governor denied and the Senate killed the bill.

As a New England manufacturer, the Governor professed to be alarmed over the tariff program of the Democratic Administration at Washington and gave out a statement in which he declared: "I want it understood that I am not and never was a free trader. I am a Protectionist." He also said the Republicans were beaten in the last election because they were Stand-patters on the tariff, and that he hoped the Democrats would learn a lesson from the Republican defeat and not endanger their own future by going to the other extreme on the tariff. As to why he sent a message on reciprocity to the Legislature a few days before, the Governor said he did so in response to President Wilson's summons to "all honest, patriotic and progressive men to counsel and sustain him." This proved to be the entering of the wedge that widened the breach between him and the Democrats and he began to work back into the Republican fold. When the

House debated his tariff message, he was roundly denounced by the Democrats for his attitude.

The Republicans passed their resolutions condemning the proposed Underwood Democratic tariff bill. Toward the end of the session the legislators took keen delight in passing measures over the Governor's veto. Of the 32 measures he vetoed, 10 were passed over his veto. Much constructive legislation was passed notwithstanding the friction between the Executive and Legislative branches and the Governor succeeded in getting through measures in which he was interested. Important among these were: the Public Opinion Act, the resolve ratifying the Federal Income Tax, and another for the direct election of United States Senators, thus ending one of the most important controversies dividing the two leading political parties for years.

Of the bills which were passed over the Governor's veto the most important were the Washburn railroad commission measure, the bill for authorizing the acquisition by the New Haven Railroad of the Western Massachusetts trolleys, and the 9 hour in 11 street railway employees measure. In the interest of labor a new Child Labor law to regulate the employment of minors was passed. It also amended the Workingmen's Compensation law and passed an act providing for joint action by the Industrial Accident Board and the Board of Labor and Industry for the treatment of occupational diseases, a subject agitated by labor leaders.

It raised salaries all along the line, in some instances from $2500 to $3000 a jump, and in the case of the Land

Court and the Railroad Commission, the members of both bodies were placed on a par with the Judges of the higher courts by the increase of their salaries to $8500 for chairmen and $8000 for members.

WALSH NOMINATED FOR GOVERNOR

By the time the Legislature adjourned, practically every Democrat, high and low, was lambasting Governor Foss. He had serious labor troubles with his Blower Works operatives. All sorts of threats were made to ruin him and his business by labor leaders, but with his usual luck he came out ahead in the controversy.

Thursday, July 3, the Railroad Commission of Massachusetts became an institution of the past. For 44 years the railroads and railways of Massachusetts had been supervised by a commission appointed by the successive Governors. The Massachusetts Railroad Commission, during its existence of almost half a century, left its impress not only on this Commonwealth but also on practically all the other States in the Union which followed its scheme of dealing with railroad corporations. On that date it yielded the field to the new Public Service Commission, created by act of the last Legislature, for the regulation of public service corporations.

The old Commission had supervision over railroads and railways. Its powers were mainly recommendatory. The new Public Service Commission was given supervision over railroad, street railway, telephone companies and steamboat companies plying between ports in this State. By virtue of one of the provisions of the act creating the Public Service Commission, the members of the old Railroad Commission were made members of the new board.

No State commission had to face more difficulties or attempt the solution of more involved problems than the old Railroad Commission. While the powers of the latter were in the main simply recommendatory, it accomplished much. During the 44 years of its existence there were only twenty appeals from its decisions and findings to the Supreme Court. In one case, the court found the mandatory act, under which the board fixed certain interstate freight rates, to be unconstitutional. This was the Berkshire coal case, back in the old Hoosac Tunnel days. In two other cases, those of the appeals of the Worcester & Nashua Railroad and the City of Cambridge, the Court's decisions were against the Board. In all other appeals the Board was sustained.

Lieutenant Governor Walsh formally entered the gubernatorial race in July and from that date he and Governor Foss became political opponents. Walsh had no opposition for the nomination. One prominent Democrat, incensed at Governor Foss, remarked that history would "record with incredulity, that such a monumental fraud escaped detection so long," quoting the late Senator Ingalls of Kansas on Grover Cleveland. The breach widened between the Governor, the Democratic State Committee and most of the leading Democrats. Late in July, it was as wide as Gunpowder River, where the Governor's Presidential boom fell overboard in June, on its way to the Baltimore convention in 1912. The hand of almost every Democratic politician, except those whom he had appointed to office, was against him openly. They dared him to come out and contest the nomination with Walsh. The State organization ignored him. His name was no longer spoken with reverent lips.

The Governor's denunciation of the labor unions further aroused the enmity of the leaders of organized labor. His tariff views and his removal of a part of his manufacturing plant to Canada, on the plea that the Underwood Tariff bill forced him to do so, because it did not include a reciprocity clause, his statement that "no man can be elected Governor of Massachusetts this year who indorses the Underwood bill," and his refusal to name Democrats to office, who were backed by the State organization, added to his unpopularity with Democratic politicians.

The day the Democratic State Committee was denouncing Foss, the latter's friends took out Republican nomination papers for him for Governor. For some weeks there had been a procession of bread and butter Republican politicians to the Executive Chamber. Self-respecting Republicans who responded to his invitation to call on him, scorned or laughed at the idea of Foss going into the Republican primary or acting as its self-appointed advisor.

The Democratic State Committee picked Richard H. Long, a shoe manufacturer, and former Republican, for Walsh's running mate, but Ex-Councillor Edward P.

Barry waged a lively campaign and defeated him.

The Republicans had their party troubles too. Just when Colonel Benton and his friends were congratulating themselves on what an easy time they would have getting the Republican gubernatorial nomination, their plans were spoiled by the announcement from Congressman Gardner that his hat was in the ring.

At this juncture, Governor Foss made two more important appointments which displeased the Democrats and didn't enthuse the Republicans. Ex-Speaker John N. Cole, Congressman Gardner's avowed political enemy, was named to fill the vacancy on the Board of Economy and Efficiency, caused by the resignation of Norman H. White of Brookline, who resigned to make an unsuccessful run in the Weeks district as the Bull Moose candidate for Congress. David A. Ellis was named a member of the Boston Transit Commission to fill the vacancy caused by the death of George G. Crocker, chairman of the commission since its creation. Ellis was not particularly strong with the Boston Democrats, although claiming to be of that political faith.

The Essex Club, Congressman Gardner's political organization, had an outing in August, at which all of the Republican gubernatorial aspirants were present. Governor Foss addressed the gathering as "Fellow Republicans."

Another batch of appointments distasteful to the Democrats was made by the Governor just before the State primaries. He named Ex-Secretary of State Langtry, Joseph B. Russell and Neil McNeil, as State House Extension Commissioners. The two latter were Democrats of a mild, inoffensive type.

GARDNER DEFEATS BENTON

GARDNER defeated Benton in the Republican primary. Foss didn't go into the Republican primary owing to defective nomination papers. Charles L. Burrill won the Republican State Treasurer nomination for which there was a three cornered contest. Frederick W. Mansfield was nominated in the Democratic primary for State Treasurer over St. Coeur.

Gardner's nomination for Governor was a genuine surprise to many seasoned politicians, who felt that he would be unable in a few weeks to undo the work of months which Colonel Benton had put in for the gubernatorial nomination. Gardner insisted on naming the chairman of the State Committee on the ground that the candidate for Governor ought to have running his campaign a man in whom he had complete confidence and who was in sympathy and harmony with the ideas of the nominee, but Chairman Hatfield, a popular and able official declined to withdraw. He had labored hard and long for party success, but he came into office at a period when the Republicans were having a streak of hard luck. Gardner wanted to run his campaign on a clean slate.

He also told the members of the Committee that he would personally go into the State convention and fight for his progressive planks and that if they had any idea that they could burden him with a colorless platform, full of ambiguities, they were mistaken. The committee passed a vote of confidence in Chairman Hatfield and Gardner proceeded to carry out his own program.

Bird, the Progressive leader, was baiting Gardner and the latter informed him that unless he ceased he would hire Faneuil Hall and administer him a walloping that he would not soon forget. Gardner hired the hall, but only good naturedly spanked his Progressive opponent, who was unable to be present and sent one of his grenadiers to represent him.

The Democratic and Republican conventions were held the same day, October 5. Under the new order of things there was nothing for the conventions to do but adopt a platform. The Democrats had a harmonious time of it. The Republicans had a monopoly of discord and exultantly "steam-rollered" Gardner. The Committee on Resolutions built a platform which didn't suit Mr. Gardner. Three planks, which he insisted should go into the resolutions, were missing, and the one on immigration was so weak that Gardner wouldn't stand on it. When the opponents of the Congressman sat down after the convention and calmly surveyed the situation, they concluded that the man who threatened to "wallop" Bird, the Progressive candidate, had been "walloped" himself.

On the last day for filing nomination papers, Governor Foss on his way home from Indianapolis, stepped off the train at Utica, New York, called the Executive Chamber in Boston and instructed his Secretary to file his papers.

Ex-Senator Albert J. Beveridge of Indiana, came into the State to help the Progressives and tackled Captain Gardner on his child labor record in Congress. Mr. Gardner claimed Beveridge garbled a speech of his, declared he stood for a Federal constitutional amendment which would give to Congress the right to prescribe maximum hours of labor and a minimum wage for workers throughout the United States. "The man is the same Beveridge who was thrashed on the floor of the Senate by Senator Bailey, whom he had insulted in debate. This is the same Beveridge, who failed to retaliate for that well deserved thrashing," declared Gardner. Nothing more was heard from Beveridge in the campaign.

The last week of the campaign Governor Foss issued a broadside against Lomasney, Riley and Fitzgerald, whom he called "the Tammany Trio" and he demanded that Bird and Gardner withdraw in his favor.

Making his 519th speech in a 36-day State-wide campaign, during which he spoke in every city and town in Massachusetts, the Progressive candidate, Bird had done what no other man ever did running for Governor and he finished in fine voice and splendid physical condition.

The election proved a Democratic landslide. The entire Democratic ticket was elected. Even the Executive Council had a majority against the G.O.P. The Republicans still controlled the Senate by a small margin, but they were seven short of a majority in the House. Gardner's vote was the smallest ever cast for a Republican gubernatorial candidate. He finished in third place.

Election night, 1913, was one of darkness and gloom at Republican headquarters. The Democrats paraded the streets with red fire and bands. The Progressives consoled themselves with the fact that they had beaten the regular Republican gubernatorial candidate to his knees and that they would hold the balance of power in the next Legislature.

WALSH ELECTED

THE election of Walsh proved that there was, after all, very little in the old bugaboo that a Catholic couldn't be elected Governor of Massachusetts. That fine example of the 20th century Puritan, Dr. Charles W. Eliot, President Emeritus of Harvard University, declared that he had voted for Walsh because only through him could he express his opinion.

The election also proved that a poor man could be elected Governor without the aid of the powerful rich or the "interests" which have axes to grind on Beacon Hill. Foss acknowledged that he spent $10,520 to get his 20,000 votes. The Republican State Committee filed returns of $21,271.17 for election expenses and Mr. Gardner's campaign treasurer declared that he had expenses of $34,692. Mr. Bird's campaign cost $92,625. Governor-elect Walsh swore that his expenses were $1539. The Democratic State Committee acknowledged spending nearly $24,000.

The political complexion of the House of Representatives made it necessary for the Republicans to bestir themselves. Speaker Cushing must have Progressive support, if he would succeed himself. He and his friends set themselves to work to secure it from the Bull Moose. In this they succeeded and organized the Legislature of 1914.

James Madison Morton, Associate Justice of the Supreme Judicial Court, resigned to take effect December 15. He was one of the State's eminent jurists. Governor Foss named Judge John C. Crosby of the Superior Court to fill the vacancy. In Judge Crosby's place he named William Hamilton of Springfield. The Governor again aroused the ire of many Boston Democrats by naming Robert W. Woods, License Commissioner, to succeed Commissioner Emery who died. Mr. Woods was well known as a settlement worker and for years head of the South End House. His views on the regulation of the sale of liquor and the conduct of saloons and cafés, differed widely from those of the liquor interests and his appointment was a blow at the "wide open" town idea.

Senator Lodge who was unable to participate in the campaign, because of a serious surgical operation, was able to be about after election and to return to Washington, resuming his senatorial duties. He let it be known that he never approved of his son-in-law's campaign for Governor.

FOSS BACK IN G.O.P.

Governor Foss was now, for a while at least, back in the Republican ranks. With all his faults the "Old Boy" had many good qualities. One of the most vacillating men who ever occupied the chair of the Chief Executive of Massachusetts, yet he had courage and at times, would stand up and fight bravely. Take for instance his judicial appointments. There isn't any question that it required considerable backbone to do what he did. His opponents said that he was playing politics for the Catholic vote; but when he declined to attend the 175th anniversary of the Charitable Irish Society, at which the President of the United States was the chief guest, because those in charge of the arrangements had assigned Cardinal O'Connell second place in the speaker's list, on the ground that a Prince of the Roman Catholic Church was a higher functionary than the Governor of the Commonwealth, he risked his popularity but they were not seriously inclined to question his attitude in that matter. They were grateful to him because of the recognition he had given them on the higher courts.

No man got more fun out of the position as Governor than Foss. At times it was hard to understand the workings of his mind. The patronage slate was more than once broken, while the Executive Councillors cooled their heels in an ante room waiting for His Excellency to make a new one.

CUSHING REËLECTED SPEAKER

THE Democratic plan was to make George Pearl Webster of Boxford, a Progressive, Speaker of the House of

1914. The Republicans once more raised the anti-Lomasney cry and pictured the great influence the latter would have in the event of Webster being Speaker. Publicly and privately the Progressives were exhorted to save the House from Democratic control. One Batchelder, prominent in dark lantern politics, had been enlisted by Speaker Cushing to assist him in rounding up Progressive votes in return, it is claimed, for Cushing's work in behalf of the sectarian constitutional amendment, so earnestly desired by Batchelder and his friends. To Batchelder many give the credit for inducing some of the Progressives to turn their backs on Webster and vote for Cushing. The six Bull Moose representatives who broke away from the Progressives and reëlected Cushing, stated that they had special reasons for doing so. The fight over the Speakership of the House of 1914 and the Democratic move to create a committee similar to the committee of the National House, taking the appointment of the legislative committees out of the hands of the Speaker, which failed by a vote of 118 to 110, delayed the inaugural ceremony two hours.

DAVID IGNATIUS WALSH
Governor 1914–1916

GOVERNOR Walsh's friends filled the House chamber eager to listen to his first inaugural address. His recommendations and observations covered a wide field. He asked the Legislature for the immediate reorganization of the financial structure of the Boston & Maine Railroad Corporation, new management of the property and divorce of the road from the New Haven system.

Provision for the calling of a Constitutional Convention to consider especially the adoption of the initiative, referendum and the recall of elective officers; biennial elections; the abolition of the Executive Council and enlarging the powers of the Lieutenant Governor; woman suffrage; rights of cities and towns to deal in necessaries of life in times of public distress; government by majority; the right of the Governor to veto special items in appropriation bills; homestead legislation; revision of the taxation system, and the making of workmen's compensation compulsory.

Party enrollment should be abolished.

Open State armories for public use.

A central purchasing agency for all State Departments.

More power for the Governor over State Commissions.

Certain boards should be consolidated.

Many other minor suggestions were made in the interest of better administration of public affairs.

The Legislature declined to follow it entirely, but several of the Governor's propositions were adopted. Much so-called "progressive" legislation was passed and by reorganizing several State boards the Governor was given an opportunity to reward his supporters.

John F. Meany, private secretary to Governor Walsh, took his place as a member of the Public Service Commission to which the Governor appointed him. He was succeeded by Thomas H. Connelly, the assistant secretary who was later made Judge of the Brighton District Court. What Governor Walsh was able to accomplish was summed up by himself in a speech at the Democratic State convention in October over which Harvey N. Shepard presided. Later Mr. Shepard was made a Civil Service Commissioner, by Governor Walsh.

Summing up what his administration had been able to accomplish in the first year in office the Governor said:—

"It has given a fair and just increased compensation to injured workingmen and workingwomen of the Commonwealth.

"It has extended the principles of home rule to our cities and towns.

"It has provided for the strict and impartial regulation and supervision of certain public service corporations, many of which until this current year were beyond the reach of supervising authorities.

"It has established a vigorous, efficient and progressive health department to safeguard and protect the public health.

"It has provided paid public officials to study the problems of the helpless and insane wards of the State.

"It has aided in forcing a dissolution of the railroad monopoly which has nigh throttled the very life and future of New England.

"It has restored to the people the right to determine in what manner their primary elections shall be conducted.

"It has kept the cost of the State government, which

HENRY I. HARRIMAN

JAMES H. BRENNAN

CHARLES H. INNES

EDWARD L. DOLAN

MORGAN T. RYAN

THOMAS C. O'BRIEN

always must be taken from the earnings of the people, within reasonable and economical limits.

"It has made it easier and less expensive for our municipalities to engage in municipal lighting.

"It has sought to increase the usefulness and efficiency of the administrative boards of the State by reorganization of the departments of the State government and by taking preliminary steps for a state-wide policy of requiring officials who are paid substantial salaries to give their entire time to the public service.

"It has encouraged, protected and promoted the agricultural industry of the Commonwealth.

"It has provided for compulsory investigation of labor disputes and giving publicity to the findings made by arbitration boards.

"It has opened to a wider and more public use the expensive armories that have been constructed by the State at a large public expense.

"It has increased the State aid to poor and deserving widows of our soldiers.

"It has compelled large foreign corporations to pay a fairer share of the expense of the Commonwealth, whose privileges they enjoy.

"It has recommended and aided the people of small means to acquire homes of their own.

"It has sought to obtain just and fair legislation in answer to the demands of labor.

"It has provided for the parole and pardon of prisoners upon a merit system rather than through financial or political influence.

"It has recommended and aided a Constitutional amendment for the reform of our taxation system, defeated heretofore by successive Legislatures, and which promises to relieve the injustice and inequality existing under the present archaic system.

"It has given the Tax Commissioner increased powers to enforce the payment of inheritance taxes.

"It has for the first time given special attention to the conservation of our natural resources by providing for the establishment and maintenance of State forests.

"It has lessened the expenses of litigation by reducing the time in which settlement might be made of estate of deceased persons."

During the year Governor Walsh removed the members of the Board of Labor Industries named by Governor Foss who failed to appoint a representative of organized labor on it, the chairman of which was James A. Lowell, a former Republican member of the Legislature and now a United States District Court Judge. A new board was named with Alfred S. Donovan, a well known shoe manufacturer as chairman.

A new and smaller Board of Port Directors of the Port of Boston was authorized and after the Legislature adjourned the Governor named Edward F. McSweeney of Boston, chairman, Joseph A. Conry of Boston and Lombard Williams of Dedham. A new Board of Insanity made up of Dr. Michael O'Meara of Worcester, chairman, Dr. L. Vernon Briggs of Boston and Charles E. Ward of Buckland was named. The reorganized Commission of Economy and Efficiency, included Francis X. Tyrrell of Chelsea, chairman, Thomas W. White of Newton and Russell A. Wood of Cambridge.

Governor Walsh also found it necessary to make two temporary appointments to fill important berths created by statutes of that year, until such time as he could make permanent appointments. He named Dr. William C. Hanson, who had been assistant to the secretary of the State Board of Health, to serve as acting Health Commissioner. The State Board of Health went out of existence under the reorganization act. Dr. Allan McLaughlin, a medical expert, of the Federal Health service was named as head of the new State Board.

Two Democrats were named for the Superior Court. Christopher T. Callahan of Holyoke, prominent and active in the Bryan days and James B. Carroll, Chairman of the Industrial Accident Board. A little later, when Justice Sheldon of the Supreme Court retired, Judge Carroll was appointed to the Supreme Judicial Court. Mr. Carroll enjoyed a high reputation at the bar in the Western part of the State. He had what the lawyers call, the "judicial temperament" and a well stocked legal mind. Mr. Carroll was a running mate of Governor Russell after General Corcoran was named to the Superior Court bench more than twenty years before. In Judge Carroll's place on the Superior Court, Governor Walsh named City Solicitor James H. Sisk of Lynn, prominent in local politics of his city for several years and a well known member of the bar.

Ex-Governor Draper died suddenly April 9, 1914, at a Southern health resort, where he had gone for rest. The

State took appropriate action and was represented at his funeral.

The last day of the year 1914, Governor Walsh made a batch of important appointments. He named Charles R. Gow for License Commissioner of Boston to succeed William P. Fowler. The same day Joseph B. Eastman was named as the successor of Clinton White on the Public Service Commission. Mr. Eastman had for several years represented a small but select body of men, banded together under the euphonious title of the "Public Franchise League," and appeared before legislative committees on transportation and other matters. Louis D. Brandeis, named by President Wilson a member of the Supreme Court of the United States was one of the group. President Wilson also named Mr. Eastman a member of the Interstate Commerce Commission where he made a fine reputation as a railroad expert. When Franklin D. Roosevelt became President in 1933, he appointed Mr. Eastman as Railroad Coördinator in his attempt to aid the railroads of the country reëstablish themselves on a paying basis.

GOVERNOR WALSH REËLECTED

GRAFTON CUSHING got into the gubernatorial nomination campaign soon after his election as Lieutenant Governor, hoping to be the Republican Moses in 1915. Samuel W. McCall felt the necessity of an early start in the contest for a renomination. Cushing as candidate for Lieutenant Governor received almost 20,000 more votes than McCall running for Governor in the last election. The year before McCall wouldn't fight for the nomination. This year he would not only fight, but he would fight to the last ditch. Cushing declared that a younger and more active man was necessary to make a successful fight for the party. Mr. McCall selected Charles S. Baxter for campaign manager. Baxter had acted in some capacity for Louis A. Frothingham in the latter's candidacies for Lieutenant Governor and Governor.

Congressman Gardner, an old friend of Cushing came out for him and arranged a meeting in his behalf on his farm in Hamilton, announcing that none of the "Big Wigs" of the party would be there—just plain, ordinary Republicans would be invited, he said. Supporting Cushing for the nomination were the "Guardians of Liberty," "Minute Men" and others of their ilk, who were advocating the sectarian amendment to the Constitution which had received the support of Mr. Cushing in the Legislature. Mr. McCall deplored the lugging of religion into the campaign and declared that he "would prefer defeat by 1,000,000 votes to victory under the black flag of bigotry."

Cushing denied that his support of the amendment was actuated by religious prejudice. To the members of the Franco-American Club he stated his position and declared that "The Constitution will operate exactly the same against Protestants, Catholics and Jews, if by any chance they seek to maintain their institutions at public expense. And the proper time to amend the Constitution is before anyone makes a demand upon the public treasury. This is not a religious question. It is a matter of sound public policy."

Ex-Governor Foss added gaiety to the campaign by announcing himself a candidate for the Republican gubernatorial nomination on a Prohibition platform. He made a few speeches and issued several broadsides of campaign literature, few took him seriously. Politically he was dead.

William Shaw, a real, simon pure Prohibitionist threatened to run the Republican primaries for the gubernatorial nomination, unless the Republican leaders came out for National Prohibition. The leaders refused to comply with Mr. Shaw's demand and he started to get into the fight but his nomination papers were defective and he had to content himself with riding on the Water Wagon at the polls.

Shortly after the Legislature adjourned, President Calvin Coolidge of the State Senate announced his candidacy for second place on the Republican ticket. Councillor Guy A. Ham of Boston was already in the field. Coolidge's entrance into the contest meant that he would have the Western part of the State. Councillor Ham made an aggressive campaign, but was easily defeated by Coolidge.

The Democrats were kept in doubt for some weeks about the candidacy of Governor Walsh. First he would and then he wouldn't and finally he put off a definite answer until his return from the Panama Exposition. There was a lot of feeling among the party leaders against

Walsh, but he didn't intend to bring on a primary fight if one could be avoided and he held off until the last moment before announcing he would run for a third term.

The Progressive party nomination went begging. It was given to Nelson B. Clark of Beverly, after some of the leaders had expostulated with him for trying to steal Cushing's thunder and making the sectarian constitutional amendment his paramount issue.

The Democrats had a little diversion on the side in their campaign this year. Congressman Dietrick of Cambridge was a candidate for the Democratic nomination on the issue of National Prohibition, announcing that he would campaign afoot from one end of the State to the other. He made a brave attempt, starting at the New York State line in Berkshire county, but his campaign petered out and he learned that preaching Prohibition among Democrats was not conducive to great enthusiasm or a large crop of votes. He received 3000 votes against 74,000 for Walsh.

Cushing carried the counties of Essex, Plymouth and Suffolk. Middlesex county, the home of McCall, where the heaviest Republican vote was cast, was split pretty fairly, the vote being Cushing, 16,277; McCall, 18,879.

Cushing accepted the result, supported McCall and presided over the State convention at Tremont Temple. There was a spirited contest on the Democratic side for the nomination of Attorney General between Joseph Joyce Donahue and Harold Williams. Joyce was nominated by a majority of more than 42,000.

WALSH'S SECOND TERM

THE day before Governor Walsh's second inauguration, January 7, 1915, Channing Cox was elected Speaker of the House and Calvin Coolidge chosen President of the Senate. In his second inaugural address, Governor Walsh called attention to the European War, saying that already its effects had been felt here by the unrest created. He asked for an appropriation of $50,000 for the unemployed, to be used to reclaim waste lands, swamps and marshes. He discussed in detail the State's finances and advocated the budget system as the only proper and business like way of handling the State's finances. He made several recommendations looking to an improvement in the tax laws and tax collections. He again demanded that the transportation, telegraph and telephone companies be compelled to bear the cost of the maintenance of the Public Service Commission. He also asked that the supervision of the telephone and telegraph companies be returned to the gas and electric light commission, but both requests were refused by the Legislature.

On the matter of calling a Constitutional Convention, he set forth his ideas of subjects which ought to be dealt with, but the Legislature declined to favor the calling of one, taking the ground that there was already a sure, safe and inexpensive method of changing the Constitution whenever the people desired to do so. Biennial elections were urged. He recommended the submission of an equal suffrage amendment, but neither one of these two suggestions were acted favorably upon. He recommended the initiative and referendum. That, too, was defeated.

He outlined a scheme of the State paying certain campaign expenses, but it was rejected. He recommended that the power to grant and regulate liquor licenses, and to control their police force, be restored to the people of Fall River. That, too, was rejected by the Legislature. Old line life insurance companies, through their powerful lobby, defeated his plan of permitting savings banks issuing life insurance not to exceed $1000. The Legislature did pass his requested appropriation for the unemployed.

The women made a gallant fight this year for equal suffrage and for the Constitutional amendment striking out the word "male" from the Constitution. The House passed it by a vote of 196 to 33. The women threw yellow flowers at the House members from the balconies and there was a great demonstration on the occasion, but their rejoicing was soon turned to sorrow for the Senate killed the proposition.

Philip J. O'Connell of Worcester, a capable lawyer and a Democrat, was appointed Judge of the Superior Court.

The Legislature passed a bill enabling the City of Boston to abolish the East Boston tunnel tolls. Inasmuch as the collection of the tolls was nominated in the bonds on which the tunnel was built, the city had to get the permission of the Legislature to enable it to appropriate an amount equal to the yearly tolls to become a part of the sinking fund to meet the bonds when they matured.

The Sectarian bill was bitterly fought this year. The

so-called "Patriotic" societies had for a long time insisted that this amendment to the Constitution was necessary to prevent private schools from getting public funds. It was aimed particularly at the Catholic Parochial schools. As in all religious contests, the feeling ran high and the fight was bitter. Leading Republican members of the Legislature fought the proposition as hard as the Democrats and it was beaten by a close vote in the House, 115 to 107.

TWO EX-GOVERNORS DIE

A FILM play, "The Birth of a Nation," shown in a Boston theatre about this time, was offensive to colored citizens. They protested to the show people in vain. They held public meetings of protest. Appealing to the Legislature and the Governor, both promptly joined in passing a law which satisfied them and prevented a repetition of such a play in this State.

The Legislature of 1915 authorized the appointment of a commission of seven persons to be known as the Pilgrim Tercentenary Commission, to devise a plan for the celebration by the Commonwealth of the 300th anniversary of the landing of the Pilgrims at Plymouth. The Governor named Ex-Governor Curtis Guild, Sherman L. Whipple, Reverend Albert E. Dunning, Ralph Adams Cram, Denis A. McCarthy, James Logan and Arthur Lord to be members of the Commission. On the death of Mr. Guild, Governor Walsh named George von L. Meyer in his place.

The State tax this year was the largest in the history of the State—$9,750,000 a $1,000,000 more than 1914.

The enactment of the bill providing for the reorganization of the Boston and Maine Railroad was a step forward and the Governor could fairly claim the credit of it as he had advocated it in his two inaugural messages. The rejection of several important taxation measures, the Governor said, was a serious omission as was the failure for the passage of a resolve for an investigation of the telephone rates by the Public Service Commission.

In April, Ex-Governor Guild died. The entire State mourned his passing. His popularity with the people had not diminished since he left public office. He had interested himself in raising funds for the Russians and the Poles in the European War and was one of the first to advocate preparedness on the part of the American people, as an insurance against war. Great respect was shown his memory by all classes and races. His body lay in state in the Hall of Flags. Thirty thousand people passed in silent review in the few hours his remains were there guarded by a detachment of the First Corps of Cadets of which he had been a popular member in his youth. Every honor the State and its officials could pay his memory was shown.

Ex-Governor Long died late this summer and Governor Walsh took appropriate notice of the event by issuing a fine tribute to him. Governor Long was one of the noblest and ablest of the Old Guard. He graced every office he ever filled. His good nature never deserted him. He was of the old school which never displays its riches or allows the public to become too familiar with their personal affairs. He was scholarly, poetic, virile, manly and upright in politics, and in his profession. A modest man, his obsequies were in keeping with this character. He was one of the most gifted sons of the State of Maine sent to the parent Commonwealth.

REPUBLICANS WIN OVER PROGRESSIVES

MR. MCCALL insisted on making the Republican platform attractive to the Progressives. To this task he gave his attention after the primaries and it required all of his tact and diplomacy to bring it about. The "Old Guard" still refused to subscribe to many of the tenets of the Bull Moose political faith. Ex-Senator Burbank, a Progressive, who had returned to the Republican party was made a member of the committee on resolutions, of which Congressman Gillett, of Springfield, a Standpatter, was chairman. The Progressives also demanded a declaration favoring an eight hour day for those employed in industries running 24 hours a day. A compromise was reached by agreeing to ask legislation for "reasonable hours" of labor for those so employed. The Old Guard was obliged to declare for a Constitutional Convention demanded by the Progressives.

Mr. McCall and his friends breathed easier after they had induced all elements to agree on the platform, but there were two recalcitrants, Ex-Governor Foss, who wanted his National Prohibition plank and Ex-Senator Seiberlich, who demanded another declaring against a loan to the European Allies to help finance the World War. Congressman Gillett, for the Committee on Resolutions, quickly reported against the resolution opposing loans to foreign countries. Mr. Gillett also reported that the committee disagreed on the resolution in behalf of National prohibition. Mr. Foss spoke for it, saying: "I am not here to make apologies for my political conduct. I am here as the representative of more than 10,000 Republicans who voted for me in this issue in the primaries. This issue of National prohibition is the compelling issue to-day and the sooner we recognize it the better. If this State is to have the greatest efficiency in its industrial establishments it must 'cut out' the liquor." The convention rejected both resolutions and stood in silence as a mark of respect to Ex-Governors Long and Guild both of whom had passed on since the last State Convention.

DEMOCRATS

THE Democrats met the same day at Faneuil Hall. Harold Williams Jr. of Brookline, defeated for the nomination for Attorney General, was the temporary chairman of the convention. Mayor Curley of Boston, was the permanent chairman. Ex-Attorney General Thomas J. Boynton, chairman of the committee on resolutions, reported the platform.

The first plank indorsed the administration of President Wilson and Governor Walsh. Other planks favored strict neutrality and the enforcement of American rights against all belligerents; "adequate preparation for National defense"; abolition of the poll tax and other sweeping reforms in the taxation system, favored a constitutional convention; favored the abolition of the executive council; reiterated the indorsement of the initiative and referendum; favored free halls for political rallies and printing by the State; free distribution of circulars setting forth the claims of political candidates; home rule; opposed the prevention of roll calls "as practiced by the Massachusetts Senate of 1915"; a thorough investigation of telephone rates; no increase in traffic rates of public service corporations unless the companies seeking the increase have been honestly capitalized and honestly and economically managed; reclamation of waste lands; encouragement and assistance for milk producers; favored savings banks life insurance; favored old age non-contributory pensions; and a reform in the administration of the Mother's Aid law; urged reforms in the prison system and favored the extension of popular education.

On motion of Professor Edwin A. Grosvenor of Amherst, the Democratic candidate for Secretary of State, who married a cousin of Ex-President Taft, the convention adopted resolutions expressing sympathy for Senator Henry Cabot Lodge in the death of his wife.

McCALL DEFEATS WALSH

McCALL and Walsh immediately began their tour of the State for votes. The Progressives flocked back to the Republican party, paying little attention to Clark, their own party candidate for Governor. The National Progressive committee looked into the situation here, saw that Charles S. Bird and others were supporting McCall and shipped Candidate Clark into the small towns in the Western part of the State where he could talk to his heart's content and do little damage to the Republican ticket.

The campaign was waged with great vigor on both sides. Senator Lodge was prevented from taking his usual active part in the debate owing to a deep domestic affliction on the very eve of the primaries. Senator Weeks contributed his organizing ability, rallying his friends to McCall's support. He talked horse sense to Republicans, reasoned with the vagabond and erring brethren of the fold and succeeded in coaxing back many of them. McCall won by a plurality of only 6000, while Coolidge exceeded by 46,000 the vote of Barry for Lieutenant Governor.

Shaw, the Prohibition candidate, received almost exactly 20,000 votes, enough to establish the Prohibitionists as a political party but much less than his supporters expected. Clark, the Progressive candidate, received 6975 votes, not enough to retain the standing of the Progressives as a political party and the Bull Moose was legally dead in Massachusetts.

The total vote of the State for Governor was more than 500,000, the largest vote ever cast, due largely to the interest in the equal suffrage amendment, which, however, was defeated by a vote of about two to one. The majority against the amendment was overwhelming almost everywhere; two or three small towns in Berkshire county were the only ones which voted in favor of it. The Suffragists were beaten by over 127,000. The entire Republican State ticket was elected. The Republicans' lead in the Legislature was increased. Governor Walsh received about 25,000 votes more than he had the year before. McCall received about 41,000 votes more than he had in 1914.

PAYS TRIBUTE TO WALSH

AFTER five years of wandering in the political desert, following false prophets, the Republicans had arrived once more on Beacon Hill and had come unto their own. After it was reasonably certain that he had been defeated, Governor Walsh did not hesitate a minute election night to congratulate his Republican opponent. Indeed, while at a banquet, where it was rumored that the election was still in question, the Governor arose, dispelled the doubt and called for three cheers for the victor. "I wish to say that I am glad that I am to have so worthy and honorable man as my successor in office next year," said the Governor to the diners. "I congratulate Massachusetts. For my own part I have no regrets. I made the best fight I could and in my heart I know that I have tried to be a faithful and conscientious Governor. I am, indeed, grateful for the magnificent vote I received. It appears that Republican Massachusetts prefers to have a Republican Governor rather than a good Democrat."

In a statement overflowing with gratitude to all who contributed to the victory, Governor-elect McCall said, "This is the greatest Republican victory since John A. Andrew. It would have been enough to contend against Governor Walsh alone, for with the exception of William E. Russell, he is the most popular Democrat who has appeared in our State politics since the Civil War."

The one discordant note was uttered by Shaw, the Dry candidate, who declared: "The organized liquor vote of Massachusetts knifed Governor Walsh to elect Samuel W. McCall, in a desperate effort to prevent the Republican party from adopting Prohibition. It was their only hope. They have apparently succeeded in electing Mr. McCall by a meagre margin, but they have failed utterly to crush Prohibition."

Governor Walsh did not share the righteous indignation of his new friend, dry Mr. Shaw.

After election the Executive Council showed a disposition not to allow Governor Walsh to have his own way on appointments. They declined to depose David T. Dickinson of the Industrial Accident Board, whose term had expired and they would not confirm the appointment of Judge O'Brien of Marblehead, as Judge of the Boston Juvenile Court, although they promptly ratified the Governor's selection of his private secretary, Thomas F. Connolly, as Judge of the Brighton District, Municipal Court.

SAMUEL WALKER McCALL
Governor 1916-1919

THE booming of cannon at noon, January 6, 1916, on Boston Common, firing a salute of 21 guns by a battery of field artillery, an ancient custom in Massachusetts, was notice to the busy passersby that a new Governor, Samuel W. McCall, the 44th under the Constitution, had taken the oath of office and another political régime had begun on Beacon Hill.

The New Governor was a man of independence with conservative Progressive leanings. He was far above the "run of the mine" politicians and could, without boasting, claim statesmanlike qualities. He was an orator, a student of public affairs, had established himself in literature by the authorship of two of his party's outstanding characters, Speaker Thomas B. Reed of Maine and Thaddeus Stevens of Pennsylvania, the latter the leader of the "Black Republicans" in Congress in the Civil War period. A lawyer by profession Mr. McCall preferred journalism and a public career.

A native of Pennsylvania, a graduate of Dartmouth

College, he settled in Massachusetts after his admission to the bar and for a number of years was chief editorial writer for the Boston Daily Advertiser a journal that clung to old fashioned Republicanism. In that period of his career, he spent his days at his law office and his nights in the editorial sanctum. Justly or unjustly, he had the reputation of being a procrastinator. A story is told of a book agent calling on him at his office to sell him a set of popular American biography. Mr. McCall was interested. "Is the set complete?" he asked the salesman. "All but one volume," said the latter. "The publishers employed a man to do the job some time ago, but he has not got around to it yet. I heard the other day that unless they receive the copy this month they will hire somebody else to write it. I think they said his name is McCall." Mr. McCall subscribed for the set of books and hastened to finish the missing volume in the series.

He served three terms in the Massachusetts House with distinction, was a delegate to the Republican national conventions in 1888 and 1892, in which year he was chosen a member of Congress, serving in that body 20 years. Sorely disappointed over his failure to be elected to the United States Senate to succeed Senator Crane, when the latter retired, he broke a long friendship with John W. Weeks, the victor of that memorable contest and failed to congratulate him on his success.

In Governor McCall's first inaugural address, he followed in the footsteps of his Democratic predecessor, Governor Walsh and urged the holding of a constitutional convention, reminding the Legislature that in the 66 years that had intervened since the last revision of the Constitution in 1853, nothing but piecemeal revision had been attempted. In his opinion, the time had come when the constitution should undergo a careful and connected revision to bring it up to date in harmony with the social and industrial changes that had taken place.

He recommended that its members be chosen without party designation and that a liberal number be selected at-large, others to be selected by political divisions of the State, such as Congressional and Senatorial districts, and, in addition, one member from each of the 240 Representative districts. He believed that such a plan would insure a notable assembly of citizens. He did not think that there was any real demand for amending the bill of rights or the articles relating to the judiciary and suggested that these sections remain undisturbed.

The cost of government, he told the members of the Great and General Court, had been increasing far out of proportion to the growth of the population. Public expenses were mounting "with frightful rapidity," he said. In 1900 the net direct debt of the State was $16,704,000; the State tax was $1,500,000 and the total expenditures of the State were $7,176,000. By 1915 the State tax had increased 600 per cent and the total expenses had almost trebeled.

In his opinion, the machinery of the State government was too complicated and expensive and much could be saved. "We have a hydra-headed system," said he, "with a minimum of responsibility." More than one hundred different commissions and departments had been set up.

EBEN S. DRAPER

Some of these creatures of the Legislature had more power than the Governor. He asked that the number of commissions be reduced and gave specific instances where he believed their creation was unjustified.

He favored extending the power of the Civil Service Commission, giving it authority to scrutinize the work done by State employees and see that their efficiency was maintained. He would also extend the Civil Service to practically all State and Court employees. With a view of strengthening the arm of the Civil Service Commission, he recommended the consolidation of the Commission of Economy and Efficiency with the Civil Service Board.

That old hardy perennial, taxation, was discussed and he recommended the imposition of a tax on the income of intangibles to relieve the burden on real estate. Elected on a platform declaring for reasonable hours of labor in industries continuously operating 24 hours, he said it was the duty of the State to conserve its citizens and he demanded that the Legislature fulfill its part of the agreement with the electorate. Stricter laws were urged to curb the greed of money lenders, especially those who made small loans to poor people, which had become a profitable "racket" with many of those engaged in that business.

The Republican party in its platform, he said, was pledged to devising a form of social insurance to protect the worker against the vicissitudes of sickness, unemployment and old age. He urged the Legislature to inaugurate such legislation and called their attention to the German system as a guide for them to follow. Better health laws were recommended. He favored the reorganization of the Board of Prison Commission and the creation of a new board of unpaid members.

The Legislative session was the shortest in 11 years. Acting on the suggestion of the Governor's inaugural, the Legislature abolished the Directors of the Port of Boston and the State Harbor and Land Commission was consolidated into a single commission under the title of the Commissioner of Waterways and Public Lands. The Commission on Economy was discontinued and a new official, Supervisor of Administration was created. The State Board of Insanity was abolished and in its place was set up the Commission on Mental Diseases. The Prison Commission was abolished and the duties given to a single commissioner, called the Bureau of Prisons.

The Governor had no difficulty in obtaining favorable consideration of a referendum on the question of holding a Constitutional Convention which the voters approved at the next State election. Two other questions also appeared on the ballot that Fall—making New Year's Day a legal holiday and whether the people desired the restoration of party enrollment at primary elections as obtained prior to last year. The Legislature voted to authorize the appointment of a Commission to study the problem of unemployment insurance. The same Commission was instructed to investigate the plan of three 8-hours shifts for "tower workers" in paper mills.

Legislation looking to improve the efficiency of the State militia was passed and the annual tour of duty was extended from one to two weeks. A regiment of Field Artillery was added to the force and the Congressional Act Federalizing the militia and creating the National Guard was accepted. To please the temperance vote, a law was passed forbidding transportation of liquor into dry territory, but the wets living in dry territory managed to smuggle in an ample supply for their needs. Twenty-five thousand dollars was appropriated for the expenses of the Pilgrim Tercentenary Commission for the celebration of the 300th anniversary of the landing of the Pilgrims at Plymouth.

The jitney bus had begun to be a problem to deal with by cities and towns where they had cut into the street railway business. The Legislature passed an act compelling owners to take out a license before they could operate. Early in the year the Governor named Frederick P. Cabot, Judge of the Boston Juvenile Court.

He vetoed a bill permitting the erection of a wooden building to provide a tabernacle for "Billy" Sunday, the famous evangelist who planned one of his characteristic invasions of sinful Boston. Mr. McCall said it would be a flouting of the fire laws of the city and Mr. Sunday was obliged to conduct his services in the Boston Arena.

Police Commissioner Stephen O'Meara of Boston was reappointed. Fletcher Ranney was made chairman of the Boston Licensing Board and Colonel Charles R. Gow, an appointee of Governor Walsh was forced out, charging that Ranney's appointment was the result of a political deal with the liquor dealers by the Governor's campaign manager. Adjutant General Charles H. Cole who had worked hard and successfully to prepare the State militia for active war service resigned and Governor McCall appointed former Adjutant General Gardner W. Pearson to succeed him.

The Legislature of 1916 had occasion to discipline two of its members—Representative Harry C. Foster of Gloucester and Simon Swig of Boston. Foster was accused of soliciting money on pending legislation. He was adjudged guilty and expelled. Swig was charged with a violation of the corrupt practices act but the House dealt leniently with him. The influence of most of the Republican leaders was thrown to Swig and he retained his seat.

Adjournment took place June 2, after 150 days of life. Speaker Channing H. Cox and President Henry G. Wells of the Senate coöperated with Governor McCall in securing much of the new Legislation suggested in his inaugural address.

An extra session of the Legislature was called for September 12 by Governor McCall for the purpose of passing legislation to enable the 7000 Massachusetts troops on the Mexican border in the service of the Federal Government to vote for National officers in the November election and to provide financial aid for their dependents. Another matter which Governor McCall deemed it necessary for the Legislature to deal with was the reapportionment of the Suffolk County (Boston) representative districts. The Supreme Judical Court had declared that the commission which had done this work had disregarded the spirit of political equality in drawing the new lines and set its work aside. Unless the work was done over again to meet the rulings of the court the largest county in the Commonwealth might be unable to choose representatives to the Legislature in the ensuing November election. The Governor said that he was advised that the Legislature had no power to revise or set aside the report of the commission which derived its power directly from the constitution. He recommended the provision be made for the nomination of candidates for the House in the county and that special primaries be provided for. These emergency measures were dealt with along the lines suggested.

NATIONAL CAMPAIGN—1916

BY 1916, many of the rebellious Republicans who had joined the Bull Moose party in 1912, were following their leader, Colonel Roosevelt back into the Republican fold, but some of them hesitated. Early in the year the Progressive party National Committee called a convention to be held in Chicago the same day in June as the Republicans fixed for their nominating convention to meet. When the Republicans met the olive branch was suspended from the entrance of the Coliseum, their convention hall. The Progressives held forth in the Auditorium. Messages of peace were exchanged by the leaders of both camps. Some of the latter nursed the hope that Roosevelt would receive the regular nomination, but T. R. himself had no such illusion and counselled his followers to mark time and await the outcome of the Old Guard convention before making a Presidential nomination. There was every indication that he was determined to make his peace with the Old Guard.

The latter were as anxious to have the Bull Moose back under the flap of the elephant's tent as the former were to find an excuse to return. Roosevelt was anxious to unite the party to beat the Democrats and eagerly accepted the invitation of the Old Guard for the appointment of a committee of Bull Moosers to confer with them, with a view of agreeing on a candidate. From his home at Oyster Bay, Mr. Roosevelt issued a statement addressed to the Republican conference committee suggesting Senator Lodge as a presidential candidate on whom both factions could unite, but he was too late. The Old Guard was committed to Judge Charles Evans Hughes. Besides, Mr. Lodge was charged with the duty of presenting the name of his Senatorial colleague John W. Weeks for the nomination and was no little embarrassed by the action of Colonel Roosevelt.

The strategy of the Old Guard was to prevent the convention from stampeding to Roosevelt. They talked Elihu Root and Hughes for the nomination, but they preferred the latter. They were resolved that Roosevelt must not have it and felt confident that they had the votes to stop him. Several States had their favorite sons, including Massachusetts which urged Senator Weeks. Senator Lodge presented his name to the convention in what seemed to be a perfunctory speech and Weeks' friends resented Senator Lodge's half-heartedness. To add to their chagrin when Weeks was placed in nomination, the Massachusetts delegation sat in their seats unmoved and inarticulate.

Judge Hughes in Washington on the bench of the highest court in the land was silent, but his ear was to the ground. Beneath the ermine there still beat the heart of the politician. He kept close watch on the happenings in Chicago. He would not lift his finger to get the nomination. It must come to him without any effort on his part. To add to the confusion, nobody in the convention city claimed authority to speak for him, but his silence was taken to mean that he was in a receptive mood.

Here in Massachusetts, the Rooseveltians put a ticket in the field in the Spring primaries for delegates-at-large, made up of Charles Sumner Bird, Grafton D. Cushing, Augustus P. Gardner and Robert M. Washburn, who contested against the Old Guard ticket of McCall, Senators Lodge and Crane and Congressman John W. Weeks. The latter group won easily. McCall topped the list with a vote of 62,470 against Cushing, high man on the Roosevelt ticket, who received 45,925 votes. Unpledged (Old Guard) delegates were also elected in all the Congressional districts except in the ninth and fourteenth.

When the delegation reached Chicago, they found the sentiment overwhelmingly for Hughes. Former Postmaster General George L. von Meyer of Boston buttonholed delegates for Roosevelt, but with little success. The permanent chairman of the Republican convention was

Senator Warren G. Harding of Ohio, who little thought that four years hence he, himself, would be the Presidential nominee and successfully lead the party back into power in the Nation.

The Progressives were milling about at their convention hall waiting for instructions from Roosevelt. Within their ranks were a number of leaders who fought at Armageddon with T. R. four years before and were opposed to any compromise with the Old Guard. They were keenly disappointed at the attitude of Roosevelt. They threatened to carry on without him. James R. Garfield, one of T. R.'s lieutenants, made a motion in the Progressive gathering that a committee be named to meet with a like committee of the Republican convention for the purpose of agreeing on a candidate for President. This move was opposed by the presiding officer, Raymond Robbins and Victor Murdock, Governor Hiram Johnson of California, and Professor Albert Bushnell Hart of Massachusetts. Robbins was for going ahead and nominating Roosevelt, but the convention adopted the motion and named a committee headed by George W. Perkins, a rich New York banker, former partner of the Morgan banking house, and one of the financial angels of the Bull Moose party who had been negotiating with the Republican committee, with the full knowledge and authority of Colonel Roosevelt.

In the midst of their turmoil, the Progressive convention wired an invitation to Roosevelt to come to Chicago and address the delegates, but the Colonel preferred to deal with the delicate situation from the end of a telegraph or telephone wire at Oyster Bay. He sent word that his attitude was set forth in his telegram to the Republican conference committee in which he had suggested the nomination of Senator Lodge. Senator Borah, who declined to follow Roosevelt out of the party in 1912, although in sympathy with the Colonel's opposition to the party management at that time, appeared and appealed to the Progressives to work with the Old Guard, accept Hughes and "march and fight together," but the convention refused and proceeded to nominate Roosevelt for President and Ex-Governor John M. Parker of Louisiana, two hours after the Republicans had nominated Hughes by a vote of $94\frac{1}{2}$ to $18\frac{1}{2}$ for Roosevelt. In the balloting in the Republican convention, Massachusetts cast 32 votes for Hughes, three for Roosevelt and one for John W. Weeks.

Roosevelt promptly declined the Progressive nomination. His refusal to run on the Progressive ticket sounded the death knell of that party, although Parker stuck to the sinking ship and went down with flying colors in the November election. Not all of the Bull Moosers went back into the G.O.P. with Roosevelt. Several of them went over to the Wilson camp where they were welcomed with open arms. Some were rewarded with high office by Mr. Wilson, notably Bainbridge Colby of New York who became Secretary of State after the dismissal of Robert Lansing from that post.

As soon as the news of his nomination reached him in Washington, Mr. Hughes resigned his judgeship in a curt note to President Roosevelt and wired his acceptance to the delegates, saying that he had not desired the nomination, but accepted it "in this critical period in our National history." He added that he stood for "the rights of American citizens on land and sea"—a jab at the Wilson administration for its neutral attitude aggravated by the sinking of the Cunarder Lusitania, by a German U boat, when the lives of several American citizens were lost. Mr. Hughes plunged into the campaign with his customary energy and enthusiasm.

DEMOCRATS

THE Democrats held their National convention in St. Louis, sending as delegates-at-large from this State, David I. Walsh, Joseph H. O'Niel, Humphrey O'Sullivan and Charles B. Strecker, pledged to the renomination of President Wilson. What was believed would be a dull gathering turned out to be a history making convention. One of the interesting side shows was the colorful parade of thousands of suffragettes in white and gold costume, carrying banners, demanding equal suffrage and a plank in the platform favoring the same. Mr. Wilson was committed to woman suffrage and the convention gratified the wish of the women and the President.

It was a Wilson bossed convention from the start to finish and contained a liberal sprinkling of Federal office holders to see that the administration's plan did not go astray. The keynoter, Governor Martin T. Glynn of New York, started the enthusiasm with his eloquent defense of the administration's foreign policy. "He kept us out of war" became their campaign shibboleth, although President Wilson never used the expression himself and believed that sooner or later the United States would have to join the Allies to "make the world safe for democracy" and "preserve civilization."

His opponents criticised him for not taking sides in the European struggle. He was accused by German sympathizers as pro-British. Mr. Wilson demanded a definite and unequivocal plank in the Democratic platform repudiating the hyphenated American, aimed at pro-Germans and anti-British factions, and got it. Irish-Americans and German-Americans were active in anti-British propaganda. The former demanded that the United States help Ireland in its struggle for freedom, but Mr. Wilson, though professing friendship for Ireland, took the ground that it was no time to throw obstacles in the path of the British when they were fighting for their lives.

When the platform was reached in the convention, Martin M. Lomasney, well known Boston Democratic politician, jumped to his feet with a plank for Irish freedom. As soon as the convention discovered his purpose, it tried to howl him down, but Lomasney was quite used to that sort of thing in politics and stood his ground. Senator James of Kentucky, the permanent chairman of the convention, announced that under the rules, the document would be referred to the committee on resolutions, but the committee on rules never met again and Ireland's champions were left to nurse their wrath.

President Wilson did his campaigning from the porch of his summer home, Shadow Lawn, on the New Jersey coast. Mr. Hughes mounted the stump and campaigned from Maine to the Golden Gate. Maine, in September, was the first State to vote and the Republicans sent there some of their biggest guns. Of course the State went Republican by a safe margin, but not as large as the Republican leaders had hoped.

WILSON REËLECTED

THE Democrats professed to be satisfied with the returns from the Pine Tree State and turned their attention to the Western front. The platform of the two parties did not differ greatly on the leading issues, but the Republicans were for immediate and a more vigorous enforcement of the neutrality laws and favored a more energetic foreign policy for the protection of American lives and American interests abroad and on the high seas.

Election night, most of the metropolitan newspapers conceded the election of Hughes—with one notable exception, the Boston Globe, which announced that the election was in doubt and that it depended on the final count in several Western States. Mr. Hughes went to bed confident that he had won and his supporters in this State paraded the streets of Boston at midnight celebrating a Republican victory. Overnight, Ohio, the Dakotas, and the other normally Western Republican States had gone Democratic and the Democrats claimed Wilson's re-election. Even rock-ribbed Republican New Hampshire went for Wilson by the slender margin of 56 votes. Massachusetts slumped to 20,000. Twenty-four hours later the same papers that had announced the election of Hughes were obliged to revise their election night claims. The result finally hinged on California. And thereby hangs an interesting tale.

During the campaign, when Hr. Hughes was touring that State, he purposely avoided meeting Governor Hiram Johnson, a Roosevelt irreconcilable, running for United States Senator. On one occasion, they were guests at the same hotel, but never met. Johnson's friends resented Mr. Hughes' discourtesy. Hughes lost the State, but Johnson was elected. They never made up. Mr. Hoover inherited the rift and in 1932 Johnson campaigned for Franklin D. Roosevelt for President. It was not until after the retabulation of the California vote, November 22, that Mr. Hughes acknowledged his defeat and sent his congratulations to President Wilson.

In the electoral count Wilson had 276 and Hughes 255 votes, the closest Presidential contest since the famous Hayes-Tilden disputed election. Mr. Wilson lost Congress, the House count being Republicans, 217; Democrats, 212, with six Independents, which meant opposition at the start of his second term.

McCALL REËLECTED

GOVERNOR MCCALL had no opposition for a renomination. The State Convention, held in Boston and presided over by Frederick H. Gillett, Speaker of the National House of Representatives, was a harmonious affair. The applause that greeted Senator Lodge as he stepped on the platform of Tremont Temple, was loud and prolonged—evidence that the senior Senator's popularity had not suffered during the recent political upheaval. Even Theodore Roosevelt was forgiven for his betrayal of the party in 1912 and the mention of his name was vociferously applauded.

Chairman Thurston of the State Committee called the convention to order and made an appeal for the reënactment of the party enrollment law. "We have lost party enrollment and thereby destroyed party integrity and the destruction of party integrity means increased growth of racial enmity and religious exploitation," said he. "Without party enrollment men can go without hindrance or detection to one side or the other at the primaries and nominate the men they think best to elect or defeat. Then they can go back to their own party on election day."

The platform was presented by Congressman John J. Rogers of Lowell, chairman of the committee on resolutions, which was a glorification of the party and a sop to the temperance vote. Senator Robert M. Washburn of Worcester moved the adoption of a resolution recommending the principle of woman suffrage. He alluded to the "trophy room" of the suffragists in this State and said they had a fine collection of political scalps coming from Milton in the east to Gardner in the West, a humorous reference to the defeat of Roger Wolcott and Levi Greenwood, who were candidates for the Massachusetts Senate in 1912. Congressman Walsh of New Bedford argued in support of the resolution as reported by the committee. He said the vote at the election of last year showed that the people of Massachusetts were not in favor of woman suffrage and the amendment was rejected by a large majority. An attempt to instruct the members of Congress from Massachusetts to favor the submission of a prohibitory amendment to the Federal constitution was voted down, under the leadership of Congressman Rogers of Lowell.

There were speeches by Governor McCall and Senator Lodge. The latter severely criticised President Wilson's foreign policy and his "autocratic rule" of the Democratic party.

Alvan T. Fuller, a prominent figure in the Bull Moose party withdrew from the Progressive ranks and announced that he would support Hughes for President and McCall for Governor. Mr. Fuller, noted for his outspoken independence said that the Progressive party no longer stood for its original ideals. Fuller was welcomed back to the Republican fold and immediately launched his candidacy for Congress as an Independent against Representative Ernest W. Roberts, defeating him at the polls at the November election. The Republicans elected 11 of the 16 Congressmen, the new members being Michael F. Phelan of Lynn and Richard Olney of Dedham, Democrats, and Alvan T. Fuller of Malden. Governor McCall was reelected by a plurality of 46,000 over his Democratic opponent, Frederick W. Mansfield. The Legislature in both branches retained their heavy Republican majorities.

Senator Lodge's Democratic opponent, John F. Fitzgerald was not regarded seriously by the Senator who ignored his candidacy and devoted his time and energy to campaigning for the National and State tickets. Mr. Lodge was reëlected by a plurality rising 32,000.

DEMOCRATS

THERE was a spirited contest for the Democratic gubernatorial nomination this year between Frederick W. Mansfield and General Charles H. Cole. The former won easily. The latter lost no time in congratulating the winner and he was the presiding officer of the State convention held at Springfield, October 7. He denied the Republican charge that President Wilson had lagged behind in preparing the country for war.

"The international rights of neutral Nations, Switzerland, Holland, Norway, Sweden as well as the United States, have been violated by both belligerents in this great European war, but not one of them have yet gone to war. The President's international policy is in keeping with that of the neutral Nations of the world," said he. "He stands today as Abraham Lincoln stood 62 years ago, calm, courageous and confident that the people will read his motives aright. Shall we change his diplomatic policy, which has kept us out of war, reserved our rights and upheld our National honor for a policy that would plunge us into war at the least theoretical violation of our rights as a neutral."

John F. Fitzgerald, the party candidate for Senator, addressed the convention and assailed Senator Lodge's public record. While Mr. Lodge was elected, the disparity between his plurality 32,000 and that of Governor McCall's, 90,000, furnished the senior Senator's friends food for thought. Had his opponent been a different type, who would have appealed to the business men of the State, the result might have been different. It was the first time that Senator Lodge was elected under the direct election law. His former elections as Senator had been at the hands of Republican legislatures.

PROGRESSIVES

ALTHOUGH most of the Progressives had returned to the Republican party and their leader, Charles Sumner Bird, no longer graced their council board and had ceased to finance the organization, there were a few of the leaders who refused to admit that the party was dead. These, headed by Matthew Hale and Professor Albert Bushnell Hart called a State Convention, in May in Boston and chose four delegates-at-large and two delegates from each of the 16 congressional districts of the State to the National Convention at Chicago, the result of which has already been told. Hale stood out against compromise to the end and the Democrats gave him their nomination for Lieutenant Governor that Fall.

McCALL'S SECOND AND THIRD TERMS

IN his second inaugural address, Governor McCall dwelt at length on the benefits and desirability of health insurance and asked that the Legislature give the subject serious consideration. "I am strongly of the opinion that there is no form of social insurance that is more humane, sounder in principle and that would confer a greater benefit upon large groups of our population and upon the Commonwealth as a whole than health insurance," he told the members of the Legislature. He recommended the establishment of a compulsory system with considerable benefit during the period of sickness and that the system be made to include members of the family as is done in many of the German funds. He also urged the extension of the old age pension system. He recorded his objection to Federal control of highways as allotted by Congress and advocated a $1,000,000 appropriation annually for five years for state highway construction.

Another one of his hobbies that he touched upon was the abolition of capital punishment, but all of these subjects were turned down by the lawmakers as was his plan to build a replica of John Hancock's house on the State House grounds to be used as a residence for the Governor. The Legislature granted his request for an appropriation of $25,000 for the 300th anniversary of the landing of the Pilgrims at Plymouth.

During the year Foster W. Stearns was appointed State Librarian and Webster Thayer was named a judge of the Superior Court. He was in the years to come to figure in the celebrated Sacco-Vanzetti murder case over which he presided. The defendents were charged with the murder of a Braintree paymaster. The trial took place when the country was stirred up over the activities of the Reds following the World War. Found guilty after a long and sensational trial and condemned to death, their friends claimed that they had not had a fair trial and that Judge Thayer showed bias. Appeal after appeal followed their convictions. There was an organized movement to free them and funds were raised for the employment of eminent counsel on their behalf. During the long waits between appeals their defenders held public meetings throughout the country. In Europe and South America demonstrations were made before American Embassies and Consulates by Reds demanding the release of their comrades, but Sacco and Vanzetti were executed after every legal question affecting their cases had been passed upon by State and Federal Courts. For years after their execution, Judge Thayer was subjected to attacks, by Sacco and Vanzetti sympathizers, culminating in the bombing of his home in Worcester, all of which so unnerved him that he was unable to sit on the bench. The State reimbursed him for the damage to his home and he died before the baffled police had discovered even a clue to the scoundrels who bombed his house and tried to kill him.

The Legislature paused long enough to pay a fitting tribute to Frank D. Sanborn, "the Sage of Concord," a man who had devoted his great talents and pen to many reforms and was the last link that bound this generation to that of Emerson and Thoreau, Wendell Phillips, Theodore Parker and John A. Andrew. He was the last of the men of the old Concord school of philosophy and politics.

The House passed a resolve backing President Wilson's efforts to protect the lives of Americans caught in the vortex of the World War. The Legislature granted the Governor's request for a $1,000,000 for the "defense of the Commonwealth," made in a special message. General Butler Ames was appointed commander of the State Guard organized to take the place of the National Guard called to the colors for the European War.

Sheriff John Quinn of Suffolk County died and Governor McCall appointed Ex-Congressman John A. Keliher to fill the vacancy. The 50-hour bill affecting women and minors in industry was defeated. In December, the City of Halifax, Nova Scotia suffered from a disastrous fire rendering many people homeless. Governor McCall promptly issued an appeal for relief and the State dispatched doctors, nurses, medical supplies, food and clothing to the stricken city. Boston opened its generous purse

EX-CONGRESSMAN
CARTER

SLATER WASHBURN

LEOPOLD M. GOULSTON

HENRY L. SHATTUCK

CONGRESSMAN TINKHAM

JAMES ROOSEVELT

and the people sent a handsome contribution to the relief fund.

The trend at the State election was still toward the Republicans, who renominated McCall and Coolidge for Governor and Lieutenant Governor respectively. The Democrats nominated Frederick W. Mansfield again. The vote for Governor was McCall, 226,145; Mansfield, 135,666; McCarty, Socialist, 16,608; Lawrence, Progressive, 4263; Hayes, Socialist-Labor, 5343. The Legislature elected was heavily Republican. Governor McCall's handling of the war problems increased his popularity with the public. People were more interested in the great European war than local politics.

McCALL'S THIRD TERM

GOVERNOR McCALL began his third and last term at a time when the World War cast its shadow over the land. The National Guard of the State had been absorbed by the Yankee Division, commanded by that gallant soldier, Major General Clarence R. Edwards, and was in the trenches of France. The part Massachusetts played in prosecuting that war at home and abroad is outlined in another chapter. In his inaugural address Governor McCall reminded the Legislature that first of all, the credit of the State must be safeguarded and every dollar possible saved for meeting the demand of war. There were then 80,000 young men mustered into the different branches of the military and naval forces of the Nation and the number was daily increasing. More than 350,000 subject to military duty were enrolled and every quota called for by the National government was promptly furnished. War created many additional civil burdens and on the 10th of February, 1917, the Governor appointed a Committee of Public Safety, the first body of its kind in the country, under the leadership of James J. Storrow, Henry B. Endicott and James J. Phelan, well known business men, prominent in all civic and philanthropic movements in Boston. That body rendered a great public service in adjusting industrial disputes, supplying help to take the places of those who went forth to war.

The last Legislature authorized the Governor to organize a State Guard to protect the peace of the Commonwealth in the event of the National Guard being out of the State. The wisdom of their legislation had become apparent. Every member of the National Guard with the exception of five officers had been called into the service of the Nation. The State Guard were given the status of the militia until such time as the National Guard were returned to the service of the State. In command of this organization he placed General Butler Ames of Lowell, grandson of General Benjamin F. Butler, who was denied a command in the National Army in keeping with his military record. It was the boast of his grandfather, General Butler, that his family had drawn their swords in every war from the French and Indian War in Colonial days and he expressed the hope that his grandson, Butler Ames, at that time a cadet at West Point, would do his share in the next war. In this General Butler had his wish. Young Ames gave a good account of himself in the Spanish-American War. His father, General Adelbert Ames, a distinguished soldier in the Civil War, served as a volunteer Brigadier General in the same war, but the military authorities in Washington could find no place in the World War for Butler Ames. He felt the slight keenly, but soldier like, accepted the command of the Home Guard.

The Governor recommended an investigation by the Legislature of the Workmen's Compensation Law with a view of remedying its defects and throwing further safeguards around workers to lessen the growing increase of injuries of those employed in industry. He again reverted to the subject to health insurance, repeating to considerable length his argument of the year before. The last legislature took the ground that the advent of the European War made it inadvisable to act and the Governor agreed with them. He again stressed the need of a state budget, and the importance of efficient transportation system in the state.

Even in the midst of war he said education must not be neglected. The physical examination of men under the Conscription Act had shown the need of physical training in the schools and he expressed the hope that the legislature would take action to improve the physical training for young people.

In accordance with the Republican custom, having had three terms, Governor McCall announced his intention to retire at the end of his present term. The smooth running party escalator carried Lieutenant Governor Calvin Coolidge to the gubernatorial landing and Speaker Channing Cox into the chair vacated by Mr. Coolidge. In the campaign of 1918, the Republicans were satisfied to go to the people on the record of Governor McCall.

DEMOCRATS

THE Democratic party was at a low ebb and as usual with a political party in distress it was willing to take on almost anybody for Governor who would pay the freight. Mansfield had no desire to sacrifice himself again and the nomination went to Richard H. Long, wealthy shoe and shoe machinery manufacturer of Framingham, who nourished a grievance against the United Shoe Machinery Company over disputed patents or infringements of shoe making machinery. The quarrel had been dragged before the Legislature in several sessions for the purpose of passing legislation to aid Long. He was currently reported to have financed the successful senatorial candidacy of James H. Vahey in a strong Republican district and he backed him for Governor.

The Shoe Machinery Company had influential friends in the Republican party and was able to prevent legislation sought by Long. The latter was reported to have made a fortune on war material contracts. Up to the time of his nomination for Governor nobody ever heard of him taking any interest in the Democratic party, but he was willing to finance the campaign and the leaders delivered the nomination to him on a platform supporting equal suffrage, Czecho-Slovak National aspirations, abolition of the Fish Trust, a New Fish Pier and competitive markets; government control of refrigerator cars and warehouses for State food distribution, reform of State transportation facilities, public ownership and control of utilities, initiative and referendum, basic eight-hour day, old age pensions, development of waterways and against biennial elections, the lobby and party enrollment.

Mr. Long's running mate for Lieutenant Governor was Joseph H. O'Niel of Boston an old time party man and a banker. Coolidge won only by a plurality of 17,000, a shock to the Republicans, the vote being: Coolidge 214,-863; Long, 197,828. Another surprise was the Cox vote which totaled almost 6000 more than Coolidge.

The Republicans elected 12 of the 16 congressmen. Ex-Congressman and Ex-Mayor John F. Fitzgerald was elected in the 10th district over Peter F. Tague in a close vote 7241 to 7003. Tague, who ran on stickers made a remarkable showing, contested the election and after a bitter, personal struggle was awarded the seat.

CONSTITUTIONAL CONVENTION

THE Legislature of 1916 voted for a State Constitutional Convention at the behest of Governor McCall and the people approved the action at the ensuing State election in November by a vote of 217,293 to 120,979. Only 41 per cent of those who went to the polls were interested enough in the calling of a convention. On the same day that the electorate passed on the question of a Constitutional Convention, the total vote cast for President of the United States was 531,823 and the combined vote for Governor was 526,421. On the same day the Constitutional amendment making New Year's Day a legal holiday in Massachusetts was carried and 425,820 voters recorded themselves on that question.

The agitation for a Constitutional Convention was before the people for some time. The Democrats favored it and had made it a part of their political platform in several campaigns. They were particularly anxious to make the initiative and referendum a part of the Constitution of the State. Republican Legislatures opposed the calling of a convention claiming that the old method of amending the Constitution afforded a safe and sane method of altering that document. To the initiative and referendum they were cold. Their party leaders were opposed to the introduction of direct legislation. In their opinion, it would be another entering wedge to weaken the representative system, but there was a growing sentiment among the younger Republicans for both ideas and the so-called progressive element of the party openly favored a convention and the initiative and referendum law.

In both of his inaugural addresses, Governor Walsh pleaded for a convention, but each time a Republican Legislature refused his request. It was not until 1915 that the Republican leaders consented to support the calling of a convention and reluctantly included a plank in their platform favoring a convention. This sudden about-face of the Republicans was due to the insistence of the gubernatorial candidate, Samuel W. McCall, who was reaching out for the support of the Progressive wing of the party, whose leader was Charles Sumner Bird. Mr. Bird was already headed back to the G.O.P. fold, but made it a condition precedent of his support of the Republican State ticket that the party go on record favoring a Constitutional convention.

The legislative act authorizing the convention followed the plan outlined by Governors Walsh and McCall. It called for the election of 320 delegates without party designation—16 to be chosen at-large, four at-large from each of the 16 Congressional districts and one each from the 240 representative districts. The primaries were held April 5, 1917 and the election May 17.

A number of well known citizens were chosen, but a majority of the delegates elected were of the small fry, political perennials variety, most of whom were after the $500 compensation. Its critics asserted that the membership of the convention was inferior to the average Legislature, but that is hardly fair. Among those elected were Brooks Adams of Quincy and Charles Francis Adams of Concord, of the famous Adams family whose ancestor, John Adams, had presided over the first Constitutional Convention in 1780. Bishop Frederick L. Anderson of Newton, relentless opponent of grants to Catholic institutions, George L. Barnes of Weymouth, Ex-

Governor John L. Bates, Sanford Bates of Boston, Charles S. Bird, Jr., Walpole, Thomas J. Boynton, Everett, Allen G. Buttrick, Lancaster, Timothy F. Callahan, Boston, Charles F. Choate, Jr., Southboro, Daniel H. Coakley, Boston, Louis A. Coolidge, Milton, John W. Cummings, Fall River; James A. Donovan, Lawrence; William Flaherty, Boston; Asa P. French, Randolph; Matthew Hale, Boston; Professor Albert Bushnell Hart, Cambridge; William S. Kinney, Boston; Daniel W. Lane, Boston; Augustus P. Loring, Peabody; John W. McCormack, Boston; Joseph F. O'Connell, Boston; Herbert Parker, Lancaster; Henry Parkman, Boston; Albert E. Pillsbury, Wellesley; Samuel L. Powers, Newton; Josiah Quincy, Boston; Joseph L. Sweet, Attleboro; Charles L. Underhill, Somerville; Joseph Walker, Brookline; Sherman L. Whipple, Brookline; George F. Willett, Norwood; Fred H. Williams, Brookline and William S. Youngman, Boston.

Among those who failed of election were President A. Lawrence Lowell of Harvard University, Moorfield Story, a leader of the bar of the State, President Harry A. Garfield of Williams College, Nathan Matthews, former Mayor of Boston, Professor Lewis J. Johnson of Harvard, foremost advocate of the I & R, Samuel J. Elder, eminent lawyer, Ex-Governor Foss, Robert M. Washburn of Worcester, a seasoned legislator, Ex-District Attorney Arthur D. Hill of Suffolk County, William H. Brooks of Holyoke, leader of the Western Massachusetts bar, Frederick P. Fish, prominent in legal and educational circles, and Chairman of the State Board of Education,

George Fred Williams and John W. Haigis, Greenfield, an experienced legislator.

It was a pity that such men were denied seats in the convention. Their recognized talents, knowledge of public affairs and the science of government would have been valuable to any gathering of public men. While the membership of the convention was chosen on a non-partizan basis the fact remained that the political affiliations of the majority of the delegates were Republicans. Necessarily, Republicans dominated the committees and the machinery of the convention from its presiding officer to the Sergeant-at-Arms. Former Governor John L. Bates was elected President of the body over Sherman L. Whipple, a Democrat, the vote being Bates, 176; Whipple, 132. The voting was by each member announcing his choice. On motion of Mr. Whipple, Mr. Bates' election was made unanimous. James W. Kimball, Clerk of the House of Representatives was elected secretary and served to the satisfaction of all.

It was early apparent that while many questions would be submitted for consideration, the two around which the most interest was manifested was the anti-sectarian and the initiative and referendum amendments. The friends and opponents of each of these subjects had organized prior to the convening of the convention. The former question proved to be the most difficult to deal with. For years the subject had aroused religious feeling in the Legislature. Every time the friends of Carney Hospital, a worthy Catholic institution, whose charity was extended to all regardless of race, color or religion, tried to secure financial aid from the State, it was denied except once, when it was given a paltry $10,000 grant. Protestant clerics and laymen feared that the growing influence of Catholics in public affairs and that the time would come when Catholic institutions, charitable and educational, would receive financial assistance from the State. Many non-Catholic institutions had received public monies from the State treasury. Only recently the State had granted $100,000 to the Massachusetts Institute of Technology and $50,000 was given the Worcester Polytechnic Institute.

Martin M. Lomasney filed the first resolve on the subject, prohibiting the use of public funds, raised by taxation, "for the purpose of founding, maintaining or aiding by appropriations . . . any church, religious denomination or religious society, or any college, educational or other institution, school, infirmary, hospital or undertaking which is not a public institution established by law." Frederick L. Anderson offered a constitutional amendment along similar lines adding the words "which in whole or in part under sectarian or ecclesiastical control." Anderson was the recognized spokesman for the evangelical churches.

The chairman of the Convention committee dealing with this subject, Ex-Mayor Edwin U. Curtis of Boston, submitted the form of an amendment reading: "No grant or appropriation of public money, property or credit shall be made or authorized for the purpose of founding, maintaining or aiding any school, college or other educational institution, any church or religious denomination or religious society or infirmary, hospital or undertaking which is not a public institution or undertaking under the order and superintendence of public officers and agents authorized by the Legislature, except that appropriation may be made for the maintenance and support of the Soldiers Home of Massachusetts."

John W. Cummings, one of the leading lawyers of the State and prominent Catholic layman, declared that the subject would be best dealt with by leaving it alone, but the Convention, after a protracted struggle, by a vote of 275 to 25 adopted a revised amendment, which satisfied all elements in the Convention. A series of meetings were held in different sections of the State by Catholics opposed to the proposed new law. Cardinal O'Connell vigorously attacked the measure as "an insult to Catholics," notwithstanding that of the 94 delegates of his religious faith only nine had voted against its adoption. As usual, when religious prejudices are aroused many harsh things were said by both sides. The proponents and opponents of the anti-aid amendment as it became to be known marshalled their forces. The Cardinal's followers differed among themselves. Some declared that they had been assured by Henry V. Cunningham, who represented himself as the Cardinal's spokesman, that the amendment agreed upon was satisfactory to His Eminence. The Cardinal himself took the stump and urged the defeat of the amendment.

The "Minute Men" and other "patriotic" organizations were strong for the amendment, with ample funds to further their side. At the election, November 6, 1917, the amendment was ratified by the people by a vote of

206,329, yes; 130,357, no, and the vexed question was removed from further political discussion.

INITIATIVE AND REFERENDUM

THE convention then tackled the initiative and referendum. The floor leader for the amendment was Ex-Speaker Joseph Walker. He had the able assistance of Ex-Governor Walsh and Sherman L. Whipple. At times the protracted debate on the subject aroused almost as much feeling as the troublesome anti-aid amendment. On one occasion the presiding officer was obliged to call for the services of the Sergeant-at-Arms to restore order. The Conservative element in the convention fought the measure at every step. Most of the ablest lawyers of the body were opposed to grafting the scheme on to the Constitution, arguing that it was subversive of representative government and had no place in the Massachusetts scheme of government, but by a vote of 163 to 125 it was adopted. Like the anti-aid measure its friends and supporters organized public opinion between its passage in the convention and the ensuing election, when it was submitted for the consideration of the voters. At the polls it was accepted by a vote of 170,646 to 162,103. The total vote for candidates at the State election was 429,447. 96,698 voters who balloted for State officers the same day refrained from voting on the I and R amendment.

The opponents of the I and R reported to the Secretary of State that they had spent $88,416.00 to defeat this measure. Rich and powerful corporations and wealthy people or their representatives contributed to the campaign to beat the I & R. The proponents of the law reported an expenditure of $3000. Labor hailed it as a great victory. As a rule the Democrats were for it and were joined by the so-called "progressive" Republicans.

Among other important changes made in the Constitution which received the approval of the voters were: providing for absentee voting; reduction of State commissions to twenty. In this matter, Ex-Governor Walsh, took a hand and ably argued for the reduction of these bodies; biennial election of State officers. Cities and towns were authorized to engage in the sale and distribution of the necessities of life in time of war, public efficiency, emergency or distress. A majority vote of the joint session of the Legislature instead of two thirds vote was substituted in submitting future proposed amendments to the Constitution. A State budget system was created.

The Convention rejected many proposed changes in the document among them the popular election of judges, now appointed by the Governor, jury verdicts in the trial of cases by less than a unanimous vote; social insurance, abolition of capital punishment.

On June 12, 1918, after the 45th, 46th and 47th amendments had been ratified by the people at the November election in 1917, the Convention reassembled and resumed its work at which session, lasting until August 21, 1918, more articles were approved and ordered submitted to the voters at the next election. These amendments embracing the 48th to and including the 66th were ratified at the polls, November 5th. On August 12, 1919, the Convention met again, pursuant to the vote of the Convention at its last session and adopted the new arrangement of the Constitution and authorized a sub-committee to correct clerical and typographical errors and prepare the text of the rearrangement of the Constitution to be submitted to the people and then adjourned sure die. The people ratified the rearrangement at the State election, November 4, 1919.

Some of the legalistic minds in the convention raised the question whether the rearrangement of the Constitution was the Constitution of the State, basing their doubt on the changing of the title of Treasurer and Receiver General to Treasurer and professing to fear that in some way it would affect the validity of the bonds of the Commonwealth. In an advisory opinion the Supreme Judicial Court held that the rearranged Constitution was not the Constitution. Later, when the issue was argued, the Court decided, Justices De Courcey and Crosby holding that the rearrangement was the Constitution while Chief Justice Rugg speaking for the majority held that it was not and that the original constitution of 1780 with its amendments was still in force and binding and the law of the State.

This tempest in the legal teapot did not disturb the people, supreme in such matters. They had formally adopted the changes proposed by the convention. The form of the rearrangement was missing in the Manual

GOV. FRANK G. ALLEN

of the General Court but the substance was retained in the changes made by this convention.

The cost of the Convention as reported by State officials was $594,284.46, but Raymond L. Bridgeman in his book "The Massachusetts Constitutional Convention of 1917" says that if the expenses of those interested in the work of the convention and the expenditures of those favoring and opposing the amendments are considered, the cost would amount to $2,000,000." Those who wish to read a more detailed story of the Convention will find it in Mr. Bridgeman's excellent book on the subject. He was not deeply impressed with the caliber of the convention and regrets that the Constitution was made a football by politicians with axes to grind.

WALSH DEFEATS SENATOR WEEKS

AFTER his defeat for Governor in 1915 David I. Walsh kept his eye on the politicians and his finger on the public pulse. In 1916 he was quite willing that John F. Fitzgerald should run for Senator against Lodge, convinced that the senior Senator was unbeatable. He did not take a very active part in the State campaigns of 1916 or 1917, contenting himself by being regular and supporting the State ticket. In the presidential campaign of that year, he took an active part as chairman of the Massachusetts delegation to the National convention and stumped the west for Wilson and Marshall.

Senator Weeks' term was expiring March 4, 1919 and he was a candidate for reëlection in the Fall of 1918. No man in recent years in either party had a better grasp on public opinion than David I. Walsh. He seemed to be able to sense what was in the minds of the voters. He felt sure that he could defeat Senator Weeks and cautiously laid his plans for the nomination. The only man in his way was Dr. Fitzgerald, but the doctor was not anxious to tackle the senatorial task again. After the usual patter about the good of the party and a desire for harmony he gave way to Walsh who kept the party big wigs guessing about his candidacy until Fitzgerald quit and he had a clear field for the nomination.

His first formal speech in the campaign was made at the Democratic State Convention held at Worcester, October 24, when he accepted the nomination and pledged himself to aid in every way he could President Wilson in the conduct of the war. He charged that Senator Weeks had been an active leader among the reactionary Senators who fought President Wilson's preparedness legislation previous to the declaration of war against Germany and that he had tried to cut down the soldiers' insurance from $10,000 to $7,500, while they were fighting the Nation's battles.

Senator Weeks could not cope with Walsh as a campaigner, and conducted the usual dignified campaign of a Massachusetts Republican Senator, running for reelection. His chief appeal was to the business interests. His friends, by no means confined to his own party, tried to put pep into his campaign, but John Weeks knew little of the art of political ballyhoo and relied on the party hacks to get out the Republican vote for him.

Aiding Walsh was Thomas W. Lawson, the State Street broker, whose daughter had married a son of Governor McCall. Earlier in the campaign it was believed that McCall would contest the nomination with Senator Weeks. McCall was still smarting over his defeat for Senator by Weeks. The anti-Weeks Republicans were encouraged to believe that McCall would enter the race. He made a speech at Southboro before the primaries, which was regarded by his friends as the opening gun of his campaign for the nomination, but he abandoned the idea if he entertained it and Lawson stepped into contest.

Walsh was the victor by a plurality of 17,632, the vote being: Walsh, 206,271; Weeks, 188,639; Lawson, 21,476. It was the first time since the Republican party came into power that Massachusetts elected a Democratic United States Senator. Only three other Democrats had been similarly honored: Joseph Bradley Varnum, 1811-1817; Nathaniel Silsby, 1826-1835 and Robert Rantoul, Jr., February 1, 1851 to March 3, 1851. All of Mr. Walsh's party predecessors, with the exception of Varnum, were about his age. Varnum was 61, Silsby, 49 and Rantoul, 46. Senator Walsh was in his 47th year when he was sworn in as Senator. Varnum was elected at the time the old Federalist party was breaking up. Silsby was a Jacksonian Democrat and Rantoul was elected by the Free Soilers and Democrats, who formed the famous coalition when the anti-slavery men of Massachusetts combined with the Democrats and routed the old Whig party of the State, making George S. Boutwell, Governor, National P. Banks, Speaker of the House, Henry Wilson, President of the State Senate and giving the long term in the Senate to Charles Sumner.

Daniel Webster's famous 7th of March speech was so unpopular with the younger element of the Whig party and the Free Soilers that he felt he no longer represented the sentiment of the State and he resigned. Rantoul was Senator for only 31 days—February 1, 1851 to March 3, 1851, when he was succeeded by Charles Sumner. Mr. Rantoul was a lifelong Democrat, who had filled many public offices of trust and responsibility, including a seat in the Massachusetts House of Representatives and United States District Attorney of Massachusetts. When his term in the Senate expired, March 3, 1851, he took his seat in the 32nd Congress, to which he had been elected. He died at Washington, August 7, 1852.

Varnum was a native of Dracut. He fought in the Revolutionary War and won a colonelcy in the fight for Independence. He was prominent and active in putting down Shay's Rebellion. He was a member of the Legislature and the Executive Council, elected to Congress, serving as Speaker from 1807 to 1811, when he was chosen as the successor of Timothy Pickering in the United States Senate. He served one term, was made President pro tem of the Senate and was acting Vice-President of the United States in 1814, succeeding Elbridge of Massachusetts who died in office. He was a member of the State Constitutional Convention in 1787 and also of the Convention of 1820. He died in 1821.

Nathaniel Silsby, the second Democrat to represent Massachusetts in the United States Senate, was an Essex County man, who amassed a fortune in shipping. He was a member of the Massachusetts Legislature for a number of years, sitting in the House and Senate and was a member of the 15th and 16th Congresses. He was elected to the Senate to succeed James Lloyd, serving but one term from 1829 to 1835. He was a firm supporter of the administration of John Quincy Adams.

Walsh was the recipient of nation wide congratulations from Democratic leaders. Senator Lodge who had labored hard for the return of his colleague, acted manfully toward his new associate and showed him every courtesy when he arrived in Washington, escorting him to the Vice-President's desk where he presented Mr. Walsh's credentials and the new Senator from Massachusetts took the oath of office.

Defeat did not sour the temperament of Senator Weeks. He continued his interest in public affairs, winning new honors as Secretary of War in the cabinet of President Harding in 1921 and served under President Coolidge until ill health forced him to resign Oct. 13, 1925. He died at Lancaster, New Hampshire, where he was born, July 12, 1926. His ashes are buried in Arlington National Cemetery, Virginia.

THE WORLD WAR

For some time before the United States declared that a state of war existed between this country and Germany, far sighted public officials were preparing the military forces of the Commonwealth for the inevitable. The declaration of war by Congress found Massachusetts ahead of many of her sister states in the preparation of her men and women for the conflict. The Massachusetts Committee of Public Safety had made a survey of the resources of the State. In February, 1917, Governor McCall named a representative committee of one hundred on Public Safety with James J. Storrow, Chairman. When the Committee organized Henry H. Endicott, a leading Boston business man was made Executive Manager.

In March, the New England Governors met to devise ways and means of putting this section of the Union in a state of preparedness. In the Council Chamber at the State House, General Leonard Wood, a Massachusetts man, Commander of the Eastern Department of the United States Army, discussed with the assembled Governors plans of putting New England on a war footing. The meeting urged the national government the need of immediate and energetic preparation for defense on sea and land.

A few days later, Governor McCall sent a message to the Legislature on the problem of common defense and that body immediately appropriated a million dollars for that purpose, the Governor pointing out that in the event of war the Federal government would reimburse the State.

The Committee on Public Safety named several subcommittees and at once tackled its task. The story of the work and activities are given in the report of its able and efficient Secretary, George H. Lyman. One of its early contributions to the Allies in the World War was the furnishing of a number of mill units, fully equipped for lumbering work in England and Scotland. Credit for procuring the volunteers, all experienced lumber men, belongs to James J. Phelan, well known Boston banker, Martin A. Brown, a leading New England lumber man and financier and F. W. Raine, Massachusetts State Forester The sum of $131,192 was raised by private contributions and New England States appropriated money for equipment and procuring 10 portable saw mills, 120 horses and 350 men. "New England's gift to Old England," as Balfour, British Foreign Minister so aptly remarked, in a letter of thanks to the New England Governors.

In December, 1917, occurred an explosion in Halifax Harbor, Nova Scotia. Two ships carrying high explosives collided wrecking the water front, killing 1800 and injuring 10,000 people. As soon as word of the disaster reached Boston, the Massachusetts Committee on Public Safety organized a relief expedition and a special train left Boston a few hours later with doctors, nurses, workers and supplies of medicine and clothing for the sufferers. A total of $716,477 was subscribed by the people of Massachusetts for relief work.

The National Guard of Massachusetts, 5152 men, 275 officers, responded to the call of President Wilson for Mexican border service in the summer of 1916. Most of them were recalled in November and mustered out of the United States service. By December 31st, the Massachusetts National Guard numbered 485 officers and 9164 men, exclusive of the Naval Brigade of 64 officers and 778 men. The war spirit was growing. By July 25, 1917, when the National Guard was again called into the Federal service, it had grown to 15,908 men and 502 officers. The Naval brigade had increased to 948 officers and men.

The 26th or Yankee Division, composed of New England National Guardsmen was organized August 22, 1917, with headquarters in Boston and General Clarence R. Edwards as Commander. His instructions were to prepare his command for France by September 1st to 15th. The first unit of the Yankee Division was ready on schedule time and arrived in France, November 12th, the first National Guard division to land on French soil.

It served in the front line 210 days and took part in most of the major engagements during that period. Its casualties numbered 421 officers and 11,534 men. The Division was fortunate in its commander. General Edwards was loved by his men and when he was relieved of his command on the eve of the armistice and sent home as a camp commander the entire division mourned his departure and resented what they believed the injustice done their gallant leader. All New England joined in the criticism of the War Department and its senators and representatives in Congress voiced the feeling of their constituents. The General's legion of friends believed that he was the victim of army politics and a clique at headquarters in France, who wished to put their own favorites in command of the Division. The popularity of General Edwards forced the War Department to change their plans and the former commander of the 26th Division was assigned to command the First Corps Area, with headquarters in Boston. He was welcomed on his return by the people of New England with great enthusiasm. Public receptions were arranged in his honor in every State at which he told the relatives of the men of the Division of the heroism of their sons and how proud he was to have commanded such "stout hearted lads" who had added new laurels to the martial glory of the New England States. To further soothe the feelings of the public over the unfair and harsh treatment of General Edwards, the War Department invited him to lead his veterans in their final review in Boston before it was mustered out.

Although a native of Cleveland, Ohio, General Edwards came of New England stock on his father's side. After his retirement on reaching the age limit, General Edwards elected to become a resident of Massachusetts and settled in Westwood on a fine estate he had purchased which he called "Doneroving." He kept in close touch with his 26th Division lads. As long as he lived he was their "Old Man." No other division commander in the A.E.F. was as beloved as Clarence R. Edwards. His death occurred February 14, 1931. He is buried at Arlington National Cemetery, beside his wife who died during his retirement at "Doneroving" and his only child, a daughter, an army nurse during the war, a victim of the flu.

On sea as well as land the men of Massachusetts gave a good account of themselves and upheld the fine reputation of the State in the Navy. The members of the Naval Brigade showed the same keen interest in the struggle in Europe as those in the army and were anxious to do their part in the event of the United States entering the World War. The Massachusetts Committee on Public Safety named a sub-committee to aid the Naval Brigade in preparing for an emergency. The first units of the naval militia were called into the Federal service late in March and were assigned to the battleships *Nebraska* and *Kearsage,* then at the Charlestown Navy Yard. The entire brigade was enrolled a few days later, the Springfield Company going to the receiving ship, Commonwealth Pier.

STATE GUARD

To provide a substitute body for the National Guard while the latter was in the Federal service, Governor McCall sent a message to the Legislature, March 22, 1917, recommending the establishment of a Home Guard, which could be used to protect domestic peace. The Legislature readily assented to the idea and the Governor named a board of military men, headed by General Butler Ames to organize the new military force. In a few weeks the board reported to the Governor that 135 companies consisting of 9000 men had been organized. These were formed into 11 regiments of infantry, a motor corps, a troop of cavalry and a medical department. Subsequently the Home Guard was changed to State Guard.

The Guard rendered valuable service in relieving distress in the Halifax explosion, in the establishment of temporary hospitals in Boston to treat the influenza cases which appeared in September, 1918, in Boston and spread rapidly to every section of the State. In the riot that followed the police strike in Boston, the entire force was mobilized for duty; maintained order and handled street traffic until the new Boston police force was recruited and organized and ready for street duty. Having performed every duty assigned to them with fidelity and efficiency, and the new reorganized National Guard having been organized, the State Guard delivered its colors to the Commander-in-Chief, at a public ceremony in the Hall of Flags, December 23, 1920, and was mustered out, praised by Governor McCall, General Ames and its three brigade commanders, Generals Clark, Samuel D. Parker and John J. Sullivan, all veteran militia officers. It was a fine body of loyal, sacrificing citizens.

HOSPITALS

MASSACHUSETTS medical men served with the British at the front before the United States entered the War. On April 28, 1917, Massachusetts authorities were notified that Base Hospital No. 5 in the French war zone would be soon ordered to mobilize and the three Massachusetts units already organized, headed by Dr. Frederick A.

Washburn of the Massachusetts General, Dr. John J. Dowling of the Boston City Hospital and Dr. Harvey Cushing of the affiliated Harvard hospitals, reported that their units would be ready in a few days to leave for France. Dr. Washburn's command sailed from Hoboken, May 11, and reached their destination, British General Hospital No. 11 in France. German air craft shelled the hospital during the night of September 4, killing four of the staff. During its service, Base Hospital No. 5 handled 45,837 sick and wounded.

Base Hospital No. 6, A.E.F., was composed of doctors and nurses of the Massachusetts General Hospital. It was originally organized as a Red Cross unit in May, 1916. It left for France, July 11, 1917, and took over the French hospitals at Talence. During its use by the Americans, its capacity was increased from 500 to 4000 patients. 25,000 cases were handled. Major Frederick A. Washburn, its commander, was relieved the following April and ordered to England to direct American hospitalization there.

The Boston City Hospital unit became Base Hospital No. 7. The Robert Bent Brigham Hospital unit as General Hospital No. 10. Both did fine work, the former in France and the latter in Boston.

OTHER ACTIVITIES

THE Fore River and Squantum plants of the Bethlehem Shipbuilding Corporation were busy places, turning out submarines, tankers and cargo vessels. At one time they had more than 16,000 hands on the payroll. It was facetiously referred to as "slackers' paradise." There is no doubt that many felt safer in the shipyards than in the trenches of France.

When war broke out in Europe many German ships were at sea. The liner *Kronprinzessin Cecile* on her regular run from New York to Germany with Plymouth, England, her first port of call. She left New York, July 28, 1914. When within about 700 miles of Plymouth, England, she got word from German authorities on the night of July 31st, that Germany and England were at war. Her captain turned about his ship and headed for the nearest American port. The first her passengers knew of the change in the course of the ship was a short time before she dropped anchor in the deep waters of Bar Harbor, Maine. As soon as the necessary arrangements could be made the ship was escorted to Boston by American naval vessels and interned here.

The *Amerika,* a Hamburg-American liner, due to sail from Boston on the eve of the declaration of war cancelled her sailing and was also interned here. The Cincinnati, another Hamburg-American liner, left her home port just before hostilities, escaped enemy war ships and reached Boston nine days later. Customs guards and police were placed in charge of the ships. Three other German ships, freighters *Kolm, Ockenfels* and *Wittekind* were added to the list.

As soon as the United States got into the war these ships were seized by the Government. The machinery of the three liners was found to be badly damaged in an effort to render them useless to the new owners, but American mechanics soon repaired them and made them fit for sea service. They were renamed and were used as transports by the United States government. In his memoirs, Count von Bernstorff, the German Ambassador at Washington, says that he gave orders to the Captains of these ships, a few hours before he was given his walking ticket by President Wilson, to render the vessels useless in case they were seized by the United States government.

Graduates of the Massachusetts Nautical Training School, a State institution, to the number of 214 served as commissioned officers in the United States Navy during the war.

This State was the first to provide a flying field for the training of navy flyers. An air service school was also established by the State at Squantum. After their preliminary training men were distributed to other flying fields to complete their training.

RADIO SCHOOLS

MASSACHUSETTS took the initiative in establishing a radio school, training radio operators, and the Committee on Public Safety paid the bills to start this important work. Most of the instructors were volunteers and 530 of its graduates entered the army and navy as radio operators.

Ten days after the United States entered the war, a naval radio school was opened at Harvard University. Before long the Navy designated this school as its official training institution for its radio operators. Barracks were erected on historic Cambridge Common and by August 18, 1918, 3400 men were under instruction in an 18 weeks' course. The government transferred its Aircraft Radio School from Pensacola, Florida, to Cambridge. More than 8000 men were graduated from the University's Radio schools.

Harvard also established a naval officers' material school, training men for the Navy. In all, 883 men graduated from this school and were commissioned ensigns in the navy. Still another school trained yeomen for the navy.

Massachusetts Institute of Technology set up a naval aviation school, giving instructions to 5210 cadets. Courses for students volunteering for navy duty were conducted by Boston University, Holy Cross, Harvard, Technology, Tufts, Worcester Technology and Williams College. 50,000 Massachusetts men served in the Navy.

CAMP DEVENS

CAMP DEVENS, consisting of 10,000 acres in the towns of Ayer and Harvard, selected by General Edwards, commanding the Northeastern Department, was the first cantonment ready to receive troops of the National or draft army. Here the 76th Division and the 151st Depot

Brigade were organized and trained for overseas. The first five percent of the draft reported there September 5th. The whole were in camp September 24th. Five hundred of the first troops were transferred to the 26th Division, September 18th.

The 76th Division began leaving for France, July 3rd, sailing from Boston, Halifax and Hoboken, and a new Division, the 12th, a regular army outfit, was organized of drafted men. In 15 weeks they were ready for overseas and reported for duty in France on the eve of the Armistice. Devens was designated as a demobilization camp at the close of the hostilities. In all 93,819 men were inducted into the army at Devens. Thirty ships carried 48,085 men from the port of Boston overseas and 97,000 returned troops landed here at the close of the war.

The Springfield Armory and Watertown Arsenal were busy places during the war. By November, 1918, the Springfield Armory was manufacturing 8250 rifles a week with more than 5000 employees. At the Watertown Arsenal heavy mobile artillery and siege guns were made. The government spent $13,000,000 to bring the plant up to date, greatly enlarging its capacity. At the peak of its activity, 3700 civilian employees were on its pay roll, the largest in its long history.

There were ordnance proving grounds at Scituate. At first the Allies provided the American army in France with artillery and its ammunition until such time as the United States could furnish its own. The country was divided into districts for the purpose of producing all sorts of war material. Levi H. Greenwood of Gardner was District Chief for New England. The total disbursements of the Boston office were $99,000,000.

CONTRIBUTION TO FEDERAL FORCES

ONE hundred ninety-eight thousand eight hundred and sixty-three Massachusetts men, 1525 army nurses and 1324 yeomen F (women) served in the Federal forces during the war. The State paid as a bonus $10 a month to 77,910 enlisted men and $100 cash to 183,020 men who served in the military forces at the conclusion of the war. 76,178 Massachusetts officers and men served overseas in the army. Her voluntary enlistments were 41,985, inductions 76,567, a total of 118,552. 10,740 were rejected, leaving a total of 83,220 who were accepted for service.

Always generous to her soldiers and sailors, the State paid to her sons and daughters of the World War more than $22,000,000. Its bill for gratuities and other expenditures on behalf of her soldiers, sailors and nurses, memorials, hospitals, burials, testimonials, regimental histories, amounted to $27,219,044.15.

The honor war shield offered by Governor McCall to the towns which should have the largest number of men in proportion to population in the military and naval service one year after the United States entered the war, was awarded to Gay Head. It had 17 men, 10.4% of its population in service. Most of its population is of Indian descent.

Following an old Massachusetts custom the flags used by Massachusetts units in the war were returned to the Commonwealth with appropriate ceremony and were placed in the Hall of Flags at the State House.

MISSIONS FROM ALLIES

DURING the war various foreign missions visited Boston. In May, 1917, a French delegation including Premier Viviani and Marshal Joffre was appropriately greeted by civic and military officials. On Boston Common, Marshal Joffre was presented $175,000, a gift of the school children of Massachusetts for the orphan children of France.

A month later came an Italian mission, headed by Prince Udine. A great crowd of Boston Italians greeted them at the South Station. In August, a Belgium mission arrived. In September the Japs, and in January the Serbians. Somebody in Washington had the wisdom to prevent a visit by the British mission. There was a feeling that Mr. Balfour who headed the British delegation might not enjoy a visit to Boston. Bostonians of Irish blood were not ready to forgive the man whose stern rule in Ireland had earned him the suggestive title "Bloody Balfour" and declared that the Irish were no more fit for home rule than the Hottentots.

A commission consisting of Adjutant General Jesse F. Stevens, Secretary of State Frederick W. Cook and State

Librarian Edward H. Redstone were appointed by the Legislatures of 1923 and 1924 to prepare a report on the part the State played in the World War. The Commission employed as the historian, Colonel Eben Putnam, historian of the Massachusetts Department of the American Legion. The result of Colonel Putnam's work was published by the State. It is a clear, concise story, reflecting credit on the author and a tribute to the wisdom of the Commission in their selection of an historian.

DEATH OF CONGRESSMAN GARDNER

DEATH claimed a knightly soul when Augustus Peabody Gardner, fell a victim of pneumonia at Camp Wheeler, Macon, Georgia, January 14, 1918. He was the son-in-law of Senator Lodge and for nearly 20 years a prominent figure in Republican politics. A wealthy man, he spent his money freely, if not always wisely, in politics. He was an officer on the staff of General James H. Wilson in the Spanish War. After his army experience he served two terms in the State Senate and then was elected to Congress, where he served as a member of the House from the old Essex district for seven terms. His popularity in his district was unbounded. There were times when no Democrat could be found to oppose him election day.

Captain Gardner, as he was popularly known in his district—"Gussie" to his intimates, was no mollycoddle. He was a fearless fighter for what he believed in and didn't hesitate to oppose the Old Guard in Congress, of which his father-in-law, Senator Lodge was an important cog. He fought Uncle Joe Cannon's House rules. He was the subject of a good many jokes in Washington because of his relationship to Senator Lodge. If the latter ever tried to control him he must have found him difficult to manage. "Gus" Gardner did his own thinking.

He was an ardent advocate of preparedness when Europe unsheathed the sword in 1914 and conducted a nation wide campaign on the subject. When the United States joined the Allies, he volunteered for service. He served at Governor's Island, New York, for a short time, was transferred to Camp Wheeler, Georgia, where he was made a Colonel in the Adjutant General's Department, but he was anxious to go overseas with a combat outfit and he was made a Major in the 131st Infantry. While his regiment was waiting for embarkation orders, he died in the camp hospital.

He was succeeded in Congress by his secretary, W. W. Lufkin, who served two terms, when he was named by President Harding as Collector of Customs at Boston, retaining that office under Presidents Coolidge and Hoover, until the administration of Franklin D. Roosevelt. His successor was Joseph A. Maynard who had served as Surveyor of Customs under the administration of Woodrow Wilson.

At the time he was appointed Maynard was Chairman of the Democratic State Committee. He was the unanimous choice of the Democratic leaders and had no opposition for the biggest Federal plum in New England, a post that had been filled by many eminent citizens of both political parties. At the Chicago convention, Maynard was for Smith for President, but accepted Roosevelt and worked hard and conscientiously to keep the State in the Democratic column. Chairman James A. Farley went on record for Maynard for Collector of the Port soon after the 1932 election and paid him high praise for his work in the campaign. President Roosevelt readily assented to the choice of the party leaders and Maynard got the first major Federal appointment in the State.

CALVIN COOLIDGE
Governor 1919-1921

CALVIN COOLIDGE, who succeeded Samuel W. McCall, was inaugurated Governor New Year's Day, 1919, in the presence of the usual inauguration day crowd that packed the chamber of the House of Representatives. A native of Vermont, he had settled in the little Western Massachusetts city of Northampton after his graduation from Amherst College in 1895, a member of the same class as Dwight Morrow, who in later years became a partner of the rich and powerful banking house of J. P. Morgan & Company. Mr. Coolidge studied law with the old Northampton law firm of Hammond & Field, entered local politics, was elected a member of the City Council, served as City Solicitor and Mayor, member of both branches of the State Legislature, President of the State Senate and Lieutenant Governor under Governor McCall. In every position he filled, he was conscientious in the discharge of his duties and was admirably equipped for the highest office in the Commonwealth.

He was not a back slapping politician and was woefully deficient in most of the arts of the office seeker, but people liked him because he kept his word and was scrupulously honest. He inherited from his Vermont ancestors, their characteristics of plain living and high thinking, thrift, taciturnity, and humor. He was not a brilliant man, was sparing of his words and had a mind of his own.

As he began to ascend the State House political escalator, he was fortunate in the friendship and backing of another Amherst graduate, Frank W. Stearns, a Boston merchant, who was anxious to see an Amherst man in the Governor's chair. Mr. Stearns helped materially and financially in paving the way of Calvin Coolidge from the State Senate to the Executive Chamber, and was the happiest man in Massachusetts when he witnessed his protégé take the oath of office as Governor. Nobody else in the inaugural crowd visioned the political future of Calvin Coolidge with the foresight of Frank Stearns. The party bigwigs used to smile when he predicted that Calvin Coolidge was destined to be President of the United States. He proclaimed him a second Abraham Lincoln and "greatest American."

Governor Coolidge's inaugural address, although concise, revealed his intimate knowledge of State affairs and public questions. In his opening, he pointed out the duty of legislators, saying:—

"You are coming to a new Legislative session under the inspiration of the greatest achievements in all history. You are beholding the fulfilment of an age-old promise, man coming into his own. You are to have the opportunity and responsibility of reflecting this new spirit in the laws of the most enlightened of Commonwealths. We must steadily advance. Each individual must have the rewards and opportunities worthy of the character of our citizenship, a broader recognition of his worth, and a larger liberty protected by order—and always under the law.

"In the promotion of human welfare, Massachusetts happily may not need much reconstruction, but, like all living organizations, forever needs construction. What are the lessons of the past? How shall they be applied to these days of readjustment? How shall we emerge from the autocratic methods of war to the democratic methods of peace, raising ourselves again to the source of all our strength and all our glory — sound self-government?"

In conclusion, he admonished the Legislature in these words:

"Let there be a purpose in all your legislation to recognize the right of man to be well born, well nurtured, well educated, well employed and well paid. This is no gospel of ease and selfishness, or class distinction, but a gospel of effort and service, of universal application. Such results cannot be secured at once, but they should ever be before us. The world has assumed burdens that will bear heavily on all peoples. We shall not escape our share. But whatever may be our trials, however difficult our tasks, they are only the problems of peace, and a victorious peace. The war is over. Whatever the call of duty now we should remember with gratitude that it is nothing compared with the heavy sacrifice so lately made. The genius and fortitude which conquered then, cannot now fail."

The return of the Yankee Division from France was an important event in the first year of Governor Coolidge's administration. He led in the enthusiastic home welcome accorded the men and paid tribute to their valor. The first bill he signed as Governor appropriated ten thousand dollars to defray the expenses of their official welcome.

He also cordially welcomed President Wilson to Boston on the latter's return from France, with the Treaty of Versailles, in February, 1919, and introduced him at a great public meeting at Mechanics Building, where Mr. Wilson made his first speech to his fellow-Americans on the Covenant of the League of Nations. Boston, it was said, was chosen by President Wilson for his first speech, because it was the chief city of the home State of Senator Lodge, chairman of the Foreign Relations Committee of the Senate, and leader of the majority party in the upper branch of Congress, who had already begun his determined fight to defeat the treaty and kill the Covenant of the League of Nations.

The State Constitutional Convention, held the year before, directed the Legislature to reorganize the top-heavy

JOHN W. WEEKS

CHARLES R. GOW

BAYARD TUCKERMAN

SAMUEL L. POWERS

GEN. EDWARD L. LOGAN

J. OTIS WARDWELL

State Commissions. The Legislature of 1919, after much backing and filling and prodding by the Governor, passed an Act reducing these bodies from 117 to about 20. It was not a job that the politicians relished. It meant the lopping off of many old official heads, whose friends besieged the State House with schemes to save them. On the whole, the reorganization task was well done, from a party standpoint. The Governor took care to reward only Republicans in the distribution of the plums and the slighted Democrats complained of his extreme partizanship.

BOSTON POLICE STRIKE

In September, 1919, occurred the Boston Police strike, during which the public got a close-up view of Governor Coolidge, and he became a national political figure, with "Law and Order" as his slogan—a phrase he used with telling effect in the turbulence of that unhappy event. The strike was the turning point in his public career. If there had been no walkout of the police, there would not, in all probability, have been any serious thought of him for higher political honors. At the end of his term as Governor, he would have joined the other political ex's of his party, to resume the practice of his profession, fading out of the political picture, except to be utilized for decorative party purposes at State Conventions and political gatherings. The police strike started him on the road to the White House.

The trouble in the Department, which led to the strike, began a year or more before, when a report reached headquarters, that members of the force were organizing a Union to be affiliated with the American Federation of Labor. The then Commissioner, Stephen O'Meara, forbade the formation of the Union. In the spring of 1919, the work of organizing a policemen's Union started anew. The men claimed that they were underpaid, that in many instances their quarters were unsanitary, and that some of the rules of the Department were unfair and unnecessarily harsh. Commissioner Curtis agreed in the main with the complaints of the men, and had induced the city government to raise their pay $200 a year, but the Mayor protested that the city could not afford at the time the improvements at the station houses which the men demanded. Late in July, Commissioner Curtis issued an order in which he endorsed the attitude of his predecessor O'Meara, taking the ground that a policeman could not consistently belong to a labor union and perform his sworn duty. Both the order and warnings of the Commissioner were disregarded, and on August 15 the Union was launched.

Shortly afterwards, nineteen policemen, connected with the Union, were placed on trial before Commissioner Curtis for violation of his order forbidding the members of the force to join a union. Mayor Peters became apprehensive over the threatening situation and named a committee of leading citizens to investigate the conditions. On September 9, the Commissioner suspended the nineteen men after a hearing. A meeting of the Union followed and a strike was voted.

All the while, Governor Coolidge was closely watching developments. He arranged with the Adjutant General of the State to have his forces ready for duty at a moment's notice. Matters were so critical on September 8th, that the Governor hastened from the Western part of the State, whither he had gone to address the State A. F. of L. convention, at Greenfield. Arriving in Boston about five o'clock, he conferred with the Mayor, the Attorney General and the Citizens' Committee. After listening to their reports, he refused to undertake to coerce the Police Commissioner into anything that might be considered as compromising the authority of the law. The Governor was at the State House all day of the 9th. That evening he established headquarters at his hotel with the Attorney General, the Adjutant General and other officials, ready to respond to any call for assistance from the Mayor. Immediately following night-rollcall at the stations, 1117 patrolmen out of 1544 in the Department "struck." Rowdyism broke out in different parts of the city soon after midnight. The police force remaining on duty was unable to cope with the situation. Matters went from bad to worse. The disorderly element grew bolder and more defiant, mocked at the authorities, looted stores, and committed other crimes.

For several hours the city was at the mercy of a mob. Lawlessness was imminent all the following day. Police Commissioner Curtis asked the Governor for the military to preserve order, requesting that they report for duty at 5:30 P.M. The Governor ordered the troops to report at once, and issued a proclamation, taking over the control of the police. Excitement was intense. The lawless element grew more defiant. There was talk of a sympathetic strike by the Fire Department and by the telephone operators. Happily, that did not take place. Conditions were such during the middle of the second day that the Governor decided it was his duty to exercise the authority vested in him by law and take full charge of maintaining order. The die was cast. Every man in the State Guard was summoned to the colors, by a proclamation in which the Governor said:

"The entire State Guard of Massachusetts has been called out. Under the Constitution, the Governor is the Commander-in-Chief thereof by an authority of which he could not if he chose divest himself. That command I must and will exercise. Under the law I hereby call on all the police of Boston, who have loyally and in a never-to-be-forgotten way remained on duty, to aid me in the performance of my duty for the restoration and maintenance of order in the city of Boston, and each of such officers is required to act in obedience to such orders as I may hereafter issue or cause to be issued. I call on every citizen to aid me in the maintenance of law and order."

President Gompers, of the American Federation of Labor, telegraphed the Governor, appealing to him to suspend the order of the Police Commissioner dismissing the patrolmen who defied the Commissioner's order and organized the Union. Mr. Coolidge replied denying the request, and laid down the doctrine that "There was no right to strike against the public safety by anybody, anywhere, any time."

The Governor did not hesitate a moment as to the course to pursue, once the issue reached him. He went vigorously about his new and unsought duties, restoring order, arousing public opinion and making hosts of friends by his courageous course. He ordered the Police Commissioner to report to him for duty and instructed him to fill the vacancies in his Department created by those who had left their posts. It was weeks afterward, December 21, before the last of the State Guard was withdrawn from the streets of the city, when the Police Commissioner had succeeded in filling the vacancies in his Department, and felt justified in notifying the Governor that he had sufficient men to maintain order and to perform the manifold duties assigned to the police.

The charge was made at the time by his political adversaries, that Mr. Coolidge played politics in handling the tense situation. But his critics do not appear to be corroborated by the record in the case. The strikers asserted that the Governor was prejudiced against them, and some of the extremists on the other side declared that he was side-stepping—"passing the buck," to the head of the Police Department. Neither was right. In the police strike, as in other matters of public policy, Mr. Coolidge was guided by his own philosophy of refraining from interfering or using his constitutional or statutory powers until the properly constituted subordinate or correlated authority had failed to bring about a settlement.

In the Police controversy, he waited until the Commissioner acknowledged his inability to cope with conditions before personally taking charge of the situation. From the moment that he stepped in, he was complete master of the case, meeting the issues promptly and fearlessly. The strike was costly in dollars and cents, and in civic pride, but Mr. Coolidge took the ground that no price was too great to pay for the upholding of the authority of the government. From all over the country he received congratulatory messages. President Wilson, then on his transcontinental trip, in defence of the Versailles Treaty and the League of Nations, denounced the strike in a speech at Helena, Montana, as "a crime against civilization." Seventy thousand people took the pains to write the Governor commending him for his vigorous course.

LAW AND ORDER TRIUMPHS

THE echoes of the police strike were still to be heard when the campaign for Governor Coolidge's reëlection opened. Then, as in the year before, no other name was thought of for Governor by his party, and thousands of Democrats and Independents now assured him of their support. The Republican State Convention was a love feast, and the Governor was easily the most popular public figure in the State.

Richard H. Long, the Democratic candidate for Governor, was quite generally supported by the leaders of the police strike and their friends. The Democratic platform in the campaign did not condone the police strike, nor did it condemn it. Mr. Long intimated that Governor Coolidge was in hiding at the most critical stage of the negotiations looking toward a settlement of the strike, a charge which the Governor promptly refuted, proving that at no time was he out of touch with his office or the legal and military authorities of the State on whom he relied for guidance in shaping the course and dealing with the situation.

He declined to enter into any personal controversy with his opponent for Governor on that or any of the other material issues of the contest. A complete refutation of Mr. Long's charge was made by Attorney General Wyman, the Governor's legal adviser, who accounted for Mr. Coolidge's movements during the strike and for several days preceding the walkout of the police. The Governor could afford to welcome the strike issue. Public opinion was on his side. He stood his ground against the reinstatement of the police who had deserted their posts of duty. At the Republican State Convention he said in his speech, that the issue of the campaign was perfectly plain.

"The Government of Massachusetts is not seeking to resist the lawful action or sound policy of organized labor," said he. "It has time and again passed laws for the protection and encouragement of trade unions. It has done so under my administration, upon my recommendation, to a greater extent than in any previous year. In that policy it will continue. It is seeking to prevent a condition which would at once destroy all labor unions and all else that is the foundation of civilization, by maintaining the authority and sanctity of the law. When that goes, all goes. It costs something, but it is the cheapest thing that can be bought; it causes some inconvenience, but it is the foundation of all convenience, the orderly execution of the laws."

The Governor was overwhelmingly reëlected, receiving the largest vote ever cast until then for a gubernatorial candidate: Coolidge, 317,794; Long, 192,673.

COOLIDGE'S SECOND TERM

MR. COOLIDGE was inaugurated Governor the second time, January 9, 1920. His inaugural address occupied a little more than thirty minutes in delivery, in which he briefly reviewed the accomplishments of his first term.

"No one year has ever witnessed like accomplishments. Considered as a whole it has been stupendous," he said. "In general, it is a time to conserve, to retrench rather than to reform, a time to stabilize the administration of the present laws rather than to seek new legislation. Not law, but perseverance and patience." His plea for the "humanizing" of industry closed with the admonition: "Change not the law, but the attitude of the mind."

The Governor was now a growing potentiality in the national political field. He attended to his official duties, keeping his eye on the departments and watching the acts of the Legislature. One of his most important vetoes of that year was of the two and a half per cent beer bill. "We have had too much legislating by clamor, by tumult, by pressure," he told the Legislature in his veto message. "Representative government ceases when outside influence of any kind is substituted for the judgment of the representative. This does not mean that the opinion of constituents is to be ignored. It is to be weighed most carefully, for the representative must represent, but his oath provides that it must be 'faithfully and agreeably to the rules and regulations of the Constitution and laws.' Opinions and instructions do not outmatch the Constitution. Against it they are void. It is an insult to any Massachusetts constituency to suggest that they were so intended. Instructions are not given unless given constitutionally. Instructions are not carried out unless carried out constitutionally. There can be no constitutional instruction to do an unconstitutional act. Can Massachusetts afford to take any position which may turn out to be, which can anywhere be interpreted to be, an act of nullification? If rights are infringed, the way to court is open."

Governor Coolidge was instrumental in securing the passage of the following laws during his second year in office:

Laws designed to check profiteering landlords.

Authorizing cities and towns to take property by eminent domain to provide dwellings for people in times of emergency.

Giving courts power to stay eviction proceedings six months in certain cases.

Prohibiting rental increases of more than 25% in any one year.

Penalizing of landlords who failed to keep agreements regarding heat, light and other service.

Extending for one year the law requiring 30 days' notice to vacate a tenement.

Establishing the office of fuel administrator.

Providing for reforestation of 100,000 acres of waste land.

Extending payments of soldiers' and sailors' $100 bonus.

Creating commission to care for graves of Massachusetts soldiers buried in France.

Regulating outdoor advertising.

Making trial of suits for less than $35 easier and less expensive.

Recognizing advancement of women in politics and public office.

Extending self-control to town governments.

Urged the ratification of the 19th Amendment to the Federal Constitution, for equal suffrage and signed the resolve June 25, 1919. Massachusetts was the eighth State to ratify the amendment. Governor Coolidge had long advocated woman suffrage.

Giving cities and towns power to establish areas in which coöperatively to operate public street railway lines.

Enlarging powers and usefulness of coöperative banks.

Creating a commission to study and report recommendations for reformation or abolition of the present system of pensions to retired public officials and employees, a problem of growing importance.

Authorizing the appointment of an unpaid commission to investigate the subject of maternity benefits and to report, with recommendations to the General Court in its extra session.

STATE TREASURER OUSTED

IN 1919, Fred J. Burrell of Medford won the Republican nomination for State Treasurer in the primaries. He was in office but eight months when a storm broke over his head. Bank officials charged that unless they placed their advertising through an agency in which Burrell was interested they could not obtain State deposits. In some cases banks lost their State deposits when they declined to give their advertising to the Burrell agency. Complaints were made to the Executive Department and Governor Coolidge ordered an investigation of the subject. The Legislature also took cognizance of the situation and conducted an investigation. Governor Coolidge announced that if evidence were furnished him showing malfeasance in office he would proceed against the Treasurer of the Commonwealth. Burrell resigned and Governor Coolidge named James Jackson a former banker to fill the vacancy until the ensuing election. Jackson was induced to become a candidate for the Republican nomination. Burrell had already filed for the nomination and the time had expired for further nominations. Jackson had to run as a sticker candidate. The feeling was such against Burrell that Jackson defeated him in a vote of Jackson, 111,634; Burrell, 51,562.

PRESIDENTIAL BEE STINGS COOLIDGE

WHILE Mr. Coolidge was busy with his official duties at the State House, his friends were not idle in furthering his fortunes in national politics. His mail continued to be heavy. His attitude and his utterances in the police strike had impressed thousands of his fellow-countrymen outside of New England. They wrote urging him to become a Presidential candidate.

The Republican Club of Massachusetts formally endorsed him for the nomination, and South Dakota Republicans named him as their choice for Vice-President, with General Wood, who claimed a residence in Massachusetts, for President. That, of course, could not be, as the Constitution forbids the selection of the President and the Vice-President from the same State. The officers of the Albany Republican Club, of Oregon, wrote asking permission to nominate Mr. Coolidge as a candidate for Vice-President. He refused to allow the use of his name.

Frank W. Stearns was as busy as the Presidential bee

that was buzzing about the Executive Chamber. The original Coolidge man was more convinced than ever that the occupant of the gubernatorial chair on Beacon Hill had the issue—"Law and Order"—which would compel his nomination for President. Mr. Stearns and other friends saw to it that the Governor's book, "Have Faith in Massachusetts," was widely distributed, and it proved a forceful campaign document.

Ex-Senator Crane encouraged the political plans of the Governor's friends. Mr. Coolidge said little, but kept himself well informed of what was going on. After a careful study of the situation, he decided that a poor man had no chance trying to outbid millionaire candidates, or those backed by soap manufacturers and chewing-gum makers. Besides, there was doubt about securing a united delegation from his home State. Just as his campaign committee was getting well started, he called a halt and ordered the closing of his headquarters, and in a statement declining to enter a contest for delegates, he said, "I have never said I would become a candidate for President. I have never accepted, unless by silence, efforts made by statesmen of more than national reputation to present my name to the convention. I have made it plain I could not seek this office.

"Some weeks ago it was represented to me that certain forces in Massachusetts desired to support me. No contest for delegates has ever been contemplated. I have no purpose to enter such contest. The probable outcome of a contest need not be considered at all. It is enough to know that some Massachusetts people intend to make one. The question is whether I ought to permit a contest in my name for delegates in my own State.

"I have taken no position from which I need to withdraw. I do not wish to embarrass anyone. I have a great desire to walk humbly and discharge my obligations. I have not been and I am not a candidate for President."

Senator Lodge headed the Republican delegation to the Chicago nominating convention. His associates were: Ex-Senator Crane, Speaker Gillett of the National House of Representatives and Chairman Thurston of the State Committee. Mr. Lodge was the keynoter and permanent chairman of the convention. There were influential men in the State who declined to enlist under the Coolidge banner. At least two of the Congressional delegation from Massachusetts refused to sign a round-robin endorsement of him. Seven or eight or more of the Massachusetts delegates were off the Coolidge bandwagon, but most of them agreed to give the Governor one or two complimentary ballots. Even Vermont, his native State, cast her lot with General Wood. With the feeling that they had a chance—and only a chance—the friends of Governor Coolidge set out for the Convention city early in June, determined to do everything possible to nominate him. While the delegates to the Convention were struggling with the problem of nominating a Presidential candidate, he remained at his desk at the State House in Boston. The only hope for Mr. Coolidge's nomination lay in the event of a deadlock. The faithful Stearns and a few others of his loyal supporters were on the scene watching every move of the party leaders.

To Frederick H. Gillett, Speaker of the House of Representatives, an old neighbor and friend, was assigned the task of making the nominating speech. Senator Lodge, who had some time before volunteered to do so, found that he had his hands full as presiding officer of the Convention, and was glad to be relieved of the task. There was no love lost between Lodge and those pushing the Coolidge candidacy.

When the little, dispirited band of Coolidge supporters entered the Convention Hall in Chicago, they knew that the chances for nominating their candidate for President were slim. But they stood loyally by him, hoping that something might happen which would swing the Convention his way.

On the first ballot Coolidge received 29 votes, all from Massachusetts. He reached his high-water mark on the second ballot, when he received 32. The stampede for Harding started on the ninth ballot, but the Coolidge delegates from Massachusetts stood pat.

NOMINATED FOR VICE PRESIDENT

Mr. Harding was named for President on the tenth ballot. Then came the nomination for Vice-President. Senator Medill McCormick, of Illinois, nominated Senator Lenroot of Wisconsin. The Senatorial oligarchy who controlled the machinery of the convention struck a snag which upset their plans. Senatorial vigilance was relaxed to permit the delegates to confer. In the din and confusion which reigned, a tall, thin, spare man in the Oregon delegation mounted a chair, shouted "McCammant of Oregon," and was recognized by the presiding officer, Senator Lodge.

"The Oregon delegation came here directed by the Republican electors of our State to present the name of the senior Senator from Massachusetts (Mr. Lodge) as a candidate for Vice-President," said he. "This distinguished stateman has requested that we refrain from presenting his name, and we feel bound to respect his wishes. There is another citizen of Massachusetts who has been much in the public eye during the past year. His nomination for the Vice-Presidency will assure the country that the Republican Party stands foursquare in its loyalty to those principles of law and order which are the foundation on which civilization is builded.

"In this tercentenary year of the landing at Plymouth, it is peculiarly fitting that we put on our National ticket a gentleman of New England birth and ancestry, whose public career exemplifies those principles of liberty under law which his forefathers brought across the Atlantic. Oregon presents the name of Governor Calvin Coolidge of Massachusetts!"

The speech took the Convention by storm. The unexpected move surprised the Massachusetts men as much as it did anybody else. But the moment the latter realized what had happened, they bestirred themselves. Some of them started to parade about the floor of the Convention with "Law and Order" banners, and quicker than it can be told, they started a great demonstration in behalf of the Governor. Delegation after delegation swung into line for Coolidge. The political wire-pullers on the platform saw that the Convention had got away from them and they were powerless to check the stampede. There was only one ballot. Coolidge swept the Convention, receiving 674½ votes; 375 were necessary for a choice.

A story has gone the rounds, that Mr. Lodge labored under the impression that Judge McCammant arose in the Convention to make an inquiry or a simple motion, otherwise he would not have been recognized, and that he was taken aback when the Oregonian proceeded to nominate Coolidge for Vice-President. But the Judge says that Mr. Lodge knew of his purpose when he gave him the floor, as he had conferred with him a few minutes before and had informed him what he was going to do to which Mr. Lodge made no objection.

Great honors came to him unsought in the domain of politics and letters that summer. The political party in which he was cradled called him to a high place in its leadership and two New England universities, Wesleyan and Vermont, conferred upon him the honorary degree of Doctor of Laws. The year also marked the 25th anniversary of his graduation from college, as it did the 15th of his marriage and the 48th of his birth.

Northampton, the home of the Vice-Presidential candidate, gave the Republican ticket a flattering vote, swamping the Democratic candidate by a vote of 1785 to 501, and Massachusetts rolled up a plurality of more than 400,000 for Harding and Coolidge.

One of the humors of the campaign was the support of the Republican presidential ticket by Richard H. Long, twice Coolidge's Democratic opponent for Governor, who announced that there was too much Wilson in the Democratic campaign and that he could no longer support the Democratic ticket. It may be that Mr. Long had in mind Mr. Wilson's congratulatory telegram to Governor Coolidge in the previous year.

Four times before the Nation had come to New England for its Vice-President, and the name of Calvin Coolidge was linked with the names of John Adams, Elbridge Gerry, Hannibal Hamlin and Henry Wilson, all New Englanders. Adams was elected as our first Vice-President, serving both of Washington's terms. Gerry was chosen with Madison in the latter's second term; Hamlin with Lincoln in 1860, and Wilson with Grant in the latter's second election.

DEMOCRATS

THE Democrats held their National nominating convention in San Francisco and sent as delegates-at-large, Senator David I. Walsh, Richard H. Long, Joseph C. Pelletier and Daniel F. Doherty. Daniel H. Coakley rounded up 21 votes for Attorney General Palmer of Pennsylvania for the Presidential nomination. Senator Walsh supported Governor Cox of Ohio, who received six votes from the Massachusetts delegation. Five voted for William G. McAdoo; Owen, 2; Bryan and Al Smith, one each. When it was evident that Palmer could not win, Coakley swung his friends to Cox on the 44th and deciding ballot, nominating the Ohio Governor. Cox's manager offered the Vice-Presidential nomination to Senator Walsh. It was represented to Senator Walsh by the Cox managers that inasmuch as the Republicans had taken their ticket from Ohio and Massachusetts and the Democrats had chosen Ohio's Governor as their standard-bearer, they would be willing to take him on to offset Coolidge in Massachusetts, but Senator Walsh resisted all arguments and persuasion brought to bear on him, saying that he was not a candidate and believed that it would be good party policy to take a man from the Pacific Coast for second place on the ticket.

ALVAN T. FULLER WINS LIEUTENANT GOVERNORSHIP

COOLIDGE'S nomination as running mate on the Harding Presidential ticket left the gubernatorial field free for Lieutenant Governor Cox and opened up a lively contest for second place on the State ticket. The candidates were Alvan T. Fuller, Albert P. Langtry, Secretary of State, and Joseph S. Warner, Speaker of the House of Representatives. Likewise the aspirations of Secretary of State Langtry threw open his position to a free-for-all, which was won by Frederick W. Cook, against a field of four opponents. He is still serving in that capacity to the satisfaction of the people.

The contest for the nomination was about the most spirited fight the G.O.P. experienced in years for a place on the State ticket. The four cornered contest soon simmered down between Speaker Warner and Congressman Fuller. In Congress, to which Fuller was elected in 1916, as an Independent, over the sitting member, Ernest W. Roberts, Mr. Fuller had attracted nation-wide attention by his assaults on the unbusiness-like methods of that body and his criticism of Old Guard Republican leadership. He shared with President Wilson the belief that world peace was desirable and necessary for the welfare of all peoples. A man of means, Fuller did not draw his salary as Congressman, accept mileage or use the franking privilege. He was soon tired of his job and decided to seek State honors at home making things lively for those opposed to him.

Mr. Fuller trained his guns on Speaker Warner, charging that the latter's law partner represented corporations at the State House on legislation. There is nothing mealy-mouthed about Alvan T. Fuller. He calls a spade a spade and graft graft, and told the voters that there was too much crooked politics in public affairs. His charges against Speaker Warner resulted in a libel suit which came to trial two years later when the plaintiff was awarded damages of one dollar. Mr. Fuller won the nomination for Lieutenant Governor leading Warner by about 3300 votes. The vote was; Fuller, 59,685; Warner, 56,346; Burrill, 52,264; Langtry, 38,147.

JOSEPH P. CARNEY

Collector Internal Revenue, Administrator C.W.A., Emergency Relief Administrator, R.F.C. Representative, Boston.

ANOTHER WALSH RUNS

RICHARD H. LONG, reputed millionaire business man of Framingham, twice an unsuccessful Democratic gubernatorial candidate, was defeated for a third nomination in the primaries of 1920, by a newcomer in the gubernatorial field, John Jackson Walsh. Walsh two years before had defeated Simon Swig for the Senate in the Eighth Suffolk Republican district. While Long was touring the State discussing Governor Coolidge's handling of the Boston Police strike, Walsh was making speeches in his district about "money bags in politics" and attempts to buy the Democratic gubernatorial nomination. Walsh's nomination for Governor was a bit of a surprise to the politicians if not himself. He pointed out in his campaign speeches that while Governor Coolidge paid $32.00 for his house in Northampton, he was obliged to pay $47.00 a month for an apartment in Boston.

The State Convention was held in Springfield. The report of the Committee on Credentials stated that 2081 delegates were entitled to seats in the convention and that 500 were present, but at no time were there more than 250 in the hall. Few of the leaders showed any interest in the gathering. They knew that with Walsh it was a forlorn hope.

At the time, affairs in Ireland interested many of the delegates more than domestic problems. By a vote of 79 to 60 it was voted to send a cable to Premier Lloyd George of England, demanding the release of Mayor

McSwiney of Cork, Ireland, then on a hunger strike in jail, but there was no rush to the cable office with the message. The permanent chairman of the convention was Marcus A. Coolidge of Fitchburg, who was nominated for second place on the State ticket.

The platform endorsed Cox and Roosevelt for President and Vice-President and commended the Wilson administration. On the League of Nations the platform had this to say:—

"We believe that the League of Nations is essential to world peace, and we further believe that the just settlement of the status of Ireland is essential to make that peace permanent. We, therefore, urge upon the Government of the United States that it present to the League of Nations as its first business the application of the principle of self-determination to Ireland, and we justify this demand by reasserting our belief in the principle contained in the Declaration of Independence that all Governments derive their just powers from the consent of the governed."

The Republican State administration was condemned as "inefficient," favored regulation of the stock exchange, non-contributory old age pensions and the abolishments of party enrollment. The result was not hard to see. The tide was running swiftly against the Democrats in State and Nation, but what Democrats there were sufficiently interested in keeping the party organization alive, put up the best fight they could, with certain defeat inevitable.

ANOTHER REPUBLICAN SWEEP

THE result of the National and State elections in November was practically a sweep for the Republicans. Harding's vote in the State for President was 681,153; Cox, Democrat, 276,691; Socialist, 32,265. Republicans elected 14 out of the 16 members of Congress and an overwhelming majority of the Legislature. Cox for Governor received 643,869 votes, John J. Walsh, Democrat, 290,350; Hutchins, Socialist, 20,079; Milligan, Socialist-Labor, 6383. The increase in the size of the vote this year was due to the adoption of the suffrage amendment permitting women to vote.

Robert M. Washburn, who had taken up the cudgels in behalf of Speaker Warner in the primary contest, accusing Fuller of resorting to unfair tactics, carried his fight to the polls election day, running as an Independent. He received 133,480 votes. The vote for Lieutenant Governor was: Fuller, Republican, 506,313; Marcus Coolidge, Democrat, 270,324; Nicholson, Socialist, 18,870; Craig, Socialist-Labor, 6,972.

Democratic Boston would have nothing to do with the League of Nations and gave the Republican electoral ticket a plurality of 33,000 votes, a rebuke such as the Democratic party had not received since it turned its back on Bryan and silver, thirty-four years before. Among the Democrats who bolted Cox were George Fred Williams, who said there were 14 reasons why he voted for Harding, and Daniel T. O'Connell, now a Judge of the Superior

Court, who could not support the Democratic candidate because he was for the Wilson League of Nations. O'Connell had taken a prominent part in advocating freedom for Ireland.

CHANNING H. COX

Governor 1921-1925

LIEUTENANT GOVERNOR CHANNING H. Cox, the first Governor to be elected under the new biennial law, one of the products of the Constitutional Convention, succeeded Calvin Coolidge as Governor and was inaugurated January 6, 1921. Congressman Alvan T. Fuller became Lieutenant Governor. The political escalator was running smoothly. Mr. Cox was schooled in the political ranks of old Ward 10, Boston, sandwiched in between the Back Bay and the South End, the bailiwick of Charles H. Innes, for many years its leader, a practical politician and one of the few Republican district leaders able to deliver a sizable block of votes election day. Cox was one of his lieutenants and Innes saw to it that when honors were being passed around Cox was not forgotten. Beginning as a member of the Old Common Council, Mr. Cox climbed steadily up the political ladder, serving as a member of the House of Representatives, twice its Speaker and followed Calvin Coolidge as Lieutenant Governor. In the Legislature he was alert and aggressive, an able debater and popular with his associates. Mr.

Coolidge was fond of him and powerful friends helped to smooth his path to the highest office in the Commonwealth.

His inaugural was long and opened with a plea for economy. The 20th amendment to the Federal Constitution, giving women the suffrage, had just been adopted and he urged legislation to provide for them a full participation in public affairs. He advocated better pay for women teachers in the public school and the fixing of the minimum salary of $550 a year for them, stricter regulation for the safeguarding of public funds and government regulation of securities offered the public. He called attention to the increasing number of accidents to children by motor vehicles and asked for a law to lessen the danger. The coal and money shortage were referred to and he asked the Legislature to authorize the State to take on all penal institutions in the interest of economy and efficiency.

He favored the short ballot, permitting the Governor to appoint the Secretary of State, State Treasurer and Attorney General. He pleaded for a suitable memorial to the World War veterans, but that had to wait several years before anything definite was done and the Legislature was cold to the short ballot plan.

The most important measures passed by the Legislature of 1921, of which B. Loring Young was Speaker and Frank G. Allen was President of the Senate, were: Extension of the law relating to educational certificates of minors employed in various occupations; a law providing for the marking and sealing of cans and containers used in the wholesale distribution of milk or cream; relating to the disposition of motor vehicle fees and fines and to appropriations for the State's share of the expense in maintaining boulevards in the metropolitan district; provision for the appointment of a special commission on the necessaries of life to study and investigate the circumstances affecting the price of fuel and other essential commodities; authorizing savings banks to establish and maintain safe deposit vaults and to rent boxes therein; game protection; assistance for feeble-minded persons.

GRAFT

DURING the Legislative session, another graft investigation flared up over charges brought to the attention of Governor Cox by Sherman Whipple, a well known member of the Boston bar, in which he alleged that members of the General Court had speculated in Boston Elevated stock while legislation was pending on the Elevated Control bill in 1918, which authorized the taking over a bankrupt, run-down transportation system, spent millions of the taxpayers' money to rejuvenate and improve it and guaranteed the dividends to its stockholders.

Representative Lomasney of Boston started the ball rolling during the debate on a resolve in the House, directing the trustees of the Elevated to report on the advisability of instituting a five-cent fare on lines of the system in South Boston and Dorchester. He charged that certain legislators "helped ravish the people when the Elevated act was passed in 1918."

Following Lomasney's charges Lieutenant Governor Fuller submitted an order in the Executive Council which that body adopted, directing the bank commissioner to report to the Council the list of unsecured notes of members of the Legislature in 1918 in the Cosmopolitan, Hanover, Prudential and Fidelity Trust Companies. The Vice-President of the latter institution was Edwin T. McKnight, President of the State Senate, a fly-by-night financier who was a controlling factor in several small banks in Greater Boston. Mr. Fuller charged that somebody had been unduly active in trying to prevent the investigation. The echoes of his fight with Ex-Speaker Joseph Warner for the Lieutenant Governorship still reverberated through the marble halls of the State House. In his opinion, Bank Commissioner Allen needed a little prodding on the matter and he got it from the peppery second in command of the Executive Department.

Governor Cox, after a conference with his advisers, including Frank G. Allen, President of the Senate, announced that while he would not knowingly do any man an injustice, "If any man has done wrong he must stand the consequences." The committee of the Legislature appointed to investigate the charges brought out the fact that McKnight's bank had loaned $450,000 to members of the Legislature, relatives and associates to assist them in stock speculation; that 36 members of the Legislature of 1918, 32 Republicans and four Democrats, had engaged in dealings with stock; that thirteen of them were members of the Senate of 1918 when the Elevated Public Control Act was passed; that nine of them were members of the Joint Street Railway and Metropolitan Affairs Committee which sat on the "El" bill; that four of them were members of the sub-committee of six dealing with the problem and that seven members of the sitting legislature were involved, namely: Senators Walter E. McLane of Fall River, Henry Clark of Boston, John Halliwell of New Bedford, Representatives George M. Worrall of Attleboro, Andrew P. Doyle of New Bedford, Ernest A. Larocque of Fall River and Clarence P. Kidder of Cambridge.

Evidence showed that Senator McLean reaped the biggest harvest in stock manipulations. Governor Cox was called as a witness. He testified that he served on the recess committee which considered the street railway question, that he believed the "service at cost" **was** the best plan submitted and supported it, but that he had never dealt in "El" other street railway stocks. The name of Vice-President Coolidge was brought into the investigation, the allegation was made that he had brought pressure to bear on at least one member of the Legislature to support the public control measure, but this he denied in a letter to the committee. He stated that he believed the public control bill was the best solution of the problem and that he had the utmost confidence in the personnel of the commission he had named under the act.

MASSACHUSETTS POLITICS 313

Representative John W. McCormack of Boston, secretary of the committee, dissented from some of the findings of his associates. In his opinion, members of the committee had used their inside official knowledge for personal profit. The committee's report was regarded as a whitewash. The bankers and brokers involved were exonerated. There was talk of the District Attorney of Suffolk taking action, but nothing was done and the matter was soon forgotten by the public.

FIRST WOMEN LEGISLATORS

In the Legislature of 1922 women sat for the first time in the history of the State. Two women members were chosen, Mrs. Susan W. Fitzgerald of Boston, a Democrat, and Miss Sylvia Donaldson of Brockton, a Republican. Mrs. Fitzgerald was the daughter of Admiral Walker, U.S.N. Both had taken an active part in the suffrage movement and were women of unusual ability, well equipped for their legislative duties.

The movement for censoring the movies was defeated on a referendum by a four to one vote at the polls. A new State Commission of administration and finance was set up and three bureaus created within the new body—a comptroller's bureau, a budget bureau and a central purchasing agency. There was a revision of the banking laws, designed to remedy the effects brought to light by the Ponzi scandal in 1920; a law was passed in an effort to relieve the congestion in the courts; a landing field for airplanes in East Boston was authorized; a new section was added to the corrupt practices act forbidding the making or publishing of false statements against candidates for public office.

SENATOR LODGE'S REËLECTION

SENATOR LODGE was up for election in the fall of 1922 for a sixth term in the Senate of the United States. In his last election he defeated his Democratic opponent, John F. Fitzgerald, by a plurality of 33,000. It was the first time Mr. Lodge ran the gauntlet of a popular vote. Much against his will, he had to take the stump. His opposition to the League of Nations embittered the followers of Woodrow Wilson. To Mr. Lodge was assigned the role of curtain dropper at the closing scene of the historic tragedy of the Wilson administration, when, as the Senate's representative, it was his duty to notify Mr. Wilson that the Senate had transacted all of its business and was ready to adjourn to make way for the coming in of the Harding régime. Those who were privileged to witness the meeting of these two opposing political leaders—Wilson broken in health and Lodge erect and militant—will never forget the memorable scene as the latter conveyed the Senate's message and President Wilson's cutting manner replying that he had no further communication to make to that body. There was a studied coolness in Mr. Wilson's curt answer as he dismissed the Republican spokesman.

Temperance Republicans were against Senator Lodge for his vote against the 18th (Prohibition) amendment. He had been against almost all of the reforms, such as the popular election of United States Senators, woman suffrage and the initiative and referendum. His opponent at the previous election stepped aside for Colonel Gaston, who made a vigorous campaign, but he lacked the enthusiastic support of Senator Walsh, who took the ground that he could not make an active campaign against his Senatorial colleague, Mr. Lodge, and confined his efforts to the State ticket.

Senator Lodge suffered from the lukewarmness of his party leaders, many of whom held aloof. He was obliged to rely on a few faithful friends to run his campaign. Towards the last of the contest he suffered from a severe attack of bronchitis which obliged him to cancel several important speaking engagements. Election day he managed to squeeze by with a plurality of 8354, the vote being Lodge, 414,130; Gaston, 406,776. The aggregate vote cast against him totalled 456,997. Of this vote, John A. Nichols, a Dry, received 24,866. The "Liberal Republican League," which was active in the campaign against Mr. Lodge, disputed the election and threatened to contest the seat. The Senator refused to take the proceedings against him seriously and nothing came of them. It was the Senator's last election. His senatorial career was drawing to a close. He had lost much of his old punch. Ere long he was to experience the ingratitude of politicians he had helped to achieve high places in the State and Nation.

COX'S SECOND TERM

In launching his candidacy for a second term in 1922, Governor Cox had reason for exclaiming: "Save me from my friends!" A group of his admirers, headed by Ernest J. Goulston, an enthusiastic well meaning supporter, arranged for a dinner to be given at the Quincy House in his honor. The local prohibition enforcement officer, Harold D. Wilson, staged a sensational raid after the Governor left the banquet and seized a small quantity of liquor. Wilson, a fanatical dry and publicity seeker, made the most of the unpleasant incident. Governor Cox satisfied his friends that he was innocent of flouting the prohibition law. The affair soon died down and shortly after Mr. Wilson was transferred to another post outside of New England. He was a dangerous official to have around for a party aligned with the Drys in a State none too strong for prohibition.

Governor Cox had to fight for his second nomination. An ambitious enemy within his own gates challenged his right to a second term. As usual, in a family row, the quarrel was bitter and personal. His opponent, Attorney General J. Weston Allen, had led the court battle for the successful removal of District Attorney Nathan A. Tufts of Middlesex County and Joseph C. Pelletier, the former prominent in the Republican party and the latter a leading Democrat. Besides the removal of these two officials, Allen and his assistants brought about the conviction of former District Attorney William J. Corcoran, Tuft's predecessor, who received a State prison sentence and the disbarment of Daniel H. Coakley, one of the best known and successful lawyers of Boston. Tufts left the State. Pelletier died soon after his removal. Coakley subsequently defended himself in court and was found not guilty by a jury of the charges in certain cases on which he had been disbarred. Always active and interested in Democratic politics, he became an unsuccessful candidate for Mayor of Boston and later was three times elected member of the Executive Council, while his petition for reinstatement at the bar was pending. Many leading citizens of the State, including Cardinal O'Connell and other churchmen, members of the bar, Governor Ely and all of his eight Republican associates in the Executive Council, joined in asking the court to grant his petition, but it was denied by Associate Justice Field of the Supreme Judicial Court.

Allen made a lively campaign against Governor Cox, charging a lack of support by the Governor in these cases because the name of Charles H. Innes, friend and political supporter of the Governor, was involved in the scandals. The Governor was incensed at Allen's charges and proved that he could fight. He took the stump and vehemently denied his opponent's statements. Most of the Republican leaders rallied to his support and he easily routed the Attorney General for the nomination and defeated his

Democratic opponent, John F. Fitzgerald, at the polls by 60,000 plurality. The vote for Governor was: Cox, 464,873; Fitzgerald, 404,192.

Lieutenant Governor Fuller was reëlected over John F. Doherty, his Democratic opponent, by 128,000 plurality. The Republicans lost one Congressional seat this year, William P. Connery, Democrat, of Lynn, winning in the 7th District.

PRESIDENT COOLIDGE

PRESIDENT HARDING left Washington late in June, 1923, on a trip to Alaska, accompanied by his wife, members of his Cabinet and his White House staff. On his way to our farthest-north possession he delivered a number of important speeches, indicating what he had in mind to recommend to the Sixty-eighth Congress, which would meet in December following. While in Alaska it was reported that Mr. Harding was suffering from an attack of ptomaine poisoning. On the return journey to California, disquieting reports reached the public regarding the President's health. Soon after arriving in San Francisco he was obliged to go to bed, a very sick man.

Vice-President Coolidge, following his annual custom, was enjoying his vacation on his father's farm in Vermont. He was engaged in doctoring a big maple tree that stands at the end of the house, removing the decayed part and making it ready to fill the cavity with cement, when tidings of President Harding's sickness reached him.

There was no railroad or telegraph at the "Notch" and the nearest long distance telephone was in the general store at the "Union," two miles down the mountain side.

The night of August 2, Mr. Coolidge retired at his usual early hour. The little town was as quiet as a graveyard. Shortly after midnight, an automobile could be heard chugging up the steep hill to the "Notch." It stopped at the little white cottage on the right of the road, on top of the hill.

The figure of a man could be faintly seen, dashing by the headlights of the car and rushing up to the front door of the Coolidge home. He pounded on the door and in a few moments a head appeared out of one of the chamber windows. It was the President's father.

"What is wanted?" he asked.

"President Harding is dead and I have a telegram for the Vice-President," said the breathless caller, a telegraph messenger, who had come from Bridgewater, six miles distant.

"I'll come right down," said Colonel Coolidge. Dressing quickly, he aroused his son and daughter-in-law, who were sleeping on the same floor.

In a few moments he opened the door and invited the messenger to step in, leading the way to the sitting room. He took the message, went back to his son's room and read to him the communication from George B. Christian, Secretary to President Harding, informing the Vice-President of the death of his chief. This was followed by another telegram from Attorney-General Daugherty, advising Mr. Coolidge to qualify as President with as little delay as possible.

Mr. and Mrs. Coolidge dressed hurriedly and soon appeared in the sitting room. The Vice-President, saddened by the unexpected and shocking information, moved noiselessly about giving instructions to the household as to what was to be done.

Word of the President's death reached the newspaper men at Ludlow about midnight. In a very short time, linemen were tapping a telephone trunk-line at the "Union" and connecting the Coolidge house. At 2.30 A.M. the Vice-President was enabled to talk with Secretary Hughes at Washington, who advised him that it was his duty to start for the capital as soon as possible, after taking the oath. At the conclusion of his telephone talk with Mr. Hughes, the Vice-President informed those present that his father, a Notary Public, would administer the oath of office.

A STRANGE INAUGURATION

THE old-fashioned clock on the mantel indicated 2.47 A.M. when Colonel Coolidge commanded his son to raise his right hand. The elder Coolidge's voice broke slightly as he read the oath, Calvin repeating it after him. When the Vice-President uttered the last word of the prescribed oath, he placed his hand on the open Bible and with great solemnity added: "So help me God!"

The 29th President of the United States turned to his wife and she embraced him. His father extended his congratulations as did the others privileged to witness the strangest of all Presidential inaugurations. For the first time in our history, a father swore his son in as President of the United States.

Calling his acting secretary, Mr. Geisser, the new President led the way to the dining room, and dictated a brief statement to the country, in which he said he would carry through the policies of the late President, and expressed the desire that members of the Cabinet remain in office in order that he might have their assistance.

The President retired shortly after 3 A.M. but sleep was out of the question. There were too many things to think about—too much to be done. He was up shortly after six. At daylight the townsfolk began to gather.

He decided to leave on the regular train from Rutland at 9.30 A.M. When all was ready for the start from Plymouth, he was seen to leave the house alone and go across the field to the little cemetery on Grandfather Coolidge's farm, adjoining that of his father. Stopping in front of a little white marble headstone, he removed his hat, bowed his head, and for three or four minutes appeared to be deep in meditation.

Rejoining Mrs. Coolidge, he bade his father farewell and gave orders to his chauffeur to drive slowly on the way to Rutland. There he was met by Governor Redfield Proctor and several other prominent Vermonters, who accompanied him to Albany, where he boarded another train for New York City. Crossing from the Grand

Central Station to the Pennsylvania Station, another special train carried him to the National capital.

At Washington he was met by Secretary Hughes and Postmaster-General New, the only two members of the Cabinet in the city at the time.

With Mrs. Coolidge and the members of the Cabinet, he met Mrs. Harding and the members of the funeral escort on the arrival of the train from San Francisco. Mr. and Mrs. Coolidge led the official mourners to the Capitol the following day and the escort of the body to the railroad station the same evening, when the funeral train left for Marion, Ohio, President Harding's home.

SETTLES COAL STRIKE

THE first important public question which Mr. Coolidge gave his attention to on his return from Mr. Harding's funeral was the threatened strike of the anthracite coal miners in Pennsylvania, scheduled for September 1st. He went about this in his customary way, calling into consultation the properly constituted authorities. He sent for the members of the Coal Fact Finding Commission, Secretary Hoover of the Department of Commerce and Commissioner Eastman, of the Interstate Commerce Commission, telling them that it was time that the Government agencies bestirred themselves and did everything in their power to prevent the threatened strike. Advised by the Attorney-General that there was no law authorizing him to interfere in the controversy, as matters stood, Mr. Coolidge referred the matter to Governor Pinchot of Pennsylvania, within whose jurisdiction the hard coal mines are situated, and who appeared to be the properly constituted authority to deal with the question.

Governor Pinchot went about his difficult task with characteristic enthusiasm and succeeded in bringing owners and workmen together. After a protracted parley, they settled their differences. Both sides made concessions. The miners gave up their demand for the continuance of the "check-off" and the owners granted a substantial increase in the wage and recognized the Union.

To be sure, the cost was passed along to the consumer, by adding a dollar or more per ton to his coal bill, but the public was glad to be assured of an ample supply at any price, and did not relish the idea of passing through another coal shortage like the year before.

The first meeting of the Cabinet was held Tuesday, August 14th, and was devoted to a general discussion of the problems confronting the Administration. By the end of the following week, Mrs. Harding had moved her personal effects from the White House and on the afternoon of the 21st, Mr. and Mrs. Coolidge took up their residence there.

LEGISLATURE, 1923

The Legislature of 1923 organized by reëlecting Frank G. Allen, President of the Senate and B. Loring Young

Speaker of the House. Both Houses reëlected their clerks and chaplains and joined in the reëlection of Charles O. Holt, Sergeant-at-Arms. For the first time two women sat as members of the House, Susan W. Fitzgerald, Democrat, from the 22nd Suffolk district and M. Sylvia Donaldson, Republican, representing the 10th Plymouth district. In thanking the members for again honoring him, Speaker Young pointed out to the Republican members the importance of legislation this year, a presidential year, and extended a cordial welcome to the woman Republican member, the members arising and cheering her. Mr. Jewett of Lowell was continued majority floor leader, John C. Hull was again chairman of the Judicial Committee and Henry L. Shattuck was chairman of Ways and Means. It was the latter's fourth year as a member of this important committee. He enjoyed the reputation of one of the leading authorities on State and municipal finance in the Commonwealth and a high type of legislator.

Edward F. Harrington of Fall River begrudgingly received the votes of 79 Democratic members for Speaker of the House, some of the Democrats feeling that he was not sufficiently aggressive on radical measures.

In the Senate, Frank G. Allen received 37 of the 40 votes for President of that branch, three Democrats refusing to join in making his election unanimous. In assuming his duties, Mr. Allen said, "I cannot commend to you too strongly the policies of our Governor and especially his desire to have all matters of State handled with true economy and on a strictly pay-as-you-go basis.

I am sure I voice the sentiments of every one of you in pledging to Governor Cox our assistance in carrying out those policies inaugurated by him during his last term and which resulted not only in lowering the State tax but also in very substantially reducing the State debt."

His closing bit of advice was: "The way to save money is not to spend it."

With the delivery of the address of Governor Cox, in which he reviewed the finances of the State and made suggestions for legislation in the public interest, the General Court of 1924 buckled down to its work, remained in session 144 days and adjourned May 26th.

Among the most important legislation of the year were: providing for the appointment of a commission to investigate jury service with special reference to the service of women on juries and the extent to which present facilities must be altered if women are made eligible for such service; requiring the consent of the mother as well as the father to the marriage of a minor; punishing bribery of police officers by forfeit of office and permanent disqualification for public office; making it unlawful to possess a revolver in a vehicle; centralizing the personnel and financial side of the government under a commission of four, under which the comptroller's bureau, a budget bureau, a purchasing bureau and a bureau of personnel, the commission to have charge of the budget and to investigate the workings of the departments; forbidding the unauthorized use of names of political parties; accepting the uniform limited partnership act approved by the National Conference of Commissioners on uniform State laws; permitting sale of pure alcohol and liquor on a physician's certificate; creating a coöperative association to facilitate marketing of farm products; permitting public officials to inspect coal and to seize that not fit for ordinary use; taxing the income of corporations making profits from real estate; forbidding discrimination based on sex among teachers in Boston. Considerable legislation looking to the widening of educational facilities of the State was passed by the Legislature of 1923, including an act aiding towns for the cost of school transportation, acts to promote civic education through courses in United States history and civics and the Constitution of the United States. The minimum salary for public school teachers was fixed at $750 a year for full time teachers.

GOVERNOR McCALL'S DEATH

Ex-Governor McCall took no active part in public affairs after his retirement from the Governorship. He was inclined to side with Woodrow Wilson's peace policy. The latter had a high regard for him and was reported to be anxious to find a place for him in his administration, but always there loomed the fear that if his name came before the Senate, both Massachusetts Senators might raise objections to him and prevent his confirmation by that body. Thus he was forced to be a mere looker-on, denied the opportunity of contributing his

SHERMAN L. WHIPPLE

JAMES J. STORROW

CHARLES F. COTTER

JOHN A. KELIHER

ALLEN T. TREADWAY

ARTHUR D. HILL

recognized talents of statesmanship and diplomacy, so much needed in post war problems. He lived quietly and unostentatiously at his Winchester home where the end came after a brief illness, November 4, 1933.

NATIONAL CAMPAIGN OF 1924
Republicans

THE task that President Coolidge faced on the death of President Harding presented many difficult problems arising out of the World War. At the start of his administration Mr. Harding invited Vice-President Coolidge to sit in at meetings of his cabinet, an innovation in National administrations, affording the Vice-President an opportunity to familiarize himself with the policies and problems of the administration.

Soon after Mr. Harding's death the country was stirred by scandals in the Veterans' Bureau, the Naval oil leases, the activities of the "Ohio gang," composed of a number of close personal friends of the late President, who operated chiefly in the Department of Justice, graft and corruption in the office of the Custodian of Alien property, taken over from German and Austrian owners when the United States entered the World War.

The first major scandal to be aired by a Senate committee dealt with graft and corruption in the Veterans' Bureau and resulted in the trial, conviction and jailing of Charles R. Forbes, its chief. It is believed that President Harding became aware of the state of affairs in that Bureau before he left on his fatal trip to Alaska. Washington had it that the President sent for Forbes and accused him of being a false friend and that the interview was a stormy one.

OIL SCANDAL

THIS was followed by the revelations of the naval oil leases and the Tea Pot Dome scandal, involving former Secretary of the Interior, Albert B. Fall of the Harding Cabinet, an Admiral of the Navy, Secretary of the Navy and his assistant, Theodore Roosevelt. Fall was convicted of bribery and served a jail sentence. Public indignation forced Denby and Roosevelt's resignations.

Then was bared graft and corruption in the Justice Department. At first President Coolidge stood by his Attorney-General whom he had inherited from Harding, but Senator Walsh of Montana succeeded in tracing the corruption closer and closer to Daugherty. Jess Smith, one of the Ohio gang, who had a desk in the Department of Justice, but no official connection with the government and was regarded as the Mr. Fixit and go-between for bootleggers and other law breakers, committed suicide. Finally, when public opinion began to insist that Attorney-General Daugherty be dropped, and no member of the Senate, except the two members from Ohio, could be found to defend him, Mr. Coolidge called for his resignation and named in his place Harlan B. Stone, a prominent New York lawyer and graduate of Amherst College, Coolidge's alma mater.

Congress rejected several of the important measures of President Coolidge. As usual, the country was with the President and against Congress. Nobody blamed Mr. Coolidge for the corruption in the Harding administration. The country as a whole was well pleased with its New England chief executive. He chose for his campaign manager an old friend, William M. Butler of Massachusetts. After the nomination Mr. Butler became Chairman of the National Committee and conducted the Presidential campaign.

LEGISLATURE, 1924

LIKE its predecessor the Legislature of 1924 was heavily Republican. There was no change in the presiding officers of either branch. When it adjourned June 5th, it had added to the "Blue Book" 510 acts and 70 resolves, much of it of little importance outside of the communities and individuals affected. Among the outstanding acts were the Northern Artery bill, a new highway, the Boston Charter amendments, extensions of the Metropolitan Water Supply system, the return of $2,000,000 to the cities and towns and the reduction of the State tax. During Governor Cox's four years, 2307 chapters of new law were added to the statute books.

It was a great year for the favorites of the presiding officers of both branches. Eight special recess commissions were named to investigate as many different subjects and report their findings to the next Legislature, for which they received liberal compensation. Chief among the laws enacted by the Legislature of 1924 were: the workmen's compensation law, further liberalized, the child labor law limiting working hours to 48 a week; eight hours a day on State contract work, extending the powers of the registrar of motor vehicles to suspend and revoke the license of any person operating a motor which causes the death of another.

COOLIDGE UNOPPOSED FOR NOMINATION
1924

No other name was mentioned for President when the convention met in Cleveland. It was a Coolidge gathering from start to finish. The Massachusetts delegates-at-large were: Governor Channing Cox, Senator Lodge, Speaker Gillett of the National House of Representatives and William M. Butler. The alternates were: General John H. Sherburne, a soldier with a fine World War record, Mrs. Anna C. Bird, widow of the late Charles Sumner Bird of Walpole, Jessie A. Hall of Worcester and Charles H. Innes of Boston. Among the District Delegates were William F. Whiting of Holyoke, a close personal friend of the President, Bernard W. Doyle of

Leominster, Congressman A. Piatt Andrew of Gloucester, Frank Baird of Malden, Thomas W. White of Newton, George L. Barnes of Weymouth and A. C. Ratshesky of Boston.

It was the first national political convention to be broadcast by radio as it was also the first to be seen by wire. Photographs were transmitted to New York in less than five minutes by the new process of telephoty. The Ku Klux Klan was represented by its Imperial Wizard, Hiram W. Evans, who was there to prevent any reference to his organization in the platform. Wayne B. Wheeler, Generalissimo of the Anti-Saloon League, was on hand to see that no encouragement was given the Republican wets. He declared that the latter would get about as many votes for a wet plank as a declaration restoring slavery. The Drys held a mortgage on both of the leading political parties at the time and both obeyed Wheeler's orders.

Before the convention met, Senator La Follette of Wisconsin gave out a statement demanding an extra session of Congress to deal with the relief of agriculture, direct primaries for the nomination of President and a declaration ruling Ex-Attorney General Daugherty out of the party. Little attention was paid to his demands. He was laying the foundation for his impending bolt and preparing the way for his independent candidacy for President on the Progressive ticket with Senator Wheeler of Montana, a Democrat running for Vice-President. Wheeler refused to support John W. Davis the Democratic Presidential nominee.

SENATOR LODGE HUMILIATED

IN this convention the Coolidgeites evened an old score with Senator Lodge. When the Coolidge-for-President campaign was launched in 1920, Mr. Lodge was lukewarm. He was an important cog in the Senate oligarchy which controlled the 1920 convention when Harding was nominated. In making their State convention slate in 1924, the President's friends put Governor Cox at the head of the group and Senator Lodge in second place. For more than 40 years Mr. Lodge had been a powerful figure in the party. His place was always at the head table. His word was law and he was wont to have a hand in dictating convention slates, but this year he was not only deprived of his power and reduced to the ranks, but humiliated by being denied a place on the platform committee. Friends interceded for him. Chairman Butler was appealed to, but he would do nothing to change the program.

Men whom Lodge had elevated to place and power in Massachusetts grinned at his humiliation and made no effort to stay the hand of the executioner. The Senator bore his punishment in silence. He was a mere looker-on at the Cleveland convention, with no voice in the committee on resolutions or the mechanics of the convention, notwithstanding he had presided over more Republican conventions and had written more platforms than any living Republican. His fighting days were over—his power gone, but he was too proud to complain, too loyal a party man to start a rift in its ranks.

Senator Fess of Ohio was the keynoter, Ex-Representative Frank W. Mondell of Wyoming the permanent presiding officer. The platform praised the administration, stressed the support of legislation in behalf of invalid war veterans, declared for the child labor amendment to the Federal Constitution, endorsed the pending "lame duck" amendment for changing the date of the meeting of Congress and the inauguration of the President from March to January, favored joining the World Court, called for the punishment of guilty Federal officials involved in the oil scandals and declared the Japanese to be "uncongenial to our industrial life." A minority report was offered by Congressman Cooper of Wisconsin, speaking for the La Follette wing of the party. He was booed and told to get out. The majority report was overwhelmingly adopted.

Dr. Marion Le Roy Burton, President of the University of Michigan, placed Mr. Coolidge in nomination and he was named on the first ballot, tabulated as follows: Coolidge, 1005; La Follette, 34, 38 of which were cast by the Wisconsin delegation, and 10 for Hiram Johnson of California, although he had withdrawn his name.

VICE-PRESIDENCY

THE Vice-Presidency was the most troublesome problem the Coolidgeites had to deal with. Senator Borah was Mr. Coolidge's first choice. The Senator had been one of the President's firmest supporters in Congress except on agriculture legislation. Mr. Coolidge often consulted the Idahoan to the displeasure of the Old Guard, who hated him. Borah was quoted as saying that Coolidge had made the White House a respectable place to live in. He could have been the convention keynoter, but he was unwilling to gloss over the scandals of the Harding régime. During the convention, Borah was summoned to the White House. Asked to run on the Coolidge ticket, he is reported to have good naturedly asked, "at which end," and refused to give up his Senate seat.

Ex-Governor Frank O. Lowden of Illinois, "Pullman's favorite son-in-law," who messed up things four years before and was forced out of the Presidential nomination contest in 1920 by an exposé of his campaign expenses, was nominated for second place on the ticket. He promptly declined by telegraph. The administration then tried to put over Herbert Hoover, but the Old Guard would have nothing to do with this newcomer. Ignoring the wishes of the President, the convention nominated General Charles G. Dawes, of Illinois, "Hell and Maria Dawes," the best advertised noncombatant hero of the World War. Concentrating all of its strength on Hoover, the administration forces led by Chairman Butler were able to cast but 334½ votes for him against 682½ for Dawes. The President accepted the decision of the convention with outward grace, but it was an open secret that he was not overjoyed at the convention's choice.

DEMOCRATS

THE Democrats held their 1924 National convention at Madison Square Garden, New York. It proved to be one of the most exciting and long drawn out gatherings of that party in years. Its first session was held June 25. Its final session 15 days later. During the turmoil there were times when fear was expressed that history would repeat itself and the party would again find itself hopelessly split, as it was in 1860, unable to agree on either a platform or a candidate, resulting in a bolt and the naming of two presidential tickets, but its final session was a love feast in which John W. Davis of West Virginia was named for President and Governor Charles W. Bryan of Nebraska, brother of William Jennings Bryan, for Vice-President.

When the leaders decided to take Davis as the nominee, the question of his bona fide residence arose. At one time in his career, Mr. Davis represented his home West Virginia district in Congress and was credited to that State when he was named as Solictor General of the Treasury in the Wilson administration. After he returned as Ambassador to England, he settled in New York and had a residence on Long Island, but Mr. Davis insisted that West Virginia was his home.

Geographically, the ticket was ideal, but the candidates had little in common. Davis was a Conservative and counsel for the Morgan banking house. The Vice-Presidential nominee stood for all of the political reforms and so-called vagaries of his brother, William. A more incongruous ticket was difficult to imagine.

Davis entered the contest for the nomination at the start, but he had only a handful of delegates outside of his native state—31 in all. As the balloting went on, day after day, Davis kept adding to this strength and earned the right to be regarded as a "dark horse" by his friends, who felt sure that after the two chief contenders for the nomination, Governor Smith of New York and William G. McAdoo of California, former secretary of the Treasury and son-in-law of President Wilson, had deadlocked the convention, the delegates would turn to Davis as a compromise.

That happened on the 103rd ballot, after a hurried consultation of a group of prominent party leaders, including Governor Smith, who declared for Davis, as the way out of the dilemma. It required 728 votes to nominate. Davis got 838½ on that ballot; Underwood, 108; Smith 7½ and McAdoo 11½. Others voted for were: Senator Thomas F. Walsh of Montana, Senator Glass of Virginia and a dozen other States' favorite sons.

The Vice-Presidency was a sop to William J. Bryan, who, a short time before his brother was named, declared with tears in his voice, "I did my best to prevent Davis' nomination." During the convention proceedings, Davis was criticized as "Morgan's lawyer" and "Counsel for the Telephone monopoly." Friends tried to counteract this propaganda by pointing out that he was American Counsel for the Irish Free State serving without compensation.

REFUSED TO CONDEMN KLAN

THE most exciting of the many episodes of the convention was the fight in the committee on resolutions and on the floor of the convention over the Ku Klux Klan. The chairman of the committee was Homer S. Cummings of Connecticut. The Committee tried to ignore the Kluxers, but Oscar Underwood of Alabama, who had fought them in their own stronghold, George Brennan, leader of the Illinois delegation, Ed. Moore of Ohio, Al Smith, Senator Walsh of Massachusetts and others insisted on condemning the organization by name. The controversy aroused intense feeling. When the Know-Nothing movement was at its height in the 50's, the Democratic party did not hesitate to condemn it by name, but now many influential members of the party founded by the author of the Virginia statute of religious freedom, fought all attempts to make the Klan an issue.

William R. Pattangall, Maine's representative on the Resolutions Committee, now Chief Justice of the Supreme Court of that State, brought in a minority report, condemning the Klan by name. He had recently emerged from a gubernatorial contest in which he made the Klan the sole issue and was defeated by Ralph O. Brewster, Republican, supported by Klansmen and their supporters. In opening the debate, Pattangall said he was "white, native born and Protestant." His people had lived in Maine 200 years. He wanted the Democratic party to send out a message to the country that "it hates bigotry and intolerance."

William J. Bryan was among those who opposed the Pattangall plank, saying that the Ku Klux Klan did not deserve to be advertised by the Democratic party. The plank of the majority report was satisfactory to the Klan representative and their agents in the convention. Massachusetts voted 35½ for the Pattangall plank and one-half vote was cast against it. The half vote was cast by Judge Welsh of Provincetown, a member of the Knights of Columbus and no friend of the hooded order. He explained that he was angry over making the Klan an issue and that he believed in ignoring them. Judge Pattangall's wife, his alternate in the convention, also voted against her husband, not, she said, because she approved of the Klan, but she was opposed to advertising the order. Had Delegate Welsh and Mrs. Pattangall voted for the minority report the Klan would have been condemned by name. As it was, it had a narrow escape, the vote being for the majority report, 542; for the minority report, 541 3–20.

SMITH BAY STATE CHOICE

THE long drawn out fight between Smith and McAdoo disgusted many of the delegates, some of whom found their pocketbooks nearly empty because of the long drawn out contest. They demanded that the bickering among the leaders cease and the convention transact the business for which it was convened. After the 71st ballot, July 5, when McAdoo had a big lead over Smith, an attempt was made to adjourn to Kansas City, July 21. The McAdoo forces particularly wanted to get away from Smith's bailiwick, where friendly doorkeepers were accused of packing the galleries with Smith shouters. Westerners feared the influence of Wall Street, but the motion to shift the scene to the mid-West failed and the balloting was resumed with McAdoo still leading and Smith a poor second. A motion to eliminate the lowest candidates from the balloting was howled down. Smith got 33 of the Massachusetts 36 votes through the tedious balloting. On the 103rd ballot its 36 votes were cast for Davis in the rush to make the nomination unanimous.

The delegates-at-large from Massachusetts were David I. Walsh, Arthur Lyman, Joseph B. Ely, John F. Doherty, Helen A. McDonald, Susan W. Fitzgerald, Mary E. Meehan and Charles H. Cole. The latter and Joseph B. Ely from the start voted for Smith. Each delegate was free to exercise his or her own judgment. Senator Walsh, the leader of the Massachusetts delegation, was active and prominent in the party councils and made one of the best speeches in behalf of the minority report on the platform.

The keynoter of the Convention was Senator Pat Harrison of Mississippi. He did not spare the Republicans or the administration. He smeared the enemy with oil and praised the Democratic Senators prominent in the exposé of graft and corruption under Harding. Newton D. Baker, Secretary of War under Woodrow Wilson, made an eloquent appeal for the League of Nations plank in the platform, invoking the name of Woodrow Wilson, but the convention voted it down.

During the convention Calvin, youngest son of President Coolidge, died at a Washington hospital. By a rising vote, a resolution of condolence was adopted and ordered wired to Mr. and Mrs. Coolidge.

The independent candidacy of Senator La Follette of Wisconsin for President, running as a Progressive, supported by the extreme radicals of all parties, was the only thing that gave the Republicans any uneasiness. La Follette's running mate was Senator Wheeler of Montana, Massachusetts born, who bolted Davis because of his Wall Street connections. The election turned out to be a Coolidge landslide. The Republicans got 382 electoral votes, the Democrats, 136, all in the South, and La Follette got 13, all of them from his home State.

Massachusetts gave Coolidge a vote of 703,475; Davis, 280,831; La Follette, 141,225. The total popular vote for President was: Coolidge, 15,748,356; Davis, 8,617,454; La Follette, 4,686,681. Massachusetts Democrats elected but three Representatives to Congress, Connery, Douglas and Gallivan.

STATE CAMPAIGN OF 1924

LOCAL interest in the Senatorship and Governorship this year overshadowed the outcome of the Presidential contest, which was a foregone conclusion. The former contest was between Speaker Frederick H. Gillette of the National House of Representatives and Senator David I. Walsh, whose term was expiring the following March.

The contest for Governor was between Lieutenant Governor Fuller, who had defeated Ex-State Treasurer James Jackson for the nomination by a plurality rising 48,000, and Mayor James M. Curley of Boston unopposed for the Democratic nomination.

William S. Youngman defeated six opponents in the primary for Treasurer. There was the usual drive in the Republican primary against the renomination of State Auditor Alonzo B. Cook, but he was renominated over two opponents. John J. Cummings secured the Democratic nomination for Lieutenant Governor, defeating two aspirants.

Curley assailed his Republican opponent as unsympathetic to the less fortunate members of society and promised, if elected, to introduce what he called Curleyism at the State House, "a kindly, considerate and humane treatment of the poor, the sick and the unfortunate." He charged that Mr. Fuller's record "of silence and evasion and absenteeism in Congress stamped him as a pacifist, slacker and enemy of free government." He also charged that Mr. Fuller was the Klan candidate and pointed to the fiery crosses that were burned as evidence of the Klan's interest in the Republican candidate, but the latter ridiculed the claim and declared that Mr. Curley seemed to have inside knowledge of the cross burning. Mr. Fuller, whose wife and children are members of the

Catholic church, said Mr. Curley was trying to hide his administration at City Hall behind the Ku Klux Klan smoke screen.

"It is for the voters to decide whether they want to have the Republican policies continued or put a spendthrift into the office of Governor," said he. If the Curley program were carried out, said Mr. Fuller, the State would be saddled with $40,000,000 additional debt. He analyzed the growth of the debt of the City of Boston under Curley and outlined the financial accomplishments of Cox by which the State debt had been substantially reduced. "We cannot afford to invite a government of scandal on Beacon Hill," said he. In his handling of the financial issue in the campaign, Mr. Fuller was ably assisted by Representative Frederick H. Shattuck of Boston, an outstanding Republican member of the Legislature, who later succeeded Charles Francis Adams as Treasurer of Harvard College, when the latter became Secretary of the Navy in the cabinet of President Hoover.

Mrs. Fuller added to the interest of her husband's campaign by her singing at Republican meetings. She was a well known opera singer before her marriage and continued her interest in her former profession, but limited her public appearances largely in behalf of charitable organizations and institutions.

Although Curley was not Senator Walsh's choice for Governor, the latter gave him his full support and said at the opening of the campaign in the Western part of the State that "the people were never offered a stronger, abler, more eloquent or more courageous candidate for Governor than James M. Curley."

Mr. Curley's preëlection predictions were wide of the mark. He said he expected to defeat Fuller by 100,000. Instead, Mr. Fuller had a plurality of 160,000. The vote for Governor was: Fuller, 650,817; Curley, 490,010; John J. Ballam, Workers' party, 9506; James Hayes, Socialist-Labor, 4854; Walter S. Hutchins, Socialist, 6292. The rest of the Republican ticket was elected by rousing pluralities. Frank G. Allen, President of the Senate, was moved up to the Lieutenant Governorship by a vote of 648,373 against 413,898 for his Democratic opponent, John J. Cummings. The Legislature chosen was heavily Republican. Thirteen of the 16 Congressmen were Republicans.

PRESIDENTIAL ELECTION

THE dissension and acrimony developed at the Madison Square Garden Democratic convention made the nomination practically worthless. In John W. Davis the Democrats had a fine upstanding candidate, an able lawyer, a man with many admirable personal qualities, a polished public speaker, a gentleman in every sense of the word, but many radicals were suspicious of him because of his connection with the great banking house of Morgan. He had been and was at the time of his nomination, an advocate of the League of Nations, Woodrow Wilson's pet hobby, which many Democrats declined to embrace. Mr. Davis enthusiastically accepted the task of leading another Democratic forlorn hope. He made a brilliant talking campaign, while President Coolidge remained in Washington and said little. From the start the Democratic campaign was hopeless. Mr. Coolidge had the confidence of the public. People liked his simple mode of living, his rustic Vermont background and his preachments on government economy and personal thrift. The public absolved him of any guilt in the Harding scandals. General Dawes did the barnstorming for the ticket and with righteous indignation condemned the grafters and the "Klan" in general, but pointed out that in certain localities like Oklahoma and Illinois, the Klan came into being as champions of law and order, nevertheless he was against the order because it appealed to racial, religious and class prejudice, he told Maine voters in his tour of that State in its September election.

DEATH OF SENATOR LODGE

SENATOR LODGE died at the Massachusetts General Hospital the night of November 10, 1924. He had been ailing for some months and was unable to take an active part in the Presidential campaign. Notwithstanding his harsh treatment at the hands of President Coolidge's friends at the Cleveland convention, he sincerely desired to see his party win the election by a decisive vote. When he was told of the Republican victory in November he lay on his death bed, a smile came over his drawn features. He called for his secretary and dictated his congratulations to President Coolidge. Soon after he sank into a coma from which he never rallied. The acknowledgment of his message he never saw for he had passed to the Great Beyond when it arrived.

His death came as a great shock to the people of the State whom he had represented in Congress for a generation. Mr. Lodge was a man of strong likes and dislikes. He was not popular with a considerable element of his own party and many Democrats cordially hated him. He was a partizan. It was enough for him to know that a candidate had received the Republican nomination to gain his support and yet, because of his genuine Americanism, he could count on the votes of Democrats when he came up for election. He was easily the foremost champion of Republicanism in Massachusetts.

Senator Lodge keenly felt the defeat of his colleague John W. Weeks by David I. Walsh in 1918, but he did not permit his political prejudice to manifest itself in his personal relations with his Democratic colleague and treated him with courtesy. When the sharp tongued, rabid old Senator John Sharp Williams of Mississippi cast reflections on Senator Walsh in the League of Nations controversy on the floor of the Senate, Mr. Lodge went to the defense of his colleague and repelled the insinuation that his associate was actuated by other than patriotic and conscientious motives in his stand against the League. A grateful State has erected on the capital grounds a monument to him.

GILLETT DEFEATS SENATOR WALSH

In opening his campaign for reëlection in 1924, Senator Walsh frankly recognized the popularity of President Coolidge and acknowledged his discretion, ability and high character. Early in his campaign for reëlection, Ex-President Wilson sent a letter to a correspondent in which he said that Walsh should be defeated because he did not support his League of Nations. In his first election to the Senate, six years before, Mr. Walsh received the vote of many independents who favored the foreign policy of Mr. Wilson, but the Wilson letter was a two-edged sword. Many Democrats were opposed to the League of Nations and upheld Walsh's course in that historic battle. Walsh's course in the Senate had been marked by considerable independence. He stood for a moderate tariff and justice for the war veterans of all wars.

Gillett was the personal choice of President Coolidge and the National administration gave him all the support it could command. He had to fight two popular opponents for the nomination—Louis A. Coolidge and Representative Frederick W. Dallinger. It was a lively contest in which personalities figured. His opponents twitted him on his age—74—and that he had been in

Congress more than 30 years. His answer was although he was past the Biblical age he would match his wits, his brains and his agility with either of his two primary opponents.

Louis A. Coolidge was treasurer of the United Shoe Machinery Company. He had been a Washington newspaper correspondent and Secretary to Senator Lodge and Assistant Secretary to the Treasury. He was a liberal on the dry issue. His brother, William H. Coolidge, was one of the ablest and best known railroad lawyers in Massachusetts.

Dallinger had served in Congress from the Cambridge district for several terms, and was a Dry, from which source he drew most of his support. Gillett became a Dry in the campaign and won the nomination by a plurality of more than 51,000, the vote being: Gillett, 145,879; Coolidge, 93,680; Dallinger, 82,250.

Walsh was unopposed for his party nomination. In a hotly contested campaign for the election in which he practically had to fight alone while his opponent had the support of a majority of the press of the State and the powerful influence of the National and State administrations, the wealthy and the corporation interests, he went down to defeat in the Republican sweep. Gillett, 566,188; Walsh, 547,600, a remarkable tribute to the Democratic candidate when one considers that Coolidge for President had a Republican plurality of 522,000.

In an interview the day following his election Mr. Gillett said he took his hat off to his Democratic opponent.

"We had a clean fight and I take my hat off to my Democratic opponent, who was gentlemanly all the way through the contest," said he. "We fought it out on our public records and the record of our parties. The people of Massachusetts voted in favor of Republican principles, as I felt sure that they would if they were explained to them."

BUTLER NAMED SENATOR

GOVERNOR COX hurried back from the funeral of Senator Lodge and announced the appointment of William M. Butler to fill the Senate vacancy to serve the unexpired term, a little more than two years to run. Friends of the late Senator criticized the Governor for his haste. Butler belonged to the Crane wing of the Republican party and had managed the Coolidge campaign for the nomination and election. Mr. Butler began his political career as a member of the Legislature in 1891. He served two terms as President of the Senate and then returned to his law practice.

The appointment of Butler and the election of Gillett restored Republican control of the two Senate seats from Massachusetts in Congress. Mr. Butler took office on the reassembling of Congress in December and when Walsh's term expired in March became the senior senator from this State.

ALVAN T. FULLER
Governor 1925-1929

ALVAN T. FULLER brought to the Governorship a wealth of experience in business and public affairs when he was inaugurated January 7, 1925. A pioneer and leader in the automobile industry, he had accumulated a fortune and built up an extensive business and established a reputation for square dealing. He began business life in a humble capacity in a rubber shoe factory in his home city Malden. He engaged in the bicycle business for himself, had the vision to see that the age of the horseless carriage had arrived and imported the first two automobiles at the port of Boston. From that modest beginning he became the largest dealer in automobiles in New England if not the United States.

With little chance to go to school, yet he is a cultivated gentleman, a devotee of art, a brilliant conversationalist, a liberal giver to charity and education. He has always found time to take a personal interest in public affairs and to lend his influence to encourage good government. He served in the Legislature and Congress before becoming Lieutenant Governor. For the latter office and his seat in Congress he had to fight the entrenched politicians, but he enjoys a fight not for the sake of fighting so much as to prove that the machine-made politician can be beaten and routed, if his opponent has courage and stamina. His entrance into the Congressional and Lieutenant Governorship field upset the plans of the politicians and he was as welcome in both contests as a Jewish white goods salesman at a meeting of the Ku Klux Klan. He had never drawn his salary in any public office and held to the same course while Governor.

"I went to Washington with the avowed intention of warring against the abuse of the franking privilege by Congressmen," he once said.

"I made war upon the practice of Congressmen in appointing their relations to various posts, some serving as secretaries of committees or of the Congressmen themselves.

"The abuse of the mileage allowance in Congress was the subject of an attack by me. It can be readily understood that in order to do all this it was necessary for me to keep my own record absolutely clear. That I did. I did not take advantage of any of these privileges. I went a step further and declined to accept any salary.

"That made my position absolutely impregnable. I did not need the salary and so, when I became Lieutenant Governor of Massachusetts, and later Governor, I continued the practice."

His first inaugural was an able paper stamped with the individuality of the man who had worked his way to the top by his own sheer ability and independence. He maintained that every reasonable aid and encouragement should be given to the industries of the State in order to stimulate business and that the law makers should cease hampering business, with a proper regard for the rights of the public. As a step in the right direction he urged a

JOSEPH A. MAYNARD
Collector Port of Boston

lessening of the burden of taxation on business. He advocated the encouragement of agriculture; the revision of the Corrupt Practice Act to prevent the large expenditures of money in elections; the establishment of a sinking fund for an insurance fund to be contributed to annually; a tax on gasoline used in automobiles; increased penalties for carrying concealed weapons and for forcibly resisting a police officer; requiring owners and drivers of automobiles to furnish security for liability for personal injuries or death caused by their motor vehicles; appointment of an emergency fuel administrator; better service by the Boston Elevated Railway Company; participation of women in government on equal terms with men; warning signals at unprotected grade crossings; control of bovine tuberculosis; amendment to the civil service laws permitting removals for incompetency and inefficiency. A lifelong advocate of temperance, he said it was his purpose to enforce the prohibitory laws.

The Legislature organized with Wellington Wells, President of the Senate, and John C. Hull, Speaker of the House.

LEGISLATURE OF 1925

THE Legislature of 1925 passed 348 Acts and 40 Resolves. The Governor vetoed 14 of its measures and allowed one Act to become law without his signature. All of Governor Fuller's vetoes were sustained. Prorogation occurred May 1, the earliest in 45 years, due to the insistence of the Governor, the prodding of the presiding officers of both branches and the floor leaders of the majority party in House and Senate. His own party leaders were not especially friendly to the Governor and more than once were reluctant to back him up, but they realized that they were dealing with a man of independence who would not hesitate to appeal from the Legislature to the public, if he believed his stand was in the public interest.

Among the important laws enacted were: compulsory automobile insurance, additional legislation governing the operation of motor vehicles on the highways, including punishment for drunken driving; an act authorizing the Boston & Maine Railroad Company to issue preferred stock, make certain bonds convertible and extend the maturity of other bonds; a new bank tax raising more than a $1,000,000 revenue; increasing tax on motor trucks; creation of a refuge and sanctuary for wild birds on Egg Rock Island, Nahant, as a memorial to the late Senator Lodge, a resident of that town; a number of laws for the conservation of game; authorization of the building of the Southern Artery from Mattapan Square in the Dorchester District of Boston, through Milton and Quincy to the South Shore, a companion measure to the Northern Artery legislation passed the year before; Morton Street, Boston, widening, regulation of aviation, arbitration of commercial disputes; creation of two new Judges for the Superior Court; addition of four Assistant District Attorneys for Suffolk County; acquirement of the Wakefield Rifle Range for the National Guard; a bill giving added powers to the Commissioner of Conservation in cases of forest fire and increasing subsidies to municipalities for fighting such fires; removal of the special preference given to veterans in the public service under which it was practically impossible to discharge a hopelessly inefficient employee, putting them on the same basis in the matters of removals as all other employees. Formerly they had to appeal to political bodies, such as city councils and boards of selectmen, and in almost every instance the appeal was sustained; permitting railroads to enter the bus business upon receiving a certificate of public necessity and convenience from the Department of Public Utilities; the Commission on Necessaries of Life was continued for two more years; resolves were passed accepting busts of John Adams and Ex-Governor Samuel W. McCall and a portrait of Ex-Governor Coolidge; $160,000 was appropriated for the purchase of the Laurence Estate to be added to the Middlesex Fells Reservation.

Much legislation proposed by Governor Fuller was rejected, but on the whole he fared pretty well at the hands of the law makers.

During the summer of 1925, there were threats of a strike by the employees of the Boston Elevated Street Railway. The trustees became scared and rushed to the Governor for advice and guidance. Mr. Fuller issued a public statement that he would remove every trustee willing to permit a strike and that he would not allow any employee to return to work who deserted his post.

The 1,500,000 car riders of the El were entitled to service, he said, and he proposed to see that they had it. There was no strike.

He slashed $200,000 off the State budget by reducing appropriations which in no way reduced the effectiveness of the activities of the Commonwealth. He warned the 12,000 State employees belonging to the Service Association of the consequences if they persisted in their plan of compelling the State to increase their salaries.

FULLER REËLECTED, 1926

GOVERNOR FULLER was unopposed for a second term in the Republican primary in 1926. The Democratic candidate for Governor, Colonel William A. Gaston, put up a stiff battle against him in the election. It was Colonel Gaston's last appearance as a candidate for public office. He inherited his Democracy from his father, who was elected Governor in 1875. Colonel Gaston was a member of Governor Russell's military staff. He was always a generous giver to his party campaign chest. A man of wealth and high standing in business, at the bar and social circles, he had for years nursed the ambition to be Governor. He was the soul of honor and possessed an attractive personality, but his corporation connections, which, in a Republican candidate, would commend him to the public, was used against him by his opponents as an effective weapon. Then, too, he always seemed to pick the wrong year to run.

Fuller made the most of Gaston and his law firm's connection with the unpopular Boston Elevated Railway. The bankers and lawyers interested in unloading that crippled road with its worn out rolling stock had succeeded in getting the State to take it over for a limited time with a State appointed board of trustees to manage it and provided that in the event the system didn't earn enough for its 6% guaranteed dividends to the stockholders, the cities and towns in which the road operated could be called upon to furnish the necessary funds. It was a great bargain for the stockholders but a poor one for the public. The manipulators were preparing to seek to extend the plan for 30 years and the next legislature would deal with the problem. Although Colonel Gaston had disposed of his El stock long before his gubernatorial campaign, Governor Fuller insisted that he and his law firm were large beneficiaries of the exciting and proposed El plan.

"Mr. Gaston is the former head of the Elevated," said the Governor in his initial attack on his opponent. "His partner, Mr. Snow, is the dominating figure on the board. In those years that the Elevated was spending thousands of dollars on legislation at the expense of the people, Mr. Gaston was directing its campaign. His law firm is still deep in Elevated affairs. His election would mean that the great financial interests would have their own man at the helm. He cannot give the public a square deal.

"I will never support or sign any bill which I believe is not in the interests of the people. I will not consent to allow the Elevated stockholders to make their own bargain at the expense of the people. No extension of financial guarantee on the part of the State to the Elevated will be sanctioned by me unless it includes a progressive program for better service and looks—when the money can be found—to replacing elevated structures with subways. If there are financial sacrifices to be made, I shall insist that the stockholders share them instead of putting the whole burden on the public."

Colonel Gaston answered saying that he was no man's man and when elected Governor he would deal with the El problem in the interests of the public. Those who knew Colonel Gaston believed him, but the public was in no mood to believe anything good of the El or its management. Governor Fuller also charged that Gaston's associate directors in the Telephone Company were responsible for increasing telephone rates, which he tried to prevent.

The Governor declared that he was proud of the financial showing of his two years in office, saying:—"Massachusetts is the only State in the Union that has not in 1926 an increase in taxes over those of 1919. Not only has a tax of $12,000,000 been retained, when it was $14,000,000 as far back as 1921, but, starting my administration with a million dollars and a half in debt, we have paid all of that indebtedness out of current revenue and have maintained the State service in every department on a higher level than ever before, and have reduced the State debt $2,500,000."

Colonel Gaston fought a good fight, but Fuller cantered

back to Beacon Hill with a plurality rising 187,000 votes, the vote being: Fuller, 595,006; Gaston, 407,389.

The rest of the Republican ticket did even better, except Allen for Lieutenant Governor, whose plurality was 167,000 and State Auditor Cook, who had 153,000 over his Democratic opponent, Strabo V. Claggett. Cook was unpopular with his own party leaders but despite their ill will he continued to get elected. The hold of the Republicans in both Legislative branches and Congress was unshaken.

LEGISLATURE OF 1926

THE 144th General Court convened for its second annual session January 6, 1926, under the same presiding officers of the previous year and remained in session until May 29—28 days longer than the year before. In the five months that it sat, there was little coöperation between the Executive and Legislative branches. It was necessary to redivide the State into Congressional districts, always a difficult political task. Also, this year the lines of the Councillor and Senatorial districts had to be redrawn and the State representatives reapportioned among the counties.

Additional water supply for the Metropolitan District and the City of Worcester was provided costing millions, was enacted; the criminal laws were tightened to enable the authorities to meet the crime wave; an act was passed regulating night clubs and roadhouses, constantly increasing under the Prohibition Law, which encouraged clandestine drinking. These resorts often became the rendezvous of the underworld; the bill allowing savings banks to invest in railroad equipment securities bonds, vetoed by the Governor last year, was amended, passed and signed by the Chief Executive; certain Trust Companies were authorized to establish branches outside of their chartered locations and the Blue Sky Law was strengthened: $100,000 was appropriated to complete the State's memorial at St. Mihiel, France, in honor of the Massachusetts soldiers who participated in that campaign in the World War. Due to the efforts of Senator John W. McCormack of South Boston, a cancer hospital was established at the Norfolk State Hospital.

WALSH DEFEATS BUTLER FOR SENATE

DAVID I. WALSH kept his ear to the ground after he left the Senate following his defeat by Frederick H. Gillett in 1924. In the interim between his defeat for reëlection and his candidacy for another term in 1926, he maintained his contacts in local politics and found plenty of opportunities to inform the voters of his views on public questions. He had no opposition for the Democratic nomination and entered the campaign confident of victory. He regarded Senator Butler as a weaker candidate than Gillett, his opponent two years before. Organized labor was opposed to Butler, who had, as a member of the Legislature and the United States Senate and as President of the Arkwright Club, an organization composed of cotton manufacturers, opposed measures for the benefit of labor. His corporation connections made a good target for labor leaders to shoot and they rallied behind Walsh.

In the United States Senate, Butler lined up with the standpat Republican element and on important administration matters was regarded as the spokesman of President Coolidge. He was also the chairman of the Republican National committee, which gave to his attitude and votes a further tinge of administration and party authority. Butler's official position in the party organization made the senatorial contest in Massachusetts this year of great National importance. His election would mean to the country that the Coolidge administration had not lost its popularity. His defeat would be a heavy blow to the administration.

The party organization in Massachusetts and the Administration forces got behind him and gave him every ounce of support in their power, but it was soon evident that he was no match as a campaigner against Walsh. It is true that he was more aggressive than Gillett, but he had a more vulnerable political record. Mrs. Constance Gardner-Williams, widow of Congressman Gardner and only daughter of Senator Lodge, announced in a letter to the *Boston Herald* that she would vote for Walsh, a bid for other friends of the late Senator to do likewise.

President Coolidge and Mrs. Coolidge came on from

Washington to Northampton to cast their votes for Butler, but not even the great weight of the influence of the National administration could carry him to victory and Walsh was the winner by 56,000 plurality.

FIRST MASSACHUSETTS CONGRESSWOMAN

REPRESENTATIVE JOHN JACOB ROGERS of Lowell, easily the ablest member of the State's delegation in the House of Representatives, died in November, 1925. As a member of the Committee on Foreign Relations, he interested himself in legislation, designed to take politics out of the diplomatic and consular service and with a view of attracting young men, possessed of education that fitted them for a diplomatic career, by making it possible to climb steadily to the top. While the Rogers Act did not do all that its promoter hoped, yet it did encourage qualified young men to enter the service with reasonable assurance that they would be advanced as fast as vacancies occur, provided, of course, that the appointing power is in sympathy with the law.

Having voted to go to war with Germany, Mr. Rogers, never a man to ask his fellow citizens to do anything he would not do himself, enlisted as a private in the army and was in a training camp when peace was declared. Mustered out of the service he returned to Congress and was one of the most active members on the Republican side. Popular in his district and in Washington, his untimely death was a great shock to his friends and constituents.

A special election was held to fill out his unexpired term. The Republicans nominated his widow, Edith Nourse Rogers. No Democrat in the district could be found to run against her. During the war Mrs. Rogers was active in Red Cross work, spending most of her waking hours among the returned soldiers in and about Washington. Her devotion to the sick and maimed soldiers earned for her the sobriquet of "The Angel of Walter Reed Hospital," the largest government hospital in the national capital. The soldiers idolized her.

Although he was not a resident of the district, ex-Governor Foss stepped up and offered himself as the vicarious sacrifice. Mrs. Rogers was literally swept into office, carrying every city and town in the district. In Congress she distinguished herself as a hard working, intelligent, progressive member. The people of the district are so well pleased with their woman Congress representative that they have retained her ever since.

MR. DOOLEY DEFEATS MR. ELY

ONE of the amusing sidelights of the State campaign of 1926 was the nomination of Harry J. Dooley of Boston, a young business man for Lieutenant Governor on the Democratic ticket, defeating Joseph B. Ely of Westfield. After entering the primary contest, Mr. Dooley was induced by Democratic leaders to withdraw in the interest of Mr. Ely, but by the time Mr. Dooley decided to accede to the wishes of the party leaders, the time for his withdrawal had expired and his name appeared on the primary ballots. He campaigned for Ely but when the primary votes were counted it was found that an unknown young man had defeated one of the best known and popular members of the party in Western Massachusetts by 6000 votes. Mr. Dooley refused the nomination and under the authority of the law the State Committee substituted Joseph B. Ely for Dooley.

Both Dooley and Ely were good natured over the situation. Each claimed that they voted for one another in the primary. Mr. Dooley was engaged in the automobile sightseeing business in Boston at the time and was a member of the board of directors of the Gray Line. Soon after the episode he moved to Chicago and is now President of the transportation company and prominent in Chicago civic affairs.

District Attorney Arthur K. Reading of Middlesex County made his first appearance as a candidate for State office, winning the nomination for Attorney General over two opponents.

In Democratic Suffolk County there was strife over the District Attorneyship and the Shrievalty. In the former contest William J. Foley was the winner in a field of six candidates and in the latter fight Sheriff John A. Kelliher defeated five opponents for the Democratic and two for the Republican nomination.

The Legislature repealed the law giving veterans preference on the Civil Service lists, but the ex-service men appealed to the voters under the initiative and referendum law and won their fight at the polls.

FULLER'S SECOND TERM

In his address to the Legislature of 1927, Governor Fuller recommended changes in court procedure in dealing with criminals in capital cases, pointing out that it occasionally happened in capital cases, after the courts have set the period within which the sentence is pronounced by them shall be carried out, that hearings on exceptions or other court proceedings necessitate postponing the execution of the sentence. "The power of respite should at such times belong to the courts," said he. He also advocated the repeal of the statute precluding the prosecuting officer from commenting on the failure of the defendent to take the witness stand. Legislation should be passed which would minimize the use of pistols and revolvers by criminals, he said.

Another important recommendation was that in criminal cases, except those growing out of killings of human beings, the agreement of eleven jurymen should be sufficient to convict.

The Governor's suggestion regarding the power of respite grew out of the famous Sacco-Vanzetti case, which attracted world wide attention because of the agitation of Communists and Reds in Europe, who claimed that they were not guilty of murder and that they had not had a fair trial, but the Legislature did not agree with the Governor on any of the three suggestions. He recommended that the Nautical Training School be abolished as being useless and an unnecessary expense to the State. On that question the Legislature also disagreed with him and it is still functioning.

"Gas and electric companies are receiving earnings which, in many instances, seem excessive," said he. "The Department of Public Utilities should be authorized upon its own initiative, as well as upon complaint, after a hearing, to reduce rates for gas and electricity, whenever it deems such rates unjust or unreasonable. I recommend that legislation to this effect be enacted."

The gas and electric companies had more influence with the Solons on Beacon Hill than the Governor and nothing was done. He asked for a law limiting the Legislative session to 90 days, until the State should adopt bi-annual sessions. That too was refused him. He asked that the Blue Sky Law be amended further to protect the investing public. He gave it as his opinion that the State could be properly run on a $12,000,000 annual budget and urged that Departments keep down their expenses to that figure.

Many more recommendations were made looking to the betterment of State activities, including adequate auditing of municipal accounts, budgets and control, agriculture, animal industry, control of the gypsy moth pest, advocacy of tree planting and the self supporting of departments, for a gasoline tax, increasing the capacity of

GOV. ALVAN T. FULLER

hospitals for the insane, and concluded with an appeal for the enforcement of the prohibition law.

LEGISLATURE OF 1928

FIVE women sat in the House of 1928, two of them reelected, the others were newcomers. The women members who were reëlected were Miss M. Sylvia Donaldson of Brockton and Miss Martha N. Brooks of Gloucester. Mrs. Mary Livermore Barrows of Melrose, Mrs. Emme E. Brigham of Springfield and Dr. Marion Cowan Burrows of Lynn were newcomers.

It was an extraordinary session in many respects. Attorney General Reading was impeached, but permitted to escape punishment by resigning. Frank A. Goodwin, Registrar of Motor Vehicles, was removed from office by Governor Fuller for meddling with legislation and criticism of the administration.

Representative Francis X. Coyne of Dorchester, one of the most active and prominent Democratic members, resigned when the Legislature was about to start an investigation of the activities of the lobby. Rumors were abroad that money had been paid by lobbyists for killing certain bills.

Daniel J. Kiley, a lawyer and well known Democratic Boston politician in former days, made the charge that Judge Charles L. Long of the Hampden County Probate Court had altered the record of evidence in a case before him. Kiley sought legislation to prevent such action. Two or three other lawyers, members of the Legislature scathingly denounced the Judge, citing their own experience in Long's court, but the committee which heard the evidence decided that no legislation was necessary. The publicity given the case had a deterrent effect on the Judge and he mended his court ways.

Day Baker, legislative agent for a number of trucking firms, who appeared before a committee protesting a gasoline tax, sent each member of the Legislature two tickets for the Boston automobile show. Several of the members resented the largess of Mr. Baker and regarded it as an attempt to bribe them. He was summoned before the Committee on Rules and questioned and denied that he was trying to bribe any of the honorable members of the General Court. It was his custom, he said, to send members of the Legislature tickets to the automobile show every year, but this was the first time anybody had refused them or sought to regard them as a bribe. He was asked to write a letter of apology to the General Court, complied with the request and that ended the silly charge of attempted bribery.

It was a jumpy year. The air of Beacon Hill was filled with rumors. State employees charged that seized liquor stored at the Capitol had been removed by State troopers and distributed among State officials and members of the Legislature. Governor Fuller ordered Charles F. Howard, Chairman of the Commission on Administration and Finance to investigate. Mr. Howard reported he found no basis for the charge, but Frank A. Goodwin, the deposed Registrar of Motor Vehicles, counsel for the State employees who brought the charge, branded the report as a "barefaced whitewash."

Governor Fuller urged the passage of a bill dealing with the Boston Elevated Street Railway and set forth his views of the terms of the proposed legislation, declaring that until a measure was passed protecting the interests of the public, he would keep the Legislature in session, but either because of outside influence or the lack of brains to deal with the question, the Legislature of 1928 passed the buck to a new committee of fifteen to try to frame a satisfactory bill for action at the next session.

The ten year public control bill of the Eastern Massachusetts Street Railway was to expire this year and the road returned to its private owners, but the company had pull enough with the members to have the arrangement extended another five years.

The Legislature refused to back the initiative petition of the Constitutional Liberty League, seeking a referendum on the repeal of the prohibitory amendment of the Federal Constitution.

The initiative petition, filed by the American Legion, making November 11 a legal holiday, fared better and was approved and became a law, but the day is honored more in the breath than in the observance. Among Boston Department storekeepers only two observe it, one "where you bot the hat" and the other a high class establishment dealing in women's wear, whose proprietor was an intimate friend and political godfather of the late President Calvin Coolidge.

Mayor Curley's East Boston vehicular tunnel bill was passed. Completed six years later, it cost $19,000,000, and proved to be a financial white elephant. Its first year deficit, according to Mayor Mansfield, will amount to $500,-000. The public complained of the high toll charges. One solution of the problem suggested is to declare it to be a public highway and assess its cost and upkeep on the cities and towns of the Metropolitan district.

The Boston and Maine Railroad corporate powers were enlarged to permit it to carry out its terminal plans for the new North Station, including a hotel and arena for sporting and amusement events.

The height of Boston buildings for the benefit of "sky scrapers" was enacted. Another boost in the tax limit for Boston was approved. Automobiles were the subject of new and important legislation, including a gasoline tax, an excise tax, regulation of parking and for better and uniform brakes.

The Drys got practically everything they asked for, including the padlock law, permitting the authorities to close a place for a year, where there has been three convictions for illegal sale of liquor.

A non-contributory old age pension law was passed. Salaries in the higher courts were raised making that of the Chief Justice of the Supreme Judicial Court, $15,000, associates, $14,000; the Chief Justice of the Superior Court, $13,000, associates, $12,000.

The word "pauper" was eliminated from the State laws.

Important banking laws of the year included the branch

trust company measure and the broker-director bill. Under the branch bill, subject to the approval of the Board of Bank Incorporation, a trust company in a municipality of less than 50,000 population may have one branch, from 50,000 to 100,000 two branches, and more than 100,000 no limit. Under the broker-director bill, a trust company may have business relations with a brokerage house in which an officer or employee is also a director in the trust company, under certain restrictions. Both measures were designed to bring the Trust company law into conformity with the National Banking act.

ATTORNEY GENERAL READING IMPEACHED—RESIGNS

ON February 28, 1928, the House adopted an order to inquire into the acts and conduct of Attorney General Arthur K. Reading and the Speaker named Representative George F. James of Norwood, Chairman. Reading was comparatively a newcomer in Massachusetts. He had been District Attorney of Middlesex County, succeeding Nathan A. Tufts, removed for malfeasance in office by the Supreme Court. He was prominent in the government proceedings against Daniel H. Coakley and Ex-District Attorney William J. Corcoran. The first inkling of wrongdoing by the Attorney General came out in a suit brought in the New York Courts by J. B. Monjar, a promoter of what was called the Decimo Club, a fraternal organization in which Reading's name was coupled with several other defendants. Monjar accused Reading of accepting a secret fee of $25,000 from the Decimo Club for legal services, after the Attorney General's office had investigated its activity in Massachusetts and given it a clean bill of health.

A Democratic member of the House, Rev. Dr. Roland D. Sawyer of Ware, first called attention to the charges of Monjar against Reading and a hearing was given the Attorney General by the Rules Committee of the House. Reading declined to answer questions propounded by Slater Washburn of Worcester, a member of the committee, but he admitted to Speaker Hull that he had accepted a $25,000 check from the Decimo Club, made payable to a third person, but denied that this had any connection with the conduct of his public office. It was, he said, a fee obtained in the course of his private practice for legal services rendered outside the Massachusetts jurisdiction. He said that he had received other fees from the same source, though no other check was made payable to a third person.

It was the first time in more than a century that an incumbent of this high and honorable office had been accused of using its power to enrich himself. The press of the State demanded Reading's impeachment. At first he sneered at the Rules Committee. His array of counsel, among whom was Robert G. Dodge, prominent in the Bar Association, was imposing. As his accusers and the committee drew the net of guilt about him tightly and impeachment seemed certain, he began to weaken.

MASSACHUSETTS POLITICS 371

In his report of the findings of the Committee, Chairman James did not spare the Attorney General, saying: "Let those apologists for the betrayal of official faith and honor, let those moralists who cannot distinguish between innocent indiscretion due to misplaced intelligence, and a sordid, mercenary, deliberate, yet secretly contrived betrayal of official trust, know that the people of Massachusetts do not hold the great honors she confers upon her officials at so cheap a price as blandly to forgive those who have betrayed her faith, dishonored her service, her credit and repute at home and abroad, and prostituted the virtue of the commonwealth for their own sordid and mercenary gain."

Mr. Reading was cited before the bar of the Senate for trial, but resigned his office. So far as the Legislature was concerned, the case was ended, and Joseph E. Warner became the new Attorney General by choice of the Legislature.

At the ensuing election Mr. Warner was elected to that office. After the Legislature had transmitted its report on Reading to the Supreme Court, Frederick W. Mansfield, representing the Bar Association and by appointment of the Court, succeeded in disbarring Reading.

1928 PRESIDENTIAL PRIMARIES

GOVERNOR FULLER insisted that in the 1928 primaries the voters be permitted to indicate on their ballots their

Presidential preference. The Legislature passed an act which gave the voters this opportunity and they expressed themselves in no uncertain terms. The striking thing about the preference voting was that Governor Smith of New York, the leading Democratic candidate, received more than 2500 votes in the Republican primary. President Coolidge got over 7000 votes and Governor Fuller 1600. There were votes for Louden, Borah and Hughes. Herbert Hoover's Democratic admirers numbering 150 voted for him in the Democratic primary. Senator Thomas J. Walsh and Senator James A. Reed of Missouri were favored by a small minority in the Democratic primary. Mr. Hoover and Governor Smith were the overwhelming choice of the Republican and Democratic voters, respectively.

The successful delegates-at-large chosen were:

Republican

William M. Butler, Frederick H. Gillett, Channing H. Cox, Eben S. Draper, Pauline R. Thayer, Minnie R. Dwight, Grace H. Nagley, Frederick L. Anderson.

Alternate Delegates

Louise M. Williams, Mary Pratt Potter, Eliot Wadsworth, Frederick H. Prince, Butler Ames, Edwin F. Leonard, Raoul H. Boudreau.

The Governor came out for the nomination of Hoover in an appeal to the Republican voters. There was talk of urging the Massachusetts Chief Executive to become a candidate for Vice-President on the Hoover ticket, but the Governor refused to regard the mention of his name as more than a personal compliment and laughed off the suggestion.

REPUBLICAN PRIMARY NOMINATIONS, 1928

WHILE Republicans were practically unanimous over their Presidential ticket, such was not the case when it came to selecting their State ticket. Lieutenant Governor Allen was opposed by Frank A. Goodwin, Registrar of Motor Vehicles for Governor, who put up an aggressive campaign and rolled up the amazing vote of 169,000 votes against Allen's 267,000. Former State Treasurer William S. Youngman had seven opponents for Lieutenant Governor, Speaker Hull of the House of Representatives, Ex-Congressman Robert M. Leach of Taunton, General John H. Sherburn, Peter G. Holmes, Charles L. Burrill, George A. Bacon and Wycliffe C. Marshall. For the Republican nomination for United States Senator, B. Loring Young defeated Eben S. Draper and Butler Ames by a plurality of 21,000, the vote being Young, 162,634; Draper, 141,525; Ames, 92,182.

John W. Haigis of Greenfield was nominated for State Treasurer on the Republican ticket over four rivals, one of whom was a discredited ex-Treasurer, Fred H. Burrell, who pulled a vote of 102,000 votes against Haigis' 111,000.

State Auditor Alonzo B. Cook achieved another single handed victory in the face of fierce personal opposition, winning by a plurality rising 79,000 in a six-cornered contest. Attorney General Warner was opposed by Clarence A. Barnes, but the former won by a plurality of 161,000.

PARKMAN BEATS INNES

HENRY PARKMAN, JR., of Boston, challenged the supremacy of the leadership of Charles H. Innes in a contest for delegates in the 11th Congressional district. Parkman's running mate was an unknown, Gordon Watt. Parkman fought the Innes organization on the ground that its leader represented a minority of the party, and that he had made a business out of politics. Parkman proved himself to be a good campaigner and succeeded in defeating Innes' ticket by 1000 votes. Parkman, a member of the Boston City Council, came from an old line family. Francis Parkman, pioneer and author of "The Oregon Trail" and other such volumes, was a relative and George F. Parkman, who left the citizens of Boston the annual income of a $5,000,000 fund for upkeep of parks and playgrounds, was his granduncle. His father, Henry Parkman, was active in Republican politics a generation before and served as Chairman of the Republican City Committee when Boston used to elect Republican mayors on a Republican platform. It was a severe blow to the political prestige of Innes but he took it good naturedly and philosophically.

HOOVER REPUBLICAN PRESIDENTIAL CHOICE

ALMOST a year before the Republicans gathered in Kansas City early in June, 1928, President Coolidge had announced at his summer camp in the Black Hills, that he did not choose to run again. The decision, made without consultation with any of the leaders of the party, startled the entire country. At first Mr. Coolidge's decision to retire from the Presidency was regarded by many as meaning that while he did not choose to run he would accept if nominated. Right up to the opening of the convention many of his admirers harbored the belief, at least the hope, that the convention would disregard his wishes and again name him for President. Some even believed that Mr. Coolidge secretly desired another term. Meanwhile, several candidates took the field. First and foremost Herbert Hoover, Secretary of Commerce, whose department contained a goodly sprinkling of practical politicians, chief among whom was Assistant Secretary Walter F. Brown of Ohio, who knew his way around. He was one of the most active politicians in his State and had been close to the unfortunate Harding. For months the Department of Commerce was a political clearing house for Hoover's nomination. President Coolidge named William F. Whiting of Holyoke, Massachusetts, to succeed Mr. Hoover, when Mr. Hoover resigned to prosecute his candidacy. Whiting, a wealthy paper manufacturer, had long been a Coolidge admirer.

Senators Curtis of Kansas, Goff of West Virginia and Watson of Indiana threw their hats in the ring. President Coolidge was neutral as was his Secretary of the Treasury, Andrew W. Mellon, who refused to declare his position until he arrived in the convention city. Importuned for an interview by newspaper reporters he fixed on the day and hour when he would divulge his well kept secret. Besides the 70 odd Pennsylvania delegates who awaited his declaration, big business was anxious to know whom he favored for the nomination but as soon as Boss Vare of Philadelphia heard that "Uncle Andy" planned to deliver the Keystone delegation, he beat him to it coming out for Hoover, thus minimizing the influence of Mellon's declaration.

Although it was apparent that Hoover had the votes to nominate, his opponents kept up a warfare on him. Senator Curtis said that if Hoover were nominated Republicans would be kept busy apologizing for him. Senator Watson declared that it was not possible for a man to live in England 23 years and not be inoculated with the views of free trade. Senator Goff hired a theatre to publicly denounce Mr. Hoover. Even the keynoter of the convention, Senator Fess of Ohio, had said disparaging things about Mr. Hoover while the latter was Woodrow Wilson's food administrator in the World War. The permanent chairman of the convention, Senator Moses of New Hampshire, used to flippantly refer to the man he

MASSACHUSETTS POLITICS 377

then favored for the nomination as " 'Erbert 'Oover."

Western farmers, smarting under the recent veto of their pet McNary-Haugen bill designed to aid them in their plight by President Coolidge swarmed into Kansas City demanding farm relief and threatening vengeance on the nominee who refused their request. Senator Reed Smoot of Utah drafted the platform, which followed the ritual lines of G.O.P. platforms of the past and omitted specific reference to the McNary-Haugen bill or its fee scheme. The farmers set up a howl and had the support of Senator Borah, but the convention paid no attention to their demands and accepted the platform as submitted.

Senator Borah also appeared as the champion of the Drys and nailed the dry plank with one of his forcible and eloquent speeches. He was pitted against Nicholas Murray Butler of New York, who argued for repeal, but the plank favored by the Anti-Saloon League was adopted. The Drys were masters of the situation from beginning to end and Mr. Hoover was nominated on the first ballot. Massachusetts threw her 39 ballots for him. Thirteen Illinois delegates and four from Oklahoma voted for Coolidge. Senator Curtis received 64 votes, Louden 74, Norris 23, Goff 18 and Watson 45.

Senator Curtis, who voiced his suspicions of Hoover's Republicanism, did not hesitate to accept the offer of the Vice-Presidency. His nomination was a sop to the farmers and was satisfactory to Big Business. The convention over, Dr. Hubert Work of Colorado, Mr. Hoover's choice, succeeded William M. Butler as chairman of the National Committe and Louis K. Liggett, prominent

Boston business man, was chosen Massachusetts member of the National Committee.

SMITH FOR PRESIDENT

FOUR years had wrought a great change in Democratic sentiment. Smith was so far ahead in the contest for the Presidential nomination that when the convention assembled at Houston, Texas, in June, 1928, he had no serious contenders for the nomination. A few State favorite sons remained in the field hoping that political lightning would strike them. Chief among this class was the veteran Senator James A. Reed of Missouri. Reed, who had always fought the Drys and was unalterably opposed to the Prohibition amendment in the Federal Constitution, issued a statement on his arrival at Houston in which he declared that "the 18th amendment will stand until and unless the moral forces of the Nation become convinced that there is some better way to deal with the liquor problem." He was at once charged with catering to the Drys and allying himself with Daniel C. Roper, a 1924 McAdoo man and the recognized spokesman of the anti-Smith element in the convention. But even more significant than that was the twist he gave the Tammany Tiger's tail, when he denounced "criminal conspiracies masquerading as political organizations, which gain and keep power by the protection of the criminal classes and exist by the tribute of the underworld."

It was a new rôle for Reed, soon to retire from the Senate when the Hoover administration was inaugurated, on the ground as he himself is alleged to have put it: "with a Britisher in the White House (Hoover), an Indian in the Vice-President's chair (Curtis) and a colored man in the House of Representatives (De Priest), it is time for a self respecting Missourian to return to private life."

Smith's foes were unable to marshal more than a corporal's guard against him. The Drys concentrated their efforts to again commit the party to prohibition in the enforcement of the 18th amendment. The committee on Resolutions held a long and heated session struggling for 48 hours, day and night, with the subject. That and the wording of the farm relief problem were the two most troublesome questions with which the Committee had to deal.

Smith's moisture and opposition to the 18th amendment was well known, but the leaders of both wings were willing to do anything in reason to prevent another 1924 debacle. The Smithites agreed to an enforcement plank drawn by dry Senator Glass of Virginia. Senator David I. Walsh, the Massachusetts member of the committee, one of Smith's spokesmen, labored hard for harmony. The only vote in the committee against the Glass resolution was Governor Moody of Texas. Senator Glass read the resolution over the 'phone to Governor Smith in Albany, who approved it.

The convention opened with Claude M. Bowers of New York, a transplanted Hoosier, journalist and historian, now American Ambassador to Spain, sounding the keynote. He fed the Democracy ample red meat.

The Republicans, he said, were no longer part Lincolnian, but were wholly Hamiltonian, and he indicted that philosophy for all the major evils in our national life and for the scandals of the little green house on K Street, for Daugherty, Fall, Forbes and the "black horse cavalry, whose hoof beats have made music in Pennsylvania Avenue during the last eight years." He singled out Secretary Mellon as the head center of Hamiltonianism and called him "the Pittsburgh Bratiano," who has "decided to make Rumanian peasants of American farmers to fill the coffers of a purse-proud caste."

Mr. Bowers drew a word cartoon in which he contrasted the Hamiltonian and Jeffersonian concept: "They (the Hamiltonians) could crowd their Nation into one corner of this vast hall and the Nation that we know includes cities and towns and countryside and 118,000,000 people in the homes of men. We are interested in the Babbitts and they in the bulls and bears."

For three days the convention dragged. On Thursday, with the Resolutions Committee still at loggerheads, it looked as if the nominations would not be reached until Friday. Smith's friends regarded Friday as an unlucky day and hastened the convention proceedings to avert such a hoodoo on their candidate. The presiding officer, Senator Joseph T. Robinson of Arkansas, already agreed upon as Smith's running mate on the ticket, joined in the movement to nominate Thursday night.

When the nominations were reached, there was a slight commotion on the stage. Men and women arose and applauded. The tall figure of a giant man made his way slowly to the chairman's desk, supporting himself by two stout canes. As soon as the audience recognized him cheers and deafening applause resounded in the great hall. It was Franklin D. Roosevelt, who arose to place the name of Governor Smith before the convention, the third time he had appeared in that rôle, the first time at San Francisco in 1920, the second time at Madison Square Garden, New York, in 1924 and now, for the third time, in the first Democratic convention held below the Mason and Dixon line since 1860, when that party became hopelessly split on the slavery issue, broke into two opposing camps and lost the Presidency to the new Republican party with Lincoln as its nominee for President.

When the applause subsided he began his speech: "I come for the third time to urge upon a convention of my party, the nomination of the Governor of the State of New York. The faith which I held I still hold. It has been justified in the achievement. The whole country now has learned the measure of his greatness."

He then hurriedly sketched the career of Smith and lauded his political career, his administrations as Governor of New York and concluded by saying:—

"America needs not only an administrator but a leader, a pathfinder, a blazer of the trail to the high road that will avoid the bottomless morass of crass materialism that has engulfed so many of the great civilizations of the past. It is the privilege of Democracy not only to offer such a man, but to offer him as the surest leader to victory.

"To stand upon the ramparts and die for our principles is heroic. To sally forth to battle and win for our principles is something more than heroic. We offer one who has the will to win, who not only deserves success but commands it, victory is his habit, the happy warrior, Alfred E. Smith."

Governor Ritchie of Maryland was among the seconders. Smith was nominated on the first and only ballot, the vote being: Smith 849⅔; Senator George of Georgia, 52½; Reed of Missouri, 52; Cordell Hull, Tennessee, 51.

For the Vice-Presidency a number of names were presented but the Smith managers had agreed on Senator Joseph T. Robinson and he received 1035 votes and declared the nominee. Thus, the Democrats presented a ticket of a wet and a dry. During the latter part of the convention proceedings, it was whispered that Smith would write his own liquor plank and that he would send it to the convention. Immediately after the nominations, Franklin D. Roosevelt reappeared on the stage and was soon surrounded by a group of party leaders. They wanted to know about Smith's message, but Roosevelt assured them he had not seen it. While the convention was engaged in passing complimentary resolutions to the people of Houston for providing such a fine meeting place and the galleries were emptying, the Smith message was read in which he said he believed that there should be changes in the prohibitory law and that such changes should be made by the people themselves or through their legislative representatives.

Before a discussion of the message could begin Mr. Roosevelt moved for adjournment, cutting off any discussion. The Drys felt that they had been tricked and the Wets applauded what they regarded as a courageous course of the nominee, but the Drys outside of the convention were not to be dismissed so easily, as we shall see in the campaign that followed.

The Massachusetts delegates at large to the convention were: David I. Walsh, James M. Curley, Andrew J. Peters, Charles H. Cole, Helen A. MacDonald, William J. Foley, Edward J. Kelley, Lawrence F. Quigley. Alternates: Charles H. McGlue, Strabo V. Claggett, Joseph Santosuosso, Bernard M. Wolf, Elizabeth C. McInerney, Dorothy Whipple Frye, James A. Donovan, Raymond V. McNamara.

MASSACHUSETTS FOR SMITH

INTEREST in the two leading party conventions during the early part of the year 1928 overshadowed all other political events. The Massachusetts Republican organization was as overwhelmingly for Herbert Hoover as the Democrats were for Alfred E. Smith. Governor Fuller took an early stand for the Secretary of Commerce for the Presidential nomination and predicted that Mr. Hoover would be elected by a big plurality.

Both Presidential candidates came to Massachusetts and spoke during the campaign. Each side tried to outdo the other in demonstrations. Smith's reception was the noisiest and biggest. Boston outdid itself. No Presidential candidate in a generation made such an appeal to the reason and emotions of Massachusetts Democrats as Alfred Emanuel Smith. The story of his lowly birth, his struggle to get on in life, his rise from a poor East Side boy to the Governorship of the Empire State, his wonderfully attractive personality and wide knowledge of the affairs of government, combined to make him a popular idol with the masses. They felt that Smith was another Jackson and that his election to the Presidency would bring their Government nearer to the people than it had been since Lincoln's time.

Smith himself said that he had never seen anything in his political career that equalled Boston's reception to him. Thousands were turned away from his meetings and had to content themselves with a fleeting glance of their political idol as his motorcar crept through the crowded streets. Coming to Boston from Albany, he was met by cheering crowds at every stop. There were brief breaks in his journey at Springfield, Worcester and Newton. Admirers fought for the privilege of shaking hands with him.

Mr. Hoover's supporters tried to equal Smith's reception for their candidate and those charged with the task of staging the demonstration did well, but the sedate, shy Republican candidate was not in Smith's class in arousing enthusiasm and attracting crowds. Smith talked issues in which the common man and woman were vitally interested—the repeal of the prohibitory amend-

ALFRED E. SMITH

ment and social welfare legislation. Mr. Hoover's speech dealt mainly with the tariff, taking care not to hurt the feelings of the manufacturers.

Smith proved to be the more attractive candidate election day, carrying the State by 17,000, the first time a Democrat had carried the State in a straight out, cleancut contest. The Wilson victory in 1912 was due to the Republican–Bull Moose split. Smith even carried the Cape by a slim plurality. Berkshire joined the Democratic column as did Bristol and Hampden. Suffolk gave him a load of more than 105,000. The vote for other Presidential candidates was Thomas, Socialist, 6,262; Foster, Workers' Party, 2461; Reynolds, Socialist-Labor, 772. More than 32,000 voters failed to vote for President.

The country as a whole was anti-Smith. It was inevitable that the religious issue would figure in the contest. Smith met it frankly and courageously and with the aid of the late Father Duffy, Chaplain of the New York regiment that Colonel William (Wild Bill) Donovan, a prominent member of the Republican party, commanded, set forth his credo answering the claims of opponents that a President professing the Roman Catholic faith could not be loyal to its institutions.

Secretly, the Republican National Committee encouraged and financed the Ku Klux Klan campaign against Smith. A reporter of the New York *World* proved the connection between the two. The South was a fruitful field for the Klan and states in that section, notably Texas, joined the Hoover forces, casting their electoral vote for the first time for a Republican Presidential candidate. Mr.

Hoover was urged by friends to denounce the religious issue but failed to do so until toward the end of the campaign and then only half-heartedly when a circular, issued by a Virginia woman supporter, urging voters against Smith on religious grounds, found its way into the newspapers, but the connection of the Klan and the Republican National Committee continued. Col. Mann of Tennessee, liaison officer between the Klan and the Republican National Committee, who expected to distribute much of the Federal patronage in the Klan-controlled States was given the cold shoulder by Mr. Hoover after inauguration and parted company with the President. Strange to relate, both Col. Mann and his wife embraced the Catholic faith and he died in the church he had vilified.

Smith lost his own State and the adjoining State of New Jersey. The vote against him was emphatic. Hoover's total of the popular vote was 21,392,190 to Smith's 15,016,433. Thomas, Socialist, received 267,420; Foster, Workers' Party, 48,770. Mr. Hoover had 444 electoral votes to 87 for Smith. It is estimated that there were about 5,000,000 Catholic voters in the United States so that 15,000,000 Protestants must have cast their ballots for Smith.

In addition to the opposition to him on religious grounds, Smith's advocacy of the repeal of the 18th or Prohibitory amendment to the Federal Constitution cost him many Democratic votes in dry territory. By the time that the next Presidential election rolled around the South had punished several of the leading Anti-Smithites, notably Senator Tom Heflin of Alabama and Senator Simmons of North Carolina, both of whom were later deprived of their Senate seats by their party. Texas also hastened to dethrone those who bolted Smith.

The Democratic candidate took his medicine manfully and soon after the election gave his support to the movement headed by Chairman John J. Raskob of the Democratic National committee to organize the Democratic forces for 1932. Headquarters were kept open and staffed by efficiency aids, financed by Raskob and directed by Jouett Shouse of Kansas. Charles Michaelson, head of the New York *World* bureau in Washington, was put in charge of publicity and for the first time in many years the Democratic headquarters continued to function and watch the Republican administration in between elections, with the result that the Republicans were kept busy explaining, always a dangerous thing for a politician.

WALSH DEFEATS YOUNG FOR SENATE

SENATOR WALSH's term of office was expiring March 3rd, 1929. Two years before he had defeated Senator Butler, named by Governor Cox on the death of Senator Lodge to fill the office, until the people could elect. Walsh's big majority over Butler was notice to the Republicans that a younger man with progressive leanings must be pitted against him if they wanted his seat. Three candidates entered the primary for the Republican nomination—Ex-Speaker of the House of Representatives, B. Loring Young, Eben S. Draper, son of the late Governor Draper, and General Butler Ames, a senatorial perennial. The Republican State Committee and its allies favored Young. He was nominated in the primary by a vote of 162,634 against 141,525 for Draper and 92,182 for Ames. The combined vote of the opposition left Young a minority nominee by more than 8000 votes. Draper and Ames fell into line and preserved their regularity with their tongues in their cheeks.

From a public service standpoint Young was well equipped for the office. He was aggressive, in his early 40's, a good talker, an able lawyer, democratic in his ways and popular with his party. He presided over the House of Representatives for three sessions, came of a good family and was connected with the well known law firm of Ropes, Gray, Loring & Perkins, specialists in big business, numbering among their clients several public service and power companies, depending on politicians for favors.

Walsh had no opposition for his renomination, but soon sensed that in Young he was confronted by an opponent who could not be easily brushed aside. Senator Walsh lost no time in getting into action and the contest was lively. Organized labor took the field against Young because of his labor record in the Legislature. Walsh accused him of trying to ride both horses on the wet and dry issue and discussed his labor record in detail. He demanded to know how Young if elected would vote on the Vare contested Pennsylvania Senatorial seat then before that body. Walsh was for refusing to admit Vare because of fraud and corruption in the election. Young made a typical lawyer's reply, saying that if elected he would consider the case carefully and be guided by the evidence submitted before the Senate investigating committee, a safe answer for a lawyer, but not for a politician seeking votes. The country believed with Walsh that Vare should be denied his seat.

In his enthusiasm, Mr. Young at times forgot his own senatorial contest and rushed to the defense of President Coolidge's economy program and upbraided Smith, the Democratic Presidential candidate, for poking fun at the White House savings by omitting the stripes on the mail bags, using lead pencils until they were stubs, utilizing the reverse side of discontinued government blank forms for copy paper, exercising more care in the use of rubber bands and shutting off the electric lights when not needed by government workers.

The trend was Democratic and election day Senator Walsh rolled up a plurality of more than 125,000 and hung another Republican scalp on his belt.

DEMOCRATS NOMINATE COLE

Senator Walsh had no opposition for the Democratic nomination. General Charles H. Cole defeated John J. Cummings for the Democratic nomination for Governor by 125,000 plurality and John F. Malley won the nomination for second place on the Democratic State ticket. The Democrats nominated Ex-Lieutenant Governor Barry for Attorney General over William F. Scharton. Dr. Joseph Santosuosso was the unanimous choice of the Democrats for Secretary of State. His nomination gave the Italian people a representative on the Democratic ticket. For years Dr. Santosuosso had taken a prominent part in Boston politics and was one of the first of his race elected to the old Common Council. He practiced medicine among the Italian people of the North End for several years and at the same time studied law and qualified as a practicing attorney.

STATE CONVENTIONS 1928

REPUBLICANS and Democrats enjoyed enthusiastic gatherings the night before their State Conventions. The Republican Club staged a big dinner, presided over by its President, State Senator Henry Parkman, Jr., at which Ogden Mills, Under-Secretary of the Treasury, was the chief speaker. The Democrats held forth with Charles Dana Gibson, the famous artist and illustrator, who paid his respects to Senator Moses of New Hampshire, presiding officer at the Kansas City Convention, which nominated Hoover and Curtis, vowing that there hadn't been a man named Moses who had amounted to much since the great old fellow in the incident of the bulrushes, "but Senator Moses made a slip in that speech that will get him a place in history, if nothing else does," he declared. "Mr. Moses' words are conclusive evidence that Moses and the Republicans don't think much of the common people, who are mostly made up of Jones, Robinsons, Browns, Smiths—and the people will rise in their might November 6 and say so," said he. "These are common names enough, but there are few Americans who can climb into their family trees without shortly meeting up with one of these names."

The Democrats put on a great banquet attended by 1500 men and women, who listened to speeches by Frances Perkins, destined to become the first woman to sit in the Cabinet of a President of the United States, and Senator Pat Harrison of Mississippi, who told of "the devilish whispering campaign," the country over, of "bales of copies of the insidious *Fellowship Forum,*" KKK organ, discovered in circulation and of 250 batches of pamphlets of "religious" character circulated through the South by the Republicans.

The Republicans held their State Convention in Boston and were addressed by Governor Fuller and their candidates for United States Senator, B. Loring Young, Senator Gillett and the candidates on the State ticket. The keynoter was Ogden L. Mills. Loring Young came in for the lion's share of attention and applause and was hailed as the next Senator.

The resolutions, read by John C. Hull, dodged the prohibition issue by name, but the platform makers resorted to the old dodge of pledging the party to a "vigorous enforcement of the provisions of the Constitution" and denied "the right of anyone to destroy these provisions by nullification and subterfuge."

The religious plank in the platform read: "We agree with our Presidential candidate, Herbert Hoover, that 'the glory of our American ideals in the right of every man to worship God according to the dictates of his own conscience.' We stand to-day, as always, for no distinction of race, color or creed as qualifications for holding public office." A message from President Coolidge was read in which he praised all of the candidates—State and National. Mr. Hoover also sent a telegram in which he thanked Massachusetts Republicans for the work they had done and were doing in his behalf.

The Democrats also held their State Convention in Boston, with ex-Mayor Andrew J. Peters as presiding officer. As soon as Chairman Frank J. Donahue finished reading the call for the gathering, Rufus B. Dodge, a Republican ex-mayor of Worcester, was chosen temporary chairman, who told the delegates why he had left that party and joined the Democrats. "Harry Daugherty, Harry Sinclair and Albert B. Fall had wrought more havoc in the Harding administration than could be traced to the door of Tammany Hall," he declared. He said that the country needed the application of the "torch of purification" and that no man was better to apply it than the Democratic Presidential candidate, Alfred E. Smith.

Mrs. Francis B. Sayre of Cambridge, a daughter of Woodrow Wilson, was a member of the Committee on Rules. When her name was called the Convention applauded. She stood up and made a brief speech, saying that she appreciated the tribute to her father and herself, adding: "I feel we are under a great and courageous leader." There were stirring speeches by Senator Walsh, Mayor James M. Curley and General Charles H. Cole, the gubernatorial candidate.

Professor Eugene Waumbaugh of the Harvard Law School was chairman of Resolutions. The platform ratified the Houston Convention proceedings, praised Smith, the Presidential candidate, General Cole and Senator Walsh. It declared among other things for old age pension, a retention of annual sessions of the Legislature and extension of the benefits of the Workmen's Compensation Law.

FRANK G. ALLEN
Governor 1929-1931

GOVERNOR FULLER was ready to retire at the end of his second term, which expired in January, 1929, and did everything he could to smooth the path of Lieutenant Governor Frank G. Allen to succeed him. Allen, another successful business man and popular with the politicians, launched his campaign for the Republican gubernatorial nomination early in the summer of 1928. He had a formidable opponent in Frank A. Goodwin, the former Registrar of Motor Vehicles, removed from his office by Governor Fuller. The contest for the nomination was spirited. Not in years had the G.O.P. experienced such a lively contest for its State standard bearer. Goodwin's sharp tongue ridiculed Allen's public record and made light of the duties of the Lieutenant Governor—a one day a week job, he claimed. Allen, he said, had spent his life making dollars with politics as a plaything, while he had served in the City Council of Boston, the office of Street Commissioner and Registrar of Motor Vehicles. At times, because Republican committees failed to invite him to speak at their gatherings, he "crashed the gates" and assailed the "machine gang" at the State House.

The Lieutenant Governor contented himself with citing his public record as a member of the Senate, as Lieutenant Governor and his standing as a successful business man. His vote in the primary for the nomination was 267,588 against Goodwin's 169,673. The latter's big vote was a disturbing eye opener for the Allen supporters and gave them plenty of food for thought. Goodwin was not a political joke.

William S. Youngman was nominated for Lieutenant Governor in a field of eight candidates. There was a hot battle for Attorney General with Clarence A. Barnes opposing Attorney General Warner, but the latter won easily. State Auditor Alonzo Cook, opposed by the State Committee, won handily by a plurality of 79,000. John W. Haigis was successful as a candidate for State Treasurer in a four man fight. His competitor was ex-State Treasurer Fred J. Burrill, who polled 111,000 votes despite his malodorous record in that office a few years before. Haigis' lead over him was only 9000. Russell Wood and J. Ernest Kerr also ran.

ELECTION

GOODWIN accepted the verdict of the primary with good grace and refused to run as an Independent for Governor, thus clearing the Republican political atmosphere. His quarrel was more with Governor Fuller than with the Lieutenant Governor. The next we hear of Mr. Goodwin is a year later, when Governor Allen appointed his Chairman of the Boston Finance Commission, a body set up by a Republican Legislature to watch the finances of the capital city. Goodwin took the place of John C. L. Dowling, a Democrat, whose reappointment was urged by his two Republican associates on the commission. There was a lot of talk in political circles about Goodwin being Curley's man. It was true that he had supported Curley for Mayor and that the latter had named him as one of Boston's street commissioners. At all events, Governor Allen took him into camp and thereby removed from the field one who might create no end of trouble for him in the next election. The Governor's friends resented the latter charge, but the public regarded Goodwin's appointment as smacking of politics. At any rate, the Republican strategists seemed pleased at the thought that henceforth Goodwin would be shooting at Democrats instead of Republicans.

General Cole's army buddies made things lively and worked hard for him. His friends kept a sharp eye on several Boston Democratic ward politicians, who had served in the Legislature with Allen and were known to be friendly with him. There was evidence of some disloyalty to Cole election day in the home wards of those suspected. It was a great disappointment to General Cole's friends election night to learn that he was defeated by 19,235 in a total vote of more than 1,500,000. The entire Republican State ticket with the exception of the candidate for Senator was elected by pluralities as high as 104,000 in the case of the Secretary of State, Frederick W. Cook. The Republicans elected 13 of the 16 Congressmen. The only new face in the new Congressional delegation was William K. Kaynor of Springfield, elected in the Second District. The three sitting Democratic members, William P. Connery of Lynn, John J. Douglas and John W. McCormack of Boston, were reelected.

Soon after election Governor Fuller, who had a high personal regard for the Democratic gubernatorial candidate, awarded him a consolation prize of a place on the board of trustees of the Boston Elevated Railway Company. Democrats made substantial gains in the Legislature. The previous Senate contained five Democrats, four from Boston and one from Holyoke. They retained all of those seats and added five, thus doubling their representation in the upper branch of the General Court. The total vote was the largest ever cast, due to the great interest in the Presidential contest. The big increase in the Democratic vote was attributable to the popularity of their Presidential candidate. Nearly 97% of the registered vote was cast—a high-water mark for Massachusetts.

The referendum act to permit professional sports on Sunday carried: Yes, 577,353; No, 304,738. On the question of instructing State Senators to favor the repeal of the 18th amendment, the vote was overwhelmingly wet. Thirty-six out of the 40 Senatorial districts voted for repeal; 15 out of the 16 Congressional districts joined the wet procession. The only district voting No was the sixth, represented by A. Piatt Andrew, by no means a dry. This test of public opinion of the prohibitory law was fathered by the Constitutional Liberty League.

AN ADAMS SECRETARY OF THE NAVY

ONE of the surprises in the formation of the Hoover cabinet was the selection of Charles Francis Adams of Massachusetts for Secretary of the Navy. Mr. Adams, a member of the family which gave to the country two Presidents, John and John Quincy Adams, a minister to England, Charles Francis Adams, and others in the public service, was generally regarded as a Democrat. His father, John Quincy Adams, was a lifelong member of that party. He accepted the Democratic nomination for Governor of Massachusetts in Civil War days and later when there was no hope of election. His son, exemplifying that independence for which the family was noted, regarded himself as an Independent in politics. The first the public knew of his selection for the Cabinet was when he called on the President-elect after the election at a

Florida resort, in company with Louis K. Liggett, National Committeeman for Massachusetts, and the fact that Mr. Hoover offered him the Navy portfolio leaked out through a sports writer of the Boston *Post,* William H. Cunningham, who wired his paper to check up on the story at this end, adding that all he knew the Adams Mr. Hoover had in mind was not the Charles F. Adams prominent in business and sports circles.

PASSING OF FROTHINGHAM AND GALLIVAN

Two of the State's most popular and useful public men, Congressmen James A. Gallivan and Louis A. Frothingham passed away within a few months of one another in 1928.

There was no more colorful figure in Massachusetts politics or in Congress than Representative James A. Gallivan, who represented the South Boston and Dorchester districts in Washington for nearly 14 years. He was a native of South Boston, a graduate of Harvard College, class of '88. He engaged in reportorial work on Boston papers until he went into politics and was elected to the State House of Representatives and to the State Senate. For 14 years, from 1900 to 1914, he was a member of the Boston Board of Street Commissioners, at which time he was elected to the vacancy in Congress created by the resignation of James M. Curley, elected Mayor of Boston.

At home, Gallivan was a power in city politics. As a campaigner he had few equals. In Congress he distinguished himself as a champion of measures affecting his cosmopolitan district. In the World War, when he believed that General Pershing and General March were unfair to the commanding officers of the Yankee Division, composed of New England troops, he took the floor in Congress and denounced them. The sudden about face of the high command in France in its treatment of the Division, was due in no small part to Gallivan's attack on the War Department and what he characterized as "the typewriter brigade safely housed behind the lines at Chaumuont, France."

He was from the first, an opponent of prohibition and spoke against it every time an opportunity presented itself in Congress. Whenever it was known that "Jim" Gallivan was going to address the House on liquor or any other subject, he was assured of a capacity audience, but prohibition was well entrenched in those days and while his speeches were eloquent, witty, and informative and often exposed the hypocrisy of the Drys in and out of Congress, he never could muster more than a handful of votes against the enforcement measures and the accompanying huge appropriations.

His last public speech was delivered March 17, 1928, before the Charitable Irish Society of Boston, celebrating St. Patrick's Day, on the same subject. He died April 3, 1928, sincerely mourned by his constituents and a wide circle of friends and admirers in and out of the State. He was succeeded in Congress by John W. McCormack, who had unsuccessfully opposed him for the nomination at his last election. It was no easy task to fill the Congressional shoes of Jim Gallivan, but John McCormack made good, though less colorful than Gallivan. He was soon recognized as the spokesman for New England in party councils and given a place on the important Ways and Means Committee, which makes the tariff. He is now serving his third term, his political statue still growing as a national political figure.

Louis A. Frothingham Lieutenant Governor of Massachusetts for two years, Speaker of the House 1901–1905, unsuccessful candidate for Mayor of Boston and Governor of the Commonwealth, Lieutenant of Marines in the Spanish-American War and Major in the United States Army in the World War, a member of Congress seven years, representing the 15th District, died suddenly while on a yachting trip on the Maine coast, August 23, 1928. Mourned by a wide circle of devoted friends, he had long been a popular figure in Republican politics and champion of good government. Governor McCall made him Chairman of a State Commission to visit the soldiers and sailors in France in 1918. He took an active interest in the affairs of the American Legion and served as State Vice-Commander. He was a graduate of and an Overseer of Harvard University at the time of his death, a position he had filled for 18 years. Mr. Frothingham was a fine type of public servant. He took his politics seriously and always attracted to his standard the best element in his party.

GOVERNOR FULLER'S COURAGE

THE four years that Alvan T. Fuller spent as Governor were by no means a bed of roses. In reality, the Republican leaders never wanted him, but when forced to take him, they pretended to enjoy his company. The fear always haunted them that he would refuse to do their bidding and in this they were justified by his record for independence, but aside from lecture now and then to department heads and a Legislature unresponsive to public opinion, he had no serious dispute with his party leaders.

His courage was put to a severe test in the carrying out of the sentence of death in the famous Sacco-Vanzetti murder case and he did not flinch.

April 15, 1920, a factory paymaster and his guard were held up, robbed and brutally murdered at South Braintree. Nicola Sacco and Bartolomeo Vanzetti were arrested, charged with the crime and found guilty at a long drawn out trial presided over by Judge Webster Thayer of the Superior Court and sentenced to die in the electric chair. Sacco and Vanzetti were Radicals or "Reds" as they were called.

Their conviction aroused the Reds of the world who kept up an agitation for their freedom and contributed to a defense fund in their behalf. Demonstrations were made against American embassies and Legations in different parts of the world by their Radical sympathisers, until the case became of international interest and importance and at the time the most celebrated case in the criminology of Massachusetts. They appealed to the Governor to save them from the chair.

Their plea for clemency was supported by an organized committee of men and women of Radical tendencies. Some of the more "advanced thinkers" among their friends threatened the life of officials connected with the prosecution of the case, including Governor Fuller. The Governor spent weeks looking into the case and concluded that the verdict of the jury was just. To make doubly sure, he summoned to his aid three unprejudiced prominent citizens, President Abbott Lawrence Lowell of Harvard University, Judge Robert Grant, a retired Justice of the Suffolk County Probate Court and President Samuel W. Stratton of the Institute of Technology, to examine into the case and report to him their findings. They agreed with the Governor that the verdict was just. Buttressed in his opinion by the jury, the courts and the special commission, Governor Fuller declined to interfere with the action of the court.

Then began a series of protest meetings by Radicals, many of whom came from other States. There were street parades and meetings and a propaganda in their behalf which deluged the Governor with appeals to save the lives of the convicted men. For a time the State House was a veritable arsenal. Many arrests were made of the more boisterous of the friends of the condemned men. The police broke up several outdoor meetings. Excitement reigned for days, while awaiting the Governor's decision. Petitions by letter, telegraph and cable poured into the Executive Chamber, many from recognized leaders in world affairs, asking the Governor to interfere, but he refused to be swerved from what he believed to be his duty. The men had been justly convicted, he maintained and the sentence of death was carried out by the warden of the State Prison.

From every nook and corner of the country came messages of gratitude and congratulations to the Governor for his courageousness.

While his decision in this Sacco-Vanzetti case was the outstanding achievement of his administration, he showed himself to be a fearless executive, who spoke his mind at all times and acted for what he believed to be the best interest of the State and its people, a type of Governor altogether too rare.

GOVERNOR ALLEN SWORN IN

FRANK G. ALLEN of Norwood was inaugurated as the 51st Governor under the Constitution, January 3, 1929, with the customary ceremonies. A battery of the 101st Field Artillery proclaimed the advent of a new Governor of the Commonwealth by firing a salute of 17 guns on the Common. The oath was administered by the Secretary of State, Frederick W. Cook, in the presence of a distinguished crowd that filled the House Chamber.

In opening his inaugural, Governor Allen advised members of the Legislature against mistaking the "loud voice of the minority" for the opinion of the majority. "To ignore public sentiment is inexcusable, regardless of how lofty the motive. Mistaking the sentiments of a few for public opinion is a danger against which we cannot too strongly entrench ourselves."

"Skillful propagandists have often promoted pet measures under the guise of public opinion. Every Legislative session reveals attempts in this direction. Occasionally, they succeed. Such practices are an imposition on our public men and a fraud on the people. It is our first duty to accurately determine the true state of public opinion and our next duty to respond to it in an appropriate manner. Legislation which cannot muster public support represents wasted effort.

"Having served as a member of both branches of the General Court," he continued, "I know and appreciate the importance of coöperation between the Chief Executive and the Legislative branches of our Government. I am convinced that there are solutions for the many problems which confront us. Nothing can hasten us in solving them more than a relationship based on coöperative effort and mutual respect."

The chief points and recommendations of his address may be summarized as follows: "Public opinion on important public matters is usually right. . . . Rejections of legislation by the people indicate that there has been either a willful disregard of public sentiment by the Legislature or a failure of our public men properly to judge such sentiment. To ignore public sentiment is inexcusable, regardless of how lofty the motive."

He recommended continuation of the policy of private ownership and public control of the Boston Elevated, "extending this method for a definite term." He urged construction of the East Boston vehicular tunnel.

"The motor vehicle owners of this Commonwealth can never be convinced that rates based upon data furnished by the insurance companies are just, reasonable and nondiscriminatory," said he. "They are justified in their opinion that in this important matter the records of all companies, both foreign and domestic, should be examined in the same manner as the law now requires the Commonwealth to examine the domestic companies."

He favored legislation to provide that no injunction relief shall be given in labor disputes unless both parties have an opportunity to be heard on the facts on which the petition for the injunction is based. The State House, he declared, is not the proper depository for confiscated liquor and he proposed a suitable warehouse for the storage of this commodity be found elsewhere.

He recommended the appointment of a commission to study the feasibility of coöperating the administrative work of State and local governments in the Metropolitan district with motor traffic, crime, fire and disease.

Other recommendations for legislation were: Regular inspection of automobiles; more drastic examination of applicants to operate automobiles and possible reëxamination of license holders to see if they are still in a fit condition to drive an automobile safely. Permanent revocation of the license of a driver involved in a fatal accident while under the influence of liquor. Legislation to prevent recurrence of the milk-borne epidemic of last year. A census of crippled children to give benefit of State's facilities and training to those now without them. Abolition of grade crossings "ought not to be abandoned merely because the railroads are in poor financial condition."

In concluding his address he observed: "There is no greater honor than the badge of public office. There is no greater regard than the gratitude and respect of our fellow-citizens. The former is ours to enjoy; the latter is ours to earn. He who covets no vain celebrity, who strives to fulfill the obligations of his trust with moral courage and intellectual honesty, bears within himself his own reward, and is conscious of having served well his Commonwealth."

The Legislature organized with Gaspar G. Bacon, President of the Senate, Leverett Saltonstall, Speaker of the House, scions of two old families whose members had rendered fine public service to the Commonwealth and Nation. Bacon's father was a close friend and political supporter of Theodore Roosevelt. He served for a short time as Secretary of State in the Roosevelt cabinet and was Ambassador to France under President Taft, was a volunteer staff officer in the A.E.F., serving with distinction and died before peace was declared. He was a partner in the great banking house of J. P. Morgan of New York.

Speaker Saltonstall's antecedents were Democrats until the Bryan era. Grover Cleveland appointed his grandfather Collector of the Port of Boston in his first Presidential term against the wishes of many Democrats, who favored Peter Butler, an old line Democrat.

The Senate Democrats voted for Robert E. Bigney for President of that body, which made him the minority floor leader of the session. Leo M. Birmingham of Brighton received the Democratic vote in the House for Speaker.

The Legislature remained in session until June 8, adjourning late in the evening after the Governor signed the new Elevated bill. The principal features of the bill were the three-way referendum on the questions of public control, public ownership or private ownership, the creation of a district council and a new board of trustees to study the need of improvements and extensions to take over existing subways. The General Court remained supreme in final settlement of the problem. The referendum to the voters in the Metropolitan district served by the road at the State election in 1930 was intended to be only a guide for the 1931 Legislature.

The members did not forget themselves and provided for 28 special investigating committees to sit during the interval between adjournment and the meeting of the next Legislature in 1931. They appropriated $143,000 for the expenses of these committees.

LEGISLATURE OF 1930

When the Legislature met January 2, 1930, Governor Allen pleased the Drys and angered the Wets by taking strong grounds against the repeal of the State enforcement law known as the "Baby Volstead Act." There was an initiative petititon before the Legislature for the repeal of the law. But the G.O.P. was wedded to the dry cause and the Governor declared that the repeal of this act "would not change the fundamental situation with regard to Prohibition." It "would be an incentive to violate the law" and "breed and nourish lawlessness."

The enforcement act was placed in the Massachusetts statute book only after a Republican President, Mr. Harding, had lectured the Governors of the States and insisted that a refusal to coöperate with the Federal authorities in enforcing Prohibition was "tantamount to flouting the supreme law of the land." The Wets claimed that there was no moral or legal obligation imposed upon the States by the 18th amendment to pass enforcement acts and even if the Massachusetts statute were repealed, the Federal act would remain unimpaired and it was as much the duty of the Federal government to enforce the Volstead Act as any other law enacted by Congress.

The State act had never been enforced. Indeed, it was unenforceable and those charged with enforcing it knew it, but it was regarded as good politics by the Republican leaders to praise the act with high sounding phrases and refuse, with affected righteous indignation, to permit any weakening of that law. The party was committed to prohibition and it must at least pretend to be its guardian. True, nothing that the State could do, except through its representatives in Congress would affect the Federal

MAYOR FREDERICK W. MANSFIELD OF BOSTON

law, but a repeal of the local Volstead Act would be notice to the powers that be at Washington that Massachusetts was against trying to make people better morally by law. This Legislature refused to do anything about repeal, but those behind the petition, headed by the Constitutional Liberty League and the Liberal Civic League, opposed to prohibition, took the fight to the people in the November election. The result was the repeal of the Baby Volstead Act carried by a majority of 281,000, demonstrating how poorly Republican leaders adjudged public opinion.

The legislature adjourned May 29th after a 24 hour session, in which Governor Allen bombarded it with five veto messages, the first of which dealt with physical examination for the classified labor services in cities and towns. The second forbade oral examinations for promotion in a police department. The third increased salaries of Justices and Clerks of District Courts. The fourth and fifth were also civil service changes. All were sustained.

Among the most important new laws passed among the 426 acts passed were:

The old age assistance bill.
The bill to extend the subway under Governor Square.
The bill for elimination of grade crossings.
The fire prevention bill.
The resolve for drafting of plans for a new Supreme Court building.
Resolves for a number of recess commissions, including one to investigate boxing, parks, limited town meetings,

habit forming drugs, bridges, marine fisheries, a Gloucester fish pier, taxation, Fort Point channel and Boston war memorial.

Compromise book censorship bill.

Bill taking away from civil service commission approval of appointees of Mayor of Boston.

Among the measures rejected were:

Investigation of Boston police department.

Practically all compulsory automobile insurance legislation.

Revision of the taxation laws.

Everything of consequence relating to power and light.

Jury service for women.

The legalizing of "yellow dog" contracts.

Adjournment was taken until October 20th, when the body met to appropriately observe the 300th anniversary of the establishment of the General Court, at which time Chief Justice Rugg of the Supreme Judicial Court delivered the principal address.

1930 A DEMOCRATIC YEAR

REPUBLICANS got little comfort out of the 1930 election. The country elected a Democratic Congress. In Massachusetts the Republicans lost their Second Senatorial seat, the Governorship, State Treasurer and State Auditor. The Hoover administration at Washington was doomed. The loss of Congress clearly indicated that. A President who loses his midterm Congress has little chance of being reëlected. The financial debacle of 1929 was followed by a severe economic depression causing a great increase in unemployment and its attending ills. The country was not satisfied with the way the Republicans handled the situation and turned them out of office. The casualty list was filled with the names of Republican Governors and members of both houses of Congress.

In Massachusetts the warning of what was going to happen in 1930 was sounded months before. Representative William K. Kaynor of Springfield, serving his first term in Congress, was killed in an airplane accident. A special election was held in February 1930 to fill the vacancy and William J. Granfield, Democrat, was elected over Frederick D. Griggs, the Republican candidate, by a plurality of more than 6000. Granfield made the repeal of the dry law his chief issue. Griggs was dry as dust. The district had been represented by Senator Gillett for 30 years. The result was regarded as significant victory for the Democrats and the Wets and when Granfield appeared in Washington to be sworn in he was lionized by the members of his party. The new Representative had served in both branches of the State Legislature and before his admission to the bar had been a professional baseball player.

The Democrats had a wealth of candidates in 1930 for United States Senator, Governor and all of the other places on the State ticket, eager to run the gauntlet of the primary. They sniffed victory in the air and were willing to fight for a chance of participating in its fruits.

Not only did every movement of the National political barometer indicate a trend to the Democrats, but those who controlled the Republican party machinery were still under the spell of the Anti-Saloon League and either side-stepped the issue or insisted on a vigorous enforcement of the dry law. Massachusetts had more than once indicated its disapproval of Prohibition. Still, the Republican organization clung tenaciously to this unpopular law and paid the penalty of loss of office and power and the respect of many voters of their own party.

TWO TERCENTENARIES 1930

THERE were two tercentenary celebrations in 1930 of historical importance—one the 300th anniversary of the founding of the Massachusetts Bay Colony, the other the 300th anniversary of the settlement of Boston. The former, directed by a representative committee headed by Herbert Parker was a State wide affair, while the latter was confined to Boston and the annexed cities and towns which make up the present municipality. Ex-Mayor Fitzgerald was chairman of the latter committee.

The celebrations program was spread over a week, beginning Sept. 14 to and including Sept. 17, the latter date being the date of the changing of the name from Tri Mountain to Boston. Mayor Curley invited Lord Mayor Salter of Boston, England, and a number of the high ranking officials of the English municipality to be the guests of the committee on the occasion. There was a monster civic and military parade September 17, the Chief Marshal of which was General Edward L. Logan the gallant-soldier who commanded the 101st Infantry in France.

During a halt of the parade, Mayor Curley sent to King Edward of England a good will message through the Governor General of Canada and he and Lord Mayor Salter exchanged similar radio messages with London officials. Mme. Schumann-Heink came all the way from California to sing at the reception to Lord Mayor Salter's banquet at which there was more handshaking across the sea. Mayor Curley made a happy speech and Salter replied in kind. Before the expiration of Mayor Curley's term of office, he made a return visit of courtesy to Boston, England, where he was accorded all of the honors reserved for distinguished visitors and guests of the quaint little English city after which Boston, Massachusetts, was named.

All of the suburban sections of the city had their own local celebrations and every racial group was given an opportunity of celebrating after their own customs and ideas. Some of the outstanding events of the week's celebration were: an evening electrical parade; dedication of the memorial tablet to the founders upon Boston Common; a town meeting and reception at the Boston Garden; dedication of the West End Health Unit; banquet by members of the Boston Typographical Union; a field day at Franklin Field.

DEMOCRATS NOMINATE ELY FOR GOVERNOR

JOSEPH B. ELY of Westfield, who didn't hesitate to advocate the election of William J. Bryan for the Presidency, when he was a student at Williams College, inherited his Democracy from a father, who was a lifelong Democrat in a strong Republican section of Western Massachusetts. When Walsh was Governor he named Ely to fill a vacancy in the office of District Attorney in his home section. That was the only public office he had ever held when he entered the primary for the Democratic gubernatorial nomination. He was popular in the Western part of the State, where he was well known, but in the Eastern part of the Commonwealth he was a comparative stranger except to a few of the party leaders. A few years before, he was a candidate for the nomination for Lieutenant Governor and as already related, was defeated by Harry J. Dooley. This time he entered the fight better prepared and with an organization made up of a group of personal friends, who were ready to stay with him to the end of the battle for the nomination. There were two other candidates in the field, Ex-Mayor John F. Fitzgerald and John J. Cummings, the latter a young Boston attorney who had been in the Legislature, was a good campaigner and a hard fighter.

It was a busy summer for the gubernatorial candidates. They toured the State and flooded it with oratory. The fight got so hot and personal, it was suggested that a convention be held at Worcester for the purpose of discussing the situation with a view of uniting on some one for the nomination for Governor. The conference was held in Worcester but it accomplished nothing and the contest was resumed with more acrimony than ever. Mayor Curley of Boston redoubled his efforts on behalf of Fitzgerald, making Ely the target for his sharp shooting. Curley supporting Fitzgerald was laughable in view of what each had said of the other in previous political fights. Just before primary day, Fitzgerald was taken sick and he issued a statement saying that his physician had forbidden him to campaign any more and withdrew from the race, but his name was on the ballot and Curley kept up the fight for him, saying that a big vote for John F. in the primary would do more to restore him to health than a doctor's medicine.

In the closing hours of the contest, Curley made a savage onslaught on Ely, branded him as an enemy of the Irish, charged that he had slurred them at the State Convention in 1920, when he championed a plank in the platform favoring the League of Nations. Ely hotly denied the silly racial charge and the fight went on to a finish, resulting in the nomination of Ely, the vote being: Ely, 117,548; John F. Fitzgerald, 84,744; John J. Cummings, 12,701. Fitzgerald accepted the verdict and campaigned for the ticket. Curley, who was wont to refer to Ely as "the boy from the sticks" showed little enthusiasm for the gubernatorial nominee and there was a feeling among Ely's followers that the Mayor of

Boston would shed no tears if Governor Allen were re-elected. He and the Governor were very friendly and some of Curley's close friends were charged with treachery to the ticket.

MARCUS A. COOLIDGE FOR SENATE

THE Democratic contest for the nomination for the United States Senate was almost as animated as the fight over the gubernatorial nomination in 1930. Senator Gillett did not care to run again and had announced his intention to retire some months before the primaries. He had been a member of Congress for 35 years and desired to return to private life. There were five entrants for the Democratic nomination, Marcus A. Coolidge of Fitchburg, Joseph F. O'Connell, Thomas C. O'Brien, an Ex-District Attorney of Suffolk County, Ex-Governor Eugene N. Foss and Peter J. Joyce, all of Boston. In the midst of the campaign when the contest was at its height, O'Connell was stricken by illness and was unable to continue.

Coolidge's forte is not public speaking. He and his campaign manager, Daniel F. O'Connell, busied themselves in organizing Coolidge sentiment throughout the State. Marcus Coolidge needed no introduction to the Democrats of Massachusetts. For years he had been a prominent figure in the Councils of the party. He came of Hunker stock. His father was one of the wheel horses of the Cleveland and Russell Democracy and was elected to Congress in the Democratic landslide in 1890, serving one term.

Marcus Coolidge accumulated a tidy fortune as a builder of electric railways in the days when that means of transportation was popular. In the World War period he engaged in manufacturing machinery and material used in the war and added to his wealth. He was a liberal contributor to the Democratic campaign fund and after sending him on a mission to Poland President Wilson offered him the Ambassadorship to that country but Mr. Coolidge felt compelled for family and business reasons to decline the honor. He stood as candidate for Lieutenant Governor on the ticket with James M. Curley in 1924, when there was no hope of election. He served as mayor of his home city, Fitchburg. His opponents used as an argument against him that Senator Walsh was also a registered voter of Fitchburg and that two Democratic Senators from a little Republican city was unthinkable, but he headed the voting primary day, winning the nomination by more than 16,000 plurality, the vote was: Coolidge, 84,451; O'Connell, 54,289; O'Brien, 45,272; Foss, 12,824; Joyce, 5,680.

CLAGGETT FOR LIEUTENANT GOVERNOR

STRABO V. CLAGGETT of Newton, an investment broker, little known among the politicians, won the second place on the Democratic State ticket in a four cornered fight, the result of the voting was: Claggett, 50,192; Michael E. O'Neill of Everett, 50,091; John F. Malley of Newton, 47,141; Charles S. Murphy of Worcester, 44,155. For Secretary of State, Charles J. O'Brien of Boston was named over Joseph Santosuosso and Arthur G. Flynn. Charles F. Hurley of Cambridge won the nomination for State Treasurer over two competitors. Francis X. Hurley of Cambridge was nominated for State Auditor and Harold W. Sullivan of Boston for Attorney General.

REPUBLICAN PRIMARY

GOVERNOR ALLEN was opposed by John D. Devir of Malden, a new and unknown comer in the Republican party, but this opposition was not serious. His vote totaled but 22,996 against the Governor's 311,043. Devir was never heard of again. Lieutenant Governor Youngman, Attorney General Warner and Secretary of State Cook were unopposed for renomination. State Auditor Cook easily defeated his opponent, Joseph N. Carriere of Fitchburg. The surprise of the Republican primary was the nomination of Ex-State Treasurer Fred. J. Burrell over eight other candidates. Burrell got 58,768— 2,000 more than his nearest competitor, Ex-State Treasurer Charles J. Burrill, one of the best vote getters in his party.

BUTLER WINS SENATE NOMINATION

THE Republican fight for the Senatorial nomination overshadowed all other G.O.P. contests. Ex-Senator Butler insisted on another trial of his strength in this field. He felt that with Calvin Coolidge no longer President, he would have a freer hand than he had before. The Old Guard, almost to a man, lined up for him. As soon as Senator Gillett announced his intended retirement at the expiration of his term, Eben S. Draper, son of former Governor Draper, threw his hat into the ring. Later in the contest Mayor "Bossy" Gillis of Newburyport entered the list of aspirants. There was considerable mystery surrounding Gillis' candidacy. Some believed it was designed to draw votes away from Draper, who openly espoused the repeal of the 18th amendment. Butler, personally wet, was politically dry. Draper claimed that Prohibition transcended all other issues. Next in importance, he said, was industrial welfare and insisted that business management "must progress with the changing conditions of the 20th century" and the Republican party heed the call of the times.

The Draper campaign attracted many of the younger and more progressive Republicans, including Ex-State Treasurer James Jackson and B. Loring Young. The latter, no longer a candidate for public office, turned turtle on the liquor question and was now a dripping Wet. Draper's war buddies of the Yankee Division in which he served as a Captain of Artillery, made things lively. He got quite a boost from a letter Senator Lodge's daughter, Mrs. Constance Gardner Williams, endorsing his candidacy and scoring Mr. Butler for the way he used her father at the 1924 Cleveland convention. She emphatically denied the story originating with Senator Moses of New Hampshire, that Mr. Lodge desired Butler to succeed him in the Senate. When Walsh defeated Butler in 1926, Mrs. Williams voted for the Democratic candidate for the same reason. In her letter to candidate Draper, Mrs. Williams said:—

"Senator Lodge arrived at Cleveland to find himself treated like a pickpocket, at the orders of Mr. William Morgan Butler, the chairman at that time of the Republican committee. It was carried so far that his accommodations were unfit and insufficient and his one-time secretary, the late Louis A. Coolidge, insisted on changing rooms with him. The convention was in June of 1924, and in November of 1924 my father died. It has always been the belief of the Lodge family and friends that this treatment of an old and distinguished statesman, with years of devoted service behind him, was a deliberate act for Lodge's refusal to make way for Butler in exchange for Butler's help in 1922. If anyone is thinking of voting for Mr. Butler because he says he is the logical successor of Henry Cabot Lodge, he, or she, had better think again. They would be voting under a total misapprehension of the truth."

Butler denied the accusations in Mrs. Williams' letter, which was made public a week before the primary and must have helped Draper, though it did not defeat But-

GOV. JOSEPH B. ELY

ler, for he was nominated by a plurality of 6000, the vote being: Butler, 163,336; Draper, 156,745; Gillis, 22,996. Mr. Butler nor his friends could extract much comfort from the primary returns. Draper must be brought or whipped into line if Butler was to be elected.

ELY DEFEATS GOVERNOR ALLEN

THE nominations settled, the next thing demanding the attention of the candidates of both parties was to restore harmony in the ranks and see that the perfunctory State Conventions were kept within bounds. The Democrats held their State convention in Boston, September 27. William G. Thompson, a well known Boston lawyer, aligned with radical progressive groups, was temporary presiding officer, Senator Walsh the permanent chairman and Ex-Mayor Andrew J. Peters, chairman of Resolutions. The first public move to get Mayor Curley into line was the appointment of a Committee by the convention to wait on him and invite him to attend the convention. He came willingly and gave no outward signs of the strained relations existing between him and Chairman Donahue of the Democratic State Committee and candidate Ely.

The liquor plank of the platform demanded the repeal of the 18th amendment and the Volstead Act "to end the appalling orgy of crime and corruption and the restoration to each State of the authority to deal with the liquor problem in accordance with the mandate of its citizens."

It also recommended that at the election the people vote for the repeal of the so-called State "Baby Volstead Act." The convention voted against the return of the old saloon. In his speech to the delegates, the gubernatorial candidate criticised the Republican administration for failing to do anything substantial to aid unemployment or industrial recovery and held it responsible for the high automobile insurance rates.

Mr. Ely lost no time in forcing the fighting for Governor. It was soon evident that in him the Democrats had a vigorous campaigner and courageous fighter. He possessed a vein of dry humor and could enjoy a joke on himself as well as poke fun at his adversaries. He never lost his temper in public and was a master of sarcasm, which he didn't hesitate to employ at the expense of his opponent. In him the Democrats had a candidate who could give and take hard blows. He would not compromise with Republicans and spoke his mind freely about certain members of his own party who were covertly against him. He captured the fancy of his audience when Mayor Curley, who had savagely denounced him in the primary campaign, presided at a rally in Boston towards the end of the campaign and introduced him as "the clean, able, brilliant leader of the Democracy from Western Massachusetts."

While the audience chuckled at Curley's eulogy of the gubernatorial candidate, the latter referred to the presiding officer as "the great Mayor of Boston" and good naturedly referred to the primary contest when things were not as pleasant as they might have been, adding, "however, a little fight was a good thing for the party." Laughingly he recalled that he had been called by Mayor Curley, "a hick from the sticks" and that he rather liked it. "Now," he said, "they say I'm a tiger, masquerading in the garments of a Yankee Democrat."

He put the Republican party on the defensive. The main issue, he insisted, was unemployment and he assailed Governor Allen for his failure to adequately cope with the problem, with 250,000 Massachusetts people out of work. He promised that if elected he would call a conference of business men and industrial leaders to deal with the serious unemployment situation.

He also promised to lead a call for a convention of the States for the repeal of the 18th amendment. He quoted official figures which seemed to dispute Governor Allen's claim that in his two years in office 600 miles of new highway had been constructed. Mr. Ely asserted that only 74 miles of new roads had been built and that the balance consisted of widening and resurfacing of old highways. He charged the Governor with using Judicial appointments to pay his political debts and mentioned the appointment of William H. McDonnell of South Boston, as Associate Justice of the Charlestown District Court. McDonnell had served with Allen in the State Senate. Ely also charged that McDonnell was one of a group of Allen Democrats who had knifed General Charles H. Cole, Democratic candidate for Governor in 1928.

He assailed Governor Allen for not making a sincere

attempt to settle the Boston Elevated Street Railway problem. Allen's only solution of the vital question to the people of Metropolitan Boston, he declared, was to "pass the buck" to the car riders and make them carry the heavy financial burden of the company by which is known as "public control," instead of compelling the owners, "who have reaped the profits in the past to shoulder the responsibility and now are guaranteed their dividends taken from the pockets of the taxpayers."

Governor Allen deferred his campaign speech making until the middle of October. On the stump and by radio, he rendered an account of his two years stewardship. He told his audiences that he had conducted the office of Governor regardless of race, creed or class and declared that his appointments were based entirely on character and merit. He had continued the "pay as you go" financial policy of his Republican predecessors. The State debt was under $10,000,000 and if this policy were continued it would not be long before the State would be free from debt. In 1929 and 1930, he was proud to say, he had financed the greatest building program in the history of the State without resorting to borrowing. But it was not entirely from a dollars and cents standpoint that he based his claims for reëlection. "I feel that the humane side deserves a preference in our consideration," said he.

Replying to Ely's charge that the State police force for protecting automobilists was inadequate, the Governor said that under his administration 40 additional State police were appointed and that 40 additional motor vehicle inspectors were allowed the Registrar of Motor Vehicles for safety work on the highways. He denied Ely's claim that the old age assistance bill was put through by the Democrats. In his campaign in 1928, he said, he favored such a law and as Governor had signed it. Under his administration the Public Utilities Commission had reduced the price of gas and electricity.

Replying to Ely's charge that he had failed to act in the matter of unemployment, Governor Allen read letters of recommendation from the Mayors of Boston, Waltham, Westfield and Fitchburg, relative to what the State Employment Agency had done to find work for people. He added that he had "prodded the authorities in Washington to expedite the carrying out of all contracts for public buildings in Massachusetts." He told of enlistment of the coöperation of the towns and cities; creation of the Massachusetts Industrial Commission and organization of local employment agencies. A total of 32,230 persons obtained employment through the State public employment offices during the year ending September 30, he said.

Answering Ely's charge regarding the McDonnell appointment, Governor Allen said that he had known the appointee as a member of the Legislature and that he bore a good reputation. "The fact that he was a Democrat was not unusual," said the Governor. "I have elevated other Democrats to the bench, among whom are Judge Hanify of Fall River of the Superior Court, Judge Good of the Boston Municipal Court, Judge Michael J. Connolly of the Waltham Court and Judge Joseph

Donovan of the Boston Municipal Court." He listed his judicial appointments and said that he believed that the list was the best indication of his judgment in the choice of members of the Judiciary as follows:

Supreme Judicial Court—Fred T. Field of Newton.

Superior Court—Thomas J. Hammond of Northampton, John M. Gibbs of Waltham, Raoul H. Beaudreau of Marlboro, Edward F. Hanify of Fall River, Abraham E. Pinanski of Brookline.

Probate Courts—Arthur W. Davis of Edgartown, Herbert M. Chase of Oak Bluffs, John A. Denison of Springfield, George M. Poland of Wakefield.

Municipal and District Courts—Harold L. French of Clinton, Abner L. Braley of Edgartown, Frank Vera of New Bedford, Winfield Temple of Marlboro, Michael J. Connolly of Waltham, Frederick A. Crafts of Weston, Daniel B. Ruggles of Nantucket, Benjamin Cook of Fall River, Edward T. Murphy of Fall River, Frank L. Riley of Worcester, Albert T. Wall of Worcester, Elijah Adlow of Boston, Edward T. Simoneau of Marlboro, William H. McDonnell of Boston, George F. James of Norwood, Joseph E. Donovan of Boston, Frank S. Deland of Boston, Albert L. Saunders of West Medway, Henry L. Harrington of Adams, James E. Luby of Framingham, Paul Stoelzel of Adams, Francis S. Wyner of Brookline, Howard A. Wilson of Maynard, Edward B. Caiger of Concord, Pierre A. Northrup of Lexington, Joseph W. Lewandowski of Holyoke, Francis J. Good of Cambridge, Albert E. Lewis of Westboro.

Ely won the election by a plurality of 16,664. The vote

for Governor was: Ely, 606,902; Allen, 590,228; Aiken, Socialist Labor, 14,603; Lewis, Socialist party, 8,222; Carter, Communist Party, 5,051.

SENATOR COOLIDGE

COOLIDGE had long been a name to conjure with in Massachusetts politics. The Democratic nominee for Senator was a kinsman of Ex-President Calvin Coolidge and had some of his characteristics. A man of rugged honesty, successful in business, he appealed to the electorate. He stood squarely on the Democratic platform and had a good labor record.

Mr. Butler was unable to coax his late primary opponent, Eben S. Draper, to his standard. After reading the platform adopted at that gathering Draper issued a statement in which he plainly indicated that he could not conscientiously support the Republican nominee for Senator. His statement said that the prohibition plank was "a meaningless straddle." "It can satisfy neither the so-called drys nor wets within the Republican party. It is beyond my belief that the voters of Massachusetts can accept a candidate who has one platform for a primary campaign in September and then the same candidate standing on another platform in the election campaign in November. I have been a life-long Republican. I have never hesitated, whether in victory or defeat, to give my utmost to my party. However, there comes a time in the life of any individual who is true to himself, when principle must be made paramount."

That was a hard blow for Butler. Draper was denounced as a traitor to the party—a traitor to his family, whose members had help found the party in this State, but he bore the assaults from his former political associates smilingly.

Election night was awaited by both sides with mixed emotions. From the first returns it was evident that Massachusetts would have two Democrats in the United States Senate. The final figures in the Senatorial contest were Coolidge, 651,939; Butler 539,226; plurality for Coolidge, 112,713.

There was great rejoicing among Democrats. Gloom settled over the G.O.P. early. Mr. Draper awaited the returns with almost as much interest as the two rival candidates. When they were in he said: "I am satisfied, that the people of Massachusetts are against Federal prohibition and the hypocrisy of candidates for high office. I trust the Republican party will face the facts and reorganize on a basis which will sincerely and honestly represent the views of the great majority of its members."

Lieutenant Governor Youngman was reëlected by the greatly reduced plurality of 18,000. Charles F. Hurley, Democrat, and Francis X. Hurley were elected Treasurer and Auditor, respectively. Charles F. Hurley's plurality over Burrell was 193,000 and Francis X. Hurley beat Alonzo Cook by 49,000. At last a Democrat, aided by disgusted Republicans, dislodged from office a Republican State Auditor whom his own party had been unable to defeat in many trials.

In the case of Charles F. Hurley, thousands of Republicans voted for him but not a single outstanding Republican leader could be found during the campaign to take an open stand against Burrell, a man whom they knew to be unfit to hold the office. The Republican State Committee supported Burrell after his nomination, notwithstanding his record as State Treasurer.

Both Secretary of State Cook and Attorney General Warner were reëlected by reduced pluralities, the former by only 25,000 and the latter by 41,000.

The anti-steel trap law was placed on the statute books by a majority of 327,616.

The proposed constitutional amendment relating to the system of apportioning Senatorial and Representative districts was adopted by a majority of 291,419.

The cities and towns served by the Boston Elevated Railway voted in favor of the continuation of the present system of public control. The vote was merely advisory and was taken to provide the Legislature with an expression of the opinion of the voters in these municipalities.

There was no change in the political complexion of the Congressional delegation. Granfield, Democrat was reëlected in the Second District. All of the Republican Representatives suffered severe cuts in their pluralities—except Tinkham, the greatest vote getter.

GOVERNOR ELY'S FIRST INAUGURAL

JOSEPH B. ELY was inaugurated January 8th, 1931, in the presence of an audience that filled the House Chamber to its capacity and overflowed into the Gardner Auditorium. The day was appropriate in that it was the anniversary of the Battle of New Orleans, in which General Andrew Jackson routed an invading British army, an event "Old Hickory's" Democratic admirers always celebrate in his honor. Massachusetts Democrats had not had a Governor of their own since David I. Walsh succeeded Governor Foss in 1914 and was himself defeated for reëlection in 1915 by Republican Samuel W. McCall. In the 15 years that elapsed since the last Democratic Governor on Beacon Hill, the Democrats experienced many ups and downs in politics. An occasional victory in State and Nation seemingly is all that is necessary to rejuvenate that historic old party which elected its first President in 1800 and its first Governor of Massachusetts six years before, in Samuel Adams, "The Father of the Revolution." He was the first Lieutenant Governor of Massachusetts, serving under that other Revolutionary patriot, Governor John Hancock. When the latter died, Adams succeeded him.

The retiring Chief Executive, Frank G. Allen, received his successor in the Executive Chamber, where he handed over the ancient keys of the State House and the Butler Bible and wished his successor a successful administration. Mr. Allen adhered to the old custom of the retiring Governor leaving the capitol by the front door and walking down the flight of steps leading to Beacon Street.

One of the issues of the recent campaign was unemployment. To that subject Governor Ely devoted a large part of his address to the Legislature. He asked for a bond issue of $20,000,000 for construction of public works to furnish needed employment "and thereby tend to revive prosperity." While commending the "pay as you go" policy of the State, in such times as the present, he said, the emergency must be met even if a well established policy must be laid aside. Of the amount of money he asked, he suggested half of it be spent for necessary public buildings and the balance for trunk line highways, particularly the completion of the line from Worcester to Boston, one of the finest roadways in the country.

He reminded his hearers that public works were not a cure-all and that the State Highway Department would require months to complete highways plans. For immediate relief work he asked for $1,000,000 which he should be allowed to spend at his discretion. He asked for an expenditure of $300,000 for improvement of State forests, work along public ways and other sundry matters to furnish work for the unemployed during the depression.

He asked for the appointment by the Governor of an unpaid commission to make a full and complete survey of the problem of unemployment and means for its avoidance and relief, giving particular attention to the possibility of adopting some form of employment insurance. He anticipated necessary changes in the Old Age Assistance Act, including a reduction in the age limit, to make it of real value to those it was designed to assist.

A study by the Legislative committee regarding the proper regulation of holding companies "which are now the means of circumventing the present laws of the Commonwealth in reference to the regulation and ownership of utilities," was recommended. "Such investigation would "determine the extent to which this control over our railroads has extended" and "devise such methods as may be available to counteract or prevent it." "Moreover, such an inquiry may establish that the consolidation has been attempted in violation of the purposes of the National Railroad law," he added.

On the liquor question he said: "The position of Massachusetts should be plainly stated by our Legislature to the point of asking a modification of the Volstead Act and the enactment of such legislation as will put the matter of intoxicating liquors on a reasonable, sane and enforceable basis, in the interest of temperance and sobriety and the peace and good order of the Commonwealth and the country."

"Decision on the question of duration of public control of the Boston Elevated rests," he said, "upon the requirements of the people and the company. It should be borne in mind that the chief object and real justification of the present method of doing business with the Boston Elevated Railway is to provide continuity of reasonable service rather than to protect the interests of private investors in the securities of the company."

He favored the "short ballot" and appointment by the Governor of the Secretary of State, State Treasurer, State Auditor and Attorney General. He would have each Governor choose membership of the Commission of Administration and Finance to serve during his incumbency, abolish the office of Controller and transfer the duties to State Auditor. Also, he would abolish injunctions and restraining orders in labor disputes except after a hearing of the parties.

The Sale of Securities law should be strengthened and the bureau transferred from the already overcrowded Department of Public Utilities to some other department.

"It may be that coöperation is the battle ground of the future," said he in closing his address. "It may be that Government must place a check upon the devastation of competitions. But in any event, America must go to work—and the profit of her labor must be more equitably distributed."

GOVERNOR ELY'S FIRST TERM

For his secretary Governor Ely named De Witt Clinton DeWolf of Chester a veteran Democrat who had long been one of his admirers and political supporters. For Assistant Secretary he selected Morgan T. Ryan of Boston, a young man of promise who had been in the thick of the fighting for him. For adjutant General he chose a young Yankee Division officer, John H. Agnew of Lynn. Lieutenant Colonels John B. Atkinson and Terrell M. Ragan of Brookline were named as personal aides. Both had served in the World War, the former in the army in France and the latter in the navy.

For the next six months the Governor had a Legislature on his hands and it was a continuous struggle on his part and his friends in the House and Senate to get enacted progressive legislation along the lines suggested in his inaugural.

His request for a $20,000,000 bond issue aroused Republican politicians and business men. The proposition was generally opposed by the Republican and independent newspapers of the State. Ex-Representative Henry L. Shattuck an authority on State finances appeared before the Ways and Means Committee of the House, representing no interest but himself, he said, and offered an alternative plan which would combine a $2,500,000 increase in the State tax, a one cent increase in the State gasoline tax and the issuance of one, two and five year notes to net the desired revenue. He praised the budget system inaugurated 11 years before, giving it credit for the present excellent condition of the Commonwealth's financial condition and the State credit. He did not agree with the Governor that the cost of public improvements such as highways and buildings should be passed on to future generations. He was not opposed to a moderate outlay to meet the needs of the depression. In his opinion the depression had not much longer to run. Borrowing, he remarked, only fooled the people who will have to foot the bills in the long run.

After six weeks of consideration of the subject, the Committee on Ways and Means reported a bill for one-cent increase in the gasoline tax for four years, beginning May 1, 1931 and expenditure of $10,000,000 for a new building for the State Department of Public Works, financed by short-term notes, which must be paid by April 30, 1935.

These items were recommended by the Governor in his budget message, but the committee substituted notes instead of bonds. Considering that the Republicans controlled both branches, the Governor did remarkably well and succeeded in getting not all that he asked for, but enough to undertake his program of aiding unemployment, welfare relief and his public building program.

At first the Republican leaders were inclined to holdfast to the "pay-as-you-go" policy, but as soon as they began to hear from their constitutents they relented and begrudgingly gave in to the Governor's program. In the end, most of the leading Republican legislators were on friendly terms with the Governor and when the Legislature was prorogued, the night of June 11, he sent to the presiding officers of the House and Senate a letter which they read to the members complimenting them upon the diligent performance of their duties. They had passed 460 acts and 67 resolves which received the Governor's approval. Of his 11 vetoes, only one act objected to by the Governor became a law.

During the final hours of the session the Governor

signed a supplementary budget totaling $1,811,812.89, a tax bill of $7,500,000 and a bill providing for a bond issue for highway construction and improvements in the Metropolitan district. Instead of the $20,000,000 that he asked for the Governor got $12,759,000, borrowed on four and five year notes and additional revenue by one cent increase on gasoline.

Another feature of the financial program was the relief of the cities and towns, for a period of two years, from the assessments which are usually levied upon them for the maintenance and repair of State highways. Almost one-half of the additional one cent gasoline tax was to be devoted to this relief, amounting to about $4,500,000 a year.

The second major achievement of the 1931 Legislature was the solution of the Boston Elevated problem. For the last 10 years this problem had baffled as many Legislatures. The problem was created by the unusual and unsatisfactory Public Control act passed by the Legislature in 1918, due to the emergency which existed at that time. A contract between the Boston Elevated Railway and the State was entered into at that time, which unduly favored the stockholders of the company. This year's Legislature modified the terms of the contract, eliminated the preferred stocks, supposed to save the State $1,000,000 a year and benefit the car rider. The bill extended "public control" of the road for 28 years in which time it is computed that a two per cent sinking fund invested at four per cent interest will be sufficient to pay off the bonds issued for the retirement of preferred stocks. Governor Ely insisted on a provision in the bill, Section 23, which compels the company to pay back to the cities and towns the deficit for which they were assessed. Also, the company is required to use its assets to pay back to cities and towns the balance of money previously assessed.

As many as 30 acts were passed on the recommendation of a special commissioner named by Governor Allen designed to help delinquent children. Of these laws President Bacon said in reviewing the work of the Legislature of 1931:

"When all the other legislative deeds of 1931 may have faded from the public conscience, still there will remain in the minds of many persons the remarkable contribution that this session has made to the welfare of children."

Legislators had begun to defy the fanatical Drys and this session passed an act providing that no dwelling house shall be entered for the search of intoxicating liquors without a warrant. It had become necessary during this prohibitory era to emphasize the old English law that a man's house is his castle.

The State was redistricted for the election of members of Congress. The State had lost one representative under the reapportionment act of Congress. Congressman Dallinger of the Cambridge district found himself in the same district with Congressman Luce. Dallinger didn't like the idea and threatened to fight for another nomination. The Republican leaders preferred Luce in Congress to Dallinger, so the latter was named to a life job on the bench of the Customs Court and this provided a clear congressional field for Luce's return.

Other important laws passed were: regulation of boxing and sparring matches; to make lawful the playing of golf, other than miniature golf, on Sunday; to permit Sunday baseball games to begin at 1.30 instead of 2 and to run until 6.30 instead of 6; to permit fishing for other than commercial purposes on Sunday; legalizing cash prizes at card games when conducted for educational, charitable, civic, fraternal, military or religious purposes; changing the name of Massachusetts Agricultural College to Massachusetts State College; for a $1,000,000 fish pier at Gloucester, toward which the State was to pay $660,000; for a pier in the Cape Cod Canal to cost $250,000.

Thirteen recess committees were created to study as many subjects. One of these committees was to study plans for a memorial to General Clarence R. Edwards who commanded the Yankee Division in France and died at his Westwood home in February, 1931. Provision was made for the representation of the State at the Yorktown, Virginia, Sesquicentennial celebration and $10,000 was appropriated for the bicentennial of George Washington's birthday.

A temporary arrangement was made for the raising of funds required for the old age pension act until the next Legislature. The last Legislature passed an old age act fixing the age at 70, but made no appropriation for a pension fund. The law itself was far from satisfactory to its advocater, who wanted the age fixed at 65, but they had committed the State to the scheme and trusted to the next Legislature to provide the funds.

LIEUT. GOV. GASPAR G. BACON

SPECIAL SESSION 1931

FAILURE to pass Legislation to relieve automobile owners from high compulsory insurance rates at its first session, Governor Ely, in response to a wide-spread demand, called a special session of the Legislature September 28, for the purpose of making changes in the existing law. When the call for the extra session was issued, the Insurance Commissioner had published the rates for the coming 12 months and they were met with a storm of protest and denunciation. Every section of the State was up in arms over the high rates and when the Legislative committee gave their public hearings the committee room was crowded with protestants and committees representing different communities appointed to demand lower rates.

The Governor addressed the Legislature on the subject briefly outlining the history of the compulsory insurance law of 1925. He pointed out that by the provisions of the act, it is a prerequisite to the registration of an automobile that it be insured against personal injury to others in a sum not less than $5000 for personal injury to any one individual and $10,000 if more than one individual is so injured.

"Because the rates recently promulgated by the Commissioner, effective January 1, 1932, appear to me to create a burden disproportionate to the risk of insuring 92 percent of motor vehicle operators," said he, "because the law as at present constituted does not permit the commissioner to modify the contract or the rates; and because the welfare of the public is so vitally affected thereby, I have called you in special session to consider amendments of the acts which will make it permissible to modify the contract of insurance, as well as to impose a great proportion of the cost of such insurance upon those who are guilty of improper operation."

In concluding this address the Governor summarized the changes in the law he deemed advisable and necessary to the insured and insurer as follows:—

1. The adoption of a law which will permit a system of demerit rating.

2. The adoption of a law which will permit the Commissioner to authorize a deductible policy so-called.

3. A law which eliminates from operation under the stand compulsory policy recovery by a guest. In other words, the elimination of the guest cases, so-called, from the operation of this particular law.

4. A requirement that the claimant give notice of the time and place of injury and the nature of the injury sustained within a limited number of days from the date of the accident. This provision should be so worded as to permit the court to waive the provision where the facts present seem to warrant the exercise of such a judicial discretion.

5. The law requiring the insured to give notice to the company, in the event of an accident, should be strengthened."

After five weeks of investigation hearings, studying and debating the subject, the mountain brought forth a mouse in the form of a single change in the existing law, which provided for a four days notice to the insurance company in cases defaulted in court by the insured person. All other proposed changes, including those indorsed by the Governor were rejected. Although automobile insurance legislation was supposed to be the sole subject to be considered at this session, several other bills were passed, including an appropriation of $245,000 for three projects to provide work for the unemployed. The cost of the special session was $139,126.50.

The unemployment relief measure, recommended by the Governor was passed in the form it came from him, to be used for clearing the woodlands in the Metropolitan Park District, $100,000 for the furtherance of mosquito control work by the State Board of Reclamation and $65,000 for the removal of ships' hulks from the East Boston waterfront and Chelsea Creek.

"The Great and Generous Court," as Frank W. Buxton, leading editorial writer on the Boston *Herald,* dubbed the members of this session, voted themselves $400 extra compensation, awarded the two presiding officers $800 each, and made liberal gifts to the employees of the Legislature. This in addition to their regular compensation. Only one member, Senator Joseph F. Monahan of Belmont, Democrat, objected to such liberality with the taxpayers' money at a time, he said, when the whole land was suffering from its greatest financial and economic depression in the history of the United States. He did not feel that he had earned $400 and he announced that if the extra compensation were voted, he would donate his share to charity in his district. He could not get a handful of senators to stand with him for a roll call on the bill and it was passed by both houses and received the signature of the Governor.

GARRETT CASE

THIS is a brief story of a Boston police officer, Oliver B. Garrett, head of the liquor squad in Prohibition days, who banked more than $122,000, owned a $70,000 farm, a town house and automobiles on a salary of $40.36 a week. In his meteoric brief career in the police department he had made upwards of 15,000 arrests in numerous raids for liquor selling. He was a czar in his own field. He often defied the orders of his immediate superiors and even the Police Commissioner, Herbert A. Wilson, once prominent in Republican politics and for several terms a member of the State Senate. The department teemed with gossip about Garrett's graft. The newspapers began to print stories about Garrett's wealth and his pull with the Commissioner and high police officials.

At last Commissioner Wilson transferred Garrett and demoted him to a patrolman. Garrett refused to accept the transfer and return to the ranks. In the meantime he claimed to have suffered an injury while riding in a police car, but as a matter of fact, he was hurt, if at all, while driving one of his trotting horses and petitioned for a pension on the ground that he was incapacitated from further service. His prayer was granted. Garrett was the talk of the town. Still, police heads made no move to seriously investigate the stories about his sudden acquisition of wealth.

Senator Joseph J. Mulhern of Boston made the first definite move, demanding a legislative investigation. Mulhern's resolve was defeated by that body. Garrett had boasted that if any attempt was made to punish him he would "blow the lid" off the Police Department. Republican leaders at the State House were disturbed. The Boston Police Department was an old Republican institution, the Commissioner the creature of the Governor. Care must be exercised lest graft and corruption might be proven which would be bad politically for them. Hence it was decided to order the Attorney General's Department to look into the charges, the resolve being fathered by Senator Henry Parkman of Boston, a liberal member of the party.

Damon E. Hall was retained by the Attorney General to conduct the hearings and he did a splendid job. Shocking evidence of graft, corruption and dealings with the underworld by Garrett was offered and the report of the Attorney General found him guilty as it did of procuring his pension by fraud. The matter was then referred to District Attorney Foley of Suffolk County and Garrett was put on trial by Assistant District Attorney Fred J. Doyle, an able member of the District Attorney's staff.

When the case was called Garrett failed to appear. He managed to keep out of the clutches of the police for six months when he voluntarily gave himself up and went to trial before Judge Patrick M. Keating. The jury was unable to agree and was discharged. He was finally convicted and sentenced to the House of Correction for two years. Police Commissioner Wilson presented a sorry spectacle on the witness stand at the Attorney General's hearings in which he revealed his utter unfitness, to say the least, for the job he filled. Several of the higher-ups in the department had difficulty in convincing the public that they were entirely innocent of Garrett's activities.

The investigation cost the State and the City of Boston nearly $100,000 and resulted in the removal of Police Commissioner Wilson, whose place was filled, not by a policeman, but a civil engineer and Republican politician, Eugene N. Hultman, who endeavored to clean the augean stable and take up the slack in the leash on criminal breeding places in the city.

PRESIDENTIAL PRIMARIES 1932
Democrats

MAYOR CURLEY of Boston led the movement for Roosevelt delegates in the April, 1932, Democratic primary. Among his chief aids was James Roosevelt, eldest son of Governor Franklin D. Roosevelt of New York and a resident of Cambridge, engaged in the insurance business in Boston. Young Roosevelt inherited his love of politics. While a student at Harvard University, he took the stump for the election of Alfred E. Smith in 1928. A coolness developed between Governor Roosevelt and Ex-Governor

Smith when the former entered the contest for the Presidential nomination and ended in a severance of personal and political relations and open warfare between these two former staunch friends as the convention drew near.

Many Democrats who had supported Smith in 1928, took him at his word after that campaign that he was out of politics. They tied up with Roosevelt or their State's favorite son for the nomination in 1932. Smith's friends urged him to step out and throw his hat into the ring. He hesitated and kept his friends guessing for weeks, but he had to sign on the dotted line before a fight could be made for him in the Massachusetts primary. Governor Ely and Senator Walsh took charge of Smith's interests. They made a short, snappy campaign and the Smith delegates won easily. The vote for Senator Walsh, high man on the Smith ticket was 155,465 to 56,451 for Curley, who topped the Roosevelt ticket.

The delegates chosen were:

At Large: David I. Walsh, Fitchburg; Joseph B. Ely, Westfield; Marcus A. Coolidge, Fitchburg; William H. Foley, Boston; William P. Connery, Jr., Lynn; John J. Douglass, Boston; John W. McCormack, Boston; William J. Granfield, Longmeadow; Mary L. Bacigalupo, Boston; Helen G. Rotch, Lakeville; Charles H. Cole, Boston; John F. Fitzgerald, Boston.

District Delegates: 1. Hugh McLean, Holyoke; Michael E. Troy; W. Stockbridge. 2. Dwight R. Winter, Springfield; John D. O'Connor, Chicopee. 3. M. Fred O'Connell, Fitchburg; Joseph E. Casey, Clinton. 4. Edward J. Kelley, Worcester; Nellie Millea, Worcester.

5. Cornelius F. Cronin, Lowell; Patrick J. Meehan, Lowell. 6. John J. McCarthy, Salem; Leo F. McNamara, Haverhill. 7. Michael A. Sullivan, Lawrence; Charles F. Cotter, Lynn. 8. Francis X. Hurley, Cambridge; James E. Hagan, Somerville. 9. Daniel H. Coakley, Boston; Joseph M. Stokes, Cambridge. 10. Timothy J. Driscoll, Boston; John J. Crehan, Boston. 11. Vincent Brogna, Boston; Lawrence F. Quigley, Chelsea. 12. William P. Hickey, Boston; Daniel J. Gallagher, Boston. 13. Arthur A. Hendrick, Brockton; James A. Mulhall, Quincy; 14. Dominick F. Corrigan, Fall River; Miles J. Neff, Fall River. 15. Patrick M. Doyle, New Bedford; Thomas H. Buckley, Abington.

Republican

Lieutenant Governor Youngman won the Republican nomination for Governor in the September primary, defeating three competitors. The vote was: Youngman, 208,937; Goodwin, 178,864; E. Mark Sullivan, 17,122; Walter E. Brownell, 11,584. Gaspar G. Bacon, president of the Senate, was nominated for Lieutenant Governor by a majority of more than 66,000 over Chester I. Campbell a member of the Governor's Council. Secretary of State Frederic W. Cook and Attorney General Joseph E. Warner were unopposed in the primary. Francis Prescott of Grafton won the nomination for State Treasurer.

Alonzo B. Cook, State Auditor for many years was renominated.

In the Congressional districts, the most spirited contest was waged against the renomination of Congressman Robert Luce by two Wets, Ralph W. Robart of Cambridge and William H. Murphy of Boston. Luce, a life long Prohibitionist, refused to swerve from his dry position. Congressman Underhill of the Ninth District was not a candidate. In his place, his secretary, George H. Norton of Somerville was nominated, defeating three contenders. In the Second District, Joseph L. Brooks of Springfield was again nominated to run against William J. Granfield, Democrat, who attracted Nation wide attention when he captured the district two years before.

DEMOCRATS LOYAL TO SMITH

Mr. Curley's defeat did not prevent him from attending the convention. He was already on the ground when the Massachusetts delegation reached Chicago and he had been elected a member of the Porto Rico delegation. The Roosevelt managers saw to that. He made one of the seconding speeches for Roosevelt and with his associates in the Porto Rico delegation supported every move of the Roosevelt floor managers. Mr. Curley's appearance in the Porto Rico delegation created considerable amusement and Governor Ely referred to him as "Don Jamie."

The Massachusetts delegation joined the Smith forces at Chicago in the "Stop Roosevelt" movement. They were either blinded by prejudice or put too much faith in the representations made to them by the Smith managers. A novice in politics could have seen that Smith had little chance of being nominated and that Roosevelt had a majority of the convention to start with. All that was necessary to do to get Roosevelt the nomination was a little trading with the favorite sons, who are generally willing to quit with a promise to be taken care of in the event of victory. Roosevelt also controlled the National committee which manipulated the key committees of the convention.

The blow which staggered the Smith forces was the defeat of Jouette Shouse for permanent chairman. The Roosevelt managers were unwilling to trust their fortunes to one so close to Smith and Raskob and insisted on their own choice for chairman, Senator Thomas J. Walsh of Montana. They got him, but not without a hard fight. The vote was 626 for Walsh and 528 for Shouse. Massachusetts' 36 votes were cast for Shouse.

Smith's supporters seeing that he had no chance to be nominated sought to join forces with other candidates to stop Roosevelt, but the New York Governor was so far ahead of his competitors, they couldn't overtake him. While Roosevelt's forces were adding to their strength, the anti-Rooseveltans were unable to unite on a candidate. When the nomination of candidates was reached, Governor Ely presented the name of Alfred E. Smith in one of the most eloquent and stirring speeches heard in the

Convention, surprising his own delegation by his oratory. When he returned to his hotel, Smith awaited him, threw his arms around him and kissed him on the cheek. Smith was unable to control his emotions. "A great speech. Thanks, Governor, I'll never forget you," said Al, tears running down his cheeks.

Seven hundred sixty-eight or two-thirds of the voting strength of the convention were required to nominate. On the fourth ballot, taken at the 6th session, Roosevelt had 945 votes to 190½ for Smith. California, which had been voting for Speaker John N. Garner swung on this ballot to Roosevelt and Texas did the same clinching the nomination for Roosevelt. The Roosevelt supporters turned around and nominated Garner of Texas for Vice-President.

Massachusetts did not join the other States in making the nominations unanimous. Smith left the city in an unpleasant mood. "The Happy Warrior" was hurt. The party which he led four years before turned its back on him. He saw States in the convention that had bolted his candidacy because he was for repeal of the 18th Amendment in 1928, lined up with Roosevelt, a dripping wet.

The Massachusetts delegation, disappointed over Smith's failure to receive the nomination, left for home with little enthusiasm for the ticket, but Senators Walsh and Coolidge got aboard the party band wagon early. Governor Ely was silent. There were rumors that he would bolt. Late in July, James A. Farley, Roosevelt's campaign manager and the new Chairman of the Democratic

National Committee with ambassadorial powers, came to Springfield to confer with Governor Ely. On leaving, Colonel Farley said that they had gone over the local situation, that he had arranged for a meeting of Ely and Roosevelt at Albany and that after the Albany conference Governor Ely would make known his position. A week later Governor Ely carried out this program and issued a statement that he would support the Presidential ticket and run himself for a second term.

REPUBLICANS

THE Republican State Committee was for the renomination of President Hoover. To think of any other course would be suicidal and the slate announced by National Committeeman Louis K. Liggett was successful in the April primary. At the same time he made public the delegates' slate Mr. Liggett announced that he was not a candidate for reëlection as National Committeeman. The understanding was that John Richardson of Canton, regarded as Mr. Hoover's Massachusetts spokesman, would succeed him and in due time the agreement was ratified by the delegates. The delegation to the Chicago convention was as follows:—

Delegates-at-Large: George F. Booth, Worcester; William M. Butler, Boston; Alvan T. Fuller, Malden; Mary P. Potter, Greenfield.

Alternates-at-Large: Frank G. Allen, Norwood; Gaspar

G. Bacon, Boston; Leverett Saltonstall, Newton; Louise M. Williams, Taunton.

District Delegates: 1. William F. Whiting, Holyoke; Dennis T. Noonan, Pittsfield. 2. Joshua L. Brooks, Springfield; Mary P. Bailey, Northampton. 3. Clyde H. Swan, Barre; Katherine V. Parker, Lancaster. 4. George R. Stobbs, Worcester; Mabel C. Batchelder, Worcester. 5. Amos L. Taylor, Belmont; Walter Perham, Chelmsford. 6. Lewis R. Hover, Haverhill; Bayard Tuckerman, Jr., Hamilton. 7. Eugene B. Fraser, Lynn; Mary P. Cox, Lawrence. 8. Eugene A. F. Burtnett, Somerville; William Miller, Medford. 9. Sinclair Weeks, Newton; Albert F. Bigelow, Brookline. 10. Christian A. Herter, Boston; Walter R. Meins, Boston. 11. Harold A. Budreau, Boston; Saverio R. Romano, Boston. 12. Frank L. Brier, Boston; Luella P. Prescott, Boston. 13. John Richardson, Canton; Fred D. Rowe, Brockton. 14. Carl A. Terry, Fall River; Robert M. Leach, Taunton. 15. Oscar U. Dionne, New Bedford; Mary B. Besse, Wareham.

There was no hitch in the election of John Richardson to succeed Liggett as National Committeeman, but when it came to selecting the woman member of the Committee there were two candidates, Mrs. Nathaniel Thayer, the present member and Mrs. Frank R. Batchelder of Worcester, one of the most active women Republicans in the State. Mrs. Batchelder won.

William M. Butler was selected as a member of the platform committee. At a meeting of the Massachusetts delegation after the resolution committee had agreed on the liquor plank for which Butler voted, he was roundly criticised for his action and told that he did not fairly represent the sentiment of Massachusetts. Mr. Butler admitted that he was not personally satisfied with the liquor plank, but said it was what President Hoover wanted and as a party man he felt it was his duty to support it. Ex-Congressman Stobbs of Worcester was emphatic in his condemnation of the plank and Mayor Sinclair Weeks of Newton said: "I have no desire to do anything that will hurt President Hoover, but frankly, I don't like this indefinite proposal. It is not a plank. It is an argument. It doesn't even pledge the party to anything. Prohibition is an issue. One of our great political parties was put out of power forever because it refused to deal with slavery. We can't play both sides. There is something worse than defeat and that is not to stand up for one's convictions. To leave Chicago with such a plank is a weak attempt to straddle a great question. Personally, it makes no difference to me. I shall vote the Republican ticket, wet or dry—but this sort of cowardice is unbecoming a great party."

Bayard Tuckerman declared that the more he read the proposed plank, the more he was convinced that it was made to fool the voters. Delegate Herter pointed out some of the verbiage that could and should have been left out and remarked the country wants something done "about this liquor question, not meaningless phrases." John Richardson made the closing speech of the meeting appealing to the delegation to stand by the President, but the plank was rejected by a vote of 16 to 15.

The liquor plank was a long wordy resolution, designed

by the master strategists of the party to keep the wets in line and please the drys, but as a matter of fact it really satisfied neither and if it were not for the large number of Federal appointees in the convention, it would not have been incorporated into the platform. President Nicholas Murray Butler of Columbia University and Senator Hiram Bingham of Connecticut put up a stiff battle for repeal, but the administration had firm grip on a majority of the delegates and its liquor plank was put into the platform.

The keynoter of the convention was Senator Dickinson of Iowa and he made a good job of it; praised the Republicans, ridiculed and condemned the Democrats. "Keep Hoover at the helm, the only man who can steer our economic ship to a safe harbor," was the burden of his speech. He hammered away at the Democrats, declaring that their "Anvil Chorus" of criticism had shaken public confidence.

There was a lot of suppressed opposition to the renomination of the old ticket, Hoover and Curtis, and when Ex-Senator Joseph I. France of Maryland took the platform for the purpose of withdrawing his own candidacy and offering the name of Calvin Coolidge, he was ordered off the speaker's stand. When he refused to go Chairman Snell summoned a Sergeant-at-Arms to eject him and he was hustled to a police station. Members of the press gallery in Washington who knew France protested the rough treatment, but "orders is orders" with a Chicago policeman. During his detention at the police station Mr. France gave out a copy of the speech he would have delivered, a bitter attack on President Hoover and his policies.

There was a lot of talk about substituting General Charles G. Dawes for Vice-President Curtis on the ticket, but Dawes, at the time, was busy trying to keep the doors of his bank open. He had recently resigned his job on the Federal Reconstruction Finance Commission to which President Hoover had appointed him and had borrowed from that obliging body $90,000,000 to save his bank from the hands of a receiver, all of which was unknown to delegates who were shouting for his nomination, but in the end the old ticket of 1928 was renominated.

ELY ACCEPTS ROOSEVELT OLIVE BRANCH

GOVERNOR ELY's journey to Albany where he had a long conference with Governor Roosevelt and accepted the proffered olive branch, followed 48 hours later by his declaration that he would support the Democratic Presidential ticket and that he would be a candidate for a second gubernatorial term, cleared the Democratic atmosphere. The Governor's decision to remain regular and to run again was pleasing news to most Democrats. His refusal to rush for the Roosevelt band wagon in Chicago and his subsequent hesitancy as to his running for Governor on the same ticket with Roosevelt and Garner didn't hurt him with Smith supporters.

Not even in his own State of New York, did Smith have

more devoted followers than in Massachusetts. When the Empire State deserted him in 1928, Massachusetts gave him her 18 electoral votes. Smith had lost none of his great popularity in this State in four years. Governor Ely's great speech nominating Smith had increased his popularity with the rank and file. He had no opponent in the primary for the nomination, but his choice for running mate, John E. Swift of Milford, was hard pressed by Ex-Lieutenant Governor Edward J. Barry, who headed the list of eight candidates for second place on the State ticket. After Barry came Mayor Michael C. O'Neill of Everett, Raymond A. Fitzgerald of Cambridge, Francis E. Kelly of Boston, David J. Brickley of Boston, William I. Hennessy of Boston and John F. Malley of Newton. Swift, belying his name, was not a good runner, but he won the nomination by the slim margin of 1300 votes. The other nominees on the State ticket were Charles F. Hurley of Cambridge for Treasurer, Francis X. Hurley of Cambridge for Auditor, both renominations; John F. Buckley of Boston for Secretary of State and John P. Buckley of Boston for Attorney General.

Daniel H. Coakley won a decisive victory over six rivals for the Fourth Councillor District nomination, the only Democratic district of the eight in the State in spite of the fact that he did not live in the district. The vote was Coakley, 36,887; Edward M. Sullivan, 19,940; Robert E. Bigney, 12,388; Patrick J. Foley, 10,629; Dennis F. Reardon, 6651; John J. Collins, 3082; Leo N. Dooley, 1511. There was more than local interest in several of the contests for County sheriffs. John A. Keliher, Sheriff of Suffolk County won the Democratic nomination after a hard contest against three opponents. He was also given the Republican nomination.

DEMOCRATIC STATE CONVENTION—1932

THE Democrats held their State convention in Lowell in its fine new auditorium, with General Charles H. Cole as temporary chairman and Senator David I. Walsh as permanent presiding officer. "The people of this country are determined to sweep every Republican out of office from Hoover down and put into the White House our great humanitarian leader, Franklin Roosevelt," said Walsh.

The convention listened to an hour's keynote speech by Ex-Senator James A. Reed of Missouri. In the two day session there were but two slight incidents that marred the harmony of the convention. When Mayor James M. Curley of Boston stepped upon the platform the audience booed him. Mr. Curley smiled and bowed and took his seat in the front row occupied by the party bigwigs. A similar demonstration ensued at the close of his speech. There were still Smith men and women in Massachusetts who refused to forget his desertion of their political idol.

Senator Marcus A. Coolidge was chairman of the Resolutions Committee. Leo H. Leary of Brookline was Secretary of the convention. When Governor Ely stood up to render the account of his stewardship, he was greeted with cheers and applause and the band played "The Sidewalks of New York." The din and uproar continued for two minutes, reminding him of the scene at the Democratic National Convention in June when he nominated Smith in a speech that thrilled the entire country and earned him a high rank in oratory and the everlasting affection of the "Happy Warrior."

"Our party assembled at Chicago, in one of the great conventions of political history, formulated a concise, constructive and sane program of national principles," said he. "We must work together to work out the purposes of that program. These are times of great distress and emergency, in which other considerations must yield to party unity and party success. It would be a most regrettable incident of our political history if, facing these times, the Democratic party should fail to unite nationally and locally for the election of its chosen candidates. Having a common purpose to succeed in our undertaking you must have in mind that a single Democratic victory cannot firmly establish a victorious party. It has taken years to construct the Republican machine in Massachusetts, and no man can break it down in two years. Let us unite our strength and move on to victory with Roosevelt and Garner and the whole State ticket."

Speaking of some of the accomplishments of his own administration he declared that for the first time in 20 years the expenses of the State Government were decreased and that they must be further reduced. He told of his attempts to aid cities and towns in this period of depression and a Republican Legislature refused to go along with him. He referred with pride to his success in providing work for the unemployed, his aid to banks which found themselves in a precarious condition, the handling of closed banks, the establishment of central banks to aid savings and coöperative banks and regretted the failure of the Legislature to authorize the establishment of a central bank with $20,000,000 capital, to be used by banks when in need of assistance, the very plan, he said, that the Federal Government had adopted for similar purposes. He assured his hearers that confidence had been restored in Massachusetts banks and urged new banking laws that would further protect depositors.

He spoke of the fine spirit which the people of Fall River had shown when the State was obliged to take over its financial management. Had the Legislature followed his advice, he said, the burden on real estate would have been lifted by his suggested limited sales tax. "It is apparent that the next Legislative session should produce a different arrangement for the collection and payment of taxes," he declared. "Under the present system, a city runs nine months upon borrowed money. That should be largely eliminated. The collection of taxes should be by installments and begin very much earlier in the fiscal year, thereby saving interest charges and relieving the taxpayer of hustling for the total sum in October."

He congratulated the people on the successful efforts waged by his Administration in preserving the railroads of the State and New England, for that matter, from being swallowed by outside rail interests anxious to con-

CHARLES F. HURLEY
State Treasurer

trol this great industrial center. Discussing the repeal of the 18th Amendment, he said it "will require sane legislation on the part of the States for the manufacture, distribution and sale of intoxicating liquors. Massachusetts should prepare for this situation."

The platform gave the committee on resolutions no little trouble. The committee struggled with it late into the morning in Boston and it was gone over by the full committee in Lowell and the final draft was made by the sub-committee headed by Senator Coolidge, Senator Walsh and Governor Ely. The Governor had hoped for a shorter platform, but there were so many things which the committee felt it must deal with that they found it difficult to boil it down any further. The opening paragraph read: "Never in history has a Nation suffering from the evils of misgovernment and lack of virile leadership stood more in need of an immediate return to the liberal and progressive policies to which the Democrats of Massachusetts have been devoted since the foundation of our party." It contained an out-and-out indorsement of the Presidential ticket and Franklin Roosevelt was praised as a true Democrat.

It declared against a Federal Department of Education; called for unemployment insurance; demanded the raising of the school age; took strong ground against the "yellow dog" contract and demanded that Massachusetts put itself in line with the Federal Government on this question; Governor Ely was congratulated on his aid to Massachusetts banks and his legislation to make banking safer for the people and favored legislation to better protect depositors; lowering of electric light and power rates and legislation relieving municipalities from existing lighting monopolies at prohibitive prices were demanded.

It called for a revision of the election laws, nullifying the candidacy of any one whose nomination papers are found to be fraudulent was favored; asked a housing law for the benefit of those who wish to own moderate priced homes; favored a rewriting of tax laws and the lifting of the burden from real estate which is bearing more than its share of taxation; pledged economy in State affairs and a reduction in the cost of Government.

On motion of Representative Paul D. Dever of Cambridge, the convention stood in silence for 30 seconds in honor of the memory of the late Mayor Edward W. Quinn of that city, for many years Democratic national committeeman from this State. Similar action was taken on motion of Mayor John H. Mahoney of Worcester in memory of the late Mayor Peter Sullivan of Worcester, for many years a member of the State Committee. It was a happy gathering from start to finish. Everybody felt that another Democratic victory was in the offing.

Seventeen Presidential electors, equal to the number of Representatives and Senators of the State in Congress, were chosen, one of whom, Mrs. Jessie Woodrow Sayre of Cambridge, daughter of President Woodrow Wilson. The list was as follows:

Electors-at-Large: John F. Fitzgerald, Boston; Jessie Woodrow Sayre, Cambridge.

District-Electors: 1. Mary E. Lucey, Holyoke. 2. Dr. Justus Hanson, Northampton. 3. J. Henry Goguen,

Leominster. 4. John N. Thayer, Worcester. 5. Cornelius F. Cronin, Lowell. 6. Mrs. Alice Doyle, Salem. 7. Charles F. Cotter, Lynn. 8. Joseph J. Borgatti, Somerville. 9. Patrick J. Duane, Waltham. 10. Leo Goulston, Boston. 11. Stanley W. Wisnioski, Chelsea. 12. Miss Mildred Keene, Boston. 13. Arthur Hendrick, Brockton. 14. Grace H. Howe, Fall River. 15. Mary E. Egan, New Bedford.

ELY DEFEATS YOUNGMAN

As the gubernatorial contest of 1932 got under way, Governor Ely grew more enthusiastic over the Democratic National ticket. His own success was bound up with that of Roosevelt and he urged the support of every Democrat running from President down to members of the Legislature. At a big rally in Boston he declared: "Republican tariff, Republican extravagance, Republican unemployment and Republican depression—isn't that enough to make you vote for Franklin D. Roosevelt for President? And I want you to know that I am standing shoulder-to-shoulder with Al Smith in our efforts to elect Franklin D. Roosevelt. The Republicans are not going to be allowed, to use reverse English, to divide the Democratic party as they did in 1928."

He told what he had done to aid the banking situation which had caused so much uneasiness among depositors saying:—"No other State in the Union and no Federal

Government attempted the program that we did in Massachusetts, which, if it had been followed by other States and by the Federal Government, would have helped materially in these times of depression."

He discussed the Boston and Worcester Street Railway Company case in detail. Youngman charged that there had been collusion between the company's officials and State authorities in the settlement of the road's claim against the Commonwealth for the removal of its tracks, to make way for the new section of the Worcester–Boston super-highway. Governor Ely declared that his opponent had no regard for facts and that he "seems to have gone daffy over this matter." He spoke of the part he had played personally in aiding the banks of the State, working with the Bank Commissioner, saying that the $90,000,000 frozen in closed banks was small compared to the $4,000,000,000 in commercial banks that had been saved without the loss of a cent.

In another speech he termed as "political hokum" the claims of Youngman that his administration had been extravagant and declared that "a Democratic Governor in the eyes of some Republicans is always an expensive luxury." His answer to his opponent's charges that appointments of Judges were made with a view of helping to reinstate Councillor Coakley as a member of the bar, was a serious reflection on the Governor's probity. "Let not the ballyhoo of a political campaign warp your mind and judgment against the bald facts of my judicial appointments," said he. "They have been my own. I take the full responsibility for them and claim the credit for them as well. For 25 years I practiced my profession in the Courts of Massachusetts. In almost daily attendance during the greater part of that time, I came to know the qualities of mind and heart, the sort of training and intellectual capacity, as well as the gift of expression which are necessary in a judge who administers the laws of this Commonwealth without fear or favor rich or poor, fortunate or unfortunate, before the bar of justice. No man in all those years has ever questioned my ability to discern the workings of an improper motive, or to ward off an improper influence, until this political hour. Nor has any person, during these last two years, ever endeavored to exercise such an influence, and I challenge anyone to contradict that statement." The Governor met every charge made against him frankly, courageously. He never had any doubt about the outcome of the campaign and as he toured the State it was apparent that the only question was the size of his plurality.

Ex-Governor Alfred E. Smith of New York came into the State and campaigned for the National and State tickets and especially to ask for support of Governor Ely. He was welcomed by an immense throng and at his Boston Arena meeting he said: "I could spend a half-hour on this platform, but I can only say what comes quick to my lips from a suppressed heart, that the leading figure of the National Convention, your Governor, typified in every respect the great Democracy, the great dignity, the great loyalty and the great devotion of Massachusetts." Smith's appearance on the stump did more to solidify the Democrats than anything else.

Even Ex-Governor Allen, whom Governor Ely defeated in 1930, speaking for Youngman, acknowledged in a public address that his successor had done well, "but not nearly as well as he might have done. He did what he could, but he did not do what he promised to do" and more to the same effect.

Youngman's campaign, based largely on criticism of Governor Ely's conduct of office and no little amount of mud-slinging, failed to arouse any enthusiasm among the Republican rank and file. Ely's smashing replies to his opponent's more serious charges of graft and corruption, left Youngman with little support from the solid men of his party. The election figures were significant aside from Ely's 122,000 plurality in that Youngman fell below his running mate, Gasper G. Bacon, candidate for Lieutenant Governor, who received 744,000 votes. Ely's vote was 826,138; Youngman's 703,636.

The Democrats also reëlected their able and efficient State Treasurer, Charles F. Hurley, with a plurality rising 90,000 over Francis Prescott, his Republican opponent, who had powerful business, political and financial backing. During his term, Mr. Hurley had refused to take orders from the big Boston bankers who were accustomed to dictate loan terms to State Treasurers and compelled them to loan money to the State at the lowest rates in the history of the Commonwealth. He had brought the office closer to the people and advocated lower mortgage interest and a higher loan allowance to home owners. Indeed, he was the first public official to suggest the scheme on which the Federal Home Owners Loan

Bank was founded, of the most popular of the Roosevelt recovery policy.

State Auditor Francis X. Hurley was elected over the hardy old perennial, Alonzo Cook, by a plurality rising 114,000. Secretary of State Frederick W. Cook was reelected by the slimmest of all his pluralities—a bare 4000. Attorney General Warner fared better with 18,000.

The three referendums on the ballot, namely legalizing the practice of chiropractics in this State and of setting up a separate board of registration of chiropractors, the question of changing the Massachusetts primary law, promoting the nomination of candidates on the State ticket at a State convention as a guide to the voters in the nominating primary, and the question of amending the Federal Constitution to do away with the "Lame Duck" session of Congress were all accepted by big majorities.

The State Senate chosen was 26 Republicans, 14 Democrats. In the House the count was 144 Republicans, 96 Democrats. The previous Senate contained only 10 Democrats and the House 99 Democrats.

BURNED BALLOTS

GASPAR G. BACON emerged from the Lieutenant Governorship contest with the biggest vote cast for any State officer on the Republican ticket, although his plurality over his Democratic opponent, John E. Swift of Milford was uncomfortably close. The contest for second place, usually dwarfed by the gubernatorial contest, this year shared public interest with the Governorship fight. Mr. Bacon has served eight years in the State Senate, the last four as President of that body. His district was strongly Democratic, as evidenced by the fact that Governor Smith of New York, running for President in 1928, carried it by a large plurality, Governor Ely carried it in 1930 and 1932 and Franklin D. Roosevelt did the same in 1932.

Bacon's four elections were also evidence of his personal popularity. Each time he ran his plurality was larger. In John E. Swift he had a vigorous opponent to contend with. Swift challenged the accuracy of the returns which gave the election to Bacon by a plurality of 5397. The vote for that office was: Bacon, 744,039; Swift, 738,462. Swift demanded a State wide recount. In the recount it appeared that in the town of Milton, the day after election cartons containing 1506 ballots had been burned by the janitor, who said he was unaware of the nature of the contents. Swift filed a bill in equity in the Supreme Judicial Court in which he asked that the Registrars of voters of Milton be enjoined from filing a statement of determination which purported to be their estimate of the votes cast at the election, alleging that the vote cannot be accurately counted because a block of 1500 votes was destroyed, because the town clerk failed to deliver the total number of ballots, the registrars had failed to recount the ballots and were therefore unable to certify the number of ballots cast for the respective candidates.

Swift asked the Court to enjoin the registrars from making and signing a statement or certification of the alleged determination of issue raised in recount and that the town clerk be enjoined from recording as the official returns the alleged recount of ballots, and that he also be ordered to cancel and expunge all records of tabulation of votes cast in Milton for the office of Lieutenant Governor. The petition was heard by Justice Waite who referred it to the full bench. That tribunal dismissed the Swift petition. The Court held that "no fraud was disclosed, no intent on the part of anybody to interfere with a recount or to effect the operation and result of the election is revealed" said Justice Rugg who delivered the opinion. "To hold that these entirely guiltless acts invalidate the voters of Precinct 2 would have the effect of disenfranchising at least 1506 voters or, according to other suggestions made in argument, all the voters of that precinct, or of the entire town. Such a result would be unnatural. It would violate fundamental conceptions as to the operation of democratic institutions and the safety of our form of government."

Referring to the status of a recount the Chief Justice said: "It does not mount higher than the election itself. It arises subsequently to the election. It has no essential connection with the election. The statutes cannot be rightly interpreted to accomplish the disenfranchisement of hundreds and perhaps thousands of voters who have complied with every provision of the law, who are entitled to have force and effect given to their votes and whose votes have been once counted and returned under all the sanctions provided by the election laws."

At this same election another interesting legal question

was raised and decided by the highest State Court. Edward B. Talbot of Fall River, Democratic candidate for Sheriff of Bristol County, asked that the ballots cast in the town of Somerset be thrown out because of the failure of the canceling device of the ballot box failing to work election day. There was a similar case in the City of Quincy before the Court. This petition was also denied, the Court deciding that the voters and the election officials were blameless. "No human being intervened in the matter," the decision said, "and the statute forbade opening the ballot boxes to see if the mechanism of inking was working. To refuse to count the uncanceled ballots would lead to gross injustice to the voters who cast those ballots which, without the fault of any person, were not canceled because of some slip in a mechanism. It would tend to subject elections to perplexing technicalities immaterial to the substantial merits of the controversy. It would counteract the free action of the voters."

Mr. Swift said on hearing the Court's finding that the looseness of the election laws as disclosed in the cases brought to the attention of the Court and the irregularities in several other cities and towns of the State called for amendments to the election laws to remedy these defects, but interest in the matter soon died out and in May following, Mr. Swift was appointed a Judge of the Superior Court to succeed Judge Webster Thayer of Sacco-Vanzetti fame, who had died. The incident was soon forgotten and the case took its place in the list of concontested elections, setting another legal precedent.

MASSACHUSETTS FOR ROOSEVELT—1932

MR. HOOVER running for a second term did not come to Massachusetts in the campaign for reëlection in 1932. Four years before he lost the State to Smith by 17,000. In the last few weeks of the campaign, Ex-President Calvin Coolidge was called to aid and made a speech at the Madison Square Garden, October 1, to a capacity audience. He was not in the best of humor. Newsmen who tried to interview him when he reached New York did not have a happy time. He declined to answer questions political or otherwise. At Republican headquarters he left a copy of his speech to be distributed to the press and kept to himself, seeing only two or three old friends. The Hoover managers counted heavily on his speech in which he reasserted his faith in the Republican party "the most efficient instrument for sound, popular government ever entrusted with the guidance of a great Nation." He took issue with those who were saying that things could not be worse and favored a change in the government at Washington. Things would have been much worse he declared, "if it had not been for the vision, the courage and leadership of President Hoover." He appealed to his fellow Americans "to hold fast to that which experience has proved to be sound, just and true."

"No government," he said, "has ever yet been able to make people prosperous all the time," but, he argued, Mr. Hoover had done everything possible to encourage business and agriculture. He was opposed to "competitive tariffs" and believed that every Nation should control its own revenue laws and commerce. He took a fling at the Democratic Presidential candidate contrasting his education "by private tutors, sent through expensive schools and universities" with that of Mr. Hoover, a poor boy, born in poverty and had to work his way through school.

Democratic leaders resented this reference to their candidate and declared it to be an attempt to raise class distinction. Chairman Farley of the Democratic National Committee, however, said he was not disturbed by the Coolidge speech, pointing out that two years before, the Ex-President had made a radio speech for the election of William M. Butler for Senator, Governor Allen, running for reëlection, and for the Republican candidate for Congress in the Springfield district, and all three were defeated.

Not even Calvin Coolidge could stem the Democratic tide that was running against his party. His Madison Square Garden speech was his last appearance on the public platform. His irritability, so noticeable on that occasion, was one of the symptoms of the ailment which in a few weeks was to end his life. His death took place at his new home, "The Beeches," Northampton, January 5, 1933. He was buried in the little country roadside cemetery at Plymouth Notch, where he was born July 4, 1872. A simple white marble slab marks his grave. There is a movement on to make his birthplace a National shrine.

Under the leadership of Governor Ely and Senator Walsh the State was drifting further and further away from its time honored Republican moorings. The depression was becoming deeper and deeper and many of Mr. Hoover's former supporters had lost faith in him as a political leader. His reiteration that prosperity was returning and was "just around the corner" had become a joke. A Democratic House in Washington did not pull with him in the same direction. People wanted real leadership and they felt that Mr. Hoover had failed them.

The way in which Roosevelt swept aside the opposition to his candidacy for the Democratic nomination, his flying to Chicago to accept the nomination and telling the public where he stood on the issues of the campaign, his demand for the repeal of the prohibitory law, his views on economics and finance, railroads and agricultural problems, intrigued his fellow Americans. His triumphal Western tour, in which he discussed the campaign issues impressed not only Democrats but Republicans and Independents that he was a man of action, unafraid to take his fellow citizens into his confidence and tell them where he stood on every important public question. They liked his frankness, his good nature and friendliness.

Here in Massachusetts after Governor Ely made his peace with him, the Democrats got solidly behind their National ticket. Governor Roosevelt made a motor trip from Albany to Maine and was met by Governor Ely, Senator Coolidge and Joseph A. Maynard, Chairman of the Democratic State Committee, at the State line. He came down through North Adams, Gardner and Fitchburg and stopped overnight at Groton to see his two sons at school there. Immense crowds greeted him everywhere. The next morning he started for Portland, Maine, where he arrived at noon and addressed a rally that crowded the city auditorium. At the close of four days spent in New England he returned to Albany by way of Providence, Worcester and Springfield, through a drenching rain which soaked the thousands who turned out to see him.

In the meantime, Smith in New York was warming up and getting up steam for a speech in Providence and one in Boston. When Smith arrived here he was received with the same enthusiasm as 1928 when he was running for President. His "other State" as he came to call Massachusetts regretted that he was not again the nominee. A good many of his admirers were inclined to sulk. They argued that Grover Cleveland was nominated in 1892 after his defeat in 1888 and was victorious. They saw no good reason why Smith shouldn't have another chance at the Presidency but Smith told them publicly that he wished all of his friends to get behind Roosevelt and Garner and appealed to them to vote the ticket from top to bottom. He asked them not to pay any attention to Republican propaganda representing him and his friends as lukewarm in the contest.

There was a decided shift in sentiment among the Smith voters after his appearance in Massachusetts and from then on there was no question about the result. Roosevelt felt that he could afford to leave the Massachusetts situation in the hands of Al and his friends. All of them redoubled their efforts to retain the State in the Democratic column and on election day their efforts were rewarded with a plurality of more than 62,000 for the Roosevelt electors, who received 800,000 to the Hoover candidates, 737,000.

GOVERNOR ELY'S SECOND TERM

GOVERNOR ELY's second term began January 5, 1933, in the presence of the usual distinguished audience that custom ordains shall witness this colorful ceremony, including the Justices of the Supreme Judicial Court, the Judges of the Superior Court, ex-Governors, heads of State Departments, the Mayor of Boston and leading citizens of both of the major political parties, and the members of the Legislature. The oath of office was administered to him by President Fish of the Senate. Four Grand Army veterans, special guests of the Governor, occupied seats of honor. As the gray haired, stooped, Civil War veterans were escorted to their seats in the House chamber, the entire assembly arose and applauded. The crowd was so great that the Gardner Auditorium was used for the overflow audience. Amplifiers carried the proceedings and the inaugural address to the overflow gathering.

The Governor began by saying that economy in the cost of government was as necessary then as it was in 1932. There should be no extravagance and no spending of money outside of the usual administrative activities, except for the aid and assistance of those who were in distress. Referring to the cost of education in Massachusetts, he said that the local authorities in each community were the best judges of the needs of the schools. In Fall River, he pointed out, school costs had been reduced apparently without any impairment of educational values.

Biennial sessions of the Legislature did not meet with his approval. As a partial remedy he suggested a more intensive effort during the early days of the session thus greatly speeding up the work of that body. He served notice on the members of the Legislature that he would veto special legislation requiring appropriations for individuals, except in the case of Judge Webster Thayer, whose house was destroyed by bombing, "a reprisal for conscientious performance of duty." Judge Thayer was the presiding Justice in the famous Sacco-Vanzetti case. Governor Ely considered legislation in his behalf as justifiable on the ground that the "outrage was an attack upon the Government of Massachusetts."

He expressed himself satisfied with the public work done under last year's emergency employment relief acts and discussed the plans of the Public Works Commission for building subsidiary highways and aiding cities and towns in the construction of highways, by reducing their share of the cost. He urged the passage of legislation which would assist cities and towns in handling the tax titles problem, by allowing them to borrow money either from private bankers or the State on such securities. It was figured that the cities and towns were holding $10,000,000 of such titles. The law would be temporary and designed to tide the cities and towns through the depression, when so many people found themselves unable to pay their taxes. He also recommended that the time for the redemption of tax titles be extended. He advocated the payment of taxes by installments. Such a plan would eliminate borrowing by cities and towns in anticipation of taxes. He favored the continuance of the gasoline tax, one cent of the three collected going to the cities and towns.

He urged legislation for the relief of real estate and said he would sign any fair measure passed. He called attention to the high cost of conducting the Courts of the Commonwealth and he recommended that the entry fee be substantially increased.

Referring to the Old Age Assistance law, he sharply reminded the Legislature that "in 1930 legislation was enacted establishing the principle of old age assistance, but without provision for the income necessary to carry out the law. Makeshift methods were adopted in 1932 which were not satisfactory." "I recommend that unless you are able to provide funds sufficient to meet the requirements of this law, its operation be suspended until some Legislature is able to provide such revenue," said he.

The banking situation was still in a precarious condition and many banks needed assistance. The Governor devoted a lot of study to the problem and he recommended legislation which would make the Coöperative Central Bank set up last year at his suggestion, to aid other banks of that type, be made permanent, or its life extended for five years and permit these banks to become members of the Federal Home Loan Bank, which would enable them to borrow ample funds on real estate mortgages. He renewed his recommendation of last year for the establishment of a $20,000,000 corporation which would take over real estate mortgages from closed banks and permit them to pay their depositors.

He had a few words to say about the general excellence of Massachusetts banks. "Properly conducted and properly regulated banking institutions under proper laws should never close," he said. "Fine as the record of Massachusetts has been in comparison with other States, it has not been good enough. The State sanction of banking institutions is, in effect, taken by the depositors as a moral guarantee by the State that they may safely invest their funds therein. The moral obligation thereby created justified, it seems to me, the use of the State credit in the manner suggested in the organization of this corporation. I estimate that this plan would speedily put into circulation approximately $18,000,000 of frozen assets. This means assistance to many small merchants and manufacturers now in dangerous financial condition, who find their cash capital tied up in closed banks. Loss for these citizens means in turn, restricted purchasing, unemployment, and in the next circle, failure, welfare assistance, and all of the changes that go with a vicious downward industrial situation. A radical departure," he remarked, "but the Federal Government had adopted the Reconstruction Finance Corporation which was operating along these lines with a similar object in view."

He commended the reports made by Special Commissions of stabilizing unemployment and State planning and zoning, appointed by authority of the Legislatures of 1931 and 1932. "A properly organized public employment office system, functioning with a conscious regard for the welfare of applicants for employment as the sole objective, would be of great assistance to the unemployed in seeking the nearest available opportunity for work for which the applicant is fitted by experience and personality," said the Governor. "Such an employment system, operating as a State-wide agency in contact also with the agencies of other States, could map the trend of employment, point out those industries which are fading industries, and bring the attention of the seeker for work to more promising lines of endeavor, and save much useless and wasted effort." He asked for a law to permit of the developing housing projects with or without Federal aid.

Referring to the death penalty, he said he would approve of legislation calling for an investigation of the subject, intimating that he questioned the wisdom of capital punishment. He hoped that legislation would be passed enabling prison labor, but still preventing institution inmates competing with right living citizens.

Referring to prohibition he said: "The people of this State desire the repeal of the 18th Amendment and a change in the Volstead Act. Believing that the adoption of a model law in Massachusetts for the regulation of the liquor traffic will carry some weight with the Congress and the people of the United States in considering the necessary Constitutional changes and the modification of existing laws, I have appointed a commission to study this question and to report their findings, together with a draft of such a law."

To aid the textile industry, he asked that he be authorized to suspend the operation of certain laws if he deemed it in the best advantage of the Commonwealth and the people. He renewed his recommendations of 1931 and 1932 for the regulation of holding companies.

In conclusion, he said: "When the story of this legislative session is written, you will undoubtedly find it largely concerns that somewhat ugly conception of modern government, called the budget. I hope that consideration of it may be presented to you early, that you may approach the problems which it will this year present, as never before, with calm and judicial deliberation. We preach the doctrine of economy, but we must not forget the gospel of help for the unemployed. Nor should we look upon the necessity for economy as a blight upon our hopes for more prosperous days. The state of the public mind demands this economy—and rightly so."

REPEAL OF 18th AMENDMENT

THE final blow was given to prohibition in Massachusetts June 26, 1933, when the delegates elected to a State convention, all wets, representing both of the leading political parties, met at the Gardner Auditorium in the

POSTMASTER GENERAL JAMES A. FARLEY

State House and unanimously ratified the 21st amendment to the Federal Constitution which repealed the 18th amendment.

Governor Ely took a lively interest in the gathering and made a short speech in which he congratulated the people of the State on the positive stand they had taken for the repeal of the obnoxious prohibitory law. The Rev. Samuel A. Eliot offered prayer. Michael A. Shaw of Revere presented the name of B. Loring Young for President of the convention. Judson Hannigan, President of the Roosevelt (TR) Republican Club, nominated Mrs. Elizabeth M. Lovett, President of the Massachusetts' Women's Organization for Prohibition Reform. His motion was seconded by James Roosevelt and Eben S. Draper.

The vote for President of the Convention was: Young, 31; Lovett, 12, James Roosevelt, One. Mrs. Lovett moved to make the election of Young unanimous and it was so voted. The lone vote for James Roosevelt was cast by James H. Brennan, who took the ground that the honor belonged to a consistent opponent of the prohibitory law, rather than one who had been on both sides of the question within a few years.

Charles F. Ely, brother of the Governor, said that everybody knew what they were there for and moved that the convention ratify the 21st amendment. The vote was unanimous. The whole proceedings took but 20 minutes.

Massachusetts under the prodding of Governor Ely, had taken steps to be ready for the manufacture, sale and transportation of liquor in advance of the repeal of the Federal law. On April 7, taking advantage of the new Federal act legalizing 3.2% beer, the Legislature passed a bill making 3.2 beer legal in Massachusetts and authorized the appointment by the Governor of a Commission of three members to be known as the Alcoholic Beverages Control Commission, with power to issue license and regulate the sale of liquor. An emergency preamble was attached to the bill and it became effective immediately. Fifteen minutes after Gov. Ely signed the beer law, he named the commission consisting of:

William P. Hayes of Springfield, chairman and member for three years.

William A. L. Bazeley of Uxbridge, for two years.

John P. Buckley, Boston, former Senator, for one year.

Real booze and full strength beer, however, did not legally flow in this State until the necessary 36 of the 48 States ratified the 21st amendment, December 5. After all the promises made that the old despised saloon would never return, it came back in the guise of the so-called "tavern" with its bar and seats. The hours for the sale of liquor were extended over the old law in the pre-prohibition period. Present day drinking places are frequented by women, a rare sight in former license days. Ten years of prohibition hypocrisy, the speakeasy and the cigarette, with equal suffrage, brought about a decided change for the worse in public drinking by women. Before prohibition, women were not tolerated in saloons and few of them would think of visiting such places for drinking purposes. Now they freely mix with the men and demand their "rights" and everything is done by the vendors of liquor to attract them.

It is the old story of the swinging of the pendulum of public opinion as far to the right as to the left.

PASSING OF MARTIN M. LOMASNEY

THERE passed away in early June, 1933, Martin M. Lomasney, a unique figure in Boston Democratic politics for more than a generation, after a lingering illness, at the age of 74. To his way of thinking there could be no neutrals in a political contest. He was shrewd and vindictive and wore his heart on his sleeve, but woe be unto the daw that pecked at it. He would savagely denounce a politician this year, but in the succeeding campaign he might be found among his earnest advocates. He played politics 365 days a year, detested professional reformers and despised double-crossers. He had a long memory. While he could forget for the time, some real or imaginary injury, it was never erased from his record book. He would go to the end of a road for one who had befriended him or his kin. Ingratitude was not one of his sins.

In his 50 years of rough and tumble politics at City Hall and the State House, he gave hard blows and received them. His admirers were not confined to his own party. Republicans often paid tribute to his ability, honesty, sincerity and usefulness as a public servant. What he lacked in book education he more than made up by his natural ability to grasp a public question. His hair-trigger mind was quick to see the vulnerable points in an opponent's argument or campaign strategy. He drove many a hard political bargain and was often denounced by politicians.

He was born in the neighborhood where he lived the greater part of his eventful life, the son of a tailor who emigrated from Fermoy, Ireland—Fermoy, the town where Mayor Patrick A. Collins was born. Both parents died when Martin was a lad and it fell to his lot to care for his younger brother, Joe, who became his political lieutenant and holder of important political jobs in City and State and who survives him.

In the annals of the poor of a big city there is no more gripping story than that of these two youngsters, struggling for a foothold in life and overcoming obstacles. At 19 Martin Lomasney was a factor in ward politics, but it was only after 10 years of hard fighting that he secured control of his ward in the West End, old Ward Eight. In the meantime, he had organized the Hendricks Club, which became the political headquarters of the ward. There, in his private office, he dispensed favors and charity to the residents of the locality and made his political plans. Although for some years before his demise, the racial complexion had changed from dominant Irish to Jews and Italians, Lomasney managed to retain his political hold.

A life long teetotaler, he had few cronies and fewer confidants. He never wore evening clothes and social events had no attraction for him. He was seldom seen at a fashionable hotel dining room, preferring some little, out-of-the-way restaurant for his meals. He could not endure public banquets. He always seemed to be in a hurry when one met him on the street and he impressed strangers as a suspicious man. He didn't like to talk to those he didn't know well.

As a member of the State Constitutional Convention in 1917, he appeared at his best as a contender and demonstrated that he knew the frame work of the State Government better than most of the high priced lawyers who served in that body.

He took an important part in drafting the new provision of the revised Constitution, forbidding the granting of State financial aid to private denominational, charitable and educational institutions, a subject that had often come up in the sessions of the Legislature and had been a troublesome topic in political campaigns. Lomasney went into this fight well prepared. He found that Catholic institutions had received $49,000 while similar Protestant institutions had benefited to the tune of $18,000,000 and he joined with the element in the convention that favored cutting off such gifts. In this he ran into a stonewall of opposition of his own co-religionists, but he refused to budge and with his help the provision was made a part of the new Constitution.

In 1911 he came within a few votes of being Speaker of the House of Representatives. His last fight was in 1932, when he was the head and front of the successful campaign for the election of William M. Prendible,

Clerk of the Superior Criminal Court of Suffolk County. He never married and made his home with his brother, Joseph P. Lomasney.

LEGISLATURE OF 1933–1934

THE session of the Legislature of 1933 was the fifth longest in the history of the State. It was prorogued at 3.30 A.M. Sunday morning, July 24, but the official record is put down as 11.57 P.M. Saturday, July 23, according to the journals of both houses, a feat arrived at by the old parliamentary device of turning the hands of the clocks back. Some questioned the legality of laws passed on the Lord's Day, but Constitutional lawyers assured the doubting Thomas' that there was no doubt of their constitutionality.

The House organized by reëlecting Speaker Saltonstall and the Senate again chose Erland F. Fish as President. In the House the Democrats cast one ballot for Representative Birmingham of Boston for Speaker.

Much important legislation was passed and Governor Ely expressed his satisfaction of the work of that body in a communication sent to both branches shortly before they concluded their business. He had a right to feel pleased for he had succeeded in getting several of his important inaugural suggestions enacted into law. He told them that he believed that the records would fail to disclose any session of the General Court requiring more earnest application, resourceful and constructive thought, than the one drawing to a close.

"It has been necessary for you to meet the change in the Volstead Act, to prepare for a repeal of the 18th Amendment, to legislate for the protection of bank depositors, and to clear up the difficulties created by the bank holiday. It has been necessary for you, in the pursuit of a rigid economy, consistent with the circumstances as we found them to reduce salaries and wages," said the Governor.

"With the advent of a new Administration of the Federal Government, in the pursuit of the 'new deal,' Massachusetts has found it necessary to somewhat alter her course in order to properly coöperate with the policy of the President of the United States. This has resulted in the enactment of the Recovery bill, so called—the change in the labor law in reference to employment of women after 6 o'clock. You have met the requirements of the Federal Government and harmonized our laws, so far as a lack of harmony appeared, to meet the Federal program.

"You have rehabilitated, I believe, the credit of cities generally. You have made available as current revenue tax titles. You have provided relief, for this year at least, from the great increase in welfare payments, and have set up the machinery for a public works program, and with all, you have preserved the credit of the Commonwealth and established a State tax indicative of a preserved State Credit.

"If you had also provided the proper form of liquor

control applicable to the repeal of the 18th Amendment, in my opinion, the session would have been as nearly perfect as a legislative session could be. So far as I am concerned, I do not propose to let that failure prevent me from expressing my gratification with the coöperation you have given, and extending to you my congratulations."

One of the reasons for such a late adjournment was the fight over the disposition of $8,000,000 money received from the gasoline tax. The Governor insisted that this sum of money be turned into the General Fund and used to keep down the State tax. Some Republican leaders, especially Speaker Saltonstall of the House, wished to distribute it among the cities and towns. Up to twenty-four hours before the last day of the session the bill was drawn with this end in view, but the Governor served notice on them that he would veto such a bill. The Senate gave way and amended the measure to conform with the wish of the Governor, but the House refused to concur in the Senate amendments. All day Saturday the conference committee struggled with the problem. Republican House leaders said that the Governor's proposal would be a betrayal of the automobile owners. The gas tax had been imposed for the expressed purpose of highway construction. Representative John P. Higgins, one of the Governor's Democratic lieutenants in the House said that if the amended bill were not passed the State tax would be $17,000,000 instead of $9,000,000. There was more conferring and late Saturday night the opponents worn out by the heat and the long session surrendered. The bill, satisfactory to the Governor was passed.

Much time was spent in the closing days of the session discussing the Governor's bill for a commission to study the prevalence of crime and suggest means for its suppression. The Governor was begrudgingly given authority to appoint such a commission to serve without salary. Ten thousand dollars was appropriated for its expenses.

New bridges were authorized over Fore River between Weymouth and Quincy and over the Saugus River between Lynn and Revere to accomodate the growing automobile traffic. The so called "yellow dog" contract between employer and employee was outlawed. Acts were passed providing for appointment of a State emergency Public Works Commission to supervise the construction of projects financed to a maximum of $22,000,000 under the provisions of the Federal Industrial Recovery Act.

Cities and towns were authorized to construct public works, with the approval of the existing State Emergency Finance Board, under the terms of the Federal Industrial Recovery Act.

Facing the prospect of defaulting $5,000,000 of maturing bonds in June, 1933, and March, 1934, the Boston Elevated Railway Company was again knocking at the door of the Legislature for relief in the form of legislation authorizing the Metropolitan District to purchase these bonds. The legislature was obliging and promptly passed the necessary law.

It was 4.15 A.M. June 30, when the Legislature of 1934 finished its business and was prorogued, the Secretary of State making official announcement to a lot of tired, sleepy members. It had passed 381 acts and 44 resolves which had received the approval of the Governor. Of the 15 acts and six resolves which he had vetoed, 12 of the former and three of the latter were sustained. The State tax bill amounted to $16,000,000. Among the important new laws passed and signed in the closing hours were:

The bill legalizing horse and dog racing and the pari-mutuel system of betting. It provided for a referendum by counties as to whether such racing should be permitted within the county. An emergency preamble was attached which made the bill operative as soon as signed. As the State election would not be held until November, the emergency preamble prevented the filing of an initiative petition to delay the operation of the act. Legalizing pari-mutuel betting, also the game of "beano," providing the receipts of conducting the latter should be applied to charitable, religious or educational purposes; re-establishing the division of smoke inspection in the Public Utilities Commission, and granting package liquor stores authority to open an hour earlier, or 8 A.M. and remain open until 11 P.M. A bill making it illegal for utility companies to impose service charges for gas or electricity upon customers who use annually electricity to the value of $9 or gas to the value of $7. Representative Lewis R. Sullivan, made a determined effort to get his bill for a run-off primary for Mayor of Boston, but failed.

Sometimes Legislatures are more notable for what they

don't do than what they do. The Legislature of 1934 is notorious for the laws it refused to pass. Conspicuous of which were the following:

Providing for the ratification of the child labor amendment.

Raising the age limit at which children may leave school.

Providing for the state-wide unification and modernization of police.

Providing for reorganization of district and municipal courts.

Providing for improvements in the jury system.

Providing for unification of the Metropolitan District police.

Obligating insurance companies writing compulsory automobile insurance to post bonds in order to protect policy holders.

Obligating out-of-state insurance companies handling weekly premium policies for workers to provide for cash surrender after five years rather than after 10 as at present.

Giving the public utilities commission power to regulate utility holding companies.

Helping cities and towns establish their own electric and gas plants.

Permitting Mayor of Boston to effect economies in the city government by keeping 1934 salary cuts in operation through 1935.

Permitting same to consolidate city departments without the consent of the City Council.

Providing for the removal of police heads from politics providing life tenure of office.

Providing machinery necessary to enable Massachusetts to take part in the Federal housing program.

Establishing a "Baby NRA" in the State, whereby the codes of fair competition applicable in national industry would operate in purely intrastate enterprises.

Calling for an investigation of the county system of government.

Establishing a flat rate for compulsory automobile insurance.

Taking the schools out of politics by means of having teachers nominated by superintendents from merit lists rather than by a politically constituted school committee, as at present.

Giving the Public Utilities Commission power to regulate borrowings of utility companies for plant extensions.

Reducing the rate of interest on small loans.

Providing for a state-run lottery.

MEMBER EXPELLED

THE seat of Representative Louis N. M. Des Chenes of Fitchburg, representing the 11th Worcester district, who had been a member of the House for a number of years was contested by John J. Gilmartin, his Democratic opponent on the ground of fraud at the polls. An examination of the ballots cast showed that they had been tampered with and evidence was offered to show that somebody at the recount had marked enough of them to elect Des Chenes. The Committee on Elections discarded the tampered ballots and awarded the seat to Gilmartin. The vote for representative as finally reported by the committee was: Gilmartin, 5591; Des Chenes, 5533. The district was a double district. There was no question raised about the election of Des Chenes' associate, Henry A. Estabrook, who was high man, with 5821 votes. The other Democratic candidate running with Gilmartin was Robert E. Greenwood, son of former President Greenwood of the State Senate and son-in-law of United States Senator Marcus A. Coolidge. He received 5485 votes and was low man in the voting. Before the committee report seating Gilmartin was reached in the calendar of the day, Des Chenes resigned. He had no part in the fraudulent marking of the disputed ballots.

JUDGE STONE INVESTIGATED

REPRESENTATIVE WILLIAM C. DOLAN of Boston filed a petition with the Clerk of the House, asking the Governor to remove Arthur P. Stone, presiding Justice of the Third Middlesex (Cambridge) District Court, alleging that Stone misappropriated funds entrusted to his care. The filing of the petition created a mild sensation in legal and political circles. Judge Stone had been on the bench for more than 20 years and was well known in

Greater Boston as an outstanding defender and advocate of Prohibition. The usual method of removing a Judge is by impeachment proceedings, but the petitioner adopted the other method as set forth in the State Constitution.

The joint judiciary Committee held several public hearings on the petition giving both sides an opportunity to be heard and by a vote of 10 to 5, reported a resolve requesting Governor Ely to remove Stone. In its report the majority of the Committee, through its Chairman, Representative Horace T. Cahill of Braintree did not mince words. It read in part:—

"The committee finds that said Arthur P. Stone, by his misconduct as a fiduciary officer appointed by the Probate Court, and by his misconduct as an attorney, has forfeited public confidence and is therefore unable and unworthy to properly serve the Commonwealth in the high office of Justice of the Third District Court of Eastern Middlesex. It therefore becomes imperative as a solemn obligation upon the General Court of Massachusetts, for the maintenance of the high character and reputation of the judiciary of the Commonwealth and the public confidence in its courts, which has been held inviolate for more than a century and a half, that said Arthur P. Stone be removed from judicial office."

A minority report was filed by Senator Davis of Haverhill and four other members, which stated that they did not concur with the majority of the Committee because they felt that the case "was not the type of case contemplated by the Constitution as the subject of action by

LIEUT. GOV. JOSEPH L. HURLEY

the General Court in the exercising of this very high prerogative." Pointing out that in all the history of Massachusetts there had been only four proceedings to remove or impeach a judge, they contended that the question before the committee concerned the doings of Judge Stone as a fiduciary officer appointed by the Probate Court "and has nothing to do with the discharge of his duties as judge of the Third District Court of Eastern Middlesex." Furthermore, they were of the opinion that the case against the Judge had not been proven.

The House adopted the majority resolve by a vote of 130 to 75 after an acrimonious debate, but the Senate refused to concur by a vote of 25 to 12. Members of the bar and politicians flocked to the State House while the case was under consideration and pleaded with members of both branches to defeat the attempt to remove Judge Stone.

While the case was pending in the Legislature, Judge Stone continued for a time to hold court until Governor Ely suggested that he withdraw until the case was decided. The Stone case first attracted public attention by the publication in the newspapers in June, 1932, of the findings and decree by Judge C. C. Campbell, Probate Judge of Middlesex County, ordering Judge Stone to pay for the services of the lawyers who represented Dr. Inez L. Clarke who appeared before Judge Campbell to contest an accounting filed by Judge Stone as administrator of her sister's estate. She was represented by Professor W. Barton Leach of the Harvard Law School and William G. Thompson, chairman of the Grievance Committee of the Boston Bar Association. Allegations of misappropriation of funds of the estate and gross impropriety of action were made against Judge Stone.

At the hearing before Judge Campbell, Judge Stone in his contested account charged himself with receiving $33,848.09 as administrator and with payments of a like sum, leaving nothing for him to further account for. Judge Campbell, in his adjudicated account, charged Judge Stone with receipt of $36,943.16 and with payments of but $24,030.22, leaving him $12,912.94 to account for. He ordered Stone to pay Miss Clarke $16,227.50. With the vote of a friendly Senate Judge Stone returned to his wool sack after he had complied with the findings of Judge Campbell.

SHAKEUP IN STATE POLICE

In the early part of December, 1932, serious charges were made to Governor Ely by Joseph M. Donovan and Walter E. O'Hara of Fall River, against high ranking officers of the State police. The Governor assigned State Auditor Hurley to investigate them and report his findings to him. As a result of the State Auditor's investigation and the charge by State Treasurer Charles F. Hurley, that monies seized in raids by the State police had not been deposited with him and properly accounted for, Capt. Charles T. Beaupre, executive officer of the force was suspended and court martialed.

A week later, Charles P. Howard, Chairman of the Commission of Finance and administration reported to the Governor that $13,000 worth of uniforms and equipment of the Department had been illegally made and General Foote head of the department became involved in the enquiry. It was brought out in the investigation that the old khaki uniforms of the State police, valued at several thousand dollars had been burned and that a contract had been made for fancy new uniforms without the authority of the proper State official.

The trial board composed of members of the State police, found Beaupre not guilty, but in the opinion of Governor Ely enough had been shown to unfit him for his position and he ended the controversy by resigning. The Governor also was convinced that General Foote was not a fit man for head of the force and he was allowed to "retire" without a pension. In his place, General Daniel Needham, a fine soldier and a Republican, who agreed to accept the position for a limited time was named. He made several changes in the department, restored its morale and won back its lost public confidence. General Needham at considerable sacrifice to himself served until October, 1934, when he resigned to give his entire time to his law practice. The Governor named a young and popular member of his military staff, Lieut. Col. Paul G. Kirk as Commissioner of Public Safety. The place was offered to General Charles H. Cole but he declined. He had had his fill of police work some years before when he was a member of the Boston Police Board.

CRIME COMMISSION

BECAUSE of the prevalence of crime in Massachusetts and the apparent inability of the police to cope with criminals, Governor Ely asked the 1933 Legislature for authority to name a commission to investigate and determine the causes for the failure to arrest, convict and punish criminals. In addition, he wanted an overhauling of the system of criminal practice and procedure and suggestions for improving the law in respect to such matters. This authority was readily granted by the Legislature. An appropriation of $10,000 was made for the expenses of the commission, the members of which were to serve without pay. The act creating the commission instructed them to make their report by December, 1933.

The Governor named Professor Frank L. Simpson of the Boston University School of Law, Daniel J. Lyne, a well known member of the Boston Bar and General Charles H. Cole, a Trustee of the Boston Elevated Railway Company, who had served as Police Commissioner of Boston. The Commission organized with Professor Simpson as Chairman, John J. Ronan of Salem and James J. Caffey of Boston, counsel, and diligently tackled the subject. The Commission held public hearings to which all those interested in the subject were invited to give their views and submit suggestions.

When the Legislature of 1934 met, the report of the so-called Crime Commission was in the hands of the Governor who transmitted it to the Legislature in his annual message to that body urging them to enact the recommendations contained therein into law. The Commission did a splendid job. It exposed and condemned in plain language the organized professional criminals and pointed out many of the defects of existing law dealing with the gangster and racketeer. It declared that the police systems, public prosecutors and the lower courts inadequate to cope with the criminal element. The Commission said that in addition to the inadequacy of police and prosecuting officers to deal with the criminal forces, their investigation showed that financial and political influences could be had for the protection of illegal enterprises.

The Commission said in its report that in dealing with criminals, the police, prosecuting officers and the courts, including the jury, probation and bail systems, had broken down and that a change was necessary and "new legal machinery must be installed to meet the threat of organized professional criminalism." The police of most of the cities and towns were not only poorly equipped and trained but were "subject to political influence."

It condemned the record of the District Courts in the disposition of cases of offenders, many of them hardened criminals often defended by special justices of the court in which they are permitted to practice. Such should no longer be tolerated. It recommended that the District Courts (the lower courts) be grouped into four districts.

Grand juries, the report pointed out, had become mere rubber stamps for District Attorneys.

The Commission would not class minor automobile offenses as crimes and would make their trials simple, allowing them to appear by counsel and the Clerk of the Court to impose fines as established by the Chief Justice of the Boston Municipal Court, thus making fines uniform throughout the State.

The congestion of cases in the offices of District Attorneys resulting in "bargain days" and the practical dictation of their own sentences was severely criticised. The report was unsparing in its criticism of the delays requiring indictment by Grand juries in cases of felony, which it characterized as "unwieldly and expensive piece of legal machinery."

Referring to recent proceedings against persons charged with jury "fixing" the Commission said that these events have led some sincere and earnest people to advocate that the system be abolished and that trials by judges or boards be substituted, but this change was opposed. "The jury system at its best is not perfect," the Commission said, "but if properly administered, its defects are those of fallible human nature."

The remedy for this they said was that the selection of jury panels be taken out of the hands of the political agencies and placed under jury commissioners appointed by the Chief Justice of that court. The advantages of this change in the mode of selecting the panel, the Commission felt would be that jury service would be spread over a larger number of eligible voters; the professional juror would be eliminated; jury "fixing" would become more difficult and more dangerous; and the jurors selected would be more representative of "the country."

In criminal cases it would abolish appeals from the lower courts to the superior court for a jury trial and require a defendent to elect whether to stand trial in the inferior court without appeal or to have his case removed at once to the superior court.

Another important recommendation called for reorganizing the police systems, freeing them from political control and coördinating them so that they might be more effectively used in cases of emergency. They would place chiefs of police under a single police head, subject to the control of the Commissioner of Public Safety, would train and equip them. This provision of the proposed law proved to be fatal to the entire scheme.

The plan of the Commission met with generous support of many public men, including Ex-Governors Allen, Fuller and Foss and Mayor Curley of Boston. Mr. Foss said that he had recommended a similar plan while he was Governor, 20 years before. He also added that the police commission of Boston should be appointed by the Mayor of that city. The Massachusetts Police Association opposed the plan and a powerful police and political lobby took the field to defeat the scheme. Spokesmen for the police claimed that local police authorities were functioning well. They raised the cry of militaristic police force, but their real fear was that some would lose their jobs. The police are a powerful factor in the politics of the smaller cities and towns and many police heads secure their appointment through political pull and retain their jobs through the same influence.

The Senate supported the police coördination by the slim margin of one vote. When the bill was before the upper branch, the vote was 16 to 16. President Fish asked to be recorded and broke the tie, but the House rejected the measure decisively refusing a third reading of the bill by a vote of 125 to 84. Governor Ely gave up the fight, but said he was convinced that a great majority of the people favored the proposed law. The rest of the recommendations of the Crime Commission were buried with the police coördination bill.

BANK HOLIDAY

GOVERNOR ELY with members of his military staff and a number of Democratic friends went to Washington to participate in the inauguration of President Franklin D. Roosevelt. Because of the economic depression, Mr. Roosevelt discouraged any elaborate display and Massachusetts did not send any of her National Guard troops to join in the inaugural parade. The banking situation throughout the country was growing worse. Many were obliged to close their doors. Others were tottering. New York banks were hard pressed. Some of them had informed Governor Lehman that unless something was done to relieve the situation they feared a money panic that would engulf the Nation and destroy the credit of all with direful results to the business interests. A banker of long and wide experience, the New York Governor advised a bank holiday. Every city in the United States shared in the suppressed fears of New York bankers. If New York proclaimed a bank holiday other States would be compelled to follow suit.

There was an all night session of leading Boston bankers and Clearing House officials to consider the situation. Lieutenant Governor Gasper G. Bacon, Acting Governor in the absence of Governor Ely also attended. Bank Commissioner Guy remained on duty at the State House all night. None were admitted to the bankers conference held at the Federal Reserve Bank building unless they were vouched for by Roy Young, Governor of the First Federal Reserve Bank district, embracing most of New England. No word was given the press of the object of the meeting. None was necessary. Everybody knew that the bankers were trying to save themselves.

At five A.M. Governor Ely's telephone in his suite at the Mayflower Hotel, Washington, rang loud and long. The operator had been instructed that the Governor must be aroused. He was informed of the precarious financial condition of the banking situation. Meanwhile New York had determined on a bank holiday to permit the banks to have a breathing spell and find out where they were at. Governor Ely talked with Governor Lehman by phone. There was nothing for Massachusetts to do but follow suit. New York, so Governor Ely learned had $24,000,000 on deposit in Boston banks. If she should withdraw those deposits it would seriously hamper if not cripple some of the depositories. Governor Ely got

Lieutenant Governor Bacon on the phone and dictated to him a proclamation declaring a two day bank holiday. There was no warrant of law authorizing the Governor to order a holiday and he knew this, but nobody questioned his action.

Said Governor Ely in making public his course: "This action is made necessary for the protection of depositors of Massachusetts institutions because of conditions in other parts of the country. It is a time for our people to remember that courage and patriotism which have made Massachusetts such a great Commonwealth and the United States such a great Nation. Trying as the situation is there should be no alarm. Sober reflection will persuade all that our banks are sound and that we must all treat them in the usual way. Means will be provided for the early resumption of business."

There was no more sleep for the Governor that night. He kept in constant touch with Boston and spokesmen for the banking interests until he left his hotel at 11 A.M. to take his place in line with the other Governors to participate in the inaugural parade. At the earliest possible moment he returned to his hotel and remained in touch with his office at the State House. With him in Washington was State Treasurer Charles F. Hurley, who returned immediately to Boston to render all assistance in his power to the banks.

In the meantime Governor Ely conferred with President Roosevelt and called a special session of the Massachusetts Legislature to pass a bill giving the Bank Commissioner the same authority over commercial accounts that he had over savings accounts and coöperative banks, allowing him in an emergency to invoke the same 90 day moratorium on commercial accounts. By 10 A.M., March 6th, the new bank law was passed and signed and became effective immediately.

Thomas P. Beal, President of the Boston Clearing House issued a reassuring statement to the public in which he said:—

"This sudden and unexpected action, which became known to the Boston banks at 5 o'clock this morning, has made it necessary for the Boston clearing house committee to request the members of the Clearing House Association to remain closed today and Monday in observance of the holiday proclaimed by the Governor.

"While the condition of the clearing house banks of Boston has never been so strong as today and there has been little pressure of withdrawals on these banks, the situation in the country at large renders it advisable to take this action at this time to preserve the strong condition of these banks."

Before Governor Ely left Washington Sunday night, March 5, he spoke to the people of Massachusetts over the radio giving them a brief account of what had happened and the whys and wherefores of the bank holiday throughout the country.

"I am confident that we shall work out of our present status and that things will be back to normal next week," he said. "It was not that Massachusetts banks could not fulfill their obligations that I assented to the two day holiday, but to protect depositors and the banks. With

States all about us declaring a holiday there was nothing else for us to do."

To be sure the closing of the banks and the limitations of withdrawals were a great hardship to many, arrangements were made to meet pay rolls of depositors of commercial accounts and the Bank Commissioner allowed limited withdrawals from savings and coöperative banks for those needing fuel, medicine or necessaries of life. The banks responded willingly and no one suffered because of the restrictions. Every day saw an improvement in the banking situation and in a short time, conditions as to withdrawals were liberalized. In a few weeks banking conditions were nearly normal. Massachusetts banks had kept faith with their depositors, weathered the financial storm much better than many other States and maintained their reputation of being the soundest in the Nation.

PRE-PRIMARY CONVENTIONS—1934

MONTHS before the pre-primary convention Governor Ely announced that he would not be a candidate for a third term. Ex-Mayor Curley's campaign for the gubernatorial nomination was begun almost immediately after his term as mayor expired and by early Spring it was well under way. He made one of his characteristic, energetic canvasses. At first Governor Ely, Senator Walsh, Chairman Maynard of the State Committee paid little attention to him, professing to believe that they would be able to again defeat him in a State wide contest, as they did in 1932, when they easily swamped his ticket for delegates to the National convention. They did not get going until a few weeks before the primaries for the election of delegates to the pre-primary convention in June.

The pre-primary law was urged by representatives of both the Democratic and Republican parties on the ground that such a gathering would be a guide to the voters in the nominating primary and its action would have the stamp of party regularity on the candidates so designated.

Both conventions were held in Worcester, the Republicans on the 8th and the Democrats a week later. Hanford McNider, former United States Minister to Canada, a Hoover favorite, Iowa banker and popular Legionnaire, was the keynoter of the "night before" banquet which was attended by 1500 enthusiastic Republican men and women. After listening to the speeches there was dancing until early morning. It was a foregone conclusion that Lieutenant Governor Bacon would be nominated for Governor and former State Treasurer John W. Haigis a Greenfield banker and one time Legislator for Lieutenant-Governor. They were named by acclamation. Frederic W. Cook, Secretary of State and Attorney General Joseph E. Warner were renominated.

There were four candidates for State Treasurer, Senator Samuel W. Wragg of Needham, Herman A. McDonald of Beverly, Richard E. Johnson of Boston and Oscar M. Dionne of New Bedford, the latter a prominent French

Canadian, backed by the State Committee to please the French voters. Dionne led on the first ballot and was nominated on the second ballot.

The liveliest contest was for the office of State Auditor. Francis J. Lally of Belmont, a certified public accountant, well qualified for the office was beaten for the nomination by Mrs. Elizabeth W. Pigeon of Boston, a former member of the School Board without any knowledge of accounting or any particular training for the office. It was a political move to attract women voters.

The greatest interest was shown in the nomination for United States Senator. Every Republican who had been urged to accept the nomination had refused. The list included several leading Republicans who could see no chance of defeating Senator Walsh. For weeks the nomination went a-begging. Robert W. Washburn stepped in where other Republican angels feared to tread and announced that he would accept the nomination. It was handed to him on the first ballot which resulted as follows: Washburn, 446; Judson E. Hannigan, who had favored giving Walsh the Republican nomination, 118; Gardner W. Pearson, 37. Washburn accepted the nomination in a humorous speech, in which he said that he liked the kind of a fight he was entering because it was regarded as hopeless. "I am sure that before the campaign ends, we shall get and hang on our tepee, the scalp of the evasive David," he told the amused delegates.

Mr. Washburn must have realized that if there was the least chance of electing a Republican United States Senator from Massachusetts he was about the last man the leaders would have picked. He talked bravely, but knew that he was leading a forlorn hope.

The platform adopted had the merit of brevity. It took a stand against the tendency of local government bodies to turn their problems over to the Federal authorities, demanded a balanced National budget, the elimination of government extravagance, the removal of government restrictions on business and opposed Democratic bureaucracy "which, like an octopus thrusting its tentacles into every corner of the land, threatens the destruction of our very institutions themselves."

The party credo set forth first: a sound currency; 2nd, praise of system of tariff protection; 3rd, opposition to the spoils system; 4th, opposed lynching; 5th, favored fair treatment of milk producers; 6th, condemned the Democratic Congress for penalizing Massachusetts taxpayers for the benefit of the South and West; 7th, favored liberal and humanitarian legislation; 8th, demanded return of the "pay-as-you-go" policy; 9th, revision of tax laws to lighten burden of home owners; 10th, mandatory minimum wage law; 11th, speedier administration of justice in State courts; 12th, better police protection; 13th, a comprehensive program of conservation.

DEMOCRATS

WORCESTER had never seen or housed so many Democrats as in mid-June, 1934. For weeks, Ex-Mayor James

M. Curley had been campaigning for the nomination of Governor. The opposition, headed by Governor Ely and Senator Walsh, held off until two or three weeks before the primary before they went into action. They had complete control of the State Committee which in turn controlled the machinery of the convention.

Governor Ely went to the convention city and took personal command of the anti-Curley forces. He and Senator Walsh favored the nomination of General Charles H. Cole, who, at first, was not inclined to enter the race, but at the urgent request of Senator Walsh who wanted a "balanced" State ticket, that is, a ticket which wouldn't be all Irish, he consented the night before the convention to allow the use of his name.

There were a half dozen candidates for the gubernatorial nomination, including besides General Cole, State Treasurer Hurley, Mayor Russell of Cambridge, Professor Simpson and Joseph W. Bartlett. At the last moment a trial balloon was sent up for Joseph P. Carney, Collector of Internal Revenue and there was talk of Judge John J. Burns. The latter announced that he was ready to accept the nomination if the delegates wished him to make the fight, but the names of neither of these two were presented to the convention. In the thick of the fighting they were forgotten and the real battle raged about Cole, Hurley and Curley.

Curley's headquarters were jammed with his singing, shouting supporters who paraded the streets with bands of music. At the night before banquet, Postmaster General James A. Farley, was the chief speaker. He took no sides in the contest for Governor, announced that it was up to the Massachusetts Democracy to settle their own differences and declared that the National administration had no candidate for Governor. His only object in coming to Massachusetts, he said, was to tell the Democrats of some of the accomplishments of the Roosevelt administration and counsel harmony in the ranks.

Senator Walsh did not reach Worcester until the convention was in session. The absence of James Roosevelt, eldest son of President Roosevelt, was in compliance with the wish of his father, who was opposed to any attempt on the part of the administration forces to throw their influence behind any particular candidate.

The eleventh hour entrance of General Cole into the contest embarrassed a number of his friends, who were supporting Charles F. Hurley. Cole himself left Boston with the intention of presenting the name of the State Treasurer to the convention for Governor. His war buddy and campaign manager when he ran for Governor in 1928, Colonel George F. Gilbody, was Hurley's floor manager at Worcester. Paul F. Dever of Cambridge was substituted for Cole to nominate Hurley in the convention.

The convention was opened by Joseph A. Maynard, Chairman of the State Committee and Collector of Customs at the port of Boston, who announced the appointment of Mrs. Grace Hartley Howe of Fall River, wife of Colonel Louis McHenry Howe, President Roosevelt's Secretary, as Secretary of the Convention. Maynard sprung another surprise when he invited Ex-Attorney

General Jay R. Benton who had served as permanent chairman of the Republican convention the week previous to a seat on the platform. Benton had come to Worcester to enjoy the Democratic "Donnybrook Fair." He accepted the invitation and told the Democrats that he hoped they would nominate a good ticket. There was more honor in defeating a good ticket than a poor one, he said, and the Republicans were going to win in November.

Leo M. Harlow, was chosen permanent Chairman over Mayor Robert H. Greenwood, of Fitchburg, son-in-law of Senator Coolidge and Robert E. Bigney of Boston, "who had no father or father-in-law to help him in politics," his nominator Thomas J. Nyland, said. The vote was, Harlow, 344; Greenwood, 269; Bigney, 107. Harlow was the choice of the Cole supporters, Greenwood, Hurley's candidate and Bigney's vote came mostly from Curley's friends. For permanent Secretary William H. Doyle of Malden another Cole supporter, was chosen.

Ex-Mayor Gleason of Brockton, Chairman of the platform committee submitted the resolutions. They began with an endorsement of President Roosevelt and his administration. Senator Walsh was highly commended for his public service. Lower rates for power and electricity were demanded and periodic enrollment of voters, humanizing of the immigration laws, public ownership of the Boston Elevated, cleaner movies and abolition of the block system of booking.

Senator Finnegan of Boston offered amendments, one plank favoring further curbing of the State House lobby

SPEAKER LEVERETT SALTONSTALL

MASSACHUSETTS POLITICS 511

which was adopted. The other, for cheaper automobile insurance rates was defeated by a vote of 247 for and 440 against. The country delegates voted almost unanimously against this. Suffolk and other counties where the rate is high voted for it.

When the nominations were reached Governor Ely stepped from his listening post in the wings of the stage, concealed from the view of the delegates, and addressed the convention. He called attention to the fact that he was not a delegate himself and, therefore, was not privileged to nominate Senator Walsh for another term, but, he said, that did not prevent him speaking his praise of the senior Senator, and he proceeded to deliver what amounted to a nominating speech, calling for Walsh's nomination by acclamation. He commended the conduct of the convention and expressed the hope that it would continue to so conduct itself to the end and prove to the country that Massachusetts was behind Franklin Roosevelt.

General Cole moved the renomination of Senator Walsh by acclamation. Mayor Hurley of Fall River seconded the motion and the convention so voted amid cheering and applause. The Senator said that to be renominated unanimously was ample reward for all the personal sacrifices he had made serving in that capacity. He paid high compliment to Governor Ely, praised his administration and said that although he was retiring from public office he would never retire when Democracy needed him for its future battles in behalf of the people. Whatever the choice for Governor made by the convention he hoped for united and harmonious support for him. He eulogized President Roosevelt, praised his humanitarianism and said he would go back to Washington and assure him that he could count on the hearty and enthusiastic support of the Democracy of Massachusetts.

Late in the evening the balloting for Governor began. The first ballot was announced by Secretary Doyle until just before midnight. General Cole led, Curley was second, Hurley, third. The tabulation of the first ballot showed:

Cole	197
Curley	178
Hurley	150
Russell	82
Simpson	47
Bartlett	27
Maynard	7
Hagan	4
Connery	3
Wall	1
Ely	1
	697

Necessary for a choice 349.

There was a drift to Cole on the second ballot, but not enough to nominate. Chairman Harlow announced that after the next ballot he would entertain a motion to adjourn until 10 A.M. the next day and the roll was called for the third ballot. Curley's highest vote was 193 on the second ballot. On the third ballot he dropped to 181. All but 29 of Hurley's supporters went to Cole on this ballot after Paul Dever stepped to the platform and informed the gathering that he had been authorized by

Hurley to release all of his supporters. Eleven delegates stuck to Mayor Russell of Cambridge. Bartlett got four and Simpson three. Cole's vote on this ballot was 430 and all but Curley joined in making the nomination unanimous. At 2 A.M. the convention adjourned until 10 A.M. when the balance of the State ticket was nominated as follows: Lieutenant-Governor, Joseph L. Hurley of Fall River; Secretary of State, Joseph Santosuosso of Boston; Treasurer, Charles F. Hurley of Cambridge; Auditor, Thomas H. Buckley, Abington; Attorney General, Paul A. Dever, of Cambridge.

The Curleyites left the convention after Cole's nomination with much muttering and condemnation of the "boss ruled" gathering and open threats to defeat the convention choice in the September primary.

CURLEY DEFEATS COLE

WITHIN a week after his defeat at the Worcester pre-primary convention, James M. Curley resumed his campaigning for the Governorship and announced that he was going to defeat Cole for the nomination in the September primary. During the summer and early Fall he covered the State from the Berkshires to Cape Cod. Everywhere he had crowded halls. As a campaigner, Mr. Curley has few equals and no superiors in the State. He is always at his best when fighting for himself. The strategy of his campaign was to array his opponents as anti-Roosevelt and himself as the chosen representative of the National Administration and its New Deal policy. Governor Ely's critical attitude toward President Roosevelt lent itself to Curley's strategy. Senator Walsh was represented as only half-hearted in his support of the National Administration and General Cole was characterized as a weak candidate, who had never been elected to public office and as "a shop worn nonentity" and "the tool of the interests."

The poor showing made by Governor Ely in the delivery of delegates from his own section of the State in the pre-primary convention, due chiefly to disappointed office seekers and those with fancied grievances, encouraged Curley to believe that he could count on substantial support in Western Massachusetts. He cultivated the anti-Elyites in that section and soon had a personal organization there and in every corner of the Commonwealth.

The Cole managers were slow in getting into action. The General himself devoted several weeks to whipping his organization into shape, meeting small groups of committee men and women whom he urged to organize and register voters. Cole's friends figured that by tantalizing Curley in repeating old tales of graft and corruption at City Hall, he would run true to form and "blow up," as he had in former campaigns. But in 1934 it was a new Curley who was running for Governor. He paid little attention to the charges hurled against him but when he deigned to notice them he replied that they were unproven, fantastic yarns, emanating from his political enemies, whose political and financial plans he had frustrated.

Roosevelt and the New Deal, not Curley, was the issue he said. He praised the President and condemned the bankers and big business men who refused to cooperate with administration's efforts to restore prosperity and put men back to work.

"Work and Wages" was a catching phrase employed by Curley in his search for voters. The Worcester Convention came in for his condemnation. The pre-primary law, he said, was an attempt "to restore divine right to a few who want to lord it over the people of this Commonwealth." He charged that the convention was packed by his opponents, who had control of the party machinery and he felt no compulsion to abide by its decision. Besides, he pointed out that during the pre-primary convention for delegates that regardless of the outcome of the Worcester Convention, he would be a candidate at the polls for Governor.

Senator Walsh did not take the stump for Cole until after Labor Day. The primaries were two weeks off before he and Governor Ely got into action. Walsh refrained from mentioning Curley's name in his speeches. He called attention to the fact that all the candidates for Governor except one, Curley, had joined in making Cole's nomination at Worcester unanimous. The Worcester convention, he claimed, had been fairly conducted and its nominees deserved the support of Democrats. Governor Ely was less restrained than the Senator. The relations of the Governor and Mr. Curley had never been cordial. In one of his early speeches for General Cole, Ely characterized Mr. Curley as a man who had "acquired wealth during a life devoted to politics. Mansions, steam yachts and Oyster Harbors have never mattered to General Cole."

The Governor did not deny that he had something to do towards nominating Cole at Worcester, but in doing so, he said, he had no selfish interest to serve. He quoted reports of the Finance Commission that that body had made public regarding the settlement of a law case involving $85,000, paid by the City of Boston to a claimant, represented by a political supporter of Curley. He asked Mr. Curley what his relations were with the Mohawk Trading Company doing business with the City of Boston, again quoting from a report of the Finance Commission. He also asked about the Hanover Street widenings for the approaches of the new East Boston tunnel. He went back into Mr. Curley's municipal campaigns and quoted some of his criticisms and uncomplimentary sayings about prominent Democrats then opposed to him, but now supporting him for Governor. There was much more of this kind of campaigning.

But Curley ignored the accusations. He knew that his opponents were baiting him, but he refused even to nibble at the bait, except to cry "Shame on you, Governor Ely" and reiterate that the issue was: "Roosevelt, the New Deal, work and wages."

General Cole called Curley's campaign a "vaudeville show," accused him of carrying with him about the State an aggregation of cheer leaders and declared that

Curley's campaign consisted of "bluff, ballyhoo and bunk." He claimed that he was as good a Roosevelt supporter as his opponent and that while he had voted for Smith for the Presidential nominee in 1932, he bowed to the will of the convention and loyally supported the Democratic National ticket.

Always a great showman in politics and a resourceful politician, Curley surpassed himself in this campaign and was always several jumps ahead of his rival. As a rabble rouser, no man since John B. Moran in Massachusetts politics, can equal him. Cole's friends laughed at Curley's vote claims and they got the surprise of their lives primary day when Curley swept Cole off his feet with a plurality of 155,000. The Democratic primary vote was: Curley, 283,583; Cole, 121,111; Goodwin, 28,084. Curley had licked his own party and now he set out to lick the Republican party.

WALSH DEFEATS TWO OPPONENTS

SENATOR WALSH devoted all of his energy and time to furthering the candidacy of General Cole in the primary and paid no attention to his two opponents, Ex-Lieutenant Governor Edward J. Barry and one Donahoe, little known in politics. Many veterans were opposed to Walsh because of his failure to support legislation which the Senator believed would further cripple the finances of the country. The Curleyites encouraged the opposition to him because of his support of Cole and limiting his own campaign for renomination to a few radio speeches in which he said that if the Democratic voters approved of his course in the Senate, he would appreciate their endorsement of him in the primary. He was renominated by a plurality rising 160,000. The vote was Walsh, 268,123; Barry, 102,960; Donahoe, 50,919. This was a serious protest vote and it gave Mr. Walsh some uneasiness.

The balance of the Worcester convention slate state offices were approved.

REPUBLICANS

LIEUTENANT GOVERNOR BACON won the Republican gubernatorial nomination against Frank Goodwin by more than 95,000, the vote being: Bacon 228,651; Goodwin, 132,699. Once more Goodwin demonstrated that there was in the Republican ranks a large element who believed in his brand of Republicanism. With such a substantial following Goodwin was sure to be a real menace to Bacon. Another discouraging fact was that for the first time the Democratic primary vote exceeded the Republican by 78,000. These two facts indicated unrest in the party and danger ahead for it. Still another discouraging sign was the defeat of Mrs. Pigeon, endorsed by the Worcester Convention for State Auditor by Ex-Auditor Alonzo Cook. There was no opposition to Washburn for Senator, Haigis for Lieutenant Governor, Cook for Secretary of State or Warner for Attorney General.

CURLEY

Mr. Curley lost no time after his nomination in beginning his campaign for election. After a week's rest he got into action again. His first move was to put in Charles H. McGlue as Chairman of the State Committee. His Boston headquarters, in old Young's Hotel building, were covered with flaring signs, one of which called attention to Lieutenant Governor Bacon's connection with the banking house of J. P. Morgan and that while many worthy citizens were on the Public Welfare list, Gaspar Bacon was on Morgan's preferred list, a fact brought out in the investigation by the Senate Banking Committee of the stock market and Wall Street financiers, directed by Ferdinand Pecora of New York. Curley made the most of this bit of damaging testimony. It made no difference to the public that personally the Republican candidate for Governor profited little, if any, by being thus favored by his father's old firm, whose policy was to let their friends in on the ground floor on stock issues floated by the firm. On the same list were former President Coolidge and William H. Woodin, Roosevelt's Secretary of the Treasury.

In the state of the public mind at the time, anybody associated with a big banking house suffered in popularity. In the ensuing weeks, Mr. Curley proved his resourcefulness as a politician. He had an efficient staff to aid him. His own tremendous energy was never more apparent. His heart was in this fight. He was confident that he would win. He continued to hold fast to the tail of the Roosevelt New Deal kite, convinced that it was a winning issue. James Roosevelt took the stump for him and General Cole sent to him his personal congratulations, but took no part in the canvass. Even Mayor Mansfield of Boston, whom Curley denounced more than once, came out in support of the State ticket.

Organized labor lined up with Curley, charging that Bacon had voted against many of its legislative measures. Day in and day out, night after night, he drove home the argument that the issue was Roosevelt and eloquently defending the recovery plan of the National administration. Replying to the charge by his opponent that if he were elected gang government would flourish on Beacon Hill, he said:

"I will not lower the standards of debate to engage in a campaign of vilification or abuse. Neither will I insult the intelligence of the people of Massachusetts by defending my public record that has stood the test of far more difficult campaigns that is now being waged against me by the Republican candidate."

Citing the scandals of the Harding administration and pointing to the banking situation, the conduct of the stock exchange and the air mail contracts, he said that it was ridiculous to claim that Republicanism and honest government were synonomous.

GOV. JAMES M. CURLEY

As the campaign progressed he grew bolder and more confident of success. He staged a monster rally at the Boston Garden, Sunday night, November 5th, which packed the hall and 7000 or 8000 more were unable to gain admission. Governor Brann of Maine and Ferdinand Pecora of New York, James Roosevelt, and Senator Walsh were among the speakers, but it was purely a Curley meeting and the great crowd acclaimed their idol the next Governor.

Chairman McGlue predicted that he would win by 200,000 and that the Democrats would elect a majority of the Legislature and the Executive Council.

Mr. Curley defended his administrations at City Hall, denied that he had been extravagant as Mayor of Boston and said that Boston under him was honestly and economically run, quoting statistics to prove his contentions.

In the last week of the campaign came a telegram from Chairman James A. Farley of the Democratic National Committee addressed to James M. Curley in which he said: "We all look for a Democratic landslide in the Old Bay State, the Cradle of American Liberty." Curley closed his six months' campaign with a whirlwind tour of the Boston wards the night before election.

BACON

In its better days, when the going was easy for the Republicans and the party escalator was running smoothly,

Gaspar Bacon would have slid quietly into the Governor's chair, but these were evil days for the Grand Old Party and its candidate for Chief Executive of the Commonwealth must fight every inch of his way up Beacon Hill. He was young and vigorous and a good talker. He had ample funds to finance his campaign. In Massachusetts he talked like a real Progressive and was not uncomplimentary to the President, but unfortunately he had been induced to make a speech in August during the Maine campaign and he pitched into Roosevelt and the New Deal. After Maine voted Democratic in September, Mr. Bacon restrained his anti-administration feelings, but the Democrats kept reminding him of his mid-summer Maine speech. In the last two weeks of the Massachusetts campaign, Mr. Bacon declared that the issue was Curley and said that if his opponent was elected he would ruin the credit of State. He asked his audience to compare Curley's promises with his performances.

In one of his early speeches, Mr. Bacon laid down a 10 point program which he promised to carry out if he were elected, summed up as follows:—

1. Honest spending of the people's money.
2. Relief of the homeowner and the householder from excessive taxation.
3. Necessary relief for the unemployed.
4. Necessary financial assistance to cities and towns.
5. Necessary public works to provide jobs.
6. Insurance against further unemployment.

7. Agreement with neighboring states to raise the standards of labor in this section, minimum wages, hours and conditions of work.

8. Removal of restrictions on business so men and women can be taken off relief rolls and placed on payrolls.

9. Adequate provision for those who on account of age are discriminated against in securing work.

10. Amendment of the motor vehicle insurance law to cut down the number of fake claims, thereby reducing rates.

These issues, he declared, represented the paramount matters of genuine concern to the men and women of the State, rather than an emotional appeal to support a candidate for office whose sole attempt to interest voters was centered about the skirts of the President of the United States.

He took up the charges made against Curley by Governor Ely in the primary campaign and repeated them. Saturday night before election at a rally in Boston, he attacked the public record of Curley, bringing in one or two new charges, and asked him to explain his connection with the Mohawk Trading Company and the Legal Securities Company. He questioned him about the letters which A. G. Tomasello & Son, Inc., sent to other contractors, and the communications signed by Charles H. McGlue, Chairman of the Democratic State Committee, soliciting campaign contributions from corporations.

By this time Mr. Bacon was saying that national issues had nothing to do with the campaign. The issue was

Curleyism, he claimed. He referred to his own connection with the Morgan banking firm, saying: "My so-called connection with the House of Morgan was through my father. In 1894, because he had already made a name for himself in business in Boston, he was selected to join the firm of J. P. Morgan & Company. For ten years he devoted himself without stint to his job. In 1904, he was invited by President Theodore Roosevelt to go to Washington, first as Assistant Secretary of State, then as Secretary of State. Later, President Taft named him as Ambassador to France. At the outbreak of the War my father sailed with the first of the American Expeditionary Forces on General Pershing's staff. He served throughout the War and died as a result of his services to his country.

"In business and in public service my father left his family a fine heritage. I revere his memory and have always tried to live up to his high standards. Curley's malicious attack on one with such a record will be treated by all fair minded citizens with the contempt which it deserves.

"I have no knowledge of the business of J. P. Morgan & Company. I have never been in any way connected with this firm's business. I have never had any banking connections. Can Mr. Curley say the same? Mr. Curley is continually speaking about a preferred list. Does he wish me to discuss his preferred list of favorite contractors who expect to get some of the cream from doing business with the State during the next two years?"

Mr. Bacon paid little attention to his Republican opponent, Goodwin, the "three-way candidate" he called him, except to say he was in the contest to aid Curley and that his compulsory state automobile insurance plan had been ruled out by the Supreme Judicial Court. Most of Goodwin's other proposed reforms were unpractical, he declared.

GOODWIN

THE Republican candidate for Governor had to fight two seasoned campaigners, Goodwin having decided to stay in the fight after having lost in both the Democratic and Republican primaries, and ran as an Independent. The Republicans accused him of remaining in the contest to help his old friend Curley. The former Registrar of Motor Vehicles and ex-Finance Commissioner began his campaign in January, 1934, when he announced that he would pay no attention to the pre-primary conventions with their hand picked delegates and that his name would appear on the ballots election day, that he believed in the New Deal, and "orderly revolution under the guiding hand of our great President, Franklin D. Roosevelt."

"The Republican party leadership of Bacon and Richardson in this State," he said, "suggests more readily the House of Morgan than Abraham Lincoln; and the Ely-Bentley-Warren Stop Roosevelt leadership of the Democratic party bears no resemblance whatever to the theories of Government as practiced and preached by Thomas

Jefferson." He was against both of the old parties' leadership.

Governor Ely removed Goodwin from the Chairmanship of the Finance Commission to which Governor Allen had named him and put in his place Joseph J. Leonard, a Boston lawyer with some experience in local politics. Goodwin, however, was permitted to remain a member of the Commission. The Chairmanship paid a salary of $5000 a year. The other members of the Board serve without salary. Three weeks before the November election, Chairman Leonard called on Governor Ely to appoint a "properly qualified citizen who has the real interests of the City of Boston at heart" to succeed Goodwin and the Governor complied with the request, naming Alexander Wheeler, a lawyer, as Goodwin's successor.

Toward the end of the campaign, Goodwin changed his mind about President Roosevelt and the New Deal and became an advocate of the Townsend Plan, a California idea, which would oblige the Federal Government to pay $200 monthly to all persons over 60 years of age. The New Deal, he charged, had become a misdeal and had not accomplished what it set out to do. "There are still 10,000,000 unemployed, 8,000,000 on part time and 4,000,000 working on Public Works projects," he said. "With the exception of a few politicians and their friends this 4,000,000 are receiving a starvation dole. Seven dollars a week on C.C.C. and $12 a week on E.R.A., will not buy the necessaries of life and the future offers no hope.

"The Townsend plan will take the control of money

from the bankers and the Government will pay out over $1,000,000,000 a month to men and women over 60 years of age, on condition that they spend it at once, but on condition that they cease all gainful employment so that room may be made in industry for the employment of millions of younger men and women now unemployed. The bankers and their controlled press will deride this plan, but they cannot stop it. The Republican party and Republican candidate for Governor in California have indorsed it, as has the Governor of Colorado. It is the only ray of light and hope on our muddled horizon," he glibly chirped.

In addition to his well known plan of State funds for automobile insurance to give the owners of motor vehicles lower compulsory insurance than the excessive rates charged by insurance companies, he favored tax reform to shift the burden from home owners to the well-to-do. He scoffed at the platform promise of the Republicans to relieve the overburdened home owners.

"How will they do it?" he asked. "They do not tell you. The State street leaders of the party tried to do it this year through a sales tax on the poor—a tax on food, clothing and everything you buy. They did not get away with it and then they took $8,000,000 last year and $10,000,000 this year out of the road building fund, taken from automobile owners by force. An investigation commission at the State House, after three years intensive study, said 'the only way to relieve real estate is to tax the billions of dollars worth of stocks and bonds now dodging taxation.'" He promised if elected to make the tax-dodgers pay. "To-day almost all of the cost of Government is heaped onto the backs of home owners and automobilists."

While he attacked the Democratic gubernatorial candidate mildly, it was the Republican candidate that he lashed the hardest. Mr. Curley was not unkind to him in his speeches and this encouraged the belief that there was an understanding between him and Goodwin. The Goodwin campaign sagged. His candidacy on the Democratic ticket hurt him with the Republicans and probably accounted for his failure to receive a larger Republican vote in both the primary and the election.

CURLEY RIDES IN ON ROOSEVELT TIDE

TUESDAY, November 6th, was election day. Early returns showed a strong Democratic trend. As the night wore on the Curley vote kept mounting. His strength even in Republican strongholds was amazing and plainly indicated his election. By midnight there was little doubt of the result. Congratulatory telegrams from every section of the State began to pour into the Curley headquarters and Republican leaders reluctantly acknowledged their defeat. The Democrats made merry, marched the streets with bands of music and cheered their successful candidate. Curley had accomplished what many believed the impossible. At last his life's ambition was realized. He had a right to feel proud and he bore himself modestly, attributing his election to a desire on the part of the people to uphold the hands of President Roosevelt in his Recovery drive.

Curley's triumph was a political revolution. The entire Republican ticket with the exception of the candidate for Secretary of State, Frederic W. Cook, went down to defeat with Bacon. The Democrats elected a Lieutenant Governor and the rest of their State ticket with the exception of Secretary of State for the first time in twenty years. They also came within an ace of controlling the Executive Council, changing its political complexion from eight Republicans and one Democrat to three Democrats and five Republicans. When the Lieutenant Governor votes the political division will be five Republicans to four Democrats. The heavy Republican majority of past Legislatures was greatly reduced—the Senate of 1935 standing, 21 Republicans, 19 Democrats, and the House, Republicans, 123 and Democrats, 117.

CONGRESS

IN the Congressional field the Democrats did not do so well. They increased their representation in the House two members, Joseph E. Casey of Clinton in the Third District and Richard M. Russell of Cambridge in the Ninth District. The largest vote cast for a Republican Congressional candidate was for George Holden Tinkham in the 10th District, running for a 10th consecutive term. He polled 84,244 votes. He had the Republican and Democratic nominations. Following his custom, Mr. Tinkham went abroad after the adjournment of the 73rd Congress and did not return until after the primaries. No representative Democrat cared to run against him, although the district is invariably carried by the Democrats in Presidential, State and often in City elections. His secretary, Miss Ryan, was clever enough politician to seize the opportunity when she saw that there was no Democrat in the field and provided Tinkham stickers, which she distributed among the Congressman's Democratic friends and he received the Democratic nomination. Mr. Tinkham did not return from his European trip until just before election. He made no campaign, but that was not unusual.

For years he had refrained from electioneering. He has not made a political speech to his constituents since his first election to Congress. He has never been a dispenser of patronage and has generally been at odds with his own party leaders in Congress and the White House on important issues. He was one of the foremost opponents of the League of Nations and Prohibition. His long drawn out fight against Methodist Episcopal Bishop James Cannon of Virginia, in which he forced the churchman into the courts on an indictment for failure to make a proper return of campaign expenses in 1928, made Tinkham a national political figure.

He opposed the Roosevelt New Deal as strenuously as he fought the Hoover administration's tie-up with the Ku

GENERAL CHARLES H. COLE

MASSACHUSETTS POLITICS

Klux Klan, the Anti-Saloon League, World Court and War debts. Yet no member on the Republican side is stronger for Republican fundamentals, such as the tariff and sound money. He is one of the best informed men in Congress on international problems, a student of government and finance and a stout advocate of unadulterated Americanism and blessed with intestinal fortitude.

The 74th Congress will contain seven Democrats and eight Republicans from Massachusetts. The defeat of Frank E. Foss in the Third District was a surprise. Russell's victory over Luce in the Ninth was the most significant. The district had always been strongly Republican. Luce was one of the severest critics of the New Deal and the Roosevelt administration. The administration was anxious to defeat Luce, but few Democrats believed that likely. Mayor Russell of Cambridge, son of the late Governor William E. Russell, took the nomination at the request of James Roosevelt and stood squarely on the New Deal Roosevelt platform. The result proved that there was still magic in the name of Russell in Massachusetts and the Democratic candidate finished with a plurality of more than 4000. The largest vote given to any Republican Congressional candidate running as a straight party candidate was for Mrs. Edith Nourse Rogers of Lowell, running for a sixth term. She received 75,000 votes. A. Piatt Andrew in the Sixth District had no Democratic opponent. Congressman John W. McCormack seeking a fourth term in the 12th District got the largest vote cast for a Democratic congressional candidate, polling 78,000 votes.

SENATOR WALSH REËLECTED

SENATOR WALSH came through election night with a plurality over his Republican opponent, Robert M. Washburn, of 316,000. There were six candidates in the Senatorial contest and the official vote as tabulated was:

Albert Sprague Coolidge of Pittsfield	Socialist	22,092
W. Barnard Smith of Brookline	Prohibitionist	10,363
David I. Walsh of Fitchburg	Democrat	852,776
Robert M. Washburn of Boston	Republican	536,692
Albert L. Waterman of Boston	Socialist-Labor	8,245
Paul C. Wicks of Greenfield	Communist	5,757

Washburn, his Republican opponent, suffered the fate of most humorists in public life. People refused to regard him seriously and thousands of Republicans boasted that they had voted for Walsh. The Senator's friends had advised him before the start of the campaign to follow the example of George Holden Tinkham or to stand on his own feet for reëlection, confident that he would win in a walk, but Walsh declined to make a lone fight for reëlection. As soon as Curley was nominated he climbed aboard the latter's band wagon. Although Walsh completely ignored his Republican opponent during the contest, never once mentioning his name, Washburn, on November 11, Senator Walsh's birthday, sent him the following gracious message:

"On your 62nd natal day be assured of my honest felicitations. If I could not win, I hope that I know how to lose, in the sweet spirit of a sportsman. No man has

MASSACHUSETTS POLITICS

held Massachusetts for years as you have done. She may make you consul for life. You should be proud. Command me when I can coöperate with you for the success of the State."

OFFICIAL VOTE OF 1934

THE official canvass of the votes as canvassed by the Governor and Executive Council showed that James M. Curley had a plurality of 109,050. Curley's total was 736,463 and Bacon's 627,413.

For Lieutenant Governor, Joseph L. Hurley of Fall River had 738,626, which gave him a plurality of 72,133 over his Republican opponent, Ex-State Treasurer John W. Haigis of Greenfield, who received 666,493.

The only Republican winner on the State ticket, Secretary of State Frederic W. Cook, had a plurality of 9975. A recount of this vote by the same authorities gave Cook 11,123 plurality.

The plurality of State Treasurer Charles F. Hurley over Oscar U. Dionne was 178,483.

Thomas H. Buckley, for State Auditor, was elected by a plurality over Alonzo B. Cook, Republican, of 143,305.

Paul A. Dever had a plurality of 46,948 over Atty. Gen. Joseph E. Warner.

The greatest plurality of any of the candidates on the State-wide ballot was that of United States Senator Walsh, who received a total of 852,776 against Robert M. Washburn's 536,692. Walsh's plurality was 316,084.

Horse and Dog Racing Wins

On the referendum for the licensing of the pari-mutuel system of betting on horse racing all counties voted in favor.

On the licensing under a similar system, the betting on dog racing, all but Barnstable and Dukes Counties voted in favor.

The State-wide referendum on modifying the Antisteel Trap law was carried by 484,172 in favor and 320,543 against.

CONGRESSIONAL VOTE

First District
Charles H. Daniels of North Adams, S.	2,531
George E. Haggerty of Holyoke, D.	35,061
Allen T. Treadway of Stockbridge, R.	51,046

Second District
Charles R. Clason of Springfield, R.	42,495
William J. Granfield of Springfield, D.	47,894
S. Ralph Harlow of Northampton, S.	3,076

Third District
Joseph E. Casey of Clinton, D.	46,830
Frank H. Foss of Fitchburg, R.	46,572

Fourth District
William A. Ahern of Worcester, S.	1,456
James H. Ferguson of Worcester, D.	38,984
Pehr G. Holmes of Worcester, R.	54,601

Fifth District
Jeremiah J. O'Sullivan of Lowell, D.	46,124
Edith Nourse Rogers of Lowell, R.	75,754

Sixth District
A. Piatt Andrew of Gloucester, R.   64,610

Seventh District
William P. Connery, Jr., of Lynn, D.   62,666
Joseph Leedes of Lynn, C.   879
Joseph F. Massidda of Lynn, S.   1,593
C. F. Nelson Pratt of Saugus, R.   40,988

Eighth District
Arthur D. Healey of Somerville, D.   53,581
William S. Howe of Somerville, R.   37,873

Ninth District
Robert Luce of Waltham, R.   54,198
Richard M. Russell of Cambridge, D.   60,141

Tenth District
George H. Tinkham of Boston, D–R   84,244

Eleventh District
John P. Higgins of Boston, D.   46,383

Twelfth District
John W. McCormack of Boston, D.   78,783
Francis A. Pentoney of Boston, R.   16,370

Thirteenth District
Francis H. Foy of Quincy, D.   48,624
Richard B. Wigglesworth of Milton, R.   58,331

Fourteenth District
Joseph William Martin, Jr., of North Attleboro, R.   46,411
Arthur E. Seagrave of Fall River, D.   38,325

Fifteenth District
John D. W. Bodfish of Barnstable, D.   38,336
Charles L. Gifford of Barnstable, R.   46,446
Glen Trimble of New Bedford, S.   2,280

JUNE 17 LEGAL HOLIDAY

A BILL fathered by Representative Robert L. Lee of Charlestown making June 17th, the anniversary of the battle of Bunker Hill, a legal holiday in Suffolk County was passed by the Legislature of 1934 with a referendum to the voters and was accepted by an overwhelming majority, the vote being 192,008 for and 37,603 against, at the November election.

CURLEY DECLINED HELP FROM ELY

GOVERNOR ELY who remained silent during the entire election canvass promptly sent his congratulations to Mr. Curley after election, offered to coöperate with him and help him gather material for his inaugural address. The Governor's letter was acknowledged by Dick Grant, one of Curley's campaigners and acting as his Secretary, who wrote:

DEAR GOVERNOR:
I beg to acknowledge your communication to the Governor-elect, which I have referred to his attention.
DICK GRANT,
Secretary.

The treatment of the Governor's courteous letter plainly indicated the Governor-elect's feelings towards Mr. Ely. The Governor's recent appointment of Frederick W. Enwright a Lynn newspaper publisher and a political opponent of Curley's, as trustee of the State Infirmary at Tewksbury did not make things any pleasanter between them. Following a brief vacation the Governor-elect moved into a suite at the State House assigned to him and there he made his headquarters until he was sworn in as Governor.

Smarting at the Curley rebuff, Governor Ely made no further attempt to ease the strain on their relations and proceeded to fill every office which became vacant during the remainder of his term. In most cases his selections were displeasing to the Governor-elect and a majority of them were either Republicans or pronounced anti-Curley Democrats, "pay offs," they were termed.

His appointment of Judge Stanley E. Qua of the Superior Court as the successor of Associate Justice Waite of the Supreme Judicial Court was disappointing to many Democrats. Qua is a Republican, thus preserving the pronounced Republican majority of that Court. In Qua's place on the Superior Court, he named an old friend and able lawyer, George F. Leary of Springfield.

The appointment of Chairman Joseph J. Leonard of the Finance Commission in place of Police Commissioner Hultman and the naming of the latter, Chairman of the Metropolitan District Commission, aroused anew the wrath of Mr. Curley and brought from him a severe rebuke of Governor Ely. The Governor could not have picked two men more distasteful to Curley. The Governor-elect was one of Hultman's severest critics and repeatedly said on the stump that one of his first acts as Governor would be the removal of Hultman from office.

By naming Hultman to the District Commission, Governor Ely, it was believed, made it more difficult for Curley to dismiss him from the State's service. Leonard took a prominent part in the activities of the Finance Commission in the investigation of contracts, land takings and city contracts while Curley was Mayor of Boston. He announced that Leonard would have to walk the plank as soon as he became Governor.

Governor Ely declared that his course was not actuated by malice or spite. "When I first took the oath of office, I was sworn to follow the Constitution of the United States and the Constitution of Massachusetts and to obey its laws and regulations, some of which required me to make appointments to public office as the terms of the incumbents expired, and as vacancies occurred. But I read nothing in the Constitutions that said my term of obedience to the laws expired on election day, 1934."

The Governor-elect did not deny the right of Governor Ely to fill vacancies and to make appointments, but he remarked that in his opinion, it was poor taste on the Governor's part to make important appointments during the remainder of his term. "In matters appertaining to my future office, referring to Governor Ely's offer to confer with him, he said, "I would rather depend upon my own judgment. I don't think I shall require any advice from the State House how to run my office." The merry war continued, the Governor and the Governor-elect drifting further and further apart.

CROWDED DAYS

DURING the heated controversy, Governor Ely named the State Racing Commission under the act accepted at the November election, consisting of General Charles H. Cole, William H. Ensign of Westfield and Charles F. Connors of Boston. The appointments aroused considerable opposition and a public hearing was given their opponents before the Council voted to confirm them. The charges that Walter F. O'Hara, of Taunton, a prominent business man, a leader in sports adventures and a controlling force in the Pawtucket, Rhode Island, race track, dictated their selection were not proven. The nominees were confirmed and at once entered upon their duties.

At the meeting of the Executive Council, November 28, 46 Ely appointments were confirmed, but it declined to give their approval to Paul J. Keefe, as a member of the Boston License Board. After further delay and apparently to avoid the washing of dirty political linen in public, the Governor withdrew his name. Keefe had been designated as manager in the Ely and Cole gubernatorial campaigns and thus became a favorite target for the opposition to shoot at.

At the Council meeting, December 19th, 13 of Governor Ely's appointments were rejected, including Frank E. Lyman, Chairman of the Public Works Commission. At the next meeting Associate Commissioner William F. Callahan of Newton was confirmed as Chairman and Lyman as Associate Commissioner. Charles F. Riordan of Sharon, a veteran Democrat and party leader was okayed as Director of the Division of Animal Industry. State Auditor Francis X. Hurley became a member of the Board of Tax Appeals, taking the place of Paul F. Tierney, who succeeded Chairman Alexander Holmes, a former Republican legislator, whose term had expired.

Governor-elect Curley had a special grievance against this board, claiming that it was controlled by a clique of State Street lawyers and real estate men and that it favored the rich and powerful real estate interests of Boston to the detriment of the small home owners and taxpayers. On the stump he promised to work for its abolition, if elected Governor. Two of its members, Tierney and Hurley, are close friends of Governor Ely.

Chairman Richard Olney, State Board of Parole, Chairman Henry C. Attwill, Public Utilities Commissioner, Budget Commissioner Carl J. Raymond, and Daniel J. Kelly, State Boxing Commissioner were confirmed at the same session.

At the final meeting January 2nd, on the eve of the inauguration of Mr. Curley, the Council confirmed the five judicial appointments submitted by Governor Ely the week before, two of whom were women. Assistant Attorney General Jennie Loitman Barron of Boston, was named special justice of the District Court of Western Norfolk and Ethel E. Mackiernan of Nantucket, justice of the District Court of Nantucket, John H. Sullivan of Taunton, justice of the 4th District Court of Plymouth, M. Fred O'Connell of Fitchburg, special justice of the Fitchburg District Court and John C. Pappas of Belmont,

PRESIDENT FRANKLIN D. ROOSEVELT

special justice of Gloucester District Court. All five were immediately sworn into office by Governor Ely. More rumblings were heard in the direction of the Curley suite, but the Governor continued to appoint and the Council to confirm.

He named his Chief Secretary, DeWitt Clinton DeWolf, State Commissioner of Labor, filling the vacancy caused by the resignation of Edwin C. Smith who was made a member of President Roosevelt's National Labor Board at Washington, and he was confirmed. Two other members of his secretarial force had already been given important public posts. Morgan T. Ryan as Registrar of Motor Vehicles in Ely's first term and Frederick J. Dillon, Director of the Department of Correction and Judge of Probate Suffolk County, an additional Judgeship created by the Legislature in 1934. Arthur T. Lyman a well known Democrat succeeded him in the Department of Correction.

Another Ely worker, Daniel F. McGrath, who did yeoman service for the Governor in his first election was given the position Director of the Division of Parks, a new office created by the Legislature in the Governor's first term, but at the following session the act was repealed, on the ground that the office was unnecessary and the work turned over to the Forester.

The State having taken over the Soldiers' Home by an act of the Legislature, a new board of trustees had to be named and the Governor appointed, Col. William J. Keville of Belmont, chairman for seven years; Richard P. McCarthy of Westfield, six years; Charles R. Doyle of

Malden, five years; James A. Buchanan, Jr. of Chelsea, four years; J. Leo Sullivan of Peabody, three years; Oscar P. Dudley of Shrewsbury, two years and State Auditor Francis X. Hurley of Cambridge, one year, all of whom received the Council's approval.

Former Attorney General Thomas J. Boynton, an Old Guard Democrat and worker in the ranks, succeeded Chairman Frank A. Burke of the State Parole Board. Henry H. Pierce was appointed State Bank Commissioner to succeed Arthur Guy, who resigned to engage in banking, following the precedent of most of his predecessors in that office. Mr. Pierce had been supervisor of liquidations under Commissioner Guy.

William H. McCarthy of Rockland, himself blind, was named as Director of the Division of the blind.

When General Cole resigned his trusteeship of the Boston Elevated Railroad to run for Governor, Representatives John W. Mahoney of Boston, who had a fine reputation as a Legislator, was given that position.

JUDICIAL AND OTHER APPOINTMENTS

In the four years that Joseph B. Ely was Governor, he made a big dent in the Republican payroll on Beacon Hill and named many deserving Democrats to office, but when he turned his office over to his successor, Republicans still controlled the important key positions at the State House. There were two reasons for this. First, the Republican Executive Council, the confirming power, was in a position to prevent removals and refuse confirmation of the Governor's appointments. Second, the difficulty in finding Democrats considered capable of filling important places, calling for executive ability of a high order, it was claimed.

It is no secret that Governor Ely would have been glad to have named a Democrat of standing and ability, one who would command public confidence and respect, for Police Commissioner of Boston, long before he shifted Commissioner Hultman to the Metropolitan District Commission and named Leonard to run Boston's police, but every time that type of a man was offered the position it was refused. More than once, when the Governor succeeded in inducing a high class Democrat to accept public office it was necessary to labor with a hostile Republican Executive Council to get him confirmed.

Over 50 of his nominees were turned down by the Council during his two terms as Governor. Perhaps the most flagrant case of playing politics by the Council was that of State Fire Marshall Stephen C. Garrity, named by the Governor to succeed Sheriff Fairbain of Middlesex County, who died in office. For a year the Council battled with the Governor and Garrity rejecting him every time the Governor insisted on a vote. The excuse for refusing Garrity's confirmation was that the County had a Republican majority of 50,000 votes. There was no question about the nominee's fitness. The office was in charge of Deputy Sheriff Joseph McElroy all the while and remained unfilled for more than a year until the election in 1934, when McElroy, the Republican candidate was elected by a plurality rising 14,000.

JUDGES

THE Governor's Judicial appointments compared favorably with most of his predecessors. Here again in most instances, he had difficulty in inducing high grade lawyers to give up their lucrative practice and serve on the bench at a modest salary. To be sure, some of his Judicial appointments to the bench had a strong political tinge to them, but that was not unusual. Frank J. Donahue, named to the Superior Court, was Chairman of the Democratic State Committee in Ely's first campaign for Governor. Vincent Brogna's appointment was manifestly made to please the Italian voters on the eve of the 1934 election, as Louis Goldberg's was to cater to the Jewish element. Few, however, will quarrel with a Governor who believes that the Courts should reflect the cosmopolitan racial complexion of the State.

Nobody charged that there was politics in the naming of Justices Charles H. Donahue, Henry T. Lummus and Stanley A. Qua to the Supreme Judicial Court. All three received their appointments on the Superior Court bench from Republican Governors. They were merited promotion. The latter filled the vacancy caused by the retirement of Justice William C. Waite, because of ill health. Judge Qua's appointment caused considerable grumbling among those Democrats who believed that the Governor should have named a member of his own party. The Court has always been heavily Republican. Of the seven members, Justice Crosby is the only one who identified himself with the Democratic party. Judge John J. Burns, an early appointee of Governor Ely resigned his seat on the Superior Court bench in the summer of 1934 to become the legal adviser of the Federal Securities Commission in Washington, the Chairman of which, Joseph P. Kennedy, a former Bostonian, was named by President Roosevelt.

Few of Governor Ely's judicial appointments were more meritorious and popular as that of Probate Judge Joseph F. Monahan of Middlesex County, a good lawyer and fine citizen. He was a Democratic member of the State Senate when he was appointed and had made a name for himself as a wise and liberal Legislator.

Among the Judges of the lower Courts named by Governor Ely were Daniel A. Shay, Hingham, Second Plymouth District; P. Sarsfield Cunniff of Watertown, Second Eastern Middlesex Court; Daniel J. Caven, Haverhill, Northern Essex; William J. Hatch, Gloucester, Eastern Essex. Cuniff and Caven were promotions.

EXIT ELY, ENTER CURLEY

ONE of the last clashes between Governor Ely and Governor-elect Curley grew out of the former's effort to have the Executive Council authorize the payment of $365,000 to the bankrupt Boston & Worcester Street Railroad Company, the balance of its claim of $565,000 for the removal of its tracks, made necessary by the construction of the Boston & Worcester super highway. The company had already received $200,000 on its claim, when in 1932, Lieut. Gov. Youngman, Acting Governor, while Governor Ely was out of the State, ignoring all precedent, sent a message to the Legislature, in which he related the history of the case, claimed that the company had no legal or moral right to receive damages and that the State had the authority and right to order the removal of the tracks without the payment of one dollar to the corporation. He also urged that suit be brought to recover the $200,000 already paid.

The action of the Acting Governor created a furore on Beacon Hill. He was severely criticized for his course and when Governor Ely returned he, too, sent a message to the Legislature on the subject. A bill was passed permitting the company to sue on its claim within 90 days of the passage of the act, but the corporation failed to take advantage of the special law. Opponents of the payment contended that it had lost whatever rights it had by its failure to sue. On the eve of the expiration of Governor Ely's term, the matter was brought up in the second last meeting of the Executive Council and the motion to pay the balance of the money was lost on a tie vote. The Governor and those who voted for the payment claimed that the State had no right to take the company's property without paying for it.

Mr. Curley characterized the attempt to force payment for the same as "steal," "a raid" on the Treasury of the Commonwealth.

As the time drew near for the inauguration of Mr. Curley January 3rd, political circles were agog with excitement. Predictions were made that when Ely and Curley met face to face at the State House inauguration day the fur would fly. Happily nothing of the kind occurred. The day before inauguration the Legislature met to organize and to prepare the way for the new Governor. The House reëlected Speaker Saltonstall without any trouble. He received the votes of 121 of the 123 Republican members to 112 for Edward J. Kelly the Democratic caucus nominee. The same day the Speaker announced the committees of the House.

Representative Horace T. Cahill of Braintree was made ranking member of the House Rules Committee and Republican "whip," and Representative Martin Hays was named chairman of Judiciary and Republican floor leader.

Speaker Saltonstall increased the membership of Democrats on all committees except his "cabinet," the Committee on Rules, because of the gains made by Democrats in the House. Most of the committees have six Republicans and five Democrats but on some eight-member committees, the places were evenly divided.

The story in the Senate was different. There the 19 Democratic members put up a fight against the reëlection of President Erland F. Fish. As senior member of that body, James G. Moran of Mansfield called the upper branch to order and presided. The Democrats demanded a 50–50 division of committee places, but this Fish declined to accede to. The fight over the Presidency was still on at the noon hour Thursday the time set for the swearing in of the new Governor. From the earliest days of the Commonwealth, the custom has been for the President of the Senate to administer the oath of office to the new Chief Executive, but the Senate was still deadlocked over its presiding officer and Mr. Curley decided to go on with the set program and the oath of office was administered to him by that veteran official Secretary of State Cook.

Some there were who questioned the legality of the oath, but Mr. Curley had taken legal advice and announced that as he had been elected Governor he would carry out the mandate of the people and enter upon his duties which he did in the presence of a record crowd, after delivering his inaugural address. It was the first time in the history of the State that a Governor was sworn into office with the members of the Senate absent. That body continued to battle over its Presidency which ended 24 hours later by the choice of Senator Moran, who had agreed to give the Democrats their share of committee places.

In the mean time Governor Ely bade his friends and members of his office staff goodbye and passed out of the State House through the front door, greeted by a throng of cheering admirers gathered on the outside of the building. He lifted his hat and acknowledged the demonstration with a smile. Opinions differ as to Mr.

Ely's course in the last few weeks in office. In looking over the record of what happened at the State House after the November election, friends of both Ely and Curley might well wish that their relations could have been more friendly. Neither is free from blame. There comes to my mind, as I write these lines, a significant remark of Governor Ely's father election night, 1930. As the venerable man sat at his desk in his crowded Westfield law office, where the election returns were being read, he quietly remarked: "They'll find that Joe is set in his ideas."

Perhaps that is the explanation of some of the things that Governor Ely did after the election of 1934. The two men, Ely and Curley, differ widely on public policy and entertain different views on politics. Their personal differences were not of recent growth. Time and political events increased their dislike of one another. With Ely, politics was a side line. With Curley it is his life and living. Without a profession or a fixed business, the latter must succeed in politics or become just another ex. With Ely, if beaten in politics, he had his profession to return to with a chance of winning new laurels. One could shift his base and views to suit the whims of the public, the other finds it difficult to adopt today that which he spurned yesterday.

Before Mr. Curley took up the burdens of his new office, we glimpse the better side of the man, in his unheralded visit to the graves of his wife and children, where he tenderly lays on their snow covered last resting place an armful of roses, says a silent prayer and with tear dimmed eyes, retraces his steps to the Capitol to face a cheering multitude and be sworn in as Governor.

With characteristic boldness Governor Curley began his term of office with the delivery of a remarkably able inaugural address in which he recommended several important administrative reforms and then lopped off the heads of some of his predecessor's last minute appointees. The next two years will witness lively political times on Beacon Hill.

THE END

INDEX

A

Abandoned Farms, 43
Adams, Charles Francis, 253
Adams, Charles Francis, 342, 397
Adams, John Quincy, 265
Agnew, Adjt. Gen., 434
Allen, Charles H., 10, 11, 12
Allen, Frank G., 309, 323, 324, 343, 393, 403, 416, 421, 423, 425, 430, 431
Allen, Isaac B., 51
Allen, J. Weston, 316
Allen's Judicial Appointments, 426, 427
American Woolen Co., 161
Ames, Butler, 140, 142
Ames, Butler, Gen., 248, 249
Anderson, Bishop, 253, 256
Andrew, A. Piatt, 331, 397, 421, 531
Andrew, John A., 4
Andrew, John F., 4
Antietam Battlefield Tablet, 43
APA, 17, 31, 36, 41
Appleton, Gen. Francis H., 15
Apsley, Lewis D., 175
Archer, Dean, 192
Arkwell, Representative, 147
Arkwright Club, 161
Ashley, Henry W., 15
Atkinson, Lieut. Col., 433
Atwill, Henry C., 540

B

Baby Volstead Act, 408
Bacon, Gaspar G., 406, 437, 464, 465, 466, 501, 518
Bacon's Platform, 522, 523

Baker, Day, 366
Baker, Newton D., 339
Ballot Law Commission, 38
Ballots, Marking, 16
Bank Holiday, 501
Banks, Nathaniel P., 264
Bar Association, 370
Bar and Bottle Bill, 130, 184
Barnes, Clarence A., 374
Barnes, Geo. L., 253
Barney, Benjamin Butler, 15
Barrett, Col. Richard H., 15
Barron, Jennie Loitman, 540
Barrows, Mary Livermore, 365
Barry, Edward J., 517
Bartlett, Chas. W., 93, 110
Bartlett, Joseph W., 508
Barton, Charles J., 115
Bascom, John, 53
Bates, John L., 55, 64, 71, 72, 75, 76, 77, 83, 87, 127, 255
Bazeley, W. A. L., 480
Beal, Thomas P., 503
Beaupre, Capt., 495
Belmont, August, 54
Bennett, Frank P., 61
Bennett, Frank W., 15
Benton, Everett C., 80, 178, 197, 198
Berkshire Trolley Merger, 165
Berry, Socialist Labor, 67
Beveridge, A. J., 200
Beverly, City of, 35
Bigney, Robert E., 407, 453
Billings, Edmund, 182
Bingham, Senator, 453
Bird, Anna C., 330
Bird, Charles Sumner, 168, 178, 181, 200, 221, 243
Birmingham, Leo, 484

551

INDEX

Bishop, Robert R., 1
Blackmer, William, 2
Blacknell, H. B., 94
Blaine, James G., 5
Blue Sky Law, 358
Bond, Judge, 152
Borah, Senator, 235, 333, 334, 377
Boston bars screened, 3
Boston City Charter, 184
Boston Elevated Railway, 52, 351, 487
Boston and Maine R. R., 352, 353, 355, 367
Boston & Worcester St. Ry., 462, 546
Boston Police Strike, 285
Boston's vote, 1896, 49
Boudreau, Raoul H., 372
Boutwell, George S., 6, 96, 264
Bowers, Claude M., 379
Boynton, Thomas J., 220, 542
Brackett, John Quincy Adams, 1, 2, 3, 6, 19
Bradford, Gov., History, 52
Brandeis, Louis D., 210
Brann, Gov., 521
Breckenridge, John C., 82
Brennan, James H., 479
Brennan, James J., 191
Brickley, David J., 455
Bridgeman, Raymond L., 261
Briggs, Dr., 208
Brigham, Emme E., 365
British Embassy, 77
Brogna, Vincent, 544
Brooks, Martha N., 365
Brophy, Thomas C., 52
Brown, Gerry, 101
Brown, Walter F., 375
Bruce, Alexander B., 57, 58, 59
Bryan, William Jennings, 44, 45, 46, 49, 53, 63, 64, 78, 171, 173, 336
Buchanan, James A., Jr., 542
Buchanan, W. R., 132, 133
Bucket Shop Bill, 67
Buckley, John F., 455
Buckley, John P., 455
Bull Moose Party, 222

Burke, Frank A., 542
Burned Ballots, 466, 467
Burnett, R. M., 121
Burns, Judge John J., 508
Burrell, Fred J., 295, 296, 418
Burrill, Charles L., 198, 418
Burrows, Marion Cowan, 365
Burton, Dr. Marion, 333
Butler, Benjamin F., 1
Butler, Nicholas Murray, 377
Butler, Peter, 407
Butler, William M., 34, 329, 330, 348, 358, 359, 372, 387, 419, 420, 451
Butler's Bible, 430

C

Cabot, Frederick P., 229
Cahill, Horace T., 492, 547
Callahan, Christopher T., 49, 209
Callahan, Wm. F., 539
Campbell, Judge, 493, 494
Canadian Reciprocity, 133
Cape Cod Canoe, 54
Carney Hospital, 255
Carney, Joseph P., 508
Carriere, Joseph N., 418
Carroll, James B., 17, 31, 163, 209
Casey's torch, 12
Casey, Joseph L., 530
Cassidy, Thomas F., 139
Caven, Daniel J., 545
Chamberlain, A. F., 121
Charitable Irish Society, 203
Chase, Frederick H., 162
Chicago Convention, Democratic, 1896, 46
Child Labor Law, 193
Child, Richard W., 175
Claggett, Strabo V., 417, 418
Clark, Albert F., 75
Clark, Champ, 134, 172, 191
Clark, Gen. E. B., 271
Clark, Nelson P., 213
Clarke, Dr. Inez, 493

INDEX   553

Cleveland, Grover, 5, 18, 19, 21, 22, 46
Clifford, Walter, 63
Coakley, Daniel H., 15, 102, 303, 317, 369, 455, 462
Coakley, Timothy W., 102, 175
Cogswell, Representative, 148
Colby, Bainbridge, 235
Cole, Gen. Chas. H., 91, 230, 389, 393, 423, 495, 496, 508, 509, 511, 513, 516, 542, 548
Cole, John N., 114
Collateral Inheritance Law, 8
Collins, Edward D., 163
Collins, Patrick A., 18, 19, 21, 22, 84, 92
Columbus Day, 130
Connelly, Judge, 224
Connelly, Thomas H., 206
Connery, William P., 318
Connors, Charles F., 539
Conry, Joseph A., 109, 208
Constitutional Liberty League, 367, 409
Cook, Alonzo B., 341, 374, 428, 465, 518
Cook, Frederick W., 279, 303, 418, 429, 465, 505, 529
Coolidge, Calvin, 250, 287, 289, 290, 291, 292, 293, 294, 295, 296, 297, 298, 299, 300, 301, 303, 318, 319, 320, 321, 323, 327, 328, 329, 334, 340, 353, 359, 372, 470
Coolidge, Frederick S., 5
Coolidge, Col. John C., 319
Coolidge, Louis A., 346
Coolidge, Marcus A., 306, 416, 417, 427
Coolidge, William H., 165, 346
Coöperative Central Bank, 475
Corcoran, Gen. John W., 9, 19, 45, 57
Corcoran, Wm. J., 369
Corrupt-Practices Act, 7
Cortelyou, Secretary, 70
Cosgrove, Daniel, 179
Coughlin, Dr., 122, 169

Coughlin, John T., 127
Cox, Channing H., 214, 230, 303, 308, 310, 311, 316, 325, 330, 332, 372
Coyne, Francis X., 365
Crane, W. Murray, 47, 60, 61, 65, 67, 68, 70, 74, 80, 87, 120, 145, 169, 185, 297
Crapo, William W., 10, 19
Crime Commission, 450, 496, 497
Crocker, Courtney, 186
Crosby, John O., 3, 74, 83, 91
Crowley, Robert J., 137, 138
Cummings, John J., 341
Cummings, John W., 257
Cunniff, P. Sarsfield, 545
Cunningham, H. V., 257
Curley, James M., 144, 342, 343, 368, 393, 413, 415, 417, 421, 422, 444, 447, 456, 508, 513–517, 519, 528, 536, 537, 538, 547–549
Curley, Martin P. F., 147
Curtis, Edwin U., 127, 256, 286, 287
Curtis, Senator, 376, 377
Cushing, Grafton D., 163
Cushing, Dr. Harvey, 272
Cushing, Speaker, 202, 204, 210, 213

D

Dalton, General, 8
Daugherty, Atty. Gen., 328
Davis, Charles H., 175
Davis, Henry G., 80
Davis, John W., 336
Davis, Senator, 492
Dawes, Charles G., 334, 454
Dawes, Ex-Senator, 70, 73
Death Penalty, Electricity, 55
Decimo Club, 369
De Courcey, Charles A., 69, 158
Delegates Constitutional Convention, 1916, 253, 254
Delegates, 1928 Democratic Convention, 383
Delegates, Democratic Convention, 1932, 445

Democratic Convention, 1924, 335
Democratic Platform, 1897, 53
Democratic Platform, 1928, 421, 422
Democratic Pre-Primary Convention, 504, 507–511
Democratic Presidential Electors, 1932, 460
Democratic State Committee, 2
Democratic State Convention, 1932, 456
Des Chenes, Louis N. M., 490
Devens, Camp, 275
Dever, Paul F., 509, 511
DeWolf, DeWitt Clinton, 433, 541
Dickenson, Senator, 453
Dickinson, David T., 164
Dietrick, Congressman, 213
Dionne, Oscar M., 505
Dixon, Senator, 176
Dodge, Robert G., 370
Doherty, D. F., 122
Doherty, Daniel F., 302
Doherty, John F., 318, 339
Dolan, Wm. C., 491
Donahue Charles H., 544
Donahue, Frank J., 153, 189
Donahue, J. J., 213
Donaldson, Sylvia, 313, 324
Donovan, Alfred S., 208
Donovan, Col., 385
Donovan, James, 45
Donroving, 269
Dooley, Henry J., 361, 362
Douglas, William L., 78, 82, 83, 88, 89, 91
Dowling, Dr. John J., 272
Dowse, Rev., 76
Doyle, Bernard W., 330
Doyle, Charles R., 541
Doyle, Fred J., 443
Doyle, William H., 510
Draper, Eben S., 47, 94, 95, 97, 110, 114, 123, 127, 128, 129, 140, 141, 185, 207, 372, 388, 419, 420, 421, 479
Draper & Frothingham, 127

Draper, Gen., 94, 131
Droppers, Garrett, 160
Drys, 2
Dubuque, Hugo A., 158
Dudley, Oscar P., 542
Duffy, Father, 385
Dutton, B. F., 46
Dwight, Minnie R., 372

E

Eastern Mass. Ry., 367
Edwards, Gen., 248, 268, 269, 438
Egg Rock, Nahant, 351
Eight Hour Bill, 131
Eighteenth Amendment Repealed, 479
Elevated Control Act, 312
Eliot, Charles W., 186
Eliot, Rev. Samuel R., 479
Ellis, David A., 197
Ellis Milk Bill, 160
Ely, Charles F., 479
Ely, Joseph B., 339, 361, 362, 414, 421, 425, 430, 433, 440, 444, 448, 449, 454, 461, 473, 475, 478, 492, 496, 511, 526, 536, 538, 542, 545, 549
Emmons, Judge, 75, 83, 91
Endicott, Henry B., 248
Endicott, William, 20
Ensign, William H., 539
Essex Club, 197
Estabrook, Henry A., 491
Evans, Hiram W., 331
Everett, City of, 16
Everett, Dr. William, 5, 52, 73
Executive Council, 14

F

Fall, Albert B., 328
Faneuil Hall Convention, 49
Farley, James A., 281, 449, 470, 508
Farmers Alliance, 11
Fast Day Abolished, 34
Federal Home Loan Bank, 476
Federal Income Tax, 157

INDEX   555

Feeney, John P., 109
Field, Judge, 317
Fifty-four Hour Bill, 155
Fillmore, Millard, 81–82
Finnegan, Senator, 510
First Sweat Shop Bill, 8
Fish, Erland F., 484, 547
Fitzgerald, John F., 37, 181, 184, 187, 243, 251, 314, 318, 414, 415
Fitzgerald, Raymond, 455
Fitzgerald, Susan W., 313, 324
Flaherty, John J., 78, 91
Foley, Margaret, 159
Foley, William J., 361
Foote, Gen., 495
Forbes, Charles R., 327
Fore River Bridge, 487
Foss, Eugene N., 128, 132, 133, 134, 135, 137, 141, 142, 143, 144, 145, 150, 151, 152, 154, 156, 158, 160, 162, 169, 172, 178, 188, 189, 192, 194, 196, 197, 202, 212, 499
Foss, Frank E., 531
Foster, Harry C., 230
Fowler, William P., 189, 210
France, Ex-Senator, 453
Fraternal Beneficiary Organization, 9
Free Coinage Silver, 11
Free Railroad Passes, 7
Frothingham, Louis A., 114, 139, 140, 158, 159, 211, 398
Fuller, Alvan T., 241, 242, 303, 304, 308, 318, 341, 342, 343, 349, 353, 354, 363, 365, 366, 371, 391, 393, 401

G

Gallivan, Congressman, 98
Galvin, J. M., 117
Gardner, A. P., 114, 142, 144, 197, 198, 199, 200, 233, 279, 280
Garfield, James R., 176
Garrett Case, 441, 442
Garrity, Stephen C., 543
Gaston, Col., 74, 82, 93, 145, 355, 356

George, Henry, 11
Gilbody, Col., 509
Gillett, Frederick H., 218, 240, 341, 346, 347, 348, 358, 377, 391
Gillis, "Bossy," 419
Gilmartin, John J., 490
Glass, Senator, 379
Glynn, Martin T., 237
Goff, Senator, 376
Goldberg, Louis, 544
Gold Bugs, 48
Gold Democrats, 44, 45, 52
Gompers, Samuel, 143, 288
Goodwin, Frank A., 365, 366, 393, 518, 525, 528
Gore, Thomas P., 180
Gould, J. Henry, 4
Goulston, Ernest J., 316
Goulston, Leopold M., 246
Gov. North Carolina, 70
Governor's salary, 16
Gow, Charles R., 210, 229
Grand Trunk Railway, 155
Granfield, W. J., 411, 429
Grant, Dick, 536
Grant, Robert, 166, 402
Greater Boston, 43
Greenhalge, Frederick T., 5, 10, 31, 32, 33, 35, 37, 39, 41, 42
Greenwood, Levi H., 163, 241, 276
Greenwood, Robert H., 491, 510
Greylock Reservation, 55
Griggs, F. D., 411
Grinnell, James S., 40
Grosvenor, Edwin A., 220
Guardians of Liberty, 211
Guild, Curtis, Jr., 47, 72, 74, 94, 95, 97, 104, 113, 115, 119, 148, 185, 217
Gurney, British Diplomat, 77
Guy, Arthur, 542

H

Haggerty, Charles, 121
Haigis, John W., 255, 373, 505

Haile, William H., 10, 17, 18
Hale, Mathew, 175, 243
Halifax Relief Work, 267
Hall, Damon E., 443
Hall, Frank S., 94
Hall, Walter Perley, 158
Hamlin, Charles S., 23, 74, 79, 132, 183
Hamlin, Wolcott, 17
Hammond, John Hays, 119
Hanna, Mark, 47
Hannigan, Judson, 479, 506
Harding, Warren G., 234, 299, 318, 327
Harlow, Leo M., 510
Harrington, Edward F., 324
Harris, Judge, 69, 132, 152
Harrison, Pat, 391
Harrison, President Benjamin, 19, 20
Hart, A. Bushnell, 175, 234, 243
Hart, Thomas N., 31
Harvard College, 6
Hatch, William J., 545
Hatfield, Chairman, 198
Hayes, William P., 137, 138, 139, 480
Hays, Martin, 547
Hearst, W. R., 79, 101
Heflin, Tom, 387
Hendricks Club, 482
Hennessy, William I., 455
Higgins, John P., 486
Hill, Arthur D., 175
Hill, David Bennett, 18, 19, 46, 63
Hisgen, Thomas L., 108
Hitchcock, Frank H., 120
Hitchcock, Judge, 76
Hoar, E. Rockwood, 4
Hoar, Senator, 4, 35, 36, 38, 66, 74, 85, 86, 87
Hoar, Sherman, 4
Hoar, Walter J., 116
Holden, Walter J., 75
Holman, Dudley M., 163
Holmes, Lemuel L., 69
Holmes, Oliver Wendell, 69
Hooker, Gen., Statue, 43, 77
Hoover, Herbert, 322, 375, 376, 384, 391, 452, 469, 470, 473
Hospitals, World War, 271
Houghton, Albert C., 19
Howard, Charles F., 366
Howard, Charles P., 495
Howe, Grace Hartley, 510
Hughes, Charles Evans, 232, 238, 239
Hull, John C., 324, 351
Hultman, Eugene N., 444, 538, 543
Hurley, Charles F., 418, 428, 455, 464, 502, 508, 509, 512, 513
Hurley, Francis X., 418
Hurley, Joseph L., 511
Hyde Park Annexation, 156

I

Income Tax, 193
Industrial Accident Board, 193
Initiative and Referendum, 258, 259
Innes, Charles H., 308
Irish Home Rule, 190
Irwin, Richard W., 162

J

Jackson Day, 6
Jackson, James, 296, 419
James, George F., 369
John Hancock House, 9
Johnson, Hiram, 234

K

Kaynor, William K., 411
Keating, Patrick M., Judge, 158, 443
Keefe, Paul J., 539
Keliher, John A., 109, 144, 246, 456
Kelly, Daniel J., 540
Kelly, Francis E., 455
Keville, Col., 541
Kiley, Daniel J., 109, 366
Kimball, Charles E., 11
Kimball, James W., 42, 255
King Edward, England, 413
Kirk, Col. Paul G., 495

INDEX 557

Knowlton, Judge, 69, 158
Ku Klux Klan, 331, 337, 342, 385

L

Ladd, Charles R., 4
La Follette, Senator, 331
Lally, Francis J., 506
Langtry, Albert P., 152, 153
Lawrence, George P., 55
Lawson, Thomas W., 108, 263
Leach, Barton, 493
Leary, George F., 539
Legislation, 1931, 436, 437
Legislative Mileage, 16
Legislature 1893, 18
Legislature 1930, 408, 409
Legislature 1931, Special Session, 439, 440, 441
Legislature 1933-34, 484-490
Leonard, Joseph J., 526, 537
Lewis, Prohibitionist, 67
Lewis, William H., 189
Liggett, Louis K., 377, 398, 450
Liliuokalani, Queen, 36
Little Apples, 12
Littlefield, Congressman, 20
Lodge, Henry Cabot, 5, 10, 12, 47, 63, 64, 80, 81, 120, 133, 142, 145 179, 198, 240, 241, 242, 261, 300 301, 314, 315, 332, 344, 420
Loan Shark Bill, 155
Logan, General, 413
Lomasney, Joseph P., 482, 483
Lomasney, Martin M., 121, 149, 237, 256, 481, 482, 483
Long, John D., 24, 49, 50, 80, 81
Long, Richard H., 197, 250, 291, 302
Long, Judge, 365
Loring, Clifton, 137
Lotteries, 16
Lovering, Congressman, 132
Lovett, Elizabeth M., 479
Lowden, Frank O., 334
Lowell, A. L., 402
Lowell, President of Harvard, 148
Luce, Robert, 114, 140, 159, 161, 437, 531

Lufkin, W. W., 280
Lummus, Henry T., 544
Lyman, T. Arthur, 339
Lyman, Frank E., 539
Lyman, George H., 267
Lyne, Daniel J., 496

Mc

McAdoo, Wm. G., 336
McCall, Samuel W., 15, 16, 64, 185, 186, 210, 211, 213, 218, 219, 221, 222, 223, 224, 225, 229, 230, 233, 240, 241, 242, 244, 246, 247, 249, 250, 253, 263, 270, 326, 353
McCarthy, Charles F., 149, 150
McCarthy, Richard P., 541
McCarthy, Wm. H., 542
McCormack, John W., 313, 358, 400, 531
McCormick, Medill, 299
McDevitt, John J., 190
McDonnell, Wm. H., 423
McElroy, Joseph, 543
McEttrick, Michael J., 18
McGlue, Chairman, 521
McGrath, Daniel F., 541
McInerney, James H., 148
McKinley Tariff, 2, 11
McKinley, William, 12, 14, 20, 45, 49, 64, 67
McKnight, Edward T., 311
McLane, Walter E., 312
McLaughlin, Edward A., 41
McLaughlin, John D., 152
McNary-Haugen Bill, 377
McNary, William S., 166
McNeil, Neil, 197
McNider, Hanford, 505
McSweeney, Edward F., 164

M

Mackiernan, Ethel E., 540
Macleod, Frederick J., 135, 137, 158
Madden, Luke J., 70
Mageenis, James F., 175
Mahoney, John W., 542

Malley, John F., 150, 183, 390
Malone, Dudley Field, 166
Mann, Col., 386
Mansfield, Frederick W., 136, 139, 198, 247, 250, 371, 520
Marden, George A., 42
Marshall, Thomas M., 174
Mass. Institute of Technology, 256
Mass. State College, 438
Mass, Troops, Baltimore, 56
Mathews, Nathan, Jr., 2
Maynard, Joseph A., 137, 183, 280, 471
Meany, John F., 160, 187, 205
Medford, 16
Meehan, Mary E., 339
Mellon, Andrew W., 376
Metropolitan Sewer and Water Board, 66
Von L. Meyer, George L., 15, 34
Meyers, James J., 61, 66
Michaelson, Charles, 387
Miles, Gen., 89, 90, 91
Mills, Ogden L., 391
Minute Man, 211, 257
Mission from Allies, 278
Mitchell, John J., 183
Mohawk Trading Co., 523
Monahan, Judge, 545
Mondell, Frank W., 333
Monjar, J. B., 369
Moody, Gov., 379
Moody, W. H., 102
Moran, James G., 547
Moran, John B., 100, 114
Morse, Elijah A., 39
Morton, Judge, 202
Moses, Senator, 376
Mother's Aid, 220
Mugwump Movement, 5, 6
Mulhern, Joseph J., 443
Murdock, Victor, 234
Murphy, John R., 178
Murray, M. J., 147
Murray, William F., 144
Music Hall Democratic Convention, 48, 49

N

National Campaign, 1896, 44
Nautical Training School, 364
Naval Brigade, 16, 268
Needham, Gen., 495
New Haven R.R., 100
North Adams, City of, 39
Northern Artery, 351
Nyland, Thomas J., 510

O

O'Brien, Thomas C., 416
O'Brien, William H., 144
O'Connell, Cardinal, 257, 281
O'Connell, Daniel F., 416
O'Connell, Joseph F., 109, 416
O'Connell, Judge, 307
O'Connell, M. Fred, 540
O'Connell, Philip J., 215
O'Donnell, James B., 64
O'Hara, Walter F., 539
Oil Scandal, 328
Old Age Assistance, 475
Old Home Week, 69
Olin, William M., 152
Olney, Richard, 21, 66, 79, 540
O'Meara, Dr. Michael, 208
O'Meara, Stephen, 99, 157, 229
O'Neil, Joseph H., 4, 251
O'Neill, Michael E, 418
O'Reilly, John Boyle, 92
Osborne, William H., 14
Osgood, W. N., 116
Overtime Bill, 102

P

Paine, Robert Treat, 59
Pappas, John C., 540
Parker, Alton B., 171
Parker, Herbert, 412
Parker, "Jim," 15
Parker, Judge, N. Y., 79, 80
Parker, Gen. Samuel D., 271
Parkhurst, Wellington E., 15
Parkman, Francis, 374
Parkman, George F., 374

INDEX 559

Parkman, Henry Jr., 374, 443
Parks, John A., 164
Pattangall, W. R., 337
Peaceful Picketing Bill, 155
Pearson, Gardner W., 230, 506
Pelletier, Joseph C., 175, 177, 302
Peoples Party, 11
Perrin, Rev. Dr., 175
Peters, Andrew J., 115, 144, 183, 286, 392
Phelan, James J., 248
Phelan, Michael F., 241
Phelps, Judge, 76–77
Pierce, Henry H., 542
Pigeon, Elizabeth W., 506, 518
Pillsbury, Albert E., Atty. Gen., 31
Pinchot, Gifford, Gov., 323
Pink Ticket Convention, 106
Plumed Knight, 5
Plunkett, William B., 63, 185
Police Commissioners, Boston, 3, 14, 24
Potter, Mary Pratt, 372
Powers, Samuel L., 74, 117
Pratt, Nathan D., 162
Prendible, Wm. M., 483
Prescott, Francis, 465
Presidential Primaries, 1932, 444
Prince, Frederick H., 372
Prince, Frederick O., 44
Progressive Republicans, 162
Prohibitionists, 1, 2
Public Bar, 7
Public Opinion Act, 193
Public Service Commission, 195
Putnam, Col., 279

Q

Qua, Judge, 537
Quincy, Josiah, 2, 22, 67
Quinn, John, 2, 46, 163
Quinn, Joseph F., 152

R

Radio Schools, 274
Ragan, Terrell M., 434

Railroad Commission, 194
Railroad Holding Bill, 156
Railroad Leases, 62
Raine, F. W., 267
Ranney, Fletcher, 229
Rantoul, Robert, Jr., 263
Rapid Transit, Boston, 8
Raskob, John J., 387
Ratigan, John B., 158
Ratshesky, A. C., 331
Raymond, Carl J., 540
Reading, Arthur K., 360, 365, 369
Redstone, Edward H., 279
Reed, James A., 378
Reed, Thomas B., 20, 47
Reed, William M., 161
Republican Delegates 1928, 373
Republican Delegates Convention 1932, 446, 447
Republican National Convention, 330
Republican Platform 1934, 507
Republican Pre-Primary Convention 1934, 505, 506
Republican State Convention 1928, 390, 391
Richardson, John, 450, 451, 452
Riordan, Charles F., 539
Ritchie, Gov., 382
Roberts, Ernest W., 241
Robinson, Gov., 42
Robinson, Henry W., 11
Robinson, J. T., 380, 382
Rogers, Edith Nourse, 361
Rogers, John J., 240
Rogers, John J., 249, 360
Roper, Daniel C., 378
Roosevelt, Franklin D., 210, 239, 280, 380, 381, 382, 461, 466, 469, 471, 473, 511
Roosevelt, James, 444, 479, 521, 531
Roosevelt, Theodore, 15, 50, 61, 64, 66, 69, 70, 80, 81, 133, 142, 161, 166, 168, 170, 174, 177, 181, 231, 232, 234, 235
Roosevelt, Theodore, Jr., 328
Root, Elihu, 81, 170, 171, 232
Ross, Senator, 130

Rugg, Chief Justice, 158
Russell and Corcoran, 11
Russell, John E., 12, 31, 32, 36, 38, 40, 45, 73
Russell, Joseph B., 197
Russell, Mayor Richard M., 508, 531
Russell, William Eustis, 1-3, 6, 8, 13, 17, 18, 19, 23, 31, 32, 45, 46
Ryan, Morgan T., 541
Ryan, Thomas F., 172

S

Sacco and Vanzetti, 245, 363, 401
St. Mihiel, Memorial, 358
Saltonstall, Leverett, 406, 547
Sanborn, Frank D., 246
Sanders, Charles R., 61
Sawyer, Roland D., 370
Sayre, Mrs. Francis B., 302
Schofield, George A., 110
Seavy, Fred H., 163
Sewell, Arthur, 47
Scharton, Wm. F., 390
Shattuck, Henry L., 324, 434
Shaw, William, 212
Shay, Judge, 545
Sheehan, William C., 80
Sheldon, Judge, 209
Sherburne, Gen., 330
Short ballot, 433
Shouse, Jouett, 387, 448
Sieberlick, Frank, 168
Silsby, Nathaniel, 263, 265
Silver Democrats, 44
Simpson, Prof., 496
Sisk, James H., 209
Sleeper, George T., 42
Smith, Alfred E., 336, 339, 378, 380, 383, 384, 385, 386, 447, 448, 450, 463, 472
Smith, George E., 55, 61
Socialist Labor Party, 11
Soule, Rufus R., 66
South Station, 43
Spanish War Appropriation $500,000, 56

Special State Election 1889, 2
Sprague, Henry B., 6
Springfield Armory, 276
State Firemen's Fund, 16
State Guard, 270, 271, 288
State House Lobby, 7
State Piers, 438
State Police, 494
Stearns, Foster W., 244
Stearns, Frank W., 282, 284
Stevens, Eben S., 121
Stevens, Jesse M., 279
Stevens, Moses T., 5, 33
Stimson, F. J., 120
Stobbs, Congressman, 452
Stone, Judge, 491, 494
Stoneman, David, 161
Stop Roosevelt, 448
Storrow, James J., 248
Stratton, Charles E., 36
Strecker, Charles B., 183
Suffolk Law School, 191, 192
Sughrue, M. J., 100
Sullivan, J. Leo, 542
Sullivan, John A., 133
Sullivan, John H., 19, 51
Sullivan, John H., 540
Sullivan, Gen. John J., 271
Sullivan, Lewis R., 488
Sulzer, William, 173
Sumner, Charles, 264
Sunday Laws, 69
Supreme Judicial Court, 8
Swift, John E., 455, 465, 466, 468
Swig, Simon, 230

T

Taft, William H., 117, 122, 167, 179
Tague, Peter F., 251
Talbot, Edward B., 468
Tammany Trio, 200
Tercentenary Commission, 216
Textile Schools, 39
Two Tercentenaries, 411, 412
Thayer, John A., 78, 110
Thayer, John R., 135, 144, 145, 147

INDEX 561

Thayer, Pauline R., 372
Thayer, Webster, 244, 468, 474
Third House, 7
Thompson, Wm. G., 493
Tinkham, George Holden, 164, 530
Tisbury, Town, 16
Tomasello, A. G. & Co., 523
Transit Commission, Boston, 54
Treadway, Allen T., 124, 130, 150, 163
Trefry, William D. T., 4
Tucker, George Fox, 15
Tuckerman, Bayard, 452
Tufts, Nathan A., 369
Turner, Henry E., 152
Tyrrell, Francis X., 208

U

Unemployment Investigation, 44
U. S. Machinery Co., 157, 161
U. S. Senators, Election, 62, 193

V

Vahey, James H., 115, 127, 134, 135
Van Buren, Martin, 81, 82
Vare, William H., 376
Varnum, Joseph B., 263
Veterans' Preference, 39
Volstead Act, 477
Von Bernstorff, Count, 274
Vote for Governor, 1890, 1; 1891, 13
Vote for Governor, 1892, 17
Vote for Governor, 1895, 40
Vote for President, 1892, 17
Vote State 1934, 533, 534, 535

W

Waite, William C., 544
Walker, Fred H., 183
Walker, Joseph, 124, 130, 147, 149, 163, 178, 181, 185, 186, 188
Walker, Joseph H., 6
Walsh, David I., 115, 158, 161, 172, 179, 188, 195, 200, 204, 209, 210, 211, 213, 214, 221, 222, 223, 236, 252, 261, 262, 263, 302, 303, 337, 339, 346, 358, 379, 387, 421, 445, 511, 517, 532
Walsh, John Jackson, 305
Walsh, Thomas F., 328, 336, 448
Wambaugh, Prof., 393
Ward, Charles E., 208
Warner, Joseph S., 303, 304, 418, 465, 484, 505
Warren, Bentley W., 15
Washburn, Charles G., 14
Washburn, Dr. F. L., 272
Washburn, Robert M., 150, 240, 307, 506, 532
Washburn, Slater, 246
Watertown Arsenal, 276
Watson, Senator, 376
Weavers Fine Bill, 8, 16
Webster, George P., 204
Weeks, John W., 184, 233, 262, 265
Wells, Henry C., 230
Wells, Wellington, 351
Welsh, Judge, 338
West Tisbury, 16
Western Mass. Trolleys, 193
Wheatley, Dr., 132
Wheeler, Alexander, 526
Wheeler, Wayne B., 331
Whipple, Sherman L., 147, 159, 187, 255, 310
White, Clinton, 160
White, John E., 153
White, Judge, 76
White, Norman H., 158, 197
White, Thomas W., 209
Whiting, William F., 330, 375, 376
Whitney, Henry M., 93, 95, 107, 145, 146
Whitney, William C., 20, 46
Williams, Constance Gardner, 359, 420
Williams, George Fred, 4, 40, 44, 45, 46, 47, 48, 49, 52, 53, 57, 63, 78, 95, 102, 159, 254, 307
Williams, Harold, 213, 219
Williams, John Sharp, 345

Williams, Lombard, 208
Williams, Louise M., 372
Wilson, Harold D., 316
Wilson, Henry, 264
Wilson, Police Commissioner, 443
Wilson Tariff, 40
Wilson, Woodrow, 144, 166, 173, 181, 182, 190, 237, 239, 240, 261, 284
Winship, A. E., 114
Winn, Major Henry, 11
Wolcott, Roger, 17, 18, 36, 40, 42, 50, 53, 54, 56, 58, 59, 60, 65
Woman Suffrage, 191
Wood, Charles G., 160
Wood, Gen. Leonard, 266
Wood, Russell, 175, 209
Woods, Robert W., 202
Worcester Polytechnic Institute, 256
Work, Hubert, 377
World's Columbian Exposition, 9
Wylie, Walter O., 116

Y

Young, B. Loring, 309, 388, 391, 419, 479
Youngman, Wm. S., 341, 396, 418, 428, 461
Y.M.C.A. Law School, 76
Young Men's Democratic Club, 2
Yankee Division, 268